ALTRUISM RECONSIDERED

Medical Law and Ethics

Series Editor
Sheila McLean, Director of the Institute of Law and Ethics in Medicine,
School of Law, University of Glasgow

The 21st century seems likely to witness some of the most major developments in medicine and healthcare ever seen. At the same time, the debate about the extent to which science and/or medicine should lead the moral agenda continues, as do questions about the appropriate role for law.

This series brings together some of the best contemporary academic commentators to tackle these dilemmas in a challenging, informed and inquiring manner. The scope of the series is purposely wide, including contributions from a variety of disciplines such as law, philosophy and social sciences.

Other titles in the series

The Child As Vulnerable Patient
Protection and Empowerment
Lynn Hagger
ISBN 978-0-7546-7252-4

Disclosure Dilemmas
Ethics of Genetic Prognosis after the 'Right to Know/Not to Know' Debate
Edited by Christoph Rehmann-Sutter and Hansjakob Müller
ISBN 978-0-7546-7451-1

Critical Interventions in the Ethics of Healthcare
Challenging the Principle of Autonomy in Bioethics
Edited by Stuart J. Murray and Dave Holmes
ISBN 978-0-7546-7396-5

Law, Mind and Brain
Edited by Michael Freeman and Oliver R. Goodenough
ISBN 978-0-7546-7013-1

Speaking for the Dead
The Human Body in Biology and Medicine
D. Gareth Jones and Maja I. Whitaker
ISBN 978-0-7546-7452-8

Altruism Reconsidered
Exploring New Approaches
to Property in Human Tissue

Edited by

MICHAEL STEINMANN
Stevens Institute of Technology, USA

PETER SÝKORA
University of Saints Cyril and Methodius, Slovakia

URBAN WIESING
Eberhard Karls Universität, Tübingen, Germany

Routledge
Taylor & Francis Group

LONDON AND NEW YORK

First published 2009 by Ashgate Publishing

2 Park Square, Milton Park, Abingdon, Oxon OX14 4RN
711 Third Avenue, New York, NY 10017, USA

Routledge is an imprint of the Taylor & Francis Group, an informa business

First issued in paperback 2016

British Library Cataloguing in Publication Data

Altruism reconsidered : exploring new approaches to
  property in human tissue. -- (Medical law and ethics)
  1. Human body--Law and legislation--Europe.
  I. Series II. Steinmann, Michael. III. Sýkora, Peter.
  IV. Wiesing, Urban.
  344.4'04194-dc22

Library of Congress Cataloging-in-Publication Data

Steinmann, Michael, 1964-
  Altruism reconsidered : exploring new approaches to property in human tissue / by
Michael Steinmann, Peter Sýkora, and Urban Wiesing.
    p. cm. -- (Medical law and ethics)
  Includes bibliographical references and index.
  1. Preservation of organs, tissues, etc.--Law and legislation. 2. Preservation of organs,
tissues, etc.--Moral and ethical aspects. 3. Right of property. 4. Donation of organs,
tissues, etc.--Law and legislation. 5. Transplantation of organs, tissues, etc.--Law and
legislation. 6. Medicine--Research. I. Sýkora, Peter, 1956- II. Wiesing, Urban. III. Title.
  K3611.T7.S74 2009
  174.2'97954--dc22

2009015492

ISBN 13: 978-0-7546-7270-8 (hbk)
ISBN 13: 978-1-138-25530-2 (pbk)

Contents

List of Figures and Tables

Figure

Tables

List of Contributors

Jasper A. Bovenberg is Director of Legal Pathways Institute for Health and Bio-Law. He holds several degrees in law (J.D. Leiden University; LL.M, University of Michigan and Ph.D., Leiden University). His publications include: *Property Rights in Blood, Genes & Data: Naturally Yours?* (Brill-Martinus Nijhoff 2006); 'A Compulsory Government Royalty Fee; a Third Way or Double Pay?', *Nature Biotechnology* (accepted 2008); 'Honest Jim and the European Database Right', *Journal of Genomics, Policy and Society* (2005).

Roger Brownsword is Professor of Law and Director of TELOS at King's College London, and he is an Honorary Professor in Law at the University of Sheffield. He has written extensively about the regulation of emerging technologies, the implications of an increasing reliance on technology as a regulatory instrument and a variety of issues in law and ethics. His most recent books are *Consent in the Law* (2007) (co-authored with Deryck Beyleveld); *Rights, Regulation and the Technological Revolution* (2008) and *Regulating Technologies* (2008) (co-edited with Karen Yeung).

Alastair V. Campbell is Director of the Centre for Biomedical Ethics at Yong Loo Lin School of Medicine, National University of Singapore. He is a Doctor in Theology, B.D., M.A. (Hons Philosophy), former President of the International Association of Bioethics; Founding Editor of the *Journal of Medical Ethics*; Fellow at The Hastings Center, New York; and Honorary Vice President of the Institute of Medical Ethics, London. His publications include: *Health as Liberation* (Pilgrim Press, Cleveland 1995); *Medical Ethics*, 4th Edition (Oxford University Press 2005); *Medicine of the Person: Faith, Science and Values in Health Care Provision* (Jessica Kingsley Publishers 2007); *The Body in Bioethics* (Routledge-Cavendish 2009); 'The ethical challenges of biobanks: safeguarding altruism and trust', S.A.M. McLean (ed.), *First Do No Harm* (Ashgate 2006); 'They stole my baby's soul: narratives of embodiment and loss', F. Rapport and P. Wainwright (eds), *The Self in Health and Illness: Patients, Professionals and Narrative Identity* (Radcliffe Publishing 2006); 'Human tissue legislation: listening to the professionals', *Journal of Medical Ethics* (2008).

Aitziber Emaldi-Cirión holds the Interuniversitary Chair in Law and the Human Genome at the Universities of Deusto and of the Basque Country in Bilbao. She is a Doctor in Law and a Professor in Bioethics, Law and Biotechnology. Her publications include: *Juridical implications on genetic counseling* (2001);

Altruism Reconsidered

Information and clinical documents (2000); 'Regulations of Civil Law to safeguard the autonomy of patients at the end of their life–an international documentation' (Germany, 2000); 'Medical liability during the genetic counseling process' (Australia, 2002); 'Juridical liability during genetic predictive tests' (Bogotá, 2002); 'Human genome interventions and sex selection' (Spain 2002); 'Human genome regulation in Spain' (Mexico, 2002); 'Personalised medicine' (Spain, 2005); 'Data protection' (Spain, 2002).

Barbro Fröding (nee Björkman) is a Marie Curie Post Doctoral Fellow at Oxford University (Philosophy Faculty), a Hardie Post Doctoral Junior Research Fellow at Lincoln College Oxford and a Research Associate at The Wellcome Centre for Neuroethics in Oxford. She holds a Ph.D. in Philosophy from the Royal Institute of Technology KTH, Stockholm. Her publications include: 'Why We Are Not Allowed to Sell That Which We are Encouraged to Donate', *Cambridge Quarterly of Healthcare Ethics* 15 (2006); 'Bodily Rights & Property Rights', co-authored with Sven Ove Hansson, *Journal of Medical Ethics* 32 (2006); 'Bioethics in Sweden', co-authored with Sven Ove Hansson, *Cambridge Quarterly of Healthcare Ethics* 15 (2006); 'Different Types, Different Rights', *Science and Engineering Ethics* (2007).

Alison Hall is Project Manager (Law and Policy) at the PHG Foundation, the Foundation for Genomics and Population Health in Cambridge. She holds a B.A. in Human Sciences (University of Oxford) and an M.A. in Health Care Ethics (University of Manchester), as well as a diploma in Nursing and the qualification as Solicitor. She is also the Secretary of the Society for Genomics, Policy and Population Health. Her publications include: 'Ethical, legal and social issues arising from cell-free fetal DNA technologies', with S. John Bostanci, *PHG Foundation* (2009, in press); as member of the Working Party of the Joint Committee on Medical Genetics, *Guidelines on the Human Tissue Act for the clinical genetics and laboratory sciences sector* (2006); 'Beyond Bristol and Alder Hey: the Future Regulation of Human Tissue', with K. Liddell, M*edical Law Review* (2005).

Nils Hoppe is a Postdoctoral Research Fellow at the Center for Philosophy and Ethics of Science, Leibniz Universität Hannover. He studied law at Nottingham Trent University, Erlangen-Nürnberg and Göttingen. He first was a Legal Assistant in Nottingham, then a Legal Counsel at University Medical Center, Göttingen, and holds a doctorate in Law from Leibniz Universität Hannover. His publications include: *Bioequity – Property and the Human Body* (Ashgate, forthcoming); with Ch. Lenk and R. Andorno (eds), *Ethics and Law of Intellectual Property – Current Problems in Politics, Science and Technology* (Ashgate 2007).

Ján Koller is Associate Professor of Surgery at the Centre for Burns and Reconstructive Surgery, University Hospital Bratislava. He is a Medical Doctor,

Head of the Burn Center, Medical Director of the Central Tissue Bank and the principal expert on tissue transplantology for the Ministry of Health in Slovakia. He also served in the Group of Experts for Safety and Quality of Organs, Tissues and Cells of the Council of Europe and is a member of the Regulatory Committee for Tissues and Cells of the European Commission, Brussels. His publications include: 'Experience in the use of foetal membranes for the treatment of burns and other skin defects', G.O. Phillips et al. (eds), *Advances in Tissue Banking* (1998); 'The use of growth hormone in the treatment of extensive burns: a case report', *Acta Chir. Plast.* 40 (1998); 'Resorption and calcification of chemically modified collagen/hyaluronan hybrid membranes', *Polymers in Medicine* 30 (2000); 'Biocompatibility studies of modified collage', *Cell and Tissue Banking* 2 (2001); 'Membranes and hydrogels in reconstructive surgery', R.L. Reis and D. Cohn (eds), *Polymer based systems on tissue engineering, replacement and regeneration* (NATO Science Series, Kluwer 2002).

Catherine Labrusse-Riou is Professor Emerita of Law at Université de Paris I Panthéon-Sorbonne. She is a member of the Comité de Protection des Personnes d'Île de France 1, Hôpital Hôtel-Dieu, Paris, and was member of the Comité National d'Ethique pour les Sciences de la vie et de la Santé, the Commission du Génie Biomoléculaire and the Groupe européen d'éthique pour les sciences et les nouvelles technologies. Her publications include: *Ecrits de bioéthique*, textes réunis et présentés par Muriel Fabre-Magnan (PUF 2007); 'La recherche sur l'embryon, qualifications et enjeux' (en coll. B. Mathieu, N.J. Mazen) (2000); *Le droit saisi par la biologie. Des juristes au laboratoire* (ed.) (1996); 'L'homme, la nature et le droit', (eds B. Edelman, M.A. Hermitte) (1988); *Produire l'homme de quel droit? Étude juridique et éthique des procréations artificielles* (PUF 1987).

Christian Lenk studied philosophy, political science and social anthropology at the University of Hamburg. From 2000–2002 he worked in two projects in the field of medical ethics and bioethics at the Universities of Marburg and Münster, financed by the German Research Community (DFG). He received his doctoral degree for a study on the ethical issues of enhancement technologies in biomedicine at the University of Münster in 2002. Since 2002, he has been a researcher and since 2004, Assistant Professor at the Department for Ethics and History of Medicine at the University of Göttingen. He finished his habilitation at the Medical Faculty of the University of Göttingen in 2008 with a study on research ethics and is Project Leader of the international Tiss.EU project on ethics and law of tissue research in Europe. His publications include: with N. Hoppe and R. Andorno (eds), *Ethics and Law of Intellectual Property. Current Problems in Politics, Science and Technology* (Ashgate 2007); 'Donors and Users of Human Tissue for Research Purposes: Conflict of Interests and Balancing of Interests', in P. Dabrock, J. Ried and J. Taupitz (eds), *Trust in Biobanking* (Heidelberg 2009).

Caroline Mullen is a Research Officer at the School of Law, University of Leeds, working on the Reflexive Governance in the Public Interest (REFGOV) project. She has previously worked at the University of Birmingham on the Property Regulation in European Science Ethics and Law Project at the Centre for Global Ethics, and on the Database of Archives of Non-Governmental Organisations at the Centre of Contemporary Governance and Citizenship. Her doctorate is from the Centre for Social Ethics and Policy, School of Law at the University of Manchester. Her publications include: with P. Vincent-Jones and D. Hughes, 'New Labour's PPI Reforms: Patient *and* Public Involvement in Healthcare Governance?', *Modern Law Review* 72 (2009); with H. Widdows (eds), *The Governance of Genetic Information: Who Decides?* (Cambridge University Press (2009 forthcoming); 'Representation or reason: Consulting the public on the ethics of health policy', *Health Care Analysis* 16 (2008).

Christine Noiville is a Doctor in Law and a Senior Researcher at CNRS (National Center for Scientific Research). She is also Director of the 'Droit, sciences et techniques' research center at the Pantheon-Sorbonne Faculty of Law (Université Paris 1, UMR 8103). She is a member of several public committees, such as the CNRS Ethics Committee, the Comité de prévention et de precaution (Ministry of the Environment) and the Observatoire du principe de précaution. Her publications include: *Du bon gouvernement des risques* (PUF); with F. Bellivier, *Contrats et vivant* (Paris); with F. Bellivier, *Les biobanques. Que Sais-je?*(PUF); with F. Bellivier, *La bioéquité* (Paris, Autrement).

Ingrid Schneider is a political scientist who has been working since 2002 as a Senior Researcher and Lecturer at the Research Centre on Biotechnology, Society, and the Environment (BIOGUM), in the Research Group on Medicine/Neurosciences, at the University of Hamburg. She received her diploma in Political Sciences in 1987 and her Ph.D. in 1996 with a study on fetal tissue transplantation. From 2000–2002 she was a member of the German parliamentary commission (Enquete-Kommission) on 'Law and Ethics of Modern Medicine'. She has written extensively on biopolitics, technology assessment in biomedicine and on intellectual property rights and has acted as adviser to hearings of the German, Austrian and European Parliaments on various topics. Currently she is writing a book on the governance of the European patent system with special emphasis on biotechnology.

Michael Steinmann is Professor of Philosophy at Stevens Institute of Technology in Hoboken, New Jersey. Prior to this he taught philosophy at the Pennsylvania State University. In Germany, he was Co-director of the program for Basic Ethical-Philosophical Studies, Lecturer and Research Fellow at the University of Freiburg and Lecturer and Research Fellow at the Interdepartmental Center for Ethics in the Sciences and the Institute of Ethics and History of Medicine at the University of Tübingen. He holds a Ph.D. in Philosophy from the University of Tübingen and received his habilitation at the University of Freiburg. His publications include:

'Under the Pretence of Autonomy. Contradictions in the Guidelines for Human Tissue Donation', *Medicine, Health Care and Philosophy* (2009); *Die Offenheit des Sinns. Untersuchungen zu Sprache und Logik bei Martin Heidegger* (2008); with H. Raspe and A. Hüppe, *Empfehlungen zur Begutachtung klinischer Studien durch Ethikkommissionen* (2005); *Die Ethik Friedrich Nietzsches* [*The Ethics of Friedrich Nietzsche*] (2000).

Peter Sýkora is a Doctor of Natural Sciences (RNDr., Charles University, Prague), an Extraordinary Professor in Philosophy and Director of the Centre for Bioethics at the University of Saints Cyril and Methodius in Trnava. He became an Associate Professor in Philosophy at Comenius University Bratislava in 1997. Prior to this he was working on antibiotic resistance and evolution for 15 years (published in *J. Bacteriol, Plasmid, Journal of Theoretical Biology*). He also is a member of the Slovak National Ethics Committee. His most recent publications include: *Ontology of Twilight Zone* (2008), *Bioethical Challenges for Philosophy* (2008, co-edited with R. Balak), *Historical Essences and Problem of Universals* (2006) and entries on Aristotle, Darwinism – Modern, Essentialism, Sociobiology and Teleology in *Encyclopedia of Anthropology* (H.J. Birx, ed., 2006).

Jochen Taupitz is Professor of Civil Law, Law of Civil Procedure, Private International Law and Comparative Law at the University of Mannheim, and Director of the Institute for German, European and International Medical Law, Public Health Law and Bioethics (IMGB), which jointly belongs to the Universities of Heidelberg and Mannheim. He also is a member of the German Ethics Council. He received his doctorate and habilitation at the University of Göttingen. His recent publications include: with A. Pitz and K. Niedziolka, *Der Einsatz nicht-ärztlichen Heilpersonals bei der ambulanten Versorgung chronisch kranker Patienten* (Berlin 2008); with H.-L. Günther and P. Kaiser, *Embryonenschutzgesetz: Juristischer Kommentar mit medizinisch-naturwissenschaftlichen Einführungen* (Stuttgart 2008).

Richard Tutton is Senior Lecturer at the ESRC Centre for Economic and Social Aspects of Genomics (Cesagen), Lancaster University. His academic training was in literary and cultural studies before he turned to studying the social dimensions of human genetics research. After completing a Ph.D. at Lancaster University in 2002, Richard worked as a post-doc in SATSU (Science and Technology Studies Unit) at the University of York (2002–2004) and the Institute for Science and Society (ISS) at the University of Nottingham (2004–2007). His publications include: (ed.), *Genetic Databases: The Socio-Ethical Issues in the Collection and Use of DNA* (Routledge 2004).

Heather Widdows is Professor of Global Ethics at the Department of Philosophy at the University of Birmingham, and Lead Editor of the *Journal of Global Ethics*. Her publications include, with C. Mullen (eds), *The Governance of Genetic*

Information: Who Decides? (Cambridge University Press 2009); with I. Alkorta Idiakez and A. Emaldi Cirión (eds), *Women's Reproductive Rights* (London: Palgrave 2006); *The Moral Vision of Iris Murdoch* (Ashgate 2006); 'Persons and their parts: New reproductive technologies and risks of commodification', *Health Care Analysis* 17 (2009); 'Between the individual and the community: The impact of genetics on ethical models', for SI of *New Genetics and Society* (2009); 'Border disputes across bodies: How and why feminists disagree', *International Journal of the Feminist Association of Bioethics* (2009); 'Conceptualising Health: Insights from the Capability Approach', with Iain Law, *Health Care Analysis* 16 (2008); 'The Self in the Genetic Era', *Health Care Analysis* 15 (2007); 'Moral Neocolonialism and Global Ethics', *Bioethics* 21 (2007).

Urban Wiesing is Professor at the Institute of Ethics and History of Medicine, University of Tübingen. He received a doctorate in philosophy and a doctorate in medicine from the University of Münster, where he also finished his habilitation in medicine. His publications include: *Kunst oder Wissenschaft? Konzeptionen der Medizin in der deutschen Romantik* (1995); *Zur Verantwortung des Arztes* (1995); *Wer heilt, hat Recht? Über Pragmatik und Pluralität in der Medizin* (2004); with D. Schmitz, *Ethische Aspekte der Genetik in der Arbeitsmedizin* (2008); 'Immanuel Kant, his philosophy and medicine', *Medicine, Health Care and Philosophy* (accepted); 'Ethical Aspects of Limiting Residents' Work Hours', *Bioethics* 21 (2007); with H.-J. Ehni, 'International Ethical Regulations of Placebo-controlled Clinical Trials', *Bioethics* 22 (2008).

Acknowledgments

This book results from a positive confusion – a confusion produced by the European research project PropEur. The PropEur project, 'Property Regulation in Science, Ethics and Law', was charged with exploring new approaches to the promising idea of property in human tissue and other related matters. New models had to be explored, and this is where the confusion started. Donna Dickenson, who initiated the project, presented the participants with many questions, such as: which models for the regulation of property should be discussed? How are they distinguished from each other, and to what extent are they realistic? Is there a difference between donation and conditional gift? How could a trust model work? Is full commodification a viable solution? And, above all, what is the best way to protect the interests of donors? This question entails a number of further questions: what are these interests? Can they all be considered? Should they all be taken into account?

The confusion became even greater, when work was finally in full swing. As in all similar research endeavors, participants from many different countries came together and so spoke against a background of their different legal and ethical traditions, and their practical experience in regard to biobanking and donor protection. As so often occurs in Europe, many languages had to be translated and this made the confusion worse, not so much because of the linguistic but of the conceptual dimension. But the confusion proved to be positive: slowly a spectrum of possibilities became clearer, and the ways to be explored appeared in a much clearer light. Still, many questions are open and the regulation of biobanking and tissue storage still appears as a field where many solutions remain to be worked out. Many new problems which we may not even be able to foresee today will likely occur. But this volume, and with it the PropEur project, shows that there is reason for hope. Bioethics is a creative discipline that produces just the right amount of confusion needed to get a discussion started, and to put ideas to the table that might help us deal with the challenges of an ever more demanding field of biomedical research.

The editors of this volume wish to thank all the other participants in the project who have helped discuss and clarify solutions for the use of property in human tissue. They also would like to thank the speakers and participants at the different workshops in Tübingen (Germany), Smolenice (Slovakia), and Birmingham (UK), who have contributed greatly to the conception of this volume, even if not every voice can be presented here. A very special thank goes to Donna Dickenson who was the author of the PropEur project, and to Heather Widdows and Caroline Mullen, who later took responsibility for the project. Keeping so many people from so many countries together at work, and maintaining the dialogue among them, certainly was no easy task. Something of the creative atmosphere that determined the very beginnings of this book hopefully can still be sensed throughout each contribution, and hopefully it also makes clear how much we need a kind of bioethics that reconsiders dominant traditions, and that opens up the way to explore and develop new models of regulation, and new normative views.

Chapter 1

Introduction

Michael Steinmann

As the demand for human tissue is constantly rising, and biobanks are becoming ever more important for medical research, bioethics cannot but continue to engage in the assessment of this field. What is the ethical paradigm that guides the donation to biobanks? For quite a long time, altruism has been the dominating concept in understanding acts of donation in the medical field. From organ transplants to blood supply, the ethics to be followed were based on the idea that donation is a free and unrewarded gift. Organs are donated in order to give life to others, and blood is donated in order to help others in case of emergency.

But the question here is: can altruism also be the ethical model that is best suited for the case of tissue donation? The answer this volume gives is that we have to reconsider the role of altruism in regard to biobanks. Altruism cannot function here the way it does in other fields of donation. The idea of donation depends on a number of preconditions, and the most relevant of these preconditions are not properly met when biobanks assume the role of recipient.

Three preconditions seem to be of particular importance. First, altruism implies that the action is designed to benefit someone. We do not give our organs or our blood to just anyone, but only to those in need, and we presuppose that those who receive our gift are really those who need it most. Altruism is a moral concept that entails a certain obligation we feel towards others. Second, the donation is conceived as an act of free agency. We are called to donate when we actually are not obliged to give anything. Only the good reasons we have when we want to help others in need motivate us to participate in a blood drive or to donate an organ. Altruism has been so largely adopted because it actually gives us a reason why we should give parts of our body away. And third, we assume that the reaction of the recipient corresponds to our altruism. Donation relies on mutual respect: the will of donors has to be taken seriously, and all necessary provisions concerning safety and personal rights have to be taken into account; otherwise it would be risky or at least unacceptable to donate.

Giving tissue to a biobank cannot really satisfy these three conditions. On the one side, biobanks cannot respond to the moral commitment of donors because their purpose is scientific, not moral. Biobanks are research institutions, in certain cases also commercial enterprises, and they have to follow criteria that are not necessarily the same as the moral assumptions or attitudes of the donors. Obviously, neither do they have to conflict. In many cases, biobanks may allow for the realization of altruistic purposes, for example, when tissue is used to search for the treatment of a certain type of disease. And in many cases, the subjective perspective of donors simply might be that they donate for altruistic reasons, whatever the goals and methods of the bank might be. The idea that any kind of donation in the medical field is a good thing still might be widely shared.

However, there are good reasons to doubt that the donation to a biobank generally should be classified as an act of 'helping others'. Many times, there is no specific recipient of the donation. Besides the cases where tissue is directly used for transplantation, the samples are stored for purposes of research, technically engineered or even treated as a commodity. Very often there is no 'other', no 'alter' to whom my donation is directed, no 'someone in need' whom I might think of when I consent to donate. Benefits of biobanking reach those in need, if ever, only in an indirect way, and not all studies or projects involving tissue samples will actually lead to the treatment of a disease. In such cases, it is simply the wrong category to apply when the contribution to a biobank is called a 'donation'. It is a contribution, indeed, but we cannot 'donate' to something as impersonal as the general progress of science. In a certain regard the contribution here is quite similar to what we do when we pay our taxes: what we give is a share of what we own, something that is needed in order to sustain certain public activities, but it clearly is not any kind of gift.

Other cases are even more obvious. We can think of the case of ova donation, described at large in this book, where women are brought to donate their eggs with faint altruistic motivations, although the use of the eggs is commercial, or at least directed to a doubtful research agenda. Here, altruism functions as an illusion to act morally, while tissue in reality is sold or given away for purely utilitarian reasons. Applying the wrong normative principle to such cases is not only a mistake in theory, but an attempt to trump the public about one's real intentions. And also in the cases mentioned above, where the intentions might be good, although there are no direct benefits of research, the use of the wrong principle tends to mislead the decisions of donors. This might not always be harmful to them, but in the long run, misconceptions and deceptions undermine the confidence of those who need to know for what reason they are asked to give parts of their body to a bank. Hence, to ask for the right normative principle in biobanking is by no means a mere theoretical, academic question, but has far-reaching practical implications.

On the other side, it can indeed be harmful for donors when giving tissue is labeled as an 'altruistic act' which leaves them no control over the use of their body parts. There are many ways in which this can be shown. One problem that usually comes up with biobanks is the problem of consent. Biobanking very much favors a broad if not completely open form of consent, because the simple fact is that the purpose and the methods of research cannot be foreseen. This means that neither donors nor researchers can foresee what will be done with the tissue. The influence of donors on tissue samples once they are stored is minimal and very hard to realize. Several contributions in this volume will point this out. The result of this situation is a certain pressure exerted on donors to renounce as far as possible any further influence on the use of their donation. Whether it is necessary to contact donors again when the purpose of research is changed or whether they can opt out and revoke their participation is discussed controversially, and very often the answer is given in favor of the biobanks.

Another problem is that research is hardly limited to one researcher or one institution. Once data are stored and samples are available, they are very likely to circulate within the wider scientific community. But then, who can guarantee that the personal rights of donors are always upheld? Complete anonymity seems to be impossible in the digital age. Genetic diagnosis might affect the interest in confidentiality in a way that can hardly be foreseen.

Still another point concerns the growing commercial interest in tissue donation. What happens if the donation of tissue leads to a significant financial benefit? If we think of donation as an altruistic act, then the donor gives without expecting any recompense. Others, however, might very well obtain financial gains from using what has been transferred to them. There is clearly an asymmetry between the assumed moral commitment on the one side and the purely economic interest on the other. From this perspective, biobanking might also be seen to bring up conflicts of interest on the side of physicians. Once the physician is involved in a research activity, there might be an additional interest that influences the course of a therapy. He or she might be inclined to take more tissue than would be necessary for medical reasons, and treatments might be proposed that otherwise would not be carried through.

Obviously, many of these concerns are only hypothetical, and we must not assume that always the worst will occur. But still, we also cannot help articulating such concerns. There have been cases where the interest in human tissue has led to a significant disrespect of donors – who in these cases were not even 'donors' in the proper sense of the word because they were not told about this interest. The scandal of retained infant tissue in the Bristol and Alder Hey cases can be mentioned here, and also the Moore case, where the financial interest was not disclosed to the person whose cells became so valuable. (Both cases play a considerable role in this volume). These cases could be exceptional. However, they seem to result from a structural mismatch between the will of donors and the interest of research institutions and not so much from the evil will of individual scientists. It is not so much a personal failure if procedures of consent are violated as a consequence of the pressure of a scientific community relying ever more on the donation of human tissue. Therefore, there is reason to be concerned. Nor do we have any reason to assume, let alone to request, that donors give their tissue altruistically when such gift might be eventually harmful to them.

This volume shows how altruism can be reconsidered. But to show why altruism cannot function is only one aspect of the endeavor. The book is critical on one side and explorative on the other. It also looks for new models in the regulation of tissue donation. In the United Kingdom, legal certainty has been reached to a considerable degree, with the Human Tissue Act (2004) and, more recently, the Human Fertilisation and Embryology Bill (HFE Act 2008), which both stipulate precise rules for the licensing of biobanks and consent rules that have to be observed.

However, not all countries have similar legislation, and besides that, much has to be done in order to fully clarify the role of donors in regard to biobanks. The existing legislation only concerns formal requirements, but not the question to what extent donors should have an influence on the objectives and the methods of research. Many authors of this volume hope that the concept of property might be instrumental for such further clarification. Property can be used in many different ways, and there are many possibilities for regulations that might help donors to actively exert their rights. But there are also critical concerns in regard to property, both for practical and conceptual reasons, and the book also brings them into play. After all, there seems to be no easy solution to the problems in the field of tissue donation. The ethical and legal landscape explored in this volume appears to be rather complex. If the book succeeds in making this complexity manifest, if it leaves the reader confused by the richness of its suggestions and propositions, it already has fulfilled its aim.

The first part is devoted to a reflection on the notions of 'gift' and 'altruism'. Sýkora and Tutton in their respective chapters both start from Richard Titmuss's seminal book *The Gift Relationship*, published in 1970. For decades, Titmuss's model of medical donation as a charitable, altruistic giving has served as the dominating model. Its purpose was to establish a strong opposition between gift and commodity. For Sykora, however, altruistic donation and commerce, traditionally considered to be mutually exclusive black and white alternatives, rather can be seen as the opposite poles of a sort of grey continuum. In this continuum, commercial and non-commercial practices are mixed together in various proportions, blurring borders between pure altruism and commerce. This continuum has a normative dimension of its own, which lies in the concept of reciprocity. Reciprocity can be seen as the foundation for a new conceptual framework in the discourse on donation. Looking on results from evolutionary psychology helps to sustain this conclusion.

Tutton explores the role of the notion of 'gift' from a sociological perspective as a leading concept in policy making. As the case of recent UK legislation, for example, the Human Tissue Act of 2004, shows, gift as a former key word slowly has been replaced by the idea of participation. Regulations are becoming more 'participatory' in giving the citizen's interests an institutional representation. Participation and reciprocity are different, but closely related notions; both are possible ways to overcome the one-way commitment of the 'gift relationship' between donor and recipient.

The second part reflects on donation in the light of human embodiment. Insofar as the body cannot be separated from the person, even the donation of small body parts concerns us intimately. Such concern has to be reflected ethically. Campbell starts from the retained organs controversy that arose with the Bristol and Alder Hey cases where organs and body parts of dead children were withheld without the consent of parents. Especially in the eyes of those mourning their beloved ones, the body acquires a highly symbolic meaning. Since the embodiment of the person does not suddenly disappear in death, this explains the strong reaction of parents in these cases. It would be quite wrong to describe their feelings of anger and loss as merely emotional or even irrational. Rather they show the narrative dissonance of the medical and lay understandings of the body. In the face of these different narratives, medicine has to rediscover the lost dimension of respect for the human body.

Steinmann's focus lies on the normative presumptions we have in relation to our body. We feel obliged to care for our body and to act in favor of its well-being, including the well-being of others (for example, by participating in research). Where does this feeling come from? The categorical framework of 'autonomy' as it is mostly used in bioethics cannot help us here. What is needed is a shift from autonomy to an approach based on 'duties toward our bodies'. Such 'duties' have to be seen as grounds for both 'altruism' and 'donation' because they give the reason why we feel obliged to donate parts of our body. The notion of duty can be explained through a phenomenological approach to the body. The body is both an internal and an external experience for us: it is identical with our personal life, but it also reminds us or even forces us to care. From this perspective, the idea of duties also helps to shed some critical light on the idea of self-ownership in the body. From a legal point of view, property is the perfect tool to articulate the rights of donors, but ethically, all decisions concerning the body are supposed to act in the best interest of our physical condition. They are determined not by a right towards the body, but by a certain normative commitment to let the body thrive.

With the third part, the book draws on the problem of property. Property rights in the body have become an important issue in the debates on biobanking. As already has been said, many ethicists hope such rights might be the appropriate tool to safeguard the autonomy of those participating in tissue donation. Others, however, reject it just because of ethical concerns in seeing the human body as an object of property. But besides such controversies, even the legal notion of property can be discussed from different points of view as this part of the volume shows. 'Property' is only the general name for a whole bundle of social relations. Which of these relations we exactly refer to when we speak about 'property' is a question that requires us to develop a richer, more complex understanding of this term.

Brownsword unfolds the spectrum of ethical positions that are relevant for property in human body parts. Three competing ethics can be distinguished which together form what he calls the 'bioethical triangle': the utilitarian view, the human rights approach, and the dignitarian view on the person. Neither of these ethics agrees with the other, and from all of them we come to different conclusions whether proprietary rights in the body can be seen as a legitimate idea or not. There seems to be no easy solution as to which edge of the triangle should be preferred. Hence, the scope of this chapter is not to decide the question but rather to develop an analytic tool that helps us to understand where the protagonists in the debate are coming from. Much is gained if the controversy around property can be traced back to such basic disagreements.

Björkman raises some fundamental questions concerning the philosophy of law. If we have a closer look at property in the human body, it is unclear what kind of relationship to biological material we really entertain. Which rights and obligations do we have, and in what exactly? A first step that becomes necessary here is to divide ownership up into a bundle of different rights. Ownership in biological material can take many different forms, from intellectual property, like patents, to traditional ownership in objects, and rights should be granted accordingly, in a flexible way that also respects the different types of material. For example, the right to possess can be distinguished from the right to income, and this again can be distinguished from the right to sell, depending always on the nature of the body parts. Property is not an all-or-nothing relationship between the owner and an object as it has been understood in the natural rights theory, for example in Locke. We rather have to refine our notion of property in regard to both the objects that are owned and the people or institutions that are given rights. A social constructivist theory of rights seems to be the appropriate tool in order to sustain and to conceptualize such a refinement.

With Hoppe the reflection on the legal meaning of 'property' is continued in a different way. Following the author's suggestions, many problems that occur in relation to human tissue rather have to do with our terminology than with actual problems in fact. Ideas about ownership and also terms like 'commodification' or 'propertization' hardly allow for an unemotional assessment of the problems at stake. However, we do need notions like 'ownership' or 'property' in order to conceptualize the control rights donors should be assigned. Against this difficulty, the legal concept of 'possession', stating the 'entitlement' of someone in something, seems to offer a solution. We might not be the owner of our body, but we certainly have entitlements in relation to others. But the idea of 'entitlements' also yields another benefit. Property laws normally require that all ownership is held in one hand – for example, in the hand of a biobank my tissue has been given to – excluding the right to further control on the side of donors. They do not allow for flexible solutions in the favor of tissue donors. In such a case, the principle of equity could be applied. Equity comes into play when the law is unable to cover all eventualities. Donors could receive at least an equitable entitlement to control the use of their tissue. Even in the framework of strict property laws, it could be possible to grant them a certain influence on research or to share the benefits of a possible financial outcome.

With the fourth part, the book explores the creative potential of bioethical thought. An investigation into the different possibilities of regulation is made. The range of models that are discussed here, in either affirmative or critical manner, is rather wide. And even if not all of the models might turn out to be practicable, at least there is no reason to lose any hope. As bad as our feelings about the 'body market' and the exploitation of the human body might be, we do not have to assume that no better solutions could be found.

Lenk and Hoppe suggest a normative model for the use of human tissue. This model relies on the special dignity of the human body. Body parts cannot be used without the voluntary and informed consent of the donor. This means that any kind of 'blanket' consent has to be rejected. 'The normative objective', according to the authors, 'is cooperation between researcher and patient for the benefit of research', including the need to establish ways of benefit-sharing. As in previous chapters of this book, the idea of a one-way relationship between donor and recipient is replaced by a more participatory notion of their relationship.

Noiville's argument is based on the observation that even with the application of given consent rules, the control donors are able to exert is fairly limited. Apart from objecting completely to the use of their tissue, they cannot influence or negotiate its industrial and commercial exploitations. A power imbalance between donors and biobanks has taken place. The contract law seems to provide a solution to this problem as it allows donors to set up conditions for the use of their material. However, not every realization of contractual freedom might be acceptable, and therefore the solution cannot work for every case. But at least in certain cases, for example, patient groups, it seems to offer a strong instrument of control.

Another instrument is charitable trust, as it has been implemented in the legislation of the UK Biobank. Mullen offers a discussion of the different points that speak in favor of the trust model as a means of adequately responding to ethical considerations associated with biobanks. However, these points do not imply that biobanks operating on a profit-oriented basis could not also be able to respond to such considerations. Public control of such biobanks might lead to the same result as the installation of a trust. On the other side, even a charitable trust might not always work in the interests of the public but rather exhibit stark partiality or prejudice. Therefore, even in the case of non-profit organizations, it is up to the society as a whole to decide what works in its best interest.

Bovenberg inquires into the possibility of benefit-sharing. All models that have been brought up so far in the debates – the contract model, charitable trust, the non-market compensation model and the global public good model – have disadvantages. Either they are too complicated or work only with specific donor groups. In addition, all models except the global public good model raise ethical concerns, because the mechanisms of benefit only pertain to a certain group and not to everyone. In order to overcome these disadvantages, the author suggests taxation as the possibility of a both equitable and practicable way of benefit sharing.

Mullen and Widdows, finally, explain the outlines of the PropEur project that stood at the origin of this volume. The goal of the project was to confront the uncertainty regarding how to conceive of, manage, regulate and govern property. From its beginning, the project was directed to a plurality of models, such as donation, trust, benefit-sharing, commodification and conditional gift. Its underlying idea was that a single model hardly can embody ideal governance. But it also started from the assumption that the models have to be discussed in a multidisciplinary way: some of them raise practical, some ethical concerns, some of them both. The capacity to distinguish not only between the different options but also between the different criteria that are used in order to assess these options is something that can be learned from this approach.

The fifth and last part of the volume is devoted to giving a broader image of current legislation and regulations. Its goal is to show the actual practices of tissue donation and to highlight the many challenges that still persist in this field.

Emaldi begins with an overview of the role of personal rights in the relation to biobanks. Particular emphasis is laid on the Spanish situation, together with the background formed by European and other international regulations. In addition, a number of nationwide projects of biobanking are described which carry their specific ethical and legal problems. As a general conclusion, equal protection of personal rights should be applied to donors whenever they participate in projects of a larger or a smaller scale.

Labrusse-Riou draws on ambiguities that arise in French law. These ambiguities stem from the fact that the human body underlies different legal (and therefore also normative) regimes: it underlies civil law that refuses to consider the existence of any classical property right on the human body, commercial law which tends to consider the body as a commodity and, finally, health law which is perpetually swinging between the satisfaction of private interests and public needs. Which logic should prevail? In French law, certain questions, for example, whether donors are the owners of their bodies, are not decided explicitly. Traces of the organicist conception of the state and of a biological solidarity between the living and the dead have not disappeared and lead to an emphasis on the altruistic character of donation, carried out for the public good – without much concern for the individual. This situation might seem favorable for all those who are critical about commodification, but it also leaves the role of donors in regard to medical institutions unclear. The law should find a way to reconcile such different but equally valid interests and points of view.

With Schneider's contribution, the volume touches a case of tissue donation where ethical reflection seems to be more needed than ever: the case of ova donation. The increasing demand for women's egg cells leads to reproductive tourism and transnational ova trafficking. In order to understand the regulatory landscape of ova donation in Europe, it is important to see whether ova are provided within or outside of the IVF context and whether anonymity of the donor is legally possible or not. A special case is given by ova demanded for cloning research. The demand generated by the cloning research race, and ambitious national research programs, have put a certain pressure on deregulation. There is actually no consistent regulation on the European level, a situation which has led to a downgrading of ethical standards. What is needed in order to increase donor protection not only pertains to a higher safety standard for fertility clinics or to provisions regarding consent procedures and the monitoring of donor's health. It also is necessary to abolish the anonymous donation of germ cells in order to make the donor recruitment more transparent than it is. Finally, the most important problem lies in financial compensation which lures women into donation. For the author, the arguments against the commodification of ova outweigh any other arguments in its favor.

Hall shows that the regulation of tissue donation remains incomplete when it does not also include the genetic information that can be obtained from tissue samples. The chapter traces the genesis of the Human Tissue Act that came into force 2004 in the UK, after a series of scandals which brought up the idea that a fundamental change of the legal settings had to occur. The Act basically concerns the holding of cellular material for DNA analysis, but the question how genetic information should be regulated is left rather vague. In addition, it exemplifies an individualistic and autonomous model of decision making by establishing a regulatory framework which promotes the interests of the tissue donor. These interests have been challenged under the perspective of genetic information. One of the objections is that genetic information should be regarded as jointly owned by family members. The autonomous refusal of an individual could knowingly inflict harm on a relative by refusing to allow his or her own material to be tested for the other person's benefit. Another problem lies in the 'right not to know', which hardly can be dealt with in a framework based on autonomy (a patient who prefers 'not to know' does not want to be fully informed and therefore prefers not to use the full potential of his or her autonomy). Other provisions within the health care regulation, as much as existing laws for data protection, might be less focused on autonomy but do not reach a clear solution of the problems either.

Taupitz explains the position of the German National Ethics Council which has issued a long and detailed statement on the use of human tissue ('Biobanks for Research', 2004). From the legal point of view, an important distinction has to be made between property rights in the bodily material, and personal rights that might be affected by the genetic information extracted from the tissue sample. The two types of law are treated differently in current legislation: a doctor will face severe sanctions if he violates a property right, whereas infringement of personal rights has not necessarily adverse consequences. Whether the self-determination of a donor is violated or not has to be decided for each single case. It is necessary to balance the interests involved, and the high weight of the freedom of research also has to be taken into account. The use of anonymized data, even without consent, might be such a case. Following this argument, blanket or global consent appears in a much more positive light than it does in other chapters of this book. The autonomy of donors, maintains the author, cannot always overrule the public good that might be promoted by research. A general recommendation of the German National Ethics Council's statement is that donors should be able to consent to the use of their samples and data for an indefinite period. Consent to virtually every use of tissue and genetic information cannot necessarily be seen as a violation of the right of self-determination, according to this.

Koller describes the various attempts to harmonize the regulation of tissue on the level of the European Union and also of the World Health Organization. Directives issued by the European Commission in 2004 and 2006 are likely to have a major impact on biobanks. Biobanks now need to implement the requirements of the Directives into their everyday practices. This includes, among others, the necessity of new accreditation, designation, authorization or licensing of biobanks by the competent authorities. How much biobanks will be able to meet these requirements is still unsure, mainly in regard to smaller establishments like hospital banks. A new system for reporting adverse events and reactions also needs to be established. But the main point seems to be that the Directives were aimed at and adopted as technical documents. Many important normative issues, like the problem of property, are not regulated on their level at all.

At this point, it remains with the reader to decide which side of the problem seems more difficult to treat: the normative conflicts underlying the use of human tissue or the practical challenges in coming to consistent and realistic rules in health care and health legislation law. Both sides are dealt with in this book, and for both sides many different solutions are indicated. These solutions might be convincing or not. But as already has been said, much is gained if we just see how complex the landscape is that our new technologies force us to explore.

PART I
Reciprocity and Participation: Overcoming the Models of 'Gift' and 'Altruism'

Chapter 2
Altruism in Medical Donations Reconsidered: the Reciprocity Approach

Peter Sýkora

Introduction

> In these scenarios [adoption of commercial ethics and management arrangements] of changing and disappearing values, the principles of altruistic giving and commitment to a service based on reciprocity and social solidarity are absolute central. It is, above all, from this perspective – the aftermath of the most radical changes to public institutions for over a century – that the arguments of the Gift Relationship most needed to be revisited. (Oakley and Ashton 1997, 11)

Since money and other forms of remuneration were first offered for blood donation in the 1960s, there has been an ongoing debate about whether medical donations in general should be based only on pure acts of altruism or whether financial compensation should also be permissible. In the last four or five decades a general consensus has been formed that paid and unpaid donation systems are mutually exclusive and society has to endorse ethically superior altruistic donations instead of bodily commerce. Furthermore, it is believed that practicing voluntary and unpaid medical donations has a prosocial effect on the society as a whole and therefore 'a major argument for exclusive reliance on unpaid donation is that, unlike paid donation, it promotes altruism and social solidarity' (Keown 1997, 96).

The main goal of this chapter is to show that rather than two mutually exclusive black and white alternatives, altruistic donation and commerce can be considered to be the opposite poles of a grey continuum, with various coexisting donation forms between them. In my view, all these forms, including opposing poles, can be subsumed under the common denominator of the concept of reciprocity – direct or indirect, equal or partial. In order to demonstrate this, first we have to rethink the concept of altruism as it has been used in the medical donation discourse for decades. To do this we need to go back to the concept of medical donation altruism as it was formed in Titmuss's crucial book *The Gift Relationship*. Then we have to bring a broader evolutionary perspective into the discourse on altruism in medical donations.

In 1970 Professor Richard M. Titmuss (1907–1973) published his seminal work *The Gift Relationship: From Human Blood To Social Policy*. After more than 30 years Titmuss's book is still a basic reference for the debate on medical donation. The main idea of the book was to demonstrate with the help of statistical data that blood transfusion system based on voluntary and altruistic blood donation is superior in efficiency, quality, safety, cost and, last but not least, also in moral and social implications to a commercial system based on payment for blood giving. Basically, the book contrasts two different national approaches to blood procurement – the UK state system based on unpaid donors with the US system of private commercial blood banks which pay reasonable money for blood donations.[1]

The Gift Relationship received an enthusiastic worldwide acceptance and almost immediately became very influential far beyond UK borders and outside the specific field of blood transfusion policy. *The New York Times* described the 1971 American edition of the book as one of the seven best books of its time. Rapport and Maggs (Rapport and Maggs 2002, 496) in their recent study of Titmuss's archive (which is kept at the LSE library and also includes Titmuss's personal correspondence) have discovered evidence that the book played an important role in the reform of the American blood banking system during the Nixon administration. In fact, it led the US government to stimulate voluntary blood donation and to require labeling of blood from paid donors. In the UK Titmuss's book played an important role in the debate about the future of British welfare state and countered plans of state health service privatization.

The Gift Relationship articulates the central question of medical donation in a very suggestive form as a Hamlet-like dilemma: should human body parts be altruistically given to those who need them or should they be sold under the rules of a free market economy like any other commodity? Titmuss believed that if blood could be sold for money, 'then ultimately human hearts, kidneys, eyes and other organs of the body may also come to be treated as commodities to be bought and sold in the marketplace' (Titmuss 1997, 219).

For Titmuss the blood donation system is a *pars pro toto* area, a microcosm where the gift and commodification dichotomy can be studied in details and then provide more general implications. His book significantly influenced the debate on organ donation in the 1980s in the USA and also in other countries.

Titmuss explores the medical, political, social and moral consequences not only for the health system itself, but for the society as a whole if one or the other alternative were taken. His conclusion is that there are areas of social life, such as the health care system or education, which have to be saved from commercialization. There are two main reasons to protect them. Firstly, they will perform better if they stay outside the market economy. Secondly, they serve another function – forming the space where highly ethical behavior, such as behaving altruistically to strangers, can be exercised. This creative altruism, a term borrowed from P.A. Sorokin and

---

1   The US system in that time was not entirely commercialized; it was rather a mixed system which, besides commercial blood banks, included blood procurement from voluntary and unpaid donors organized by the Red Cross.

used by Titmuss, plays a crucial role in social cohesion. According to Titmuss, freedom to exercise altruistic behavior belongs to basic human rights. Since in his view there is no place for altruism in market economy, the commodification of a particular area of social life suppresses altruism as a human right.

Titmuss's argument against commodification of the body based on the social cohesion function, which exercises creative altruism in acts such as unpaid donation of body parts to strangers, complements other arguments against human body commodification. Those are the ones based on the human dignity concept, whose secular tradition goes back to Kantian morality: a human being must be treated as an end and never as means only, never as a thing. Things have prices, they can be sold and bought while human beings have intrinsic values. The common view is that the commodification of the human body violates Kant's categorical imperative and the human dignity principle which forms the core of all human rights (Politis 2000).[2] Recently his antimarket argument has been expanded into two distinct arguments: the 'contamination argument' and 'erosion of motivation argument' (Archard 2002). According to the first argument, although market and non-market regimes can coexist, 'the meaning of non-market exchanges would have been contaminated by the existence of the market exchange'. According to the second argument, 'motivation of co-citizens could be eroded by mercenary reasoning' (Archard 2002, 95 and 101 respectively).

During the decades after *The Gift Relationship* was published, a virtually worldwide consensus, usually secured by national legislation, has been built up to prohibit the buying and selling of human body parts, organs, tissues and cells. This prohibition is also supported at the international level and has been especially stressed recently in European countries. *The Council of Europe Convention on Human Rights and Biomedicine* (Oviedo 1997) states that 'the human body and its parts shall not, as such, give rise to financial gain', (Chapter VII, Article 21) and almost the same words can be found in Article 3 of *The Charter of Fundamental Rights of the European Union* (2000). Titmussian arguments have been used in favor of unpaid donation of human blood and human plasma in the EC Directive 89/381 (Keown 1997), and the principle of altruistic, voluntary and unpaid medical donation is embedded in corresponding recent European Union directives (see Article 20 in Directive 2002/98/EC on human blood, Article 12 in Directive 2004/23/EC on human tissues and cells).

For altruism 'purists' not even non-financial incentives are allowed. In his book Titmuss criticized a practice of 'fringe benefits' of various kinds in the Communist countries of the former Soviet block. For him it was a big surprise and provided evidence of deep hypocrisy in these societies. Here were the states which proclaimed a total anti-capitalistic, non-commercial way of life, yet promoted

---

2   The application of Kant's categorical imperative in biomedicine is often less clear-cut than here; see, for example, Beauchamps and Childress 1994, 351. For more complex relationship between the commodification of the body, property and human dignity, see Beyleveld and Brownsword 2001, 171–94.

this collectivistic pro-social ideology by giving extra benefits to donors. He was right to see a form of reciprocity in these benefits, and since he was accepting only unreciprocated pure altruism, this was for him the equivalent of selling and buying, just as blood donation was rewarded by money in the US (Titmuss 1997, 237–42).

The Council of Europe's policy on blood seems to follow Titmuss's legacy of pure altruistic donation. For example, Politis (Politis 2000) recently pointed out in his editorial article that 'the principle of voluntary non-remunerated blood donation as defined by the Council of Europe is not applied properly in several European countries'. He is criticizing these countries because donors are allowed extra time off from work or school, food tokens, theater tickets, free trips, extra vacation and money as reimbursement of travel expenses (for plateletpheresis and plasmapheresis donors).

For example, according to Politis it has to be among the objectives of most central and eastern European countries to include non-remunerated blood donation in their health sector reforms. Interestingly enough he points to the results of the Eurobarometer 41 survey from 1994, which showed that in Mediterranean countries such as Greece, Italy, Spain and Portugal, the most frequent motive for blood donation was the need of a relative or friend. He comments about this data that 'it may be unreasonable to expect that the principle of altruistic donation for the unknown fellow-man, as required by international organizations, can be adopted easily' in these countries with strong family bonds and a 'mosaic of nationalities or races' and history of civil wars and separatism (Politis 2000, 356).

In his view those countries face a challenge to convert family replacement blood donors to regular volunteers. The solution lies in national blood donor recruitment and retention programs – organized by trained staff, backed by active information, education and motivation campaigns – 'effective blood donor recruitment and retention should to be managed in a businesslike way by a director of blood donor recruitment' (Politis 2000, 357). Essential are good public relations in the media, presenting athletes, movie actors, TV stars, singers and church leaders as role models. And last but not least, 'the donors must also feel that their gift is useful for the community and appreciated' Politis notes that 'awards, letters of appreciation and encouragement, refreshments, ceremonies, parties, newsletters, are all valuable materials and methods which can be utilized for promoting blood donation' (Politis 2000, 357).

At the same time the situation with regard to various human body parts has changed significantly. New biomedical techniques have caused increased need for various medical donations, ranging from human cells to organs. During recent years there has been an increased demand for a greater number as well as for a broader range of usable human body parts. Various body parts considered to be just biological waste turned out to be useful substances for biomedicine, pharmacology and the cosmetic industry. Although in most countries unpaid blood donation systems prevail and are well able to cope with the increase in the need for blood, the demand for plasma products has to be satisfied on a commercial basis by paid donors and specialized multinational pharmaceutical companies trading blood products internationally. Especially in the area of human tissue and cells donations, commercial and non-commercial activities are so tightly interconnected that it is impossible to draw a clear-cut line between social and economic man, as Titmuss would phrase it. This is particularly true for the domain of human tissue, when altruistically received tissue from unpaid donors can be later traded for money, preserved, processed and used purely on a commercial basis (Waldby and Mitchell 2006).

The most obvious disproportion is between the demand for and the donation of organs for transplantation medicine. A severe shortage of both cadaveric organs as well as those from living donors is now a major obstacle for the full development of transplantation as a routine medical practice. The gap between the number of available organs and patients on the waiting list is continually growing. And it is just the tip of the iceberg, as the real disproportion is much higher since many patients are not eligible to get onto the waiting list. Thousands of patients are dying because of donor shortage. Some authors are challenging the very concept of altruism in connection with organ procurement and are talking about the limits of altruism (Wilkinson 2003, Goodwin 2006).

An international black market in human organs is a fact of life. It is an illegal but real reaction to the high disequilibrium between organ supply and demand. Globalization and the Internet opened new dimensions for patients, who can take the initiative and look for an altruistic donor worldwide with the help of their personal homepage.[3] New specialized websites connecting donors and recipients from all over the world are run as non-profit organizations and earn more than reasonable money for their keepers. Globalization also allows people to overcome the strict national legislation on organ donorship which exists in some countries. Recently a web-based company on the Internet was set up in the USA offering altruistically donated ready-made embryos for sterile women all over the world.[4]

This chapter is divided into five parts. In the first four parts Titmuss's concept of gift relationship will be deconstructed. The first part will briefly review already known criticism of Titmuss's economic arguments in which he tried to demonstrate that an altruistic blood donation system is better than a commercial one in all compared economic parameters – ability to respond to blood demand increase, efficiency of management (less donated blood is wasted), blood unit cost and quality of blood and safety.

The second part will focus on Titmuss's sociological and anthropological arguments and will argue that his arguments in favor of altruistic blood donation are incoherent because he does not distinguish between two different meanings of the gift term: the gift as a voluntary act of pure gratuitousness and the gift as a tool of social mutual relations based on reciprocation.

---

3   http://www.matchingdonors.com (last accessed 20 June 2009).
4   http://www.theabrahamcentreoflife.com (last accessed 20 June 2009).

The third part will offer a wider perspective on the problem of human altruistic behavior and will propose that medical donation discourse should incorporate some of the main insights from modern evolutionary psychology. For decades altruism has been considered to be a typical human characteristic, a result of civilization, culture and social learning, as contrasted to pure selfish biological endowment. During the conceptual revolution in evolutionary biology which started in the 1960s–70s, it was shown that altruistic behavior is not at odds with Darwinian mechanisms of evolution, and that altruistic pro-social behavior could have been selected during the last 30 million years in an evolutionary line leading to our species. Evolutionary psychologists have suggested that our brain has been designed by evolution in such a way that our emotions support altruistic (as well as selfish) behavior, depending on the conditions.

The fourth part will demonstrate that Titmuss's gift relation model for medical donations is in fact a purely altruistic charity model, a kind of alms-giving, with no expectation for return. The question is whether medical donations in modern medicine and biomedical research where nothing is for free can be based on a charity.

Finally, the concluding fifth part will propose a new conceptual framework for medical donations as an alternative to Titmuss's charitable gift model. Within the new framework it is possible to conceptualize gift and commodity as the opposing poles of the same reciprocity continuum.

Deconstructing Titmuss's Gift Relationship

There are two different kinds of arguments used by Titmuss in *The Gift Relationship*. First, he uses comparative statistical data to argue in favor of altruistic blood donation in contrast to a commercial system. From these data, it seems evident that an altruistic system is more effective from an economic and administrative point of view; it is cheaper and medically safer. Arguments of this sort were mostly addressed to his opponents from the neo-liberal think tank *The Institute of Economic Affairs* (IEA), who had been advocating privatization of the British health care system. His strategy was to beat his opponents with their own arguments. Arguments in favor of higher economic efficiency could hardly be rejected by those who promoted commercialization and a free market philosophy.

The second set of arguments is of a completely different sort. Titmuss uses ethical, anthropological and social arguments to show that we should prefer an unpaid altruistic donation system to a market system. This type of argument is called anthropological. These arguments, in contrast with the first kind mentioned above, are much more vulnerable to the accusation of being ideological. In this context it would mean that the arguments are used in order to support a socialist instead of a capitalist view on health care policy and social administration. And the way that Titmuss uses anthropological argumentation shows that such a suspicion would not be unfounded. First of all, it is obvious to him (as to many others) that altruistic donation is ethically superior to paid donation. (All things being equal, an altruistic solution should be preferred). But his main argument for a non-commercial blood donation system is not only what it does for the blood transfusion system itself, but how it could affect the whole society. He believes that it encourages altruistic and pro-social behavior in everyday life, needed in modern societies, in which the commercialization of ever broader parts of social life destroys social bonds. According to him, a non-commercial blood system opens an opportunity for people 'to make moral choices or to behave altruistically if they wish to do so' (Titmuss 1999, 386).

Part I: Titmuss's Economic Arguments

According to Titmuss 'the voluntary socialised system in Britain is economically, professionally, administratively and qualitatively more efficient than the mixed, commercialised and individualistic American system' (Titmuss 1997, 271). However, during the consecutive three decades after appearance of *The Gift Relationship*, its critics clearly demonstrated that none of these arguments was correct.

The Gift Relationship is the culmination of Titmuss's polemic with the IEA. Since its founding by F. Hayek in 1955, the IEA has become the UK's leading think-tank promoting free-market principles as a way of solving economic and social problems in society. This is the reason why Titmuss tries to keep his argument at the evidence-based level and uses economic arguments against commercialized blood donorship (represented by the US system) in favor of maintaining the British altruistic system of blood donorship within the National Health Service.

However Titmuss, as a prominent Fabian academic, sees the debate on blood donorship and health policy as a special part of a broader picture. Being an advocate of the socialist welfare state, he sees the rise of a neoliberal economic approach to society as 'the philistine resurrection of economic man in social policy' (Titmuss 1997, 60).

The reason why this book became very influential on health policy is the convincing empirical evidence it offers – but not only because of that. As Fontaine recently pointed out:

> What made for the impact of his book, however, was not merely its argument that transfusion-transmitted infections were much more common with paid than with voluntary donors, but also its reflections on what it is that holds a society together. And here Titmuss argued that a 'socialist' social policy, by encouraging the sense of community, played a central role. (Fontaine 2002, 411)

Tutton's recent comment of this aspect went further when he said that *The Gift Relationship* 'should be read as primarily a political account' (Tutton 2002).

It is true that Titmuss's major concern is the overall character of the health care system and of the society. According to him a real danger of the commercialization of blood donorship is that it can spread to other health and social services. To accept the commoditization of blood would get us on a slippery slope down towards the complete commercialization of social affairs:

> What are the consequences, national and international, of treating human blood as a commercial commodity? If blood is morally sanctioned as something to be bought and sold, what ultimately is the justification for not promoting individualistic private markets in other component areas of medical care, and in education, social security, welfare services, child foster care, social work skills, the use of patients and clients for professional training, and other 'social service' institutions and processes. (Titmuss 1997, 58)

Titmuss knew very well that only economic arguments would appeal to the economists from the IEA and the US who preferred a private market in blood. Therefore he directly addressed his economic opponents on their own terrain, reacting to the economic analysis of blood donorship commissioned by the IEA in 1968.

The main argument of the IEA study is that human blood is in fact an economic good. It has its price, and the scarcity of blood can be solved by market forces if paying money to donors is allowed.

Titmuss wants to beat his opponents with their own weapons as

> criteria of economic efficiency, administrative efficiency, cost per unit of blood and purity, potency and safety ... [We] shall try to behave like an economist. [The] way in which ethical premises are avoided by economic writers on the supposition that utilities of different persons are empirically comparable. (Titmuss 1997, 261)

For seven years he had been carefully collecting and analyzing statistical data from Britain, the US and other states, as well as doing his own empirical research on blood donorship. Therefore his book is full of statistical data on procurement, processing, distribution and use of human blood in transfusion systems focusing mostly on a single thing: to demonstrate that the unpaid British donation system is cheaper, more effective, of higher quality and safer for both donors and recipients.

All Titmuss's economic arguments have been challenged since they were published. Now, after more than three decades, it seems that none of them has survived. Titmuss uses data to show that a voluntary and unpaid British system is better able to cope with a rapid increase in demand for blood. It was really true for the years between 1951 and 1965 if one compared the US and British systems. But it was due to the messy and uncoordinated blood systems of that time in the US, one commercial and one non-commercial, rather than caused by the commercialization itself. The same was true for the efficiency parameter.

Recalculating of the data revealed that blood was wasted almost equally in both the US and British systems (Schwartz 1999).

Titmuss also pointed out the safety of blood. He argued that once blood becomes a commodity its quality is corrupted – American blood was four times more likely to infect recipients with hepatitis than British blood. Even Titmuss's critics have acknowledged he was right to point out the fact that in the specific situation of the US blood donation system, altruistically given blood was safer than blood from paid donors. But they do not agree with his argument that this particular situation is an inevitable consequence of blood commoditization itself, and that only altruistic blood donation can remove this health risk. The radical improvement in safety in the following years was due to the introduction of tests able to detect hepatitis B antibodies after 1985. The situation has radically changed with the blood donated by HIV positive donors. In contrast to what Titmuss would have expected, commercial pharmaceutical companies buying and selling blood plasma responded much more rapidly to the AIDS safety challenges than non-profit biobanks. As Waldby and Mitchell concluded in their book *Tissue Economies* 'the AIDS contamination demonstrated the inability of gift systems to guarantee the security of the blood supply' (Waldby and Mitchell 2006, 49).

In the view of present-day critics Titmuss's comparative case study failed to support his main thesis that an unpaid non-commercial blood system by its altruistic nature is more efficient, better administered, less costly and safer than its commercial counterpart. Evidence has shown that both systems are equally open to blood misadministration, waste or health risk, and that these parameters are 'ideologically' (commercial versus non-commercial debate) independent.

Part II: Titmuss's Sociological/Anthropological Arguments

The second set of arguments presented by Titmuss will now be discussed in more detail. These may be called sociological or anthropological. From empirical findings he drew a more general and profound conclusion – an altruistic blood donation system is not only better from an economic and health policy point of view, but it also plays a special role in society. It creates a place where people can exercise their moral choice (or freedom as he saw it) to help strangers. In *The Gift Relationship,* which happened to be his last work, he integrates the most important ideas about the welfare state and the role of social and health policy in it from his previous works. It therefore became the

> clearest statement of his moral philosophy: the view that a competitive, materialistic, acquisitive society based on hierarchies of power and privilege ignores at its peril the life-giving impulse towards altruism which is needed for welfare in the most fundamental sense. (Oakley and Ashton 1997, 7)

Titmuss, who was known for his wide interest and his interdisciplinary approach to problems, tries to ground his vision of the role of altruism in a modern society on the anthropological works of Malinowski, Mauss and Lévi-Strauss on gift culture in primitive societies.

Titmuss says in the introductory chapter that his study is about the role of altruism in modern society and is an attempt 'to fuse the politics of welfare and the morality of individual wills' (Titmuss 1997, 59). The biggest concern that Titmuss had was that the opportunity to exercise a moral choice altruistically – to give or not to give to strangers – is an essential human right, and that imperialistic commercialization of all areas of social life deprives us of this freedom. He is directly against the trend toward what he called the 'philistine resurrection of economic man in social policy' (Titmuss 1997, 60). Since he died in 1973, he was lucky enough not to witness how 'economic man' finally took Britain's social welfare state by storm during the Thatcherism of the 1980s.

Titmuss sees human nature as a selfish one, which has to be trained to behave altruistically. According to Titmuss we are born to be selfish, and we have to learn to behave altruistically:

> Men are not born to give; as newcomers, they face none of the dilemmas of altruism and self-love. How can they and how do they learn to give – and to give to unnamed strangers irrespective of race, religion, or colour – not in circumstances of shared misery but in societies continually multiplying new desires and syndicalist private wants concerned with property, status, and power. (Titmuss 1997, 59)

Therefore we have to give a chance for our social environment to create such a social space where altruism can be exercised. In Titmuss's view this space opens 'the opportunity to behave altruistically – to exercise a moral choice to give in non-monetary terms to strangers'. It is a kind of freedom, an essential human right. He is very likely using this vocabulary of freedom and human rights in reaction to a neoliberal vocabulary of economic freedom, which means in this context letting the state extend a free market economy to health and social service.

Titmuss believes that economic freedom cannot coexist with altruism and that a free market economy will necessarily supersede altruistic behavior, destroying a space which provides the opportunity to practice altruistic behavior. This would also eliminate the opportunity to teach people how to behave altruistically (remember, according to Titmuss, we are born selfish). With the gradual expanding of economic freedom, as it is called by neoliberal economists, to all areas of social life, we are not only losing space to behave altruistically, but also losing a way that could mold us into altruistic beings. If there is no space left to exercise altruism in a society, then people will not be shaped to be altruistic, meaning pro-social and human, at least human, as a desired ideal. Titmuss does not want (as a communist would) to have a whole society without free market economy and based on an altruistic, or, in this context, cooperative (collectivistic) behavior. He accepts a central role for the free market economy in a society, but not that selling and buying should be extended to every sphere of life. He suggests that even in a free market capitalistic society, it is necessary to have islands of altruistic behavior, areas of pro-social behavior with creative altruism, which create altruistically behaving people. Since, according to Titmuss, free market mechanisms cannot coexist with a non-market mechanism within the same social area, there have to be clear borders between market and non-market social areas.

Titmuss's Social Engineering

Titmuss, with his understanding that one has to learn to be altruistic, shares a standard position with the social sciences – we have to be taught to be human.[5] He accepts the general position of social and human sciences that human nature (if anything like this exists) is molded by social environment, by the process called socialization. Socialization is a continual process of learning how to behave in a society. From birth to death we are socialized and resocialized by family, school, peers, the mass media, religion, the workplace and by multiple networks and interactions with other people. Whether we will be altruistic or selfish depends on the social environment and the previous process of socialization during our sensitive years in childhood. If we want people to behave altruistically, first we have to teach them to behave this way, and then we have to create an opportunity to exercise such behavior. In Titmuss's view it is up to social policy to create instruments and institutions not to allow free market economy to destroy space which can serve as an opportunity to behave altruistically. This has an obvious positive role not only within the borders of such space, but also outside of it, since it creates more altruistic, more pro-social citizens.

Based on this social engineering approach, Titmuss recommends 'examining the extent to which specific instruments of public policy encourage or discourage, foster or destroy the individual expression of altruism and regard for the needs of others' (Titmuss 1997, 59). The analyses of gift-exchange systems in anthropological works have disclosed a complex social network generated by gift relationships. In the creation of a social network among strangers, Titmuss sees a basic analogy between gift-giving in these pre-industrial societies studied by anthropologists and giving blood as the gift of life in modern societies. It is not the gift itself which is important in the gift relationship but the social relationship which is created by the transfer of a gift. Therefore Titmuss is opposing those who see the gift exchanges as parallel to economic transactions in a non-monetary society. Referring to works of Lévi-Strauss and Mauss, he points out that the gift culture in primitive societies has a far more important

---

5   'Learning to Be Human: ... ' is, for example, the title of the chapter on child development in a standard sociology textbook, Brinkerhoff's and White's *Sociology* (1988).

function than in our modern societies where it was largely replaced by commercial activities, by selling and buying commodities with money. Mainly, it generates social cohesion among unrelated members (strangers) in a society (Titmuss 1997, 277–8).

Titmuss is fully aware that the gift relationship as it is described by anthropologists is not voluntary, and it is even questionably altruistic since it is always reciprocated. On the other hand, unpaid blood donation is both a voluntary choice to help others and altruistic in a much higher moral sense. Giving blood is completely voluntary and truly altruistic behavior towards a stranger. Donors remain anonymous to recipients and do not expect reciprocal rewards from them. Furthermore, altruistic blood donation in his view creates social cohesion in a similar way as the gift relationship in primitive societies.

Titmuss lists several specific attributes of unpaid blood donation which make it a unique form of gift giving and radically different from gift exchange relationship in primitive societies (Titmuss 1997, 127). In contrast to gift exchange, it is impersonal: donors and recipient do not know each other. People are not obliged to participate in the blood gift relationship, either as donors or as recipients; it is a fully voluntary system. On the other hand, there is a selection of donors (not recipients). Not everybody can give his or her blood, for medical reasons of quality and safety. Receiving blood does not create an obligation to be a donor. There are no penalties for not giving. Givers are not certain of reciprocity in the future.

The truthfulness and honesty of the giver is an important factor since it can determine whether the blood gift will be beneficial or harmful to a recipient. There is no permanent loss on the side of giver as a result of donating blood since it can be quickly replaced in his or her body. On the side of receiver, it may have the highest value – saving a life.

Blood donation in Titmuss's eyes is not only about medical treatment, saving lives or the non-commercial character of health services. For him it is a barrier to the destruction of existing non-commercial social space in modern societies, which would otherwise happen as economic calculations spread over the whole society. Blood donation is a battlefield in the war between social and economic man:

> [B]lood as a living tissue and as a bond that links all men and women so closely that differences of colour, religious belief, and cultural heritage are insignificant besides it, may now constitute in Western society one of the ultimate tests of where the 'social' begins and 'economic' ends. (Titmuss 1999, 383)

We can say that in Titmuss's hands an unpaid blood donation system turns into a social engineering tool to train people how to be human.

Titmuss's Empirical Study of Blood Donors' Motivations

Titmuss carried out a large survey in order to support his claims about people's desire to act altruistically with empirical evidence. This brings us to the question of the motivation behind blood donation and medical donation in general.

Titmuss presents the results of his survey study on the characteristics and motivations of donors in England and Wales. The study was done in the summer and autumn of 1967 with the assistance of the Ministry of Health and the National Blood Transfusion Service. It analyzes data on some 3,800 donors, which represents approximately a 50 percent return rate of questionnaires. The results are presented in two chapters of *The Gift Relationship*. One chapter is devoted to social and demographic characteristics of donors by age, sex, marital status, income group and other attributes (for example, the number of children among married donors). In another chapter entitled 'Who Is My Stranger?' Titmuss is trying to identify the motivations of donors and to interpret the data within the framework of the concept of creative altruism.

There are several questions in his questionnaire addressing this problem. Unfortunately, in his book he discussed only answers to a single question 'Could you say *why you first* decided to become a blood donor?', in which respondents were allowed to write about their motives in their own words in the space below instead of choosing from multiple answer options. He preferred to do it this way because the original answers created by respondents 'seemed to express more vividly different categories of replies than many stereotyped answers' (Titmuss 1997, 293). All these answers from about 3,800 donors were sorted into 14 categories and presented with a sample of representative quotations for each category.

For Titmuss these results are in clear support of his theory of the willingness to help strangers, because according to him nearly 80 percent of the answers can be recognized as expressing 'a high sense of social responsibility towards the needs of other members of society'. This high percentage is reached by adding up seven categories: altruism, reciprocity, replacement, duty, personal and general appeal, awareness of need (what is left are categories of gratitude for good health, war effort, Defence Service after 1945, rare blood group, miscellaneous, more than one type of answers). His final conclusion is: 'Perhaps this is one of the outstanding impressions which emerges from the survey' (Titmuss 1997, 303).

It has to be pointed out that only non-commercial motives could be discovered in this survey since paid donation was not allowed in the British system. So the questionnaire studied only those particular motives among a small fraction of people from the whole potential donor population who decided to donate without any financial compensation. In fact it is very difficult to find out solid reasons why any of these categories (except the benefit obtaining category and the miscellaneous category of frivolous answers) cannot be included in the category of social responsibility. In some cases, we might have reservations about a donor's benefit category. For example, there are cases like this example of a married woman of 20:

'I wanted to do something to convince myself I was 18 [in that time] and I always wanted to be a blood donor – snob appeal' (Titmuss 1997, 300).

Furthermore, it is highly questionable why rare blood groups or war effort donors are excluded from the category of altruists. Thus, for example, a mother of six wrote that 'maybe my blood may help some other mother'. A married man wrote 'I like to think that a life may be saved by my blood'. Or consider this answer: 'My mother is of a rare blood group and I thought perhaps I would be. I was not, but felt my blood would still be needed'. Does this answer look as if it belongs to the socially irresponsible category? Similar argument applies to the category of war effort. 'I first gave blood during the last war to try and help save people from the results of war ... prefer to preserve life as against destroying it', wrote a married woman.

Titmuss's blood donor survey has been thoroughly criticized lately by Rapport and Maggs (2002). They revisited Titmuss's survey as it was published in *The Gift Relationship* original 1970 edition, and they have revealed serious methodological inconsistencies in the design and implementation of the survey which raise questions about the validity of the study.

For example, questions Number 4 and Number 5 in the questionnaire are crucial if Titmuss is to have empirical evidence for the existence of creative altruism in the British blood donation system. Question 5 we quoted above. Here is question 4:

Please tick the *main* reasons why you give blood?

a) general desire to help people

b) to replay in *some* way a transfusion given to someone I know

c) in response to an appeal for blood

d) some of my friends/colleagues give blood and encouraged me to join them

e) another reason (please state)

As Titmuss has already acknowledged, respondents were confused by these questions. By including Question 4 (which was taken from an American Red Cross survey), he could directly compare the motivations of US and British donors. However, many donors ticked more then one answer, some even all four. That was the main reason why he ignored data from Question 4 in the final interpretation. Rapport with Maggs concluded that 'Titmuss's models [are] methodologically flawed and based on assertions that do not stand up to scrutiny' (Rapport and Maggs 2002, 502). They are astonished that 'problems surrounding questions 4 and 5 went unnoticed' and that 'whilst recognizing the general confusion in his survey, he took the answers to these dubiously worded questions as the basis for his model' (Rapport and Maggs 2002, 502).

There are other flaws in Titmuss's survey from a contemporary methodological perspective, but a study made 40 years ago can hardly be blamed for that. Rapport and Maggs concluded that it is time to revisit Titmuss's model once more and to reopen the debate on blood donation and also on new types of medical donations, such as oocytes, and take into consideration other donation schemes on the basis of evidence which is rigorous and valid.

The author fully agrees with the suggestion to look for evidence-based models of medical donation. However, at the same time, there is a need to explore a new conceptual space for some key terms used in medical donation discourse – first of all the concept of altruism. The next part will show how a new perspective on altruistic behavior as it has been developed within the framework of evolutionary psychology during the last three decades can enrich the discourse on the role of altruism in medical donation.

Part III: Altruism from an Evolutionary Perspective

The blank slate concept of human nature which is dominant in contemporary social and human sciences has been strongly criticized from the position of Darwinian evolutionary theory during the last three to four decades (Cosmides and Toobey 1992; Pinker 2002). For many outsiders it seems to be just a new wave of the (never ending) nature and nurture debate. But rapidly growing empirical evidence from the modern behavioral sciences, such as social psychology, social neuroscience, comparative ethology, behavioral ecology, experimental economics, behavioral genetics and evolutionary psychology makes a difference.

First of all, behavioral sciences work with a much broader concept of altruism as compared to the one traditionally used in human and social sciences. The traditional notion of altruism sees altruistic behavior as motivated for the well-being of other people instead of for the individual's own well-being. According to the more general concept used in behavioral sciences, however, behavior is said to be altruistic if an altruistic actor pays a cost for delivering a benefit to others. In a traditional, narrower sense, true altruists could by definition only be humans, because only humans have the capacity for conscious decisions to act in a particular way for a particular goal. This includes also their decisions (if they are willing to decide this way) to act altruistically, to bestow a benefit to somebody else while at the same time being aware of imposing the cost on themselves. Such behavior, when there is a desire for well-being of others at the very beginning of a psychological causal chain (ultimate desire) leading to an altruistic behavior, is called *psychological altruism*.

In the deontological tradition – at least since Kant – only psychological altruism is considered to have moral value. Helping behavior cannot be considered altruistic unless it has unselfish motives, regardless of the benefit it brings to the recipient. However, there is a continuing debate whether there is such thing as psychological altruism at all, as in the theory of psychological hedonism all ultimate desires are self-interested, although actors do not need to be aware of it.

On the other hand, for a broader concept of altruism we do not need to presuppose the consciousness and free will of the actors which are necessary conditions for having altruistic motives – altruistic behavior is defined in a utilitarian way by the consequences of actions, not by the intentions of actors. Therefore a broader concept of altruism also allows us to identify altruistic behavior among non-human animals and study altruism within the much wider framework of biological evolution.

This broader concept, sometimes called *biological altruism*, might sound like a contradiction in terms. The key mechanism of evolution is survival and reproduction of the fittest individuals. Any altruistic behavior in the biological world would mean increasing fitness of competing individuals at the cost of their own fitness. Such a strategy cannot be sustained in the longer term. If this strategy is somehow ultimately genetically determined, as it has to be in order for biological evolution to work, then altruistically behaving individuals would be quickly wiped out by selfish competitors. And if altruistic individuals disappear, then so do the genes responsible for an altruistic alternative. Although in each generation new altruists can appear by random mutations, they will be very quickly overtaken by selfish counterparts. Therefore it seems logically impossible to have altruistically behaving organisms, if the existence of the Darwinian evolutionary mechanism is a true premise. To put the point a bit differently, if Darwinism as a scientific theory of evolutionary mechanisms is correct, then it is logically impossible for organisms to behave altruistically. But they do behave altruistically. The altruistic behavior of animals became a paradox of Darwinian evolutionary theory.

Group Selection

The well-known nineteenth-century anarchist Peter Kropotkin was probably the first who pointed out a great insufficiency of Darwin's theory of evolution, as it was presented by 'Darwin's pit bull' Thomas Huxley. Huxley had argued in his essay of 1888, which provoked Kropotkin's reaction, that natural selection is a struggle for existence between self-interested individuals. Kropotkin did not agree:

> In the animal world we have seen that the vast majority of species live in societies, and that they find in association the best arms for the struggle for life: understood, of course, in its wide Darwinian sense – not as a struggle for the sheer means of existence, but as a struggle against all natural conditions unfavourable to the species. (Kropotkin 1903, 293, reprinted in Caplan 1978, 35–40)

Kropotkin, who denied the evolutionary mechanism based solely on selfishness, did not find followers. Darwinism was secured thanks to population genetics and the establishment of the New Synthesis in evolutionary theory, in which natural selection was conceptualized as the struggle between individual genotypes in populations and corresponding genes in a population gene pool.

However, Kropotkin's refusal to accept Hobbesian selfishness as an animal legacy and altruism as a legacy of morality and civilization was prophetic.[6] Altruistic behavior among animals is a biological fact, and during 1960s it was gradually incorporated into Darwinian theory, thanks to the concept of group selection. According to the group selection theory, an altruistic, evolutionary self-sacrificing behavior can exist because it is for the benefit of a group – a population or the species itself. However, empirical evidence as well as detailed theoretical analysis disproved the existence of group selection. Although the debate is not completely over yet, and some theorists believe that group selection can exist in rare and special conditions, according to the majority opinion of evolutionary biologists, group selection is a fallacy.

Kin Selection and Reciprocal Altruism

The contemporary evolutionary solution to the altruism puzzle is based not on a rejection of Darwinism (as usually done by some anti-evolutionists and anti-Darwinians), but a deepening of it.[7] In the enthusiastic words of David Barash, one of the early proponents of the application of this conceptual revolution in human social behavior:

> Altruism is one of the greatest mysteries of life, and its seeming solution, one of the triumphs of modern biology … [t]he scientific solution to the question of altruism generated much of the explanatory horsepower than has fuelled gene-centred biology, and which in turn has revolutionized our understanding of all living things, human beings included. (Barash 2001, 37)

From a gene's point of view there are genetic and environmental conditions when it is a better strategy (in terms of higher number of gene copies) if its carrier (an organism) helps close genetic relatives to reproduce rather than to do so itself. However, such nepotistic behavior is limited within the range of genetic relation coefficient from 1.0 to 0.25. This form of natural selection is called *kin selection* and explains how altruism among close genetic relatives can be created and maintained by Darwinian mechanisms of random mutations and natural selection. The most obvious examples are eusocial species of insects, such as bees, ants or termites. Members of sterile casts in eusocial species express ultimate altruistic behavior – either they sacrifice their own life for the benefit of the colony (a bee sting or a termite warrior defending the entry to the nest by exploding its head), or

---

6   See Ridley (1996), *The Origin of Virtue.*

7   Many popular or semi-popular books are devoted to this conceptual shift: R. Dawkins' well-known bestseller *The Selfish Gene* (1989 [1976]), as well as Ridley (1993), *The Red Queen* and Wright (1994), *The Moral Animal.*

they give up their own reproduction in order to help the queen to raise more bee sisters.[8] However, the problem of altruism is far from being completely explained by kin selection alone. Besides many examples of nepotistic behavior in animals as well as in *Homo sapiens*, a great deal of altruistic behavior among animals can be observed between genetically unrelated individuals of the same species, or even very distant species (symbiosis). This cannot be explained by kin selection theory.

In 1971 Robert Trivers (Trivers 1971) published his theory of reciprocal altruism in order to explain the existence of altruistic behavior among genetic non-relatives. The idea is very simple, and it can be expressed by the slogan 'if you scratch my back, I'll scratch yours'. Altruistic behavior which imposes a cost to the giver can be selected if it is later reciprocated by the receiver. In such a situation costs linked with altruism are mutually shared in the longer term, and both sides receive benefits which otherwise would not be received.

Important theoretical support for reciprocal altruism came later from game theory – specifically from the Prisoners' Dilemma. In this well-known game, there are two players with two options each – either they cooperate or defect. Defection corresponds to selfish and cooperation to altruistic behavior. According to a standard payoff matrix, if both sides cooperate, each player receives three points. If both sides defect, each player receives only one point. If one defects and the other one cooperates, the defecting one receives five points – the best payoff, and the cooperating one gets zero points – the worst payoff. Players do not know what decision will be made by the opponent, but they know that he can defect or cooperate.

In 1984 the political economist Robert Axelrod (Axelrod 1984) published the results of a series of computer simulated tournaments in which the iterated Prisoners' Dilemma was played by programs with various strategies of choosing between defection and cooperation in an encounter with an opponent. The winning player in a tournament was a program running a simple strategy called tit-for-tat. This strategy starts with cooperation. In the next encounter, behavior depends on the opponent's past behavior. It would retaliate with defection if the other player defected, but it returns to cooperation if the other player has cooperated.

If defection in a continuing dyadic interaction of the same two tit-for-tat players is a bad strategy, the situation is radically changed if we have a whole population of players who meet randomly in a series of single-shot Prisoners' Dilemmas. It can be clearly demonstrated that a population with cooperative, altruistic players is unstable because it can be destroyed by free rides.

The question is how to protect a population of cooperating individuals from free riders.

---

8   For more examples of altruistic behavior among animals, see Trivers 1985, Krebs and Davies 1993.

Reciprocal Altruism Has to Be Stabilized

There are two complementary ways to stabilize altruistic cooperative behavior – to support motivations by various positive incentives which lead to altruistic behavior and to build up mechanisms which discriminate against free riders. Whether the mechanisms for stabilizing altruistic behavior are biological or cultural, they all have to deal with cheating.

Trivers pointed out that the conditions for the evolution of reciprocal altruism have been met during human evolution at least for the last five million years and therefore 'there has been strong selection on our ancestors to develop a variety of reciprocal interactions' (Trivers 1985, 386). According to him natural selection selected for a human 'emotional system that underlies our relationships with friends, colleagues, acquaintances, and so on' (Trivers 1985, 386). As we all know, humans routinely help each other, share food, tools, knowledge towards only distantly related recipients and 'although kinship often mediates many of these acts, it never appears to be a prerequisite' (Trivers 1985, 386).

Anthropologists have been studying present-day stone-age cultures in order to better understand possible cultural practices among our ancestors. Among the questions that interested them was how much do people of these cultures exercise altruistic behavior. Are they more or less altruistic than people in modern societies with free market economies?

The !Kung San hunter-gatherers from Botswana in Southern Africa, together with Inuits and Australian Aboriginals, are among the very few societies which have retained the Paleolithic lifestyle which is believed to be common to our ancestors for a major part of human evolutionary history. The !Kung San people live in small nomadic bands with division of labor – men hunting animals for meat and women foraging plant food. Killed meat provides from 20 to 90 percent of calories, 40 percent on average, and all of it is shared. Although as many as ten men hunt simultaneously, only one of them needs to be successful to provide meat for the entire band. Shared food, of course, has to be reciprocated. This system has obvious advantages for each member of the band. There is much more meat from one prey than the family of a successful hunter can eat, and food in these societies cannot be stored; therefore, if it were not shared it would be wasted. Obviously not all hunters can be successful. Most probably, a majority would not be; without sharing their families would be hungry. Sharing food thus rationally distributed scarce food in a community and minimized the risk of not having any meat (for more details see Workman and Reader 2004, 198–203).

Since the beginning of the twentieth century anthropologists have collected a great volume of empirical evidence for gift exchange practices from various present pre-industrial societies. As one can see from M. Mauss's classical study of the gift (a work which influenced Titmuss very much), in all these gift relationship activities, reciprocity is a social norm. In the final chapter of his book, Mauss (Mauss 1954) quotes a fine Maori proverb to illustrate the main idea of his book: '*Ko Maru kai atu Ko maru kai mai ka ngohe ngohe*'. ['Give (gift) as well as take (gift) and all will be right'.] Or, an alternative translation: ['As much as Maru gives, so much Maru takes, and this is good, good'.] (Maru is the god of war and justice). The principle of reciprocity contained in this proverb is striking.

As Trivers pointed out, the crucial universal issue for altruism to be sustainable would be to detect and to discriminate against free riders. Evolutionary psychologists Leda Cosmides and John Tooby, based on the results of psychological experiments using the Wason selection task, hypothesized that there is an innate psychological mechanism in humans (*social contract algorithm, cheater detection module*) which is activated by social exchange problems (Cosmides and Tooby, 1992). It is reasonable to expect that our ancestors have been frequently exposed to social contract problems during human evolution – such as sharing of food, tools or other material things, helping others, cooperating in hunts or fights – where reciprocity in a longer run is crucial. This creates selection pressure for a human cognitive system to be able to judge various forms of social contracts in order not to be cheated. In the Wason selection task people are asked whether a conditional rule 'if P then Q' is violated. If P and Q have abstract content 70 percent of people answer incorrectly. If P and Q are presented in the form of a social contract situation, and solving the task is in fact detection of social cheating, then 70 percent of people answer correctly. According to Cosmides and Tooby the cheater detection algorithm is one of many human mind modules, each of which evolved in the human brain as a result of specialized adaptation to particular environmental challenges (for the discussion of cheater detection module and its criticisms see Badcock 2000, 108–10 and Barrett et al. 2002, 281–8).

Indirect Reciprocity

The prototype of human altruism is not to behave altruistically towards close kin, not even towards unrelated friends or partners, but toward strangers. This type of altruism is considered to be the most moral one. In reciprocal altruism the same two agents encounter each other many times in a series of repeated Prisoners' Dilemma situations, and they exchange altruistic acts. It is similar to a barter economy with a time-delayed goods exchange between the same two partners. An overwhelming majority of gift relationships cases mentioned in Mauss's book *The Gift* belong to this category. Three kinds of obligations mentioned by Mauss and others make perfect sense from the perspective of the theory of games and the winning tit-for-tat strategy. Firstly, the obligation to give a gift initiates cooperation. Game theorists called it a nice strategy. Secondly, the obligation to accept a gift is a necessary step for setting up a relationship. And finally, the third obligation, the obligation to reciprocate a gift, is a cultural way to avoid free riders who are parasitic upon gift givers.

Direct reciprocity, very likely an important factor in human evolution when people lived in small communities, and altruistic interactions, such as gift exchange, could be based on the fact that the people concerned know each other. But as communities become larger and interactions between people grow more complex, the model of direct reciprocity is not useful. Other models, such as indirect reciprocity, network reciprocity or group reciprocity, are needed in order to explain altruistic human behavior. In these models altruism is not expected to be returned by the recipient, but by somebody else.

A model of indirect reciprocity, a term coined by evolutionary biologist Alexander (1987), has already been forecast by Trivers. He was thinking about the possibility of a 'generalised altruism', when altruism is reciprocated not to a donor but to a third party. Trivers speculated that a human sense of justice could develop from such a system of multi-party altruism. In a similar way Alexander thought that indirect reciprocity is the essence of human moral systems, as is illustrated by universal moral norms such as the so-called Golden Rule. According to him there is no surprise that this 'third party altruism' cannot be found in the animal kingdom since it presupposes the existence of individuals with highly developed brains enabling them to plan and manipulate others (so called Machiavellian intelligence).

Recently, Nowak and Sigmund (1998) tried to find theoretical conditions for indirect altruism to evolve and stably persist, using computer model simulations and mathematical analysis. In their models they introduced a special parameter, an 'image score' for each player. The value of this parameter depended upon each player's previous behavior and increased with the players' altruistic behavior. In fact, the image score parameter reflects actors' reputations for fair (reciprocal) behavior. Image scores of each player were known to all players. They found that there is a threshold which must be met if a society is to evolve toward sustainable altruistic behavior towards third parties: the probability of knowing the image of another player has to exceed the cost-to-benefit ratio of the altruistic act. From their model it follows that information about the opponent player can be received indirectly, by observing the player interacting with other players or by talking about the players. Language can obviously help to share information about a player's reputation. Our love for gossip could have a deep evolutionary meaning – it facilitates the acquisition of information about social cheaters.

Recently, the rapidly expanding field of experimental economics seems to support evolutionary psychology claims that our emotional system built up during evolution significantly influences our decisions, whether moral or economic. Psychological experiments dealing with simple economic decisions led economists to think that real people (real in contrast to theoretical people of economic theories) are in fact not pure economic actors, as suggested by economic theories, but rather hybrids between *Homo economicus* and *Homo emoticus*. For example, in the so-called Ultimatum game, people do not behave as they would if they were only rational and selfish agents. They behave in accordance with a sense of fairness and justice, which is in discord with the behavior predicted on the basis of pure rationality.

In a very simple version of the Ultimatum game, one of two players receives an amount of money, say 100 British pounds (GBP), and it is up to him how he is going to split it with the other player. The first player proposes how the

GBP 100 will be shared, but the second player has the option to refuse or accept the offer the first player makes. They are not going to see each other again, and they cannot communicate and bargain about the offer. The central problem for the player offering a share is to determine how large a share of the money the other player would accept, which means that the first player has to put himself into the second player's position and think about how much, or how little, he would accept in his situation (theory of mind reasoning).

According to classical economics, a purely rational player should accept any offer, no matter how low, because any amount of money is better than nothing. And the prediction for the first player is that the second player will offer a minimum of money. However, two thirds of people in these experiments offer between 40 and 50 percent, and only four people from 100 offer less then 20 percent.

Why do people in the Ultimatum game think that the offer risks rejection? Rationally, they should accept any offer higher then zero. Players predict the other player's reaction by putting themselves into opponent's shoes. Such results are difficult to interpret within the borders of the *Homo economicus* framework. According to that framework, we would have to say that players who refused a small offer did not understand that it is a single encounter game.

But this explanation is not very convincing, as has been pointed out by Sigmund, Fehr and Nowak in their article for *The Scientific American* on The Economics of Fair Play (Sigmund et al. 2002). Their alternative explanation relies on the principles of evolutionary psychology. According to them our emotional apparatus has been shaped by natural selection for millions of years when our ancestors lived in small groups similar to the !Kung San hunter-gatherers mentioned earlier. In such conditions one-shot interactions were rare; people interacted regularly with people they knew – relatives, friends, colleagues, neighbors. Such social environment supports the evolution of relationships of direct reciprocity. Our human emotions were shaped for better survival and reproduction in such an environment (called by evolutionary psychologists the EEA – environment of evolutionary adaptedness – see Gaulin and McBurney 2004, 40–43).

Sigmund et al. think that this might be the reason why players in the Ultimatum game reject a dismal offer. From the point of view of emotions, players want to keep their self esteem high. Such emotions could have evolutionary meaning: if others in a small group know that I am happy with a small offer, they will also make me a small offer in the future. If they know I would get angry with such an offer, they are likely to make a higher offer. Therefore, while our emotionally driven behavior might seem irrational in the modern society with its high number of anonymous single-shot interactions, it makes perfect sense in ancestral human conditions, or even in modern social environments in which reputation and gossip make a difference. Sigmund et al. finally concluded: 'From an evolutionary viewpoint, this self-esteem is an internal device for acquiring a reputation, which is beneficial in future encounters' (Sigmund et al. 2002, 85).

However, cross-cultural studies have shown that the size of the share offer is culturally dependent. For example, in the Machiguenga tribe in the Amazon, the mean offer was 26 percent, significantly lower than 46 percent, a typical number in experiments with Western-type people. On the other hand, many members of the Au tribe in Papua New Guinea offered more than 50 percent. But these differences can be explained by local cultural traditions in gift giving. Among Au tribe the tradition of gift giving and strong obligation of accepting a gift play an important role. The cultural differences, as Sigmund et al. pointed out, do not count against the idea that humans could have evolved the emotions that prompt us to behave in ways that would have benefited either us or our group in the long run (Sigmund et al. 2002).

Marc Hauser, in his iconoclastic book on human moral instincts (Hauser 2006) has recently conceptualized the tension between the expected universality of human traits if they are to be the result of evolution on the one hand and actually observed cultural variability of the traits on the other. He suggests a new model for our moral faculty, inspired by Chomsky's idea of universal grammar. In Hauser's view, although we are born with universal and common abstract moral rules, the cultural environment sets parameters and guides us toward the acquisition of particular moral systems. This perspective does not deny cross-cultural variation, but at the same time it allows the existence of an underlying universal 'grammar' (Hauser 2006, 165 et seq.).

The Ultimatum game is admired for its simplicity. A more complex game combining cooperation and competition is the Public Goods game. In the Public Goods game players decide whether they should invest some money in a common pool, in which the money is multiplied and then divided equally among all players. Here, the rational strategy is to invest nothing. However, real people in experiments donate, although not the largest possible sum. In a setting where the Public Goods game is repeated with the same group of people, most people approaching the end of the game invest nothing and get the same share from the common pool as people who invested.

Fehr and Gächter (Fehr and Gächter 2002) found that the situation radically changed if players can punish other players in the group, for example by imposing fines. Surprisingly enough, although the act of punishment is costly to a player imposing a punishment, most players were eager to punish cheating co-players. Fehr and Gächter described this phenomenon as altruistic punishment. A corresponding mathematical model has been developed to show how altruism can evolve with the help of punishment (Gintis 2000, Bowles and Gintis 2004). The authors believe that humans have a predisposition to punish free riders, even if it is costly to the punishers. Psychological experiments with people surprisingly demonstrated that many players were even more interested in punishing free riders than in maximizing their profits. Sigmund et al. commented that: 'Punishers discipline the self-interested agents so that the group is much more likely to survive. Subjects who punish are not, of course, aware of this evolutionary mechanism. They simply feel that revenge is sweet' (Sigmund et al. 2002, 87).

This brings us to the question of the relationship between altruism and awareness. We have already said that the key feature which distinguishes psychological (and truly moral) altruism from biological is the willingness to do something altruistic. This means that the actors are fully aware that their altruistic act brings a benefit to the recipient, but at the same time it imposes a cost to them. In pure altruism no reciprocity from recipients or others is expected, and this is the reason why pure altruism is considered to be morally higher then other forms of help in which some kind of reciprocity is expected. However, it seems that there is always some reciprocity behind altruism, although the altruistically behaving actor is not necessarily aware of it.

Recently, scientists started to use available techniques of imaging brain activity to understand the neural bases of pure altruistic behavior, such as charitable donations. In an experimental design, as used in experimental economics studies, 19 participants could choose to endorse or oppose societal causes by anonymous decisions to donate or refrain from donating to real charitable organizations, and their brain activities have been measured by functional magnetic resonance imaging (fMRI) (Moll et al. 2006).

There are several distinct fronto-limbic networks which underlie decisions whether to donate altruistically or not. The mesolimbic reward system (VTA-striatum) is responsible for a general reinforcement mechanism, the other structures mediate social attachment and aversion response, and also more complex reinforcements related to altruistic decisions. Moll et al. have found that 'the mesolimbic reward system is engaged by donations in the same way as when monetary rewards are obtained' (Moll et al. 2006, 15623). Authors believe their study also supports evolutionary and neurobiological theories according to which the specific human form of pure altruism, such as an anonymous donation to charity, was shaped during human evolutionary history of the Upper Paleolithic period. However, Mall et al. did not discuss the question of how their interpretation is related to the suggested human selection for reciprocal altruism mentioned earlier.

Thinking in terms of the human brain's emotional predispositions towards altruistic behavior leads us to expect emotions to be hardwired in the brain as a result of all types of altruistic selection – kin selection, direct reciprocity selection and indirect reciprocity selection. One may expect different emotions at work in altruistic behavior towards the family, in friendships, in large in-group loyalties (ethnicities, religions) or in charitable donations (helping strangers). We might think also about a more complex picture of interaction between different kinds of emotions. Of course, more studies are needed to study the emotional background of various kinds of altruistic behavior in detail. However, the above mentioned recent discovery that the neural basis of rewarding emotions somehow makes paid and unpaid donations equal is of a great importance for our reciprocity model of medical donation. This will be discussed below.

Part IV: Titmuss's Gift Relationship is in Fact a Charity Relationship

Opposition of the gift to the commodity is the main theme of Titmuss's analysis of blood donation, which later became a paradigm for medical donation in general. Titmuss sees a clear cut division between the commercial domain of utilitarian calculations and the social domain of those unilateral and multilateral altruistic relationships, which constitute real social glue. For Titmuss, inspired by M. Mauss, the act of giving transcends the given material thing itself; it is what has been called 'a total social fact' – an activity with symbolic, economic, axiological, political, legal and religious implications, when subjective as well as objective aspects of a thing are interwoven together. The gift relationship transcends the divisions between the spiritual and the material, and generates social cohesion.

Titmuss is perfectly right that blood donorship can be seen as the modern example of a total social fact. Blood has a traditional meaning of close social bonds and a symbolic meaning as the essence of life. In transfusion the donated blood becomes not symbolic, but a real gift of life. In accordance with the conceptualization of the total social fact, Titmuss is stressing the role unpaid donorship plays in social cohesion. One may argue that Titmuss would have defended an altruistic blood donation system even had he found that a non-commercial system is less economically effective than a commercial one in his comparative study, because the social function of unpaid blood giving highly outweighs its economic drawbacks. For example, he talks about 'the social costs to American society of the decline in recent years in the voluntary giving of blood' (Titmuss 1997, 263), costs which cannot be evaluated in economic terms. Titmuss strongly believes that a decline in the 'spirit of altruism' in one sphere of human activity will cause a similar decline of altruism in other spheres. Blood donation is for him more then just one of many medical procedures; it is the indicator of where the social begins and the economic ends.

P. Singer, in his defense of Titmuss against Arrow's criticism, among other things also agreed with Titmuss that non-commercial and commercial blood systems cannot coexist. This is because a remunerated system would cause some people to become less likely to give blood 'if blood were a marketable commodity', and that 'the possibility of others buying and selling blood would destroy the inspiring force behind their own donation' (Singer 1973, 317–18). On the other hand, Frow has recently criticized Titmuss's position as well as the dominant twentieth-century view on social relationships in terms of 'opposition of the gift to the commodity' (Frow 1997). He points out that on a closer examination the 'concepts of gift and commodity seem to partake of each other' and that Mauss clearly recognized 'according to forms of calculation and interest that in some sense resemble those of a market economy' (Frow 1997, 102 et seq.). It is still an open question whether paid and unpaid systems cannot coexist. K. Heally recently tested this question (among others) by comparing various blood regimes in European countries (Healy 2000). He found that in Spain and Germany where selling of blood plasma is allowed, the likelihood of giving blood seems to be reduced as compared to the majority of countries where selling plasma is not permissible. However, on the data available it was not possible to conclude that this reduction is, for example, due to a preference of poor people to sell their plasma rather than altruistically donate blood.

Titmuss systematically ignored the 'radical ambivalence of gift exchange' documented by anthropologists, including Mauss, and continued to understand gift giving as a voluntary act of pure gratuitousness, which does not require anything in return. Although this is a common definition of contemporary dictionaries, this meaning is very likely of recent origin. It is radically different from the notion of the gift as it was understood in archaic and traditional societies, as a total social fact which relies on three kinds of obligation – to give the gift, to accept the gift and, finally, and maybe the most important obligation, to reciprocate the gift. The gift exchange relationship as a tool of social cohesion depends on reciprocation, on both direct and indirect reciprocity, as is well documented throughout Mauss's book *The Gift*.

In fact, the notion of gift giving which Titmuss has in mind is closer to the concept of charity. The English word 'charity' comes from the Old French *charité*, an equivalent of Latin *caritas*, which is a standard translation of Greek word *agape*. *Agape* means God's unlimited loving kindness to all others. In St. Paul's Christian theology, *agape* means giving to the unfortunate.[9] C. Grant in his book *Altruism and Christian Ethics* points out this link between altruism and *agape*:

> Although altruism is a modern concept, it is, of course, not entirely novel. Despite the secular context of its emergence and submergence, the basic notion behind it, of a concern for others, was integrated into the fabric of western culture through the influence of the Christian gospel. The sense that God reaches out to humanity in love, and seeks to elicit an emulating caring from us for one another, represents an obvious inspiration for a concept isolating other-regard. The obviousness of the Christian source is enhanced by an apparent lack of other prominent candidates. The notion seems to be missing from the other major pillar of the western outlook, Greek civilization. (Grant 2003, 167)

Another term for this is almsgiving – giving money, goods or time to the poor, a meaning common to Judaism, Christianity and Islam. Although almsgiving is defined as giving without expecting reciprocation, it can be conceptualized within the framework of reciprocity and exchange, as has been done by Mauss himself in *The Gift*. If one thinks of almsgiving as a form of sacrifice to the gods, then usually the giver expects to receive their favor in return. However, there is a clear difference between a reciprocal relationship with people and with divinity. Therefore we are going to understand the word gift as a generic term which includes both the giving of a thing without expectation of any return from people

---

9   See: 1 Cor 13: 3.

(act of charity, almsgiving) and the giving of a thing with the expectation of a reciprocal gift (gift exchange).

It has been shown that the notion of a charitable gift has its origin in the religious practice of sacrificing things to gods, in Christian virtue and the Christian theological concept of love (*agape*). It might be clearer within that framework, to refer to medical donations as medical almsgivings. Titmuss's linking of medical donations to gift relations, which are, in fact, according to anthropologists always reciprocal, was misleading.

Now, after we have revealed the true nature of Titmuss's concept of blood donation and medical donation in general as charitable giving, we can ask whether the only way to prevent the human body and its parts from commodification is if they will be charitably given to those who need them. Or we can ask whether modern biomedicine, biomedical research and the pharmaceutical industry can effectively rely exclusively on the charitable medical donations of the human body or its parts. Widening the gap between the need for organs, tissues and ova (maybe with few exceptions) and the supply received from unpaid and generally unreciprocated donations seems to seriously undermine the idea of the efficiency of the altruistic medical donation system.

The cost connected with a donation seems to play an important role. If the cost is relatively small, as in the case of blood donation, the system can efficiently work on altruistic basis. But this looks like an exception proving a rule. Because if the cost for the donor is a little bit higher, for example in terms of time and pain, as it is in plasmapheresis, the number of donors fall under the necessary threshold and the commercialized system plays a major role in supply. Titmuss, of course, has criticized (Titmuss 1997, 101) what was in his time a new trend, when some regular donors were paid as much as 'semisalaries' for their plasma donations. But the present reality is that multinational pharmaceutical for-profit companies based mostly in the United States and acting as brokers have a dominant position in the worldwide plasma trade. European countries also buy plasma components, such as Factor VIII, from these companies and at the same time criticize the US commercial approach as unethical, although in fact only thanks to it they can cover their needs (Steiner 2003/5, 152, Waldby and Mitchell 2006, 41–5).

As soon as Titmuss's book appeared, it was also criticized by economists for his claim that market and non-market systems cannot coexist in the same social sphere because the market would destroy the non-commercial system. Kenneth Arrow complained that Titmuss had not answered the question '*why* should it be that the creation of a market for blood would decrease[s] the altruism embodied in giving blood' (Arrow 1972, 351). In general, Arrow saw Titmuss's 'pervasive fear' that commercialization of social services would damage the entire social system as a 'mirror image of Hayek's', since they both agreed that a mixed economy is necessarily unstable (Arrow 1972, 360).

Frow, in his essay mentioned above, rejects Titmuss's original gift and market opposition as reductive and misleading. On the other hand he somehow agrees with Titmuss that society has to prepare space for exercising altruistic behavior, when he asks for paying more attention to the neglected industrial and institutional aspects of medical donation. He claims that 'altruism is socially constructed', which in this case means that one must take into account the institutional conditions which enable the human drive for altruism to express itself. For example, there are fewer living liver donors in France than in Norway and the reason is not that French people are less willing to behave altruistically, but that there is opposition to donation by living donors in general among French doctors. (Steiner 2003/5, 156–8)

Tissue donation is probably one of the best examples of where the demarcation line between non-commercial and commercial social spheres in medical donation is blurred. D. Dickenson pointed out a sort of hypocrisy in the tissue discourse, saying that 'if donors believe they are demonstrating altruism, but biotechnology firms and researchers use the discourse of commodity and profit, we have not "incomplete commodification" but complete commodification with a plausibly human face' (Dickenson 2002, 55). There is the danger that 'the whole structure of the gift relationship totters' because such one-way altruism can provoke in donors 'a sense of being duped', being exploited and can create mistrust, which may finally undermine altruistic donation for medical research in general. Therefore we need to look for alternative models (Dickenson 2008, 39–41).

The blurring of the demarcation line between altruism and commodification is one of the main ideas of a fine study by Waldby and Mitchell. They argue that recent developments in tissue exchange make Titmuss's concept of altruistic gift giving inadequate as a solution to all potential problems with medical donation in the twenty-first century. One of the most serious arguments they use is the conflict between the 'laudable principle' of unpaid tissue donation secured by legislation on the one hand, and 'the rapidly increasing commercial value of the tissue fragments *after it has been donated*', on the other (Waldby and Mitchell 2006, 23).

Donated tissue as such can be sold to pharmaceutical or cosmetics companies, or further processed into cell lines or gene sequenced, patented and then sold. 'Metaphorically, we can say that as in Austrian economic theory, the longer the path between the initial act (collecting blood) and the prescribed product, (blood on the one hand, stabilized blood products on the other), the more "capitalistic" the process is', says Steiner (Steiner 2003/5, 153).

Julia Mahoney argues in her article that 'markets in human biological materials not only exist but are for all practical purposes unavoidable' (Mahoney 2000, 166). Her major argument is that 'since markets of human biological material obviously exist, preventing payments to sources cannot be justified on the ground that bans or limitations are necessary for prevention of the commoditization of non-marketable goods' (Mahoney 2000, 211). The reality is that human body parts, human tissue and cells – thanks to the advance in biotechnology and modern biomedicine – create a value and therefore a potential for monetary returns during their transfer from a lower-value user to a higher-value user. This is especially true for human tissue. It does not matter that the tissue has been given to the transfer chain stretching from the donor to final recipient on non-commercial basis, as altruistically given. At some point it nevertheless becomes a commodity, with the right to be used and exchanged for money. For Mahoney it is an argument that preventing tissue sources from receiving financial compensation does not stop commodification of human biological material later in the transfer process (Mahoney 2000, 175). In this process, which Mahoney terms 'transfer', altruistic and profit-making motivations are mixed together. (It would be more accurate to use the term 'processing' instead of Mahoney's 'transfer', since human biological material in most cases is not transferred from the donor to the recipient intact). Human tissue which enters the transfer chain 'as a gift is frequently transformed into a commercial product – one that is sold, not donated, to its ultimate recipient' (Mahoney 2000, 175). For Mahoney this is a sort of social and moral schizophrenia, since, while on the one hand there seems to be a consensus that tissue can be only altruistically donated because financial compensation would 'dehumanize society by viewing human beings and their parts as mere commodities' as she quotes words of The Council on Ethical and Judicial Affairs of the American Medical Association (Mahoney 2000, 179); on the other hand, the tissue itself or tissue products are sold to the final recipients. As she continues:

> It is hard to argue that there is something fundamentally wrong with participating in the market by *selling* one's own tissue (or that of one's newly deceased relatives) but not with market participation that includes *buying* tissue derived from others or, in the case of intermediary organisations, both buying and selling the materials of others. (Mahoney 2000, 211)

As some critics of the gift and commodity distinction noticed, from the economic point of view there is not a real difference between for-profit and not-for-profit organizations specializing in the procurement and distribution of human tissues, if the legal system allows it. For example, it seems that the only difference in the US is that they fill out different tax forms. The same economic logic seems to penetrate the question of efficiency in charity organizations. It is clear that any charity organization needs money for effective running, since unpaid and unprofessional management of any organization, whether for-profit or non-profit does not promise efficiency. The question is what proportion from the donation it is acceptable to use for running the charity organization itself. Where is the border between the cost of an effectively working management of a non-profit organization and an overpaid management using donation resources for their own interest? For example, the British charity watchdog, the Charity Commission, starts to worry if more than 15 percent of the income is used for managing a charity. It is hardly a coincidence that some charity organizations advertise to the public that 100 percent of their donated money goes to charity.[10]

---

10   http://www.charity-commission.gov.uk/ (accessed 19 May 2009).

This question of the distribution of charity financing has its parallel in human biological material distribution. There are formidable logistical challenges on both sides, and the question is, who is going to pay for the costs linked with the transfers themselves and their coordination. In her article mentioned earlier, Mahoney argued that it would be unrealistic to run a distribution network of human biological material solely on a gratuitous basis and expect that if markets were eliminated from this social sphere then the current quantity of life-saving and health-enhancing services would be maintained (Mahoney 2000, 221).

Recently new models for organ procurement have been suggested which incorporate the reciprocity idea into the system. Thus commercial and non-commercial principles are combined together in the Ethical Market model (Erin and Harris 2003; Harris and Erin 2002) in order to increase the pool of donated organs. According to this model, human organs would be bought from donors, but not sold to recipients. A non-profit organization would mediate the organ transfer between donors and recipients. It would buy organs from donors for a fair price and then distribute them to recipients according to medical criteria used in waiting lists. Money for buying organs could come from health insurance companies and charities.

G. Siegal and R.J. Bonnie based their new model of organ procurement from deceased donors on what they call 'reciprocal altruism'. It can be expressed in the following words: 'Everyman is a potential recipient as well as a potential donor' (Siegal and Bonnie 2006, 416). Since in their view pure altruistic donation is not able to cope with the widening gap between demand and supply of organs for transplantation, they are looking for ways to increase the pool of potential donors. The model which they propose and under which they call for reframing of the Act of Organ Donation in the USA is basically a national plan for 'organ transplantation "insurance"' with the federal government as the payer of last resort, covering all costs associated with transplantation. They see the current system in the US as fundamentally unjust, since the majority of organ donors 'would not, financially, be able to receive most organs'. As they pointed out, '[r]egrettably, the reciprocal interest in an organ – a potentially powerful social and psychological instrument – has so far been overlooked in communicating with the public' (Siegal and Bonnie 2006, 416).

The 'reciprocal altruism' in their model differs from a direct reciprocity mechanism in which willingness to donate an organ is reciprocated by eligibility to receive one. The reciprocity they have in mind is a kind of indirect reciprocity with the benefits for the potential donor just being involved in the transplantation 'insurance' system.

The crucial question addressing their model is why people should participate as potential donors in the system if there is no guarantee, such as there is in real insurance, that they will receive an organ should they need one. The answer is that by participating in the system, they are increasing the overall pool of transplantable organs and indirectly increasing their own chances to get one when needed. Therefore, Siegal and Bonie are talking about reciprocity in principle (increasing the chance to be a recipient), not in a legal sense (to be a mandatory recipient). It is in everyone's rational self-interest to be a potential organ donor. An adequate analogy according to the authors would be immunization.

Part V: The Reciprocity/Solidarity Framework for Biomedical Donations

As we have seen, Titmuss's model of medical donation as charitable giving along with his opposition of gift to commodity has serious limitations in theory as well as in practice, since it is not able to cope with present biomedical and biotechnological complexities. Both the economic and anthropological arguments on which Titmuss based his model have been profoundly criticized. The main objection to Titmuss's conceptualization of medical donation is that he wants to ground the medical donation practice on pure altruism, which is practically for him a kind of charitable gift giving. At the same time, he conceptualizes it as a modern example of the gift relationship framework that creates a social solidarity, but ignores an essential part of the gift relationship logic which is the principle of reciprocity.

Aafke Komter has recently explored the relationship between the gift and solidarity. Are there similarities, for example, 'between donating blood and being a union member?' (Komter 2006, 1). She is trying to bring together two rather unrelated discourses on social ties – a sociological one on solidarity and an anthropological one on gift exchange – to show how 'both theoretical traditions may complete and enrich each other' (Komter 2006, 6). What is clear from her analysis of a gift relationship referring to classical anthropological works as well as to recent theoretical and experimental works (including her own research on gift giving and receiving in the Netherlands) is the crucial importance of reciprocity. Reciprocity as a key element of creating social bonds in a gift relationship is a standard view in anthropology. But reciprocity also plays at least as important, if not as crucial, a role in the interpretation of psychological motives to give a gift. She noticed in the study, for example, that even when respondents expressed motives that they believed were purely altruistic, such as 'friendship, love, gratitude, respect, loyalty, or solidarity', ('one wants to contribute to another person's well-being without thinking about a return service'), such gift may have 'a strategic aim'. Therefore, giving to charity not only benefits another person but may serve at the same time our own self-interest, like 'relieving our own conscience'. She points out that 'feelings of being morally obliged to return a gift and not purely altruistic motives are the main psychological impetus to reciprocal giving' (Komter 2006, 46–8). In her analysis of the motives behind gift giving, she stressed a crucial role of gratitude in establishing and maintaining social relations. She refers here to the work of sociologist Georg Simmel from the beginning of the twentieth century: 'By mutual giving, people become tied to each other by a web of feelings of gratitude. Gratitude is the motive that moves us to give in return and thus creates the reciprocity of service and counterservice' (Komter 2006, 67).

She found in her own empirical study of gift giving in the Netherlands 'a sociological pattern of reciprocity'.

As far as solidarity is concerned one can also find reciprocity playing a crucial role here too. Whether talking about 'generalized', 'balanced', or 'negative' reciprocity (using Sahlins's terms), or 'conscious or unconscious expectations of reciprocity', Komter is pointing out reciprocity to be a key and most effective factor in 'creating the cement of society' because reciprocity is 'the elegant combination of self-interested concerns with the requirements of social life' (Komter 2006, 203).

As this chapter has also demonstrated, recent analysis of altruistic behavior in humans as well as in animals can be plausibly explained from the perspective of Darwinian evolutionary theory. The core of this explanation is that there is always directly or indirectly some kind of reciprocity behind altruism towards strangers. Whether it is reciprocity in terms of ultimate evolutionary causes of higher fitness in the case of animal altruistic behavior and of the human ancestors in the evolutionary past, or in terms of proximate psychological causes such as motivation and emotions behind the altruistic behavior of modern people, there is reciprocity. It is necessary to include these conceptions of reciprocity in the discourse on medical donation.

A new conceptual framework for medical donations is suggested, an alternative one to the charitable gift relationship model. Instead of a binary opposition between gift and commodity in the charitable gift model, within a new framework one can see gifts and commodities at the opposing poles of the reciprocity continuum. On one pole of the continuum, there is purely altruistic donation, which is not reciprocated 'externally'. However it is reciprocated 'internally' through 'good feelings'. This 'inner reciprocity', the emotional reward for altruistic acts, when no 'external reciprocity' is expected, can at the neurological and psychological levels be probably of the same quality as feelings caused by 'external reciprocity', such as financial reward. This has been shown by fNMR studies mentioned above.

At the opposing pole of the continuum, there is human biological material as a commodity which can be bought and sold. Between the poles there is a continuum of situations in which commercial and non-commercial practices are mixed together in various proportions, reflecting the actual blurring of the borders between pure altruism and commerce. Tutton recalls that since the 1990s the 'gift' as a public policy keyword for tissue donation started to be replaced by the new keyword 'partner'.[11] The term partner seems to be also more suitable for the new model of reciprocity in medical donation, because it can be used across the whole spectrum from the pure altruism pole to the market one.

It is an equal and direct reciprocity situation, which can routinely be realized by the process of selling and buying. In trade there is a direct or mediated interaction between giver and receiver, and equality is constructed through the

---

11   See R. Tutton, 'Notes on Policy, Language and Human Tissue', next chapter in this book.

price negotiated by both sides. Titmuss saw the gift as the antithesis of commodity, but gift exchanges have been categorized, at least by some anthropologists and economists, as a form of barter economy in pre-monetary societies; therefore gifts are not completely out of the economic domain, as envisioned by Titmuss. If we cease to demonize money in a Marxist way, it does not matter whether money is involved in equal exchange between a giver and a receiver, or the exchange is a kind of barter economy. As Mahoney points out, 'avoiding the language of markets and property will not prevent the existence of markets, nor will attempts to describe transactions in non-commercial language inhibit efforts to realize gains from transfers of human biological materials' (Mahoney 2000, 192).

In a narrow sense, the notion of reciprocity evokes equity, a 50–50 exchange, and an expectation that the donor will later receive the same value as the one given to the recipient. However, in the much broader sense of reciprocity that is used in this work, equity in reciprocation is not necessary insofar as there is a feeling of fairness on both sides. The reciprocity could be quite robust and depend on cultural and societal factors (compare cross-cultural differences in the feeling of fairness in the Ultimatum game experiments mentioned above). It is preferable to talk about 'some reciprocity', which is a concept borrowed from Marc Hauser. Based on the results of reciprocation game experiments conducted with children, he concluded that young children are more selfish than older children, but not absolutely selfish; young children are more likely to follow 'the model of some distribution of resources, as distinct from equal distribution' (Hauser 2006, 262).

Limited and indirect reciprocity, which can be seen as an application of the solidarity principle, is in fact behind many modern welfare state policies, such as tax, pension and health care systems as well as other societal services.

There is a whole range of direct and indirect reciprocity situations between the two poles of pure altruism and free market commodity trade. For example, a kind of limited-direct reciprocity situation is financial compensation for inconvenience related to donorship. This is not a situation of trade; compensations are not the price of the donated thing. This policy is routinely practiced in many countries, for example, in the case of ova donations, and it is accepted by EU legislation. Another situation of some indirect reciprocity would be the controversial Ethical Market Model mentioned above (Erin and Harris 2002; Harris and Erin 2003). The ethical market would be limited to self-governing geopolitical areas, such as the EU. According to the authors, only citizens resident within such area could sell into the system, and they and their families would be equally eligible to receive organs. Thus, besides financial incentives, which are categorized in this chapter as direct reciprocity, there are also indirect reciprocity incentives in play when 'organ vendors would know they were contributing to a system which would benefit them and their families and friends' (Erin and Harris 2003, 138).

Furthermore, promotional tools, such as awards, letters of appreciation and encouragement, TV shows, parties with celebrities for recruitment of donors recommended by Politis for blood and plasma donation, as mentioned in the Introduction, fit perfectly into our modeling of donorship, referring to some reciprocity. All these non-financial incentives support the inner reward feelings of altruistic donors mentioned earlier in this chapter, such as self-esteem, in-group loyalty and others. But at the same time, the proposed reciprocity approach does not exclude various forms of donations for certain benefits, including financial compensation or various forms of benefit-sharing models based on principles of reciprocity, mutuality, solidarity and citizenry developed originally for genetic research and genetic databases (Chadwick and Berg 2001, Knoppers and Chadwick 2005).

It depends on various factors, including cost for donors linked to donations, cultural and moral traditions, social policy, general public attitudes, political discourse, legal situation, demands for human biological materials and progress in biomedical research. From the reciprocity approach, it follows that there is not a single universal normative rule, but rather more different medical donation policies which can coexist – ranging from truly altruistic donation to selling and buying for money on the opposing pole, although this extreme need not be implemented. The central role of reciprocity in human social behavior has been already been termed the implicit social contract. Following this idea we may say that the suggested reciprocity approach for medical donations draws on the implicit bioethical social contract.

Acknowledgments

I am very grateful to D. Dickenson, R. Brownsword and A. Campbell for their helpful comments on earlier drafts. My special thanks are owed to R. ter Meulen, R. Huxtable and B. Capps from the Centre for Medical Ethics at Bristol University for the inspiring discussions we had during my short stay in October 2007. My very special thanks go to Don Hill for his careful reading of the final draft.

Grant Support

This work was supported by the MVTS grant for the international research cooperation from the Slovak Ministry of Education.

Bibliography

Alexander, R.D. (1987), *The Biology of Moral Systems* (New York: Aldine).

Archard, D. (2002), 'Selling yourself: Titmuss's argument against a market in blood', *The Journal of Ethics* 6, 87–103.

Arrow, K.J. (1972), 'Gifts and exchanges', *Philosophy and Public Affairs* 1 (4), 343–62.

Axelrod, R. (1984), *The Evolution of Cooperation* (New York: Basic Books).

Badcock, C. (2000), *Evolutionary Psychology: A Critical Introduction* (Cambridge: Polity).

Barash, D.P. (2001), *Revolutionary Biology: The New, Gene-Centered View of Life* (New Brunswick-London: Transaction Publishers).

Barrett, L., Dunbar, R. and Lycett, J. (2002), *Human Evolutionary Psychology* (Houndmills and New York: Palgrave).

Barkow, J.II., Cosmides, I. and Tooby, J. (eds) (1992), *The Adapted Mind* (New York: Oxford University Press).

Beauchamps, T.L. and Childress, J.F. (1994), *Principles of Biomedical Ethics* (Belmont, CA: Wadsworth Publishing Company).

Beyleveld, D. and Brownsword, R. (2001), *Human Dignity in Bioethics and Biolaw* (Oxford: Oxford University Press).

Bowles, S. and Gintis, H. (2004), 'The evolution of strong reciprocity: Cooperation in heterogeneous populations', *Theoretical Population Biology* 65, 17–28.

Brinkerhoff, D.B. and White, L.K. (1988), *Sociology* (St. Paul: West Publishing Company).

Caplan, A.L. (ed.) (1978), *The Sociobiology Debate* (New York: Harper and Row, Publishers).

Chadwick, R. and K. Berg (2001), 'Solidarity and equity: New ethical frameworks for genetic databases', *Nature Reviews/Genetics* 2, 318–21.

Commission of the European Communities (2007), *Organ Donation and Transplantation: Policy Actions at EU Level* (Brussels: Commission of the European Communities).

Cosmides, L. and Tooby, J. (1992) 'Cognitive adaptations for social exchange', in Barkow et al. (eds) (1992), *The Adapted Mind* (New York: Oxford University Press), 163–228.

Dawkins, R. (1976), *The Selfish Gene* (Oxford: Oxford University Press).

Dickenson, D. (2002), 'Commodification of human tissue: Implications for feminist and development ethics', *Developing World Bioethics* 2 (1), 55-63.

Dickenson, D. (2008), *Body Shopping – The Economy Fuelled by Flesh and Blood* (Oxford: Oneworld Publications).

Erin, C.A. and Harris, J. (2003), 'An ethical market in human organs', *J Med Ethics* 29, 137–8.

Fehr, E. and Gächter, S. (2002), 'Altruistic punishment', *Nature* 415 (10), 137–40.

Fontaine, P. (2002), 'Blood, politics, and Social Science. Richard Titmuss and The Institute of Economic Affairs, 1957-1973', *Isis* 93 (3), 401–34.

Frow, J. (1997), *Time and Commodity Culture: Essays in Cultural Theory and Postmodernity* (Oxford: Oxford University Press).

Gaulin, S. and McBurney, D.H. (2004), *Evolutionary Psychology* (Upper Saddle River, NJ; London: Pearson Education).

Gintis, H. (2000), 'Strong reciprocity and human sociality', *Journal of Theoretical Biology* 206, 169–71.

Goodwin, M. (2006), *Black Market: The Supply and Demand of Body Parts* (New York: Cambridge University Press).

Grant, C. (2003), *Altruism and Christian Ethics* (New York: Cambridge University Press).

Hamilton, W.D. (1964), 'The genetical evolution of social behavior I and II', *Journal of Theoretical Biology* 7, 1–52.

Harris, J. and Erin, C. (2002), 'An ethically defensible market for organs', *BMJ* 325, 114–15.

Hauser, M.D. (2006), *Moral Minds: How Nature Designed Our Universal Sense of Right and Wrong* (New York: HarperCollins Publishers).

Healy, K. (2000), 'Embedded altruism: Blood collection regimes and the European Union's donor population', *American Journal of Sociology* 105, 1633–57.

Keown, J. (1997), 'The gift of blood in Europe: An ethical defence of EC Directive 89/381', *J Med Ethics* 23 (2), 96–100.

Knoppers, B.M. and Chadwick, R. (2005), 'Human genetic research: Emerging trends in ethics', *Nature Review/Genetics* 6, 75–9.

Komter, A. (2006), *Social Solidarity and the Gift* (Cambridge: Cambridge University Press).

Krebs, J.R. and Davies, N.B. (1993), *An Introduction to Behavioral Ecology*, 3rd Edition (Oxford: Blackwell Scientific Publications).

Kropotkin, P. (1903), *Mutual Aid: A Factor of Evolution* (New York: McClure Phillips and Co).

Kuhse, H. and Singer, P. (eds) (1999), *Bioethics: An Anthology* (Oxford: Blackwell Publishers).

Lorenz, K. (1966), *On Aggression* (London: Methuen).

Mahoney, J.D. (2000), 'The market for human tissue', *Virginia Law Review* 86 (2), 163–223.

Mauss, M. (1954), *The Gift* (London: Routledge).

Moll, J., et al. (2006), 'Human Fronto-mesolimbic networks guide decisions about charitable donations', *PNAS* 103 (42), 15623–8.

Nowak, M.A. and Sigmund, K. (1998), 'Evolution of indirect reciprocity by image scoring', *Nature* 393, 573–7.

Oakley, A. and Ashton, J. (eds) (1997), *Introduction to The New Edition. The Gift Relationship: From Human Blood to Social Policy* (New York: The New Press).

Pinker, S. (2002), *The Blank Slate* (London: Allen Lane, Penguin).

Politis, C. (2000), 'Blood Donation Systems as an Integral Part of The Health System', *Archives of Hellenic Medicine* 17 (4), 354–7.

Rapport, F.L. and Maggs, C.J. (2002), 'Titmuss and the Gift Relationship: Altruism Revisited', *Journal of Advanced Nursing* 40 (5), 495–503.

Ridley, M. (1993), *The Red Queen* (London: Viking).

Ridley, M. (1996), *The Origin of Virtue* (London: Viking).

Schwartz, J. (1999), 'Blood and Altruism – Richard M. Titmuss' Criticism on the Commercialization of Blood', *Public Interest*, Summer Edition.

Siegal, G. and Bonnie R.J. (2006), 'Closing the organ gap: A reciprocity-based social contract approach', *Journal of Law, Medicine and Ethics* 34 (2), 415–23.

Sigmund, K., Fehr, E. and Nowak, M.A. (2002), 'The Economics of Fair-play', *Scientific American* January, 84–7.

Singer, P. (1973), 'Altruism and commerce: A defence of Titmuss against Arrow', *Philosophy and Public Affairs* 2 (3), 312–20.

Steiner, P. (2003/5), 'Gifts of blood and organs: The market and 'fictitious 'commodities', *Revue française de sociologie* 44, 147–62.

Titmuss, R.M. (1970), *The Gift Relationship: From Human Blood to Social Policy* (London: Allen and Unwin).

Titmuss, R.M. (1997), *The Gift Relationship: From Human Blood to Social Policy* (original edition 1970), in Oakley and Ashton (eds), *Introduction to The New Edition. The Gift Relationship: From Human Blood to Social Policy* (New York: The New Press), 57–315.

Titmuss, R.M. (1999), 'Why give to strangers?', in Kuhse and Singer (eds), *Bioethics: An Anthology* (Oxford: Blackwell Publishers), 383–386.

Trivers, R. (1971), 'The evolution of reciprocal altruism', *Quarterly Review of Biology* 46, 35–57.

Trivers, R. (1985), *Social Evolution* (California: The Benjamin/Cummings Publishing Company, Inc).

Tutton, R. (2002), 'Gift relationship in genetics', *Science as Culture* 11 (4), 523–42.

Waldby, C. and Mitchell R. (2006), *Tissue Economies: Blood, Organs, and Cell Lines in Late Capitalism* (Durham and London: Duke University Press).

Wallace, B., et al. (2007), 'Heritability of ultimatum game responder behavior', *PNAS* 104 (40), 15631–4.

Wilkinson, S. (2003), *Bodies for Sale* (London: Routledge).

Workman, L. and Reader, W. (2004), *Evolutionary Psychology: An Introduction* (Cambridge, UK: Cambridge University Press).

Wright, R. (1994), *The Moral Animal* (London: Random House).

Chapter 3

Notes on Policy, Language and Human Tissue

Richard Tutton

Introduction

This chapter draws on sociological and anthropological analysis of policymaking to discuss the significance of the term 'gift' in policy discourses on the use of human tissue in biomedical research. The chapter suggests that in the 1990s this term was a persuasive 'keyword' in policy guidelines on the procurement and use of human biological samples by research scientists. At the end of the 1990s, however, publicity about tissue retention at a number of UK hospitals changed the policy discourse with respect to the collection, use and storage of all kinds of human tissue. The UK Government responded by drawing up new legislation, the Human Tissue Act of 2004, to regulate and license the use of tissue across a number of contexts from pathological examination to museum display.

In this new policy context, I reflect on whether the term gift retains its persuasiveness. My chapter progresses in four parts: the first outlines my analytical approach; the second discusses the influential work of Richard Titmuss in relation to gift and specifically the 'gift relationship'; the third part focuses on how gift was used and to what effect in ethical guidelines on human tissue produced during the 1990s; the final and concluding part reflects on the situation today and asks whether gift has the same significance in contemporary policy discourses.

Policy, Persuasion and Keywords

How we should think about the texts that policymakers produce has been of interest to sociologists and anthropologists. Stephen Hilgartner (2000), for example, has analyzed scientific advice in terms of being a performance, one that is enacted to an imagined audience. He suggests that in their performance, scientific advisors 'use a variety of rhetorical devices to mobilise support from the literature, and package advice persuasively' (Hilgartner 2000, 10). One highly significant rhetorical device is the 'boundary work' (Gieryn 1983) that separates science and politics. The authority of the advisors comes from being able to maintain this boundary and to place themselves on the opposing side to politics. Hilgartner concludes that '[t]he legitimacy of advisory bodies depends in persuading their audiences, not only to accept their knowledge claims and recommendations, but also to accept the rhetoric they use to define the boundary that separates science from policy' (Hilgartner 2000, 10).

Anthropology has also become interested in policy, specifically in terms of how it impinges on concerns about governance and power. Apthorpe's (1997) analysis sees policy writing as an expression of power which can be analyzed through its genres and styles. One aspect of his analysis draws on the cultural theorist Raymond Williams's notion of 'keywords'. In his classic essay of the 1970s, Williams identified and reflected on what he called a number of 'keywords' in contemporary culture and society, which were 'significant, binding words in certain activities and ... indicative of certain forms of thought' (Williams 1988, 15). Apthorpe takes Williams's idea to highlight how policy texts attempt to persuade their audiences through the use of certain keywords.

One interpretation of Apthorpe's discussion of 'policy keywords' is to consider them as being persuasive both in terms of shaping the conceptualization of the public policy problem at stake and – flowing from this – in the promotion of particular practical arrangements that should be put in place for dealing with the problem. If Williams's project was an inquiry into the significant, changing vocabulary of post-World War II culture and society, this chapter represents a contribution towards an inquiry into the vocabulary of policy advisors' discourses in relation to human tissue. It focuses primarily on the policy keyword of 'gift', which policymakers have used to conceptualize human tissue and to advance particular arrangements concerning its collection, use and retention. The following two sections explore the history to the use of this policy keyword. The concluding part of the chapter reflects on the emergence of another policy keyword which might be superseding that of 'gift' in the context of human tissue policy.

Gift: Human Dignity and Social Solidarity

'Gift' is a keyword which ethicists, lawyers and sociologists have used in relation to the human body and its parts. Bioethicists and philosophers, wanting to resist what they see as the commodification of the human body, write about the 'generous, unrestricted gifts of informed adults and their families' (Lawrence 1995, 133) that should not be treated as property and traded as commodities (Holland 2001). Their concern is that to do otherwise would be an affront to human dignity and undermine our sense of human personhood (Murray 1987). Sociologists, equally concerned with commodification, do not speak of dignity but emphasize instead the greater social good that is served from the gifting of human tissue because this implies an act of altruism and solidarity (Nelkin and Andrews 1998). Nowhere is this sentiment more clearly expressed than in the work of Richard Titmuss, who examined the policies of blood donation over three decades ago. He saw the donation of blood as revealing 'the quality of human relationships and of human values prevailing in society' (Titmuss 1997, 59) and suggested that, when voluntarily given, blood could be an expression of both individual altruism and collective cohesion.

Social scientific thinking about the provision of human organs and blood in the 1960s and 1970s was shaped by anthropological gift theory in the early part of the twentieth century. The French anthropologist Marcel Mauss' account of gift exchange ([1925] 1997) was especially influential. He had argued that the exchange of gifts, which involved obligations to give, receive and reciprocate, was not only a matter of economic relationships but was also a powerful force for creating social bonds between individuals, families and communities. The medical sociologists Renée Fox and Judith Swazey ([1967] 1978), who noted the colloquial use of the term 'gift' in medical, legal and popular discourses in relation to organ donation, drew on the anthropological literature to inform their analysis of the processes of giving and receiving donated organs. Titmuss was equally influenced by Mauss: in his understanding of the sociality of gift, Titmuss found an attractive analogue for his own proposition that the voluntary donor system in Britain could be represented as a 'gift relationship'. However, Titmuss departed from the anthropological account of gift exchange on several key points. Most crucially, he suggested that the British donor system was not defined by a set of obligations to give or reciprocate the 'blood gift'. Instead, it was organized around the principle of voluntary donation; people who gave blood did so from a sense of altruism and with no expectation of a return.

It is important to realize that Titmuss was concerned with understanding the underlying objectives of different public policies. The focus of his analysis was not at the level of the motives of individual blood donors but on the function of social institutions, especially the National Health Service, which he saw as performing an important role in the social cohesion of British society (Rose 1981). Titmuss concluded that the National Health Service, by being non-divisive, universal and free at point of access, helped create the conditions in which people would have 'the choice to give, or not to give, blood for unseen strangers' (Titmuss 1997, 292). While it might be argued that the anthropological notion of gift is not applicable to contemporary Western societies in any strict sense (Frow 1997), imaginatively applied, gift has become a persuasive keyword when speaking about the values of social equality, altruism and community. Specifically, the 'gift relationship' can be seen as essentially a political representation, from a liberal-socialist perspective, of the virtues of the welfare state vis-à-vis market-based healthcare as epitomized by the United States (Rapport and Maggs 2002). The next part of this chapter will address how the 'gift relationship' came to be evoked in the 1990s in relation to the use of human tissue for biomedical research.

Evoking the 'Gift Relationship' in Human Tissue Policy in the 1990s

In the wake of the well-documented John Moore judgment by the California Supreme Court in 1990 (Boyle 1995), there was increased interest in the status of human tissue not only by lawyers but also by sociologists, ethicists and policymakers (Beyleveld and Brownsword 2000, Frow 1997, Landecker 1999, Grubb 1998; Laurie 2002, Nelkin and Andrews 1998). This case centered on an action against doctors who had performed a splendectomy on John Moore, a US businessman, and who then retained some tissue without his knowledge and used it to develop a cell line that became commercially valuable. Moore claimed that he held a property right in the tissue used to grow the cell line, which entitled him to share in its commercial exploitation. After a number of hearings at lower courts, the Supreme Court ruled against him (see Boyle 1995 for extended discussion of the judgment).

Prompted in part by this ruling, the Nuffield Council on Bioethics established an advisory group in 1995 to draw up guidelines on human tissue across a number of contexts, ranging from whole organ transplantation to the collection of blood samples for genetic research. A few years later, the Medical Research Council (MRC) set up another group to develop its own guidelines; their work began before but concluded after the tissue retention controversy at Alder Hey Children's Hospital in the UK, with the final guidelines emerging in 2001. These later guidelines primarily focused on tissue samples provided to research studies. This chapter is limited to precisely this kind of context. There is a danger otherwise of ranging too widely so that the specificities of the tissue, the social relationships and institutional contexts involved are obfuscated.

The evocation of 'gift' and 'gift relationships' as keywords in the policy discourses of the 1990s can be explained in terms of the need to facilitate and manage commercial interests in human tissue and its products. The policy advisors of the Nuffield Council and MRC needed to come up with an 'ethical' solution to the problem of how to manage these interests in a way that met commercial demands for intellectual property protection but which did not look like naked exploitation. It is in this context that 'gift' is used to persuade us that biomedical research should comprise both voluntary and commercialized elements and where the boundary between these elements should be drawn.

Both the Nuffield Council and the MRC started from the position that the provision of biological samples for the purposes of biomedical research should not be commercialized. Instead, 'tissue samples donated for research [should] be treated as gifts' (MRC 2001, 9). As opposed to being paid, for example, to provide samples, people should be willing to provide samples from an altruistic motivation. Both sets of guidelines appealed to the idea that members of the public can assist researchers to find new treatments and to make scientific breakthroughs by voluntarily donating samples. While the policy advisors rejected the commercialization of tissue provision, they stated that these 'scientific breakthroughs' would depend on commercial involvement to ensure that they can be 'sufficiently available to benefit human health' (MRC 2001, 12). Such products require substantial long-term investment and 'will be best distributed through market structures' (Nuffield Council 1995, 52).

This distinction between the voluntary and commercial aspects of biomedical research was reinforced by what the MRC guidelines claimed was the 'factual' and legal distinction between physical tissue and the 'data or intellectual property derived from them' (MRC 2001, 12). The California Supreme Court had made a similar distinction between the cells taken from John Moore's body and the cell line grown from them, which the judges saw as being a product of human ingenuity and therefore a matter of intellectual property (Boyle 1995). As well as stressing that the provision of tissue should be voluntary, altruistic and unpaid, the guidelines were also concerned with establishing that the individuals involved could not make any kind of claim over their tissue. Given that the provision of human tissue was made as a donation, the Nuffield Council determined it was 'free of all claims' (Nuffield Council 1995, 68) and observed that donation does 'not ordinarily give rise to intellectual property rights' (Nuffield Council 1995, 74).

Through the use of the keyword 'gift', the guidelines therefore sought to persuade their audience first, that the provision of human tissue should be an unpaid, voluntary donation and second that which was being 'gifted' was the physical tissue sample and not what was derived from it, which was seen as a matter of scientific intellectual property. At the same time, both the Nuffield Council and the MRC were aware that the public 'may be particularly sensitive to the idea of a company or an individual making a profit out of the tissue that they have freely donated' (MRC 2001, 12). Therefore, to assuage these perceived concerns, both sets of guidelines proposed that the physical tissue samples gifted by individuals should be stored at universities or hospitals. In these institutions people had traditionally invested trust (Busby 2004), and these would act as custodians of sample collections and mediate between the commercial and non-commercial elements of biomedical research, guided by their professional codes of practice to ensure public confidence.

It is of interest that the MRC guidelines also use the 'gift' keyword in a very different way. As the legal theorist Graeme Laurie (2002) has observed, to conceive of donated tissue samples as gifts implies property and ownership rather than their absence (Laurie 2002). The MRC guidelines stated that, at the time of donation, 'any property rights that the donor might have in their tissue would be transferred, together with the control over the use of the tissue, to the recipient of the gift' (MRC 2001, 8). Therefore, the word 'gift' was used to describe the transfer of ownership and control to the institutions described above. The removal of any competing property claims would mean that scientists and the organizations for which they worked could make intellectual property claims without contestation and maximize any financial benefit that accrued.

In summary, this analysis shows how 'gift' was a keyword with different meanings that served two not unrelated needs in the Nuffield Council and MRC guidelines of the 1990s. Through the 'gift' keyword, these policy advisors constructed a boundary between non-commercialized and commercialized elements of biomedical research. While celebrating the voluntary and altruistic nature of tissue provision through the use of the expression 'gift relationship', the guidelines also sought to ensure that commercial interests could be facilitated and protected by ensuring that people relinquished any ownership rights over their physical tissue samples and any claims to the intellectual property produced by research.

Beyond Gift? From Donors to Participants

Since the Nuffield Council on Bioethics and the MRC worked on developing these guidelines in the 1990s, policy discourses about human tissue – its collection, use and retention – have arguably been transformed. In 1999, following evidence given at an official inquiry into clinical practices at Bristol Royal Infirmary, the long-accepted and established practice of removing and keeping some organs after post-mortem examination for education and research purposes came to public attention as a highly controversial practice (Royal Liverpool Children's Inquiry 2001). At the center of the controversy was the issue of informed consent: hospitals, principally Alder Hey Children's Hospital in Liverpool, had routinely retained organs without the proper consent of relatives.

In parallel with these events, the Wellcome Trust, MRC and Department of Health developed their plans for what became known as UK Biobank (Barbour 2003). This large-scale longitudinal project involves the collection and storage of blood and urine samples along with medical and lifestyle information from 500,000 volunteers across the country. The stated purpose of UK Biobank is to investigate the genetic and environmental factors involved in the aetiology of common, complex diseases, such as diabetes, Alzheimer's and hypertension. The partners in UK Biobank were very much aware of the potential sensitivities that surrounded this initiative; they organized public consultations and drew up an Ethics and Governance Framework (UK Biobank 2003) to ensure that the project won public confidence.

Against this background, the conclusion to this chapter argues that since the 1990s the 'gift' keyword has receded somewhat in policy discourses to be replaced by that of 'participation'. Across the contexts of healthcare, biomedical research and publishing, as well as policy advice, there is evidence of a change in the language used to describe people who take part in various kinds of research studies (Corrigan and Tutton 2006, Tutton 2007). No longer are these people referred to as the subjects of research but rather as 'participants' in it. Take, for example, UK Biobank: in its early stages, volunteers were primarily talked of in terms of being donors giving 'a gift to biomedical research' (Meade 2000, Newton 2003, Cragg, R.D. 2000). Now they are seen as 'participants' in the project (People Science and Policy Ltd 2002, UK Biobank 2003).

'Participation', as a policy keyword, can be seen as a reflexive institutional response to perceived public ambivalence towards science and expertise (see Corrigan and Tutton 2006 for futher discussion). The word 'participation' resonates with discourses of 'active citizenship', individual choice and autonomy (Tutton 2007). Policymakers use this keyword to construct an image of people not as the passive subjects of research but as partners actively engaged in the research process, with a stake in its outcomes. However, the use of the word 'participation' is very much contested, and it is a matter of contention whether its increasing use in policy texts is reflected in changes in research practices or in people's experiences of being involved in studies (Chalmers, Jackson and Carvel 1999, Williamson 1999).

However, it can be argued that some recent innovations in governance would suggest that policy advice and regulation has become more 'participatory'. Whereas the tissue guidelines of the 1990s imagined that the public would entrust institutions such as hospitals and universities to regulate the use and retention of human tissue, and to act in the public interest, recent developments suggest a departure from this arrangement. Created under the terms of the Human Tissue Act 2004, the UK Human Tissue Authority (HTA) is a statutory body responsible for regulating and licensing the use of human tissue for a range of purposes from transplantation and pathological examination, to research. The HTA emphasizes that, of its 16 members, the Chair and nine others are not from medical professional backgrounds but are individuals with experiences in the voluntary sector, NHS user involvement and patient or public advocacy groups. Another development is the UK Biobank Ethics and Governance Council (EGC), which was created to oversee the Ethics and Governance Framework that was developed in effect to regulate the activities of the project and define the terms of people's 'participation' in it (UK Biobank 2003). This Council is a semi-independent oversight body funded by the partners and is comprised of members from a number of professional backgrounds, including ethics, law, medicine, medical science and social science, as well from public consultation and community and consumer involvement.

The sociologists Salter and Jones (2005) see these kinds of developments as evidence of a move away from professional self-regulation towards a form of regulation that seeks to represent citizen interests through the inclusion of people from a wider set of backgrounds. They suggest that this indicates a strategic move to establish the legitimacy of potentially controversial research by including the public in consultations about research projects and by opening up the membership of oversight bodies to include representatives from patient or consumer advocacy organizations and other special interest groups.

Therefore, this chapter might conclude that the creation of the HTA and the UK Biobank EGC illustrate how some of the assumptions underpinning the evocation of the 'gift relationship' in the 1990s have been questioned. Arguably, in relation to the provision of human tissue for research, it is not sufficient to call upon people to be altruistic and to trust the researchers concerned to act in the public interest. Trust and confidence have to be won and secured through new forms of governance, which seek renewed legitimacy by including people positioned to represent citizen or lay interests.

While 'gift' remains a powerful word, especially in relation to organ transplantation, in policy discourses about human tissue provided for research studies, it has been displaced by a new policy keyword. 'Participation' conjures up the image of people's active involvement in research, which the idea of 'gifting' did not convey. Moreover, policy advice and regulation are represented as becoming more 'participatory' by including representatives of citizen interests. Whether this will prove to be an adequate response to what has been perceived as a lack of public confidence in the institutions of science and medicine remains to be seen. From the perspective of the social scientific analysis of policy, the rise of 'participation' as a prominent keyword is of immense interest. Analyzing how and when it is used can open up a critical space in which its competing definitions and interpretations can be explored to address the issues of ownership, control, consent, benefit-sharing and commercialization in relation to human tissue. These, after all, remain as significant today as they were in the 1990s.

Acknowledgments

This chapter draws on material from a published chapter, 'Person, Property and Gift: Exploring Languages of Tissue Donation to Biomedical Research', in R. Tutton and O. Corrigan (eds) (2004) *Genetic Databases: Socio-Ethical Issues in the Collection and Use of DNA* (London: Routledge) and an oral presentation, 'Beyond Gift: From the Gift Relationship to the Human Tissue Authority', which was given at a seminar organized by the ESRC Genomics Research and Policy Forum and the Human Tissue Authority (HTA) in London, 28 June 2006. I would like to thank my colleagues Sujatha Raman and Helen Busby who read and commented on an earlier version of this chapter.

Bibliography

Andrews, L. and Nelkin, D. (1998), 'Whose body is it anyway? Disputes over Body tissue in a biotechnology age', *The Lancet* 351, 53–7.

Apthorpe, R. (1997), 'Writing development policy and policy analysis plain or clear: on language, genre and power', in C. Shore and S. Wright (eds), *Anthropology of Policy: Critical Perspectives on Governance and Power* (London: Routledge).

Barbour, V. (2003), 'UK Biobank: a project in search of a protocol?', *The Lancet* 361, 1734–8.

Beyleveld, D. and Brownsword, R. (2000), 'My body, my body parts, my property?', *Health Care Analysis* 8, 87–99.

Boyle, J. (1995), 'A theory of information: copyright, spleens, blackmail and insider trading', *California Law Review* 80, 1415–1540.

Busby, H. (2004), 'Blood donation for genetic research: what can we learn from donor's narratives?' in R. Tutton and O. Corrigan (eds), *Genetic Databases: Socio-Ethical Issues in the Collection and Use of DNA* (London: Routledge).

Chalmers, I., Jackson, W. and Carvel, D. (1999), 'People are "participants" in research', *British Medical Journal* 318 (7191), 1141.

Corrigan, O. and R. Tutton (2006), 'What's in a name? Subjects, volunteers, participants and activists in clinical research', *Clinical Ethics* 1 (2), 101-4

Cragg, R.D. (2000), *Public perceptions of the collection of human biological samples*. Summary Report prepared for Wellcome Trust/MRC, London.

Fox, R.C. and Swazey, J. ([1967]1978), *The Courage to Fail: A Social View of Organ Transplants and Dialysis* (London: University of Chicago Press).

Frow, J. (1997), *Time and Commodity Culture, Essays in Cultural Theory and Postmodernity* (Oxford: Clarendon Press).

Gieryn, T. (1983), 'Boundary-work and the demarcation of science from non-science: strains and interests in professional ideologies of scientists', *American Sociological Review* 48, 781-95.

Greenberg, W. and Kamin, D. (1993), 'Property rights and payment to patients for cell lines derived from human tissues: an economic analysis', *Social Science and Medicine* 36 (8), 1071-6.

Grubb, A. (1998), '"I, me, mine": bodies, parts and property', *Medical Law International* 3, 299-317.

Hilgartner, S. (2000), *Science on Stage: Expert Advice as Public Drama* (Stanford: Stanford University Press).

Holland, S. (2001), 'Contested commodities at both ends of life: buying and selling gametes, embryos, and body tissues', *Kennedy Institute of Ethics Journal* 11, 263-84.

Landecker, H. (1999), 'Between beneficence and chattel: the human biological in law and science', *Science in Context* 12, 203-25.

Laurie, G. (2002), *Genetic Privacy, A Challenge to Medico-Legal Norms* (Cambridge: Cambridge University Press).

Lawrence, S.C. (1995), 'Beyond the grave – the use and meaning of human body parts: a historical introduction', in R. Weir (ed.), *Stored Tissue Samples: Ethical, Legal and Public Policy Implications* (Iowa City: Iowa University Press).

Marinetto, M. (2003), 'Who wants to be an active citizen? The politics and practice of community involvement', *Sociology* 37 (1), 103-20.

Mauss, M. ([1925] 1997), *The Gift, The Form and Reason for Exchange in Archaic Societies*. Translated by W.D. Halls (London: Routledge).

Meade, T. (2000), *After the Human Genome Project: the UK Population Biomedical Collection*, Millennium Lecture Series, St. Catherine's College, Oxford: 18 May 2000.

Medical Research Council (MRC) (2001), *Human Tissue and Biological Samples for Use in Research* (London: Medical Research Council).

Murray, T.H. (1987), 'Gifts of the body and the needs of strangers', *Hastings Law Center Report*, April 1987, 30-38.

Nelkin, D. and Andrews, L. (1998), 'Homo economicus: commercialisation of body tissue in the age of biotechnology', *Hastings Center Report*, September-October 1998, 30-39.

Newton, J. (2003), 'Address to Industry Consultation Workshop on UK Biobank', *Association of the British Pharmaceutical Industry*, London, 4 April 2003.

Nuffield Council on Bioethics (1995), 'Human tissue: ethical and legal issues', http://www.nuffieldfoundation.org/bioethics (accessed 18 May 2009).

People Science and Policy Ltd (2002), 'Biobank UK: a question of trust: A consultation exploring and addressing questions of public trust' (London: Medical Research Council and Wellcome Trust), http://www.ukbiobank.ac.uk/documents/consultation.pdf (accessed 18 May 2009).

—— (2003), *UK Biobank Consultation on the Ethics and Governance Framework* (London: Medical Research Council and Wellcome Trust).

Rapport, F.L. and Maggs, C.J. (2002), 'Titmuss and the gift relationship: altruism revisited', *Journal of Advanced Nursing* 40 (5), 495-503.

Rose, H. (1981), 'Re-reading Titmuss: the sexual division of welfare', *Journal of Social Policy* 10 (4), 477-502.

Royal Liverpool Children's Inquiry (2000), Crown Stationery Office, Norwich. http://www.rlcinquiry.org.uk/index.htm (accessed 31 May 2007).

Salter, B. and M. Jones (2005), 'Biobanks and bioethics: the politics of legitimation', *Journal of European Public Policy* 12 (4), 710-34.

Titmuss, R. (1997), *The Gift Relationship, From Human Blood to Social Policy*, in A. Oakley and J. Ashton (eds) (London: London School of Economics and Political Science).

Tutton, R. (2004), 'Person, Property and Gift: Exploring Languages of Tissue Donation to Biomedical Research', in R. Tutton and O. Corrigan (eds) (2004), *Genetic Databases: Socio-Ethical Issues in the Collection and Use of DNA* (London: Routledge).

Tutton, R. (2006), 'Beyond Gift: From the Gift Relationship to the Human Tissue Authority', paper presented to ESRC Genomics Research and Policy Forum and the Human Tissue Authority joint meeting, London, 28 June 2006.

Tutton, R. (2007), 'Constructing participation in genetic databases: citizenship, governance and ambivalence', *Science, Technology and Human Values* 32 (2), 172-195.

UK Biobank (2003), *Draft ethics and governance framework*. www.ukbiobank.ac.uk/ethics/efg.php (accessed 23 January 2006).

Wellcome Trust/MRC (2000), Public Perceptions of the Collection of Human Biological Samples. http://www.ukbiobank.ac.uk/documents/perceptions.pdf (accessed 1 May 2003).

Williams, R. (1988), *Keywords: A Vocabulary of Culture and Society* (London: Fontana Press).

Williamson, C. (1999), 'The challenge of lay partnership', *British Medical Journal* 319, 721-2.

PART II
Donation in the Light of Human Embodiment

Chapter 4

Why the Body Matters: the Symbolic Significance of Human Tissue[1]

Alastair V. Campbell

Introduction

This chapter is written from the perspective of the retained organs controversy, which was uncovered by the Bristol and Alder Hey Inquiries.[2] I was appointed Vice-Chairman of the Retained Organs Commission, which was set up by the Chief Medical Officer (CMO) for England in 2001. For me, as for most other members of the Commission, the powerful emotions generated by this controversy were an unforgettable experience. Commission meetings were held in public, and on several occasions the anger and grief expressed by affected families interrupted proceedings, on one occasion bringing them to a temporary halt. Private discussions between Commission members and relatives (from a wide variety of backgrounds) revealed even more powerfully the profound feelings of anger and sense of betrayal provoked by the discovery of past postmortem practice and by the subsequent poorly managed attempts to return retained organs.

This chapter seeks to explore the roots of this powerful reaction to the widespread practice of retaining organs and tissue without the knowledge and consent of relatives.

Two Narratives in Non-Communication

In *Doctors' Stories* Kathryn Hunter describes what she calls the 'narrative incommensurability' of doctors' and patients' accounts of illness:

> The patient's account of illness and the medical version of that account are fundamentally, irreducibly different narratives, and this difference is essential to the work of medical care. Sick people who seek a physician's advice and help are in quest of exactly this difference, for, physicians are believed not only to know more about the body but also to see its disorders clearly and without shame. Yet

---

1   This is a modified version of Campbell and Willis 2005.

2   *Interim Report of the Bristol Royal Infirmary Inquiry* 2000, *Report of the Royal Liverpool Children's Inquiry* 2001.

because it is scarcely acknowledged by either patient or physician, the difference between their accounts of the patient's malady can warp understanding between them. (Hunter 1991, 123)

As we see from this quotation, Hunter is not deploring the fact that the narratives are incommensurable – she sees this as necessary for medicine to offer help to the patient. But things go wrong when the difference between the narratives is not acknowledged and understood, and this wrong is compounded, when, as in the retained organs controversy, the medical narrative persists past the point where it is either necessary or useful.

Let us compare, then, the way relatives saw the retention of organs and tissue after postmortem examination with how it was conceptualized by some of the professional bodies, who gave evidence to the Chief Medical Officer's Summit on Organ Retention. The evidence of relatives is fully available from the Documentation of the Summit and also from the three Inquiry Reports of Bristol, Alder Hey and Isaacs. I can give only a few brief excerpts to convey the profound feelings experienced by so many families:[3]

> You relive the moment that she died over and over again. I have flashbacks of what they have done and what you imagine they have done. I had a dream the other day that I said to someone in the hospital where I work what is in the cupboard? When we opened it there were three jars: one with babies' hearts, one with babies' lungs and one, which looked like peas. When I looked closer they were eyes ... I have a great big empty void inside. (Department of Health 2001, 22)

> ...they were devastated to hear that their daughter's tongue had been retained, and father protested silently outside Alder Hey ... They describe the hospital as having stolen their daughter's body, which was 'white as driven snow. It was reduced to skin and bone by predators and it must never happen again'.[4]

Compare this testimony from relatives with some of the written evidence given by professional medical associations to the CMO's Summit:

> The fact that in the past many families have not been informed in detail about what a post mortem examination entails ... invariably reflected a simple and understandable wish to spare them further anguish and distress at the time of bereavement. (Royal College of Pathologists) (Department of Health 2001, Ref. 101)

---

3   Only extracts from the evidence of families who experienced the loss of a child are being used here, but it should be noted that there was also widespread retention of *adult* organs. Department of Health 2003.

4   *Royal Liverpool Children's Inquiry*, 421.

> It is perhaps a paradox that in an age when we have more understanding than ever before of the nature of human life and the biology of the human body, we are more distressed than at any time in human history about what is perceived as inappropriate disposal of the whole human body or part of it ... This is a philosophical puzzle. (President, Royal College of Paediatrics and Child Health) (Department of Health 2001, Ref. 119)

Perhaps this last quotation is the most powerful indication of the narrative dissonance of the medical and lay understandings of the body. The President of the Royal College of Paediatrics and Child Health cannot understand how, with such improved knowledge of the *biology* of the body, relatives can feel distressed when they discover that they have buried a body 'stripped of organs'.

Such a clash of narratives is not restricted to the medical world. The philosopher John Harris shows similar puzzlement and disapproval when considering the controversy over organ retention and the proposals for a more respectful treatment of human remains:

> A quite absurd, if understandable, preoccupation with reverence and respect for bodily tissue has come to dominate discussions of retained tissues and organs in the wake of the Alder Hey revelations. We do not normally feel this reverence for our bodily remains, tissue and organs when alive – why suddenly this morbid *post mortem* preoccupation? (Harris 2002, 546)

Harris's disrespect for respect in this situation stems from his commitment to a valuation of human life in terms of identity based on consciousness. He shares this with the philosopher John Locke, who gave an account of human identity based solely on awareness and memory. Such a view leaves no room for the significance of the body, though it lends itself well to the scientific paradigm on which medical practice is usually based.[5]

Another example of this purely materialistic approach to the human dead body can be seen in the Body Worlds exhibition of Gunther von Hagens. Here the plastinated corpse becomes a kind of entertainment or spectacle – a throwback to the era of public dissections. Von Hagens justifies it as 'education', but the boundary between genuine entertainment and showmanship seems very thin indeed!

Embodiment, Vulnerability and Loss

It would be naïve to suppose that these different ways of viewing the human body can easily be reconciled. Indeed there may be no need to do so, provided

---

5   I have explored this problem in John Harris's view of the body at greater length in Campbell 2009.

we understand that they serve different purposes and provided the feelings of the bereaved are properly respected. The medical discourse is functional for achieving the goals of scientific medicine, in which the body-as-object is required in order to create the generalizations that allow for differential diagnosis and (some kinds of) therapeutic intervention. But even in the realm of the living, it is now well recognized that such distancing and objectifying of the body has detrimental effects on health and offers only limited scope for effective recovery from illness.

When medicine extends uncritically into the realm of the dead and supposes that 'this malformed and damaged heart' (to be stored in a jar for further study) is the same as 'my child's heart' (soon to be buried with my child's body), then it loses the plot completely. The meanings attributed to the parts of the body by doctors and by the lay public are in reality completely different, and each has its own rationality. Intimate relationships never concern merely a meeting of minds or of Lockean self-valuing pools of consciousness! The physical body of the person loved is fully part of the love that parent feels for child or wife for husband. This embodiment of the person does not suddenly disappear in death, though, of course, it soon becomes necessary to let go of the body and live only with the memory and mental images of the person now dead. A mother cuddling her dead child, a husband kissing the cold brow of his wife's dead body are not acts which *deny* the death of the person. They are part of the story of human lives shared and of the pain, which comes from parting.

Emotions, the Body and the Narrative Self

At this point some lines from a poem of Philip Larkin's come to mind:

> I would not dare
> Console you if I could. What can be said,
> Except that suffering is exact, but where
> Desire takes charge, readings will grow erratic? (Larkin 1988, 32)

The striking contrast between the philosophical and medical narratives about the treatment of the bodies of the dead and the lay narratives of the same events stems from the centrality of emotion in personal relationships. In the retained organs controversy, families were criticized for letting their feelings run away with them, and it was suggested that the media were deliberately manipulating emotions to get a good story, with headlines like 'They Stole My Baby's Soul'.

This moral condemnation is echoed in John Harris's description of opposition to the use of organs as 'wicked' (Harris 2003, 133). Clearly emotions can blind our better judgment at times, and some powerful emotional reactions can have their own momentum, in which the wholeness of the self is engulfed, and our identity lost. But without emotion we are no selves at all. We become distanced from our body and unable to create personal relationships or respond to the lives of others. It is as much the continuity of emotion as the continuity of memory and consciousness that gives us that unique phenomenon we call personal identity.

So, reading again the narratives of the affected relatives, we can see how it is the emotional loading of the memory that makes it distinctively and painfully theirs: the dreadful images of the body as an empty shell, of the horrifying cupboard full of specimens that once were hearts or eyes of living babies, the depredation of a daughter's white body – these are all the responses of people in close human relationships. Not surprisingly, the traumatized relatives then extended their sense of loss and betrayal to every scrap remaining of their relative's body – even the sliver of tissue on microscopic slides. All tissue becomes symbolically related to the body of the person now lost and gone.

To philosophers like John Harris, such feelings are dangerously irrational. In his view, we should be happy for our body and its tissues to be used in any way that might be of benefit for others, for once we are dead they are of no more use to us. He describes as 'wicked' the wish to have one's body or body parts treated as special and deserving of respect:

> It is surely implausible to think that having one's body remain whole after their death is an objective anyone is entitled to pursue at the cost of other people's lives! It is implausible to the point of wickedness, not least because the objective is irrational and impossible of achievement. (Harris 2003, 133)

But in my view it is quite wrong to describe the feelings of anger and loss of relatives as 'merely emotional' and ridiculous to describe our desire for respect for the dead body as 'wicked'. There is not a sudden transition from the living to the dead in ordinary human experience. These relatives, in their anger and grief, were responding to losses that we can all recognize easily. There is no 'real' or 'better' or 'more rational' self floating above the experiences which make up our individual lives. There is only the live self, an embodied self in which reason and emotion each play a part in making us who we are. Human tissue is not 'material' in the sense we usually mean it. It carries a symbolic weight derived from the source of it in a loved person, whose identity was bodily and well as mental.

Conclusion: Embodiment and Medicine

So what might this all mean for the practice of medicine? At one level, the retained organs controversy has brought to the fore some much needed changes in medicine. New legislation in the UK (the Human Tissue Act 2006 in England and Wales and similar legislation or regulation in other parts of the UK) will ensure that the removal and use of organs without consent cannot happen again. The powerful reaction of relatives to the discovery of retention has also brought about changes in medical practice, with a better understanding of how to help people facing the trauma of bereavement. But at a deeper level, there is probably still a long way to go before medicine can rediscover the lost dimension of respect for the human body. This entails seeing the strength, but also the limitation, of the 'scientific' approach to medical practice. It requires the ability to respond to the emotional and not merely the physical aspects of people's lives.

This does not mean a total embargo on the use of human tissue for beneficial ends, nor need it mean any radical change in policies for collecting, storing and using human tissue, now that the principle of consent has been unambiguously enshrined in legislation (at least in the UK). All that it means is that biomedical science must remain humane, and being humane entails never losing sight of the embodied self in our dealings with our own and others' bodies. Symbolism is not the same as superstition, and emotions, though they may confuse us at times, are an inseparable part of a genuine understanding of human value. So we should celebrate, not deplore, the powerful symbolic force of human tissue.

Bibliography

Campbell, A.V. (2009), *The Body in Bioethics* (London: Routledge-Cavendish).

Campbell, A.V. and Willis, M. (2005), '"They stole my baby's soul": narratives of embodiment and loss', *Medical Humanities* 31 (2), 101–04.

—— (forthcoming), 'Why the body matters: reflections on John Harris's account of organ procurement', in Holm, S., Hayry, M. and Takala, T. (eds), *Life of Value* (Amsterdam and New York: Rodopi).

Department of Health (2001), Chief Medical Officer's Summit, Evidence Documentation. (London).

—— (2003), *Isaacs Report* (London).

Harris, J. (2002), 'Law and regulation of retained organs: the ethical issues', *Legal Studies* 22 (4).

—— (2003), 'Organ procurement: dead interests, living needs', *Journal of Medical Ethics* 29.

Hunter, K.M. (1991), *Doctors' Stories: The Narrative Structure of Medical Knowledge* (Princeton: Princeton University Press).

Interim Report of the Bristol Royal Infirmary Inquiry (2000), Central Office of Information. (London).

Larkin, P. (1988), *Deceptions. Collected Poems* (London: The Marvell Press).

Report of the Royal Liverpool Children's Inquiry (2001) (London: Stationery Office).

Chapter 5
Duties Towards our Bodies

Michael Steinmann

Introduction

The donation of tissue to a biobank ideally is done according to the principles of a free, democratic society. On the one hand, donors have to consent before their tissue is taken. They can freely decide to whom and for what purpose their tissue is given. In this sense, their personal and property rights are fully respected. On the other hand, scientific research is free. Science does not follow political or social requirements, but only its own standards and rules (within the given legal framework). Our democratic society protects and even encourages free decision-making on both sides, on the side of participants in research, and on the side of scientists.

Against this freedom, the question why we give our tissue away is left explicitly open. No restrictions can be set, and no one should tell us why we are supposed to donate. However, this freedom which is so important on the individual, social, legal and political levels of our life is only one side of the coin. With the focus on freedom, nothing is said about how decisions are made. Even if our decision is free, we usually need good reasons in order to decide for one thing rather than for something else. In the case in question, we have to think that donating tissue is desirable, that it is good to donate; otherwise we might not participate in the collection of tissue at all.

But the question remains: is there a standard that helps me to decide what is desirable and what is not? If I think that it might be good to donate, then my reflection follows certain normative presumptions. I assume, for example, that my tissue will be used efficiently, and I feel a certain obligation to participate in the progress of research. This chapter tries to elaborate the normative presumptions we may have. My claim is that such presumptions cannot be formulated through the categorical framework of 'autonomy', although this framework is most often used in regard to tissue donation. The framework we need relies instead on 'duties toward our bodies'. As we will see, such duties are not absolute in a Kantian sense, and they certainly are not meant to replace autonomy but rather to guide and even to foster autonomous decision-making.

'Duties' stem from the vulnerability and the sensibility of our bodies. They oblige us to care for our body and to act in favor of its well-being. We have to maintain our body, to heal it when it is sick and suffering and to improve its condition where such improvement is possible. Finally, we have to respect the body as part and extension of our personality. This care for our individual bodies does not exclude the body of others: the body, by its common biological nature, includes all similar entities. The care for my body is realized together with the care for others. The 'our' here is to be understood in a collective sense.

In general, to speak about 'duties' towards our body is nothing extraordinary or new – it only makes explicit what it means to act responsibly in relation to one's own bodily condition. But this responsibility is very rarely taken into account, and it needs a proper terminology in order to become clear. In this sense, 'duty' is a category meant to explain our concerns and normative presumptions in regard to our body.

One might be tempted to ask: why is it so important to lay out how we decide and why we participate at the collection of tissue samples? After all, everyone might do it for his or her own personal reason. But this question does have a huge practical impact. It concerns first of all the question of *control*. Recently, a lot of effort has been spent in order to find the appropriate means of control in relation to biobanks. Besides the installation of ethics committees, much importance is placed on the donor. Donors can decide not only whether they want to participate at all, but also whether to withdraw if, for example, the purpose or the methodology of research is changed, or if research is carried through by an institution other than the one to which consent was originally given. To decide means to control, and this touches a point of greater interest.

But the question why we participate also concerns the question of *legitimation*. Storing tissue is legitimate when the donor has been informed and given consent. Usually we do not ask for the scientific reason for such a collection (because we take it for granted), but want to make sure that ethical standards are being observed. In this sense, the autonomous consent of the donor is a source of legitimation; besides all usual legal standards, researchers are legitimized in carrying a project through if they found someone who considered this project acceptable and agreed to participate. For our liberal point of view, something is acceptable if it is accepted by someone, by a group of people or by virtually everyone.

From this perspective, our individual decision-making is of utmost importance, just as the normative standard we are following. We have to decide responsibly to whom we donate, and we have to be aware of our normative presumptions in order to decide what we find acceptable or not. Again, speaking about 'duties' is a way to make these presumptions a bit more explicit. Like any other approach in philosophical ethics, it is not meant to state what is right or wrong, but to clarify the questions at stake and to help in making a more responsible decision.

A final point concerns the value-laden concepts that are typically used in this context, such as 'altruism' or 'donation'. These concepts also tell us why we should give our tissue away and why we should do this in an unconditioned way. We should do it because we are 'donating', because we act 'altruistically' in favor of others. By making use of these concepts, biobanking and research on tissue rely on normative presumptions. This is important to see because it shows that the approach we have chosen is not the only one that brings value-laden concepts into play. However, 'altruism' and 'donation' are not always analyzed as much as they should, and we have good reasons to assume that the idea of 'duties' will help us to explain even these concepts a little bit more. We have to ask, for example, *why* we think that altruism is desirable and legitimate. This question might be surprising, but in fact we do not accept each kind of donation only because it is done altruistically: a donation to a racist organization would not be acceptable. This means that giving tissue to a biobank is not legitimate because it is done altruistically, but because altruism is an expression of the duties we have towards our bodies. Altruism, at least in its unqualified forms, needs to be reconsidered. 'Duties' have to be seen as grounds for both 'altruism' and 'donation'.

We will start from some preliminary points. The first point concerns the question of what it means to speak about normative presumptions. How can we say that we are having 'presumptions' if we might not even be aware of them? We have to say a few words about the methodological status of this notion. The second point explains why we actually need another normative standard in addition to the ones that are usually brought into play. Altruism will be mentioned here but also property. The commercial use of tissue banking will shed some light on the problem of altruism; the following paragraphs will take a quick look at the notion of property, which has been suggested as a category helping donors to control the use of their material. We will see that it lacks a standard of its own. This brings us to the question of the basic relation to our body. Is self-ownership the appropriate means to conceptualize this relation? Starting from some traditional theories, we can show that it has to be accompanied by the duty to care about one's body. We have to distinguish between legal and ethical points of view, and from a strictly ethical perspective, we do not so much own ourselves as we are responsible to preserve ourselves and to act in the best interest of our physical condition. The last paragraph will finally explain the notion of duties, starting from a phenomenological approach to the body. Duties stem from our mixed experience of the body – an experience which relates internally and externally to it.[1]

What are 'Normative Presumptions'?

What it means to speak about normative presumptions may not seem clear. First, who is having these presumptions? Is it everyone who participates in tissue donation? But what if not everyone agrees, what if someone denies having any presumptions at all? Does that mean that the claim that is made here is wrong? In order to clarify this point, we first have to show what the function of such presumptions is.

As already has been said, presumptions are the reason *why* I donate. Participants, donors and even relatives need some kind of motivation in order to consent. They have to *presume*, in one way or the other, that it is desirable to donate; moreover,

---

1 For an earlier approach to this topic, see Steinmann 2008.

they have to *expect* something from it.[2] But expectations or presumptions are also intrinsic to the practice of science: we expect science to work for the benefit of humanity or at least to benefit those who are affected by a certain disease. In general, we can say that presumptions about research are related to our belief in its practical fruitfulness on the one side, and its moral purposiveness on the other side. With a formulation taken from Weir and Olick, we can say that normative presumptions, and the ethical principles that might be related to them, serve as 'action-guides' for us (Weir and Olick 2004, 272).

This belief does not deny the fact that each altruistic donation is deemed to be an unconditioned one. We have to give for the benefit of others, without setting conditions about how our tissue should be used. Altruism is unconditioned, and any limitation of it would be unethical. 'You will get the tissue, but you have to do x' – this is not an acceptable condition in regard to an act of donation. Besides, the use of tissue is unconditioned as well: in the best interest of research, all kinds of projects or methodologies should be possible. Within the given legal framework and under the observation of all ethical rules, scientists should be free to do whatever they hold necessary for the progress of science.

These two sides have to be seen together: the unconditioned character of donation and the presumptions about the purposiveness of research. Although they seem to contradict each other, this contradiction very seldom becomes explicit. There are many different ways in which expectations influence our practical engagement with science, and we cannot even say that everyone has the same strong 'presumptions' in regard to scientific research. Some may have very specific expectations they want to have met. Others may have rather vague presumptions that could be realized in a future far from now. They could say that in the long run, science will find out what is beneficial and what is not. It may not correspond immediately to their expectations, but at a certain point it will. Others simply might be satisfied when their personal and property rights – for example, in regard to data protection – are being respected, without giving the scientific endeavor a second thought ('I trust in doctor x'). And others might be touched by the idea of acting altruistically ('I usually donate when I am asked').

Hence, the notion of presumptions we are using is rather vague. It goes from strong and exclusive motivations – 'I do not donate if...' – to rather open expectations – 'I hope that at the end it is worthwhile'. But the question comes up again: what if someone denies having any presumptions at all, or if the expectations are simply too vague to be taken into account? Can we really build an ethical claim on something so variable and unsure? How can we say that there are *necessarily* some kinds of presumptions that we have in regard to our body?

We can say this because presumptions are not strictly identical with the will of the donor. They are even independent from it. We can see this when we reflect on the very nature of tissue donation. Human tissue is not a resource that is naturally available. Rather it is one that requires a highly demanding social relationship

---

2   See the survey described by Jack and Womack 2003.

– highly demanding insofar as there has to be not only the positive will to donate, but also a stringent procedure of consent and withdrawal and an institution able to use responsibly what has been donated. All participants have to play rather complex social roles: information has to be given and understood, consent needs to be made reliable, procedures of data protection have to be observed, etc. In this sense, 'donation' is not so much an individual decision but a social practice: we might say it is a social game implying certain rules and obligations on all sides. And if it can be compared to a game, then there are certain conditions we agree upon whenever we participate in such an activity. Certain presumptions related to practices are constitutive for the practices themselves. We have to accept them, like it or not; otherwise it is another type of practice we create. In our case, this is even more obvious as 'donation' has a long tradition as a basic and important pattern of social behavior. Asking others for their tissue automatically echoes similar patterns or games that are played. It would be nearly impossible not to presume any of the altruistic purposes implied in these games.

From the perspective of bioethics, especially the one coming from a liberal tradition, this is by no means self-evident. Bioethics very often focuses on the individual agents – on the patient or donor, or on the physician or researcher seeking consent. This means it follows a different methodological approach, an approach according to which only those points are taken into account that matter for the individual agents. But the normative presumptions related to tissue donation cannot be explained with such a methodology. They need a social approach, focusing on expectations that are shared and incorporated in patterns of behavior, in common attitudes and traditional rules. We have to see what the social meaning of a given practice is – its function within a larger context of practices, independent of those who are actually involved, or its goals which make it a game that is repeatedly played by many different agents and in regard to many different occasions or needs.

Besides this social approach, there is an issue involved we may call anthropological. Donors are not only to be seen as agents possessing the ability of autonomous decisions. Rather, they also have to be seen as *persons*. Besides their autonomous will, they are endowed with attitudes toward social values and benefits. Without such attitudes it would be difficult, if not impossible, to motivate their will. Autonomy would be based on arbitrary acts, and there would be no sufficient reason to say why someone acts in one way or the other. This means that we have to see donors as having presumptions about what they do. We need the idea of normative expectations in order to understand ourselves as persons that are able to act according to reasoning and reflection. As we said earlier, presumptions are the reason why one donates, and reasons are what we need to ascribe to ourselves in order to understand ourselves as responsible participants in any social activity. We might not have presumptions in every specific case, but we cannot imagine ourselves as having no presumptions at all in what we repeatedly do.

It now should be clear what it means to speak about normative presumptions. Presumptions can be seen as a rather open concept. However, they imply a certain methodological approach, taking the social and anthropological conditions of our practices into account. Now we can move on to a more specific question, the question why we need a moral standard based on 'duties' and not on 'altruism' or 'property'.

Altruism and the Commercial Use of Tissue Samples

Altruistic donation most often is described as praiseworthy, both for its act (the pure act of donation) as well as for the consequences it brings for others. Altruism fits the requirements both of deontological and consequentialist ethics. But its moral worth is not as obvious at it seems. We can show this in regard to an example: the commercial use of tissue samples.

In recent times, the interest in collecting human tissue has been widely directed to public institutions. All over the world, ambitious projects have been set up, not only in hospitals or at universities, but even on a national level. Examples for this national interest in biobanks are the Iceland Health Sector Database, the Estonian Genome Project or the UK Biobank. The growing importance of tissue banking has been accompanied by broad public discussions. But besides this there is an important branch of tissue banking that lies in the private sector, in private companies or laboratories. Companies producing tissue devices, like skin or cartilage replacement, also can be seen as tissue banks, even if they function on a lower scale: they are keeping tissues from various donors for various forms of use and, presumably, for an indeterminate time. Tissue is not only needed for the very production of tissue devices but also for experimentation, product testing and documentation. The know-how a company builds up requires the archiving of material and information.

As a general principle, it is widely accepted that the human body and its parts should not be used for any commercial purpose. ('Parts', in our context, has to be understood in a wider sense than usual, as any amount of cells that contains the biological information of a donor). Selling or buying body parts is held unethical. Hence, the donation to private companies or private tissue banks has to be altruistic and free, just like it is in the case of public banks. However, as soon as the material that has been donated belongs to a tissue bank or company, they are free to use it according to their commercial or non-commercial interests. Tissue must not be donated under commercial conditions, but once donated it can be used commercially.

There is clearly a discrepancy between these two sides – between the obligation to donate freely and altruistically and the freedom of commercial exploitation. On the one side, the dignity of the human body makes it necessary to prohibit any form of commercial exploitation. We are not allowed to sell parts of our body to someone else. But on the other side, as soon as parts of the body are separated, they become objects of financial interest. The recipient is allowed to treat tissue as being property in the full sense – including all consequences, like commercial benefit, resale to others or destruction.

For the question of altruism, this means that altruistic donation is getting abused. Research on human tissue depends on the altruism of others. There must be the free donation of material, not only once but constantly; otherwise there would be no input for new insights or experimentations. In this sense, research has to *depend* on altruism; it has to take altruism for granted. Obviously, one could say that counting on altruism does not constitute an ethical problem as such. All charitable organizations have to count on donations, and social networks between friends let us rely on the help of others in case of need. We know that others are not forced to help, but more or less we know they will do.

But there is a difference between these cases. Charitable organizations have no other purpose than help; they do not keep for themselves what they receive. On the contrary, commercial organizations use the altruistic gift in order to sustain themselves. It is their rationale to transform it into capital; otherwise they could not exist. In this sense, they have to abuse the altruism of donors – not intentionally, that is, not by evil will, but simply through the way in which they work.

To be clear: this argument is not about the question whether it is legitimate or not to combine scientific research with commercial interests. We have to take it for granted that there is a commercial interest in tissue banking. Nor is the argument about the question whether companies are to be blamed for their abuse of altruism. The argument is only about the value of altruism in the case of tissue banking. As we can see, altruism is a moral requirement that does not entirely fit the context in which it is used. Its morality is binding only for one side, for the donor, but not for the other. This means that altruism is an ethical standard that is useless in our case because it cannot be generally applied. It does not help us to establish ethical rules that are valid for *all parties* involved. If we want to set a standard that also fits with what private companies do, it is clearly not altruism that can give us any orientation.

This is not so much a moral, but a methodological argument. We do not want to say that donors should give up all their altruistic motivations. Altruism is inadequate only because it does not help us to *explain* the normative presumptions we have in regard to the *whole* process of tissue banking. Questions that arise here are: why should tissue be taken at all, how should it be treated, what kind of consequences should its storage have, etc.? All these questions need to be answered, and they require an ethical standard that altruism cannot give. As we will see, the concept of duties can help us to integrate all the different aspects and to conceptualize their underlying moral implications.

Another thing that we do not want to say is that altruistic motivations on the side of donors should be given up. All we want to say is that altruism cannot be the *only* motivating principle for participating in tissue donation. But once it is accompanied by other moral reasons, there is no problem in saying that one also gives 'for the benefit of others'. Motivations, in the sense of psychological facts, are often not very clear, and one should not even try to reduce them to one principle.[3]

An attempt to find a moral standard that is valid also for companies has been expressed in the discussion of benefit sharing. Benefit sharing is often named as reaction to the discrepancy between the altruism of donors and financial profit. Individual benefit sharing is thinkable here, but also the tribute of companies to larger communities, like patient groups or the healthcare sector as such. It seems to be a question of justice for a profit-making company to pay back some of the earnings it made with the material given from others.

But benefit sharing has several disadvantages, all of which are often named in the debates. Just a few of them shall be mentioned here. In individual cases, when the possibility of recompense is involved, donation would become a form of selling. Recompense could become the motivation to donate. This would contradict not only the principle according to which body parts should not be sold. It also could bring participants into a situation where they undergo higher risks and have a lower standard of protection for their personal rights. But even the case of collective benefit sharing is problematic. For instance, how can we establish the amount of a due recompense in relation to the material received? Is there a reliable calculation telling us how much a company has to 'pay back'? It seems there could only be an arbitrary answer to this question.[4]

We cannot enter this discussion in more detail. The reference to benefit sharing has the only purpose to show that the idea of distributive justice is not a good candidate either for a general moral rule. There might be single cases in which it works, but generally the idea of distributing profits to donors or communities does not help to balance the disproportion between altruism and commercial exploitation. However, it gives us a hint at a principle that respects the social dimension of tissue banking better than altruism does. Profit-sharing is an attempt to act according to the common responsibility of those who depend on the altruism of others. But we can see that the notion of duties is a much better means to conceptualize this responsibility than justice is. The question is not whether companies should 'pay back' a certain amount and how large that amount could be, but whether they act in a reasonable and beneficial way in regard to what they have received. What we actually need is not the sharing of benefits but a guarantee that the material coming from human bodies is used for the common good. It is necessary to set ethical standards and to control their application through commercial entities. Tax reduction might be an incentive here, or perhaps even a sort of 'ethical rating' of companies.

---

3   See Batson 1998 for such mixed motivations. One flaw of this study is its being based on the dichotomy of altruism-egoism. Hence, every motivation that is not altruistic is egoistic. This point of view is much too narrow. Following a duty is clearly not altruistic, but it is likewise not egoistic.

4   For a critical discussion of benefit sharing see Bovenberg 2005; for a more positive account Dickenson 2005.

'Property' between Ethics and Law

In recent discussions, the category of property has been suggested as a means to stipulate rules for the regulation of tissue donation. In this sense it is not only a moral standard but also a legal tool helping to articulate the concerns of donors. Again we cannot enter into much detail here. Our basic question is whether this tool is able to bring satisfying solutions for all aspects relevant to tissue banking. This means the question is again more methodological than moral.

The attractiveness of property stems from the fact that it can be conceived as a bundle of relations. Having property in something gives us not only one but many different entitlements, for example, a right to use, to manage, to alienate or even to destroy. This means property is not an all-or-nothing relationship to something.[5] There could be a right to use without the right to income, or a right to income without the right of transfer. How many different 'sticks' there are in the 'bundle' is an open question among scholars which we do not have to dwell upon.[6] In any case, it is possible to think that only certain entitlements are given when tissue is donated to a bank, while others are being withheld. For many ethicists, this seems to be the appropriate tool to protect the interests of donors. Donors would not have to renounce any influence on the exploitation of their tissue. They could keep certain rights in relation to the recipient, the right to participate in financial gains (for example, when patents are filed) or the right to decide about the most charitable way of using tissue samples (for example when specific patient groups or diseases are involved). The bundle theory of ownership seems promising with all these different legal tools, even if many of them are still hypothetical.

Obviously, there will be a lot of practical problems when it comes to stipulating the choice of 'sticks' from a legal standpoint. How can biobanks or companies, and also public research institutions, be brought to accept that they are not entrusted with the whole bundle of relations? Is it possible for a biobank to accept only limited access to property? Some ethicists claim this would be detrimental for any long-term project of research.[7] And how can donors exert their rights: for instance, how can the use of different entitlements be adequately controlled? These are only a few questions that arise in this case. But they are not what is most interesting for us. A much deeper problem lies in the fact that property is just another expression of autonomy. Ownership in something means being able to decide about it. Property has a moral value insofar as it actualizes autonomy. Hence, it presents us with the same difficulty as autonomy: it gives us no criterion about how to decide. In order to know which 'sticks' of the bundle I want to withhold, I have to establish what the most appropriate expression of my autonomy would be. In short, I need

---

5   See Dickenson 2005, 44. For a broader account see Christman 1994, 6-7.

6   See Björkman 2005, 19 for an overview on different conceptions. The main reference in this discussion is Honoré 1961.

7   See, e.g., German Research Foundation 2003, 44, 46. In general, researchers often claim that 'implied consent should suffice' (Furness 2003).

to know the purpose of my donation. 'Property', however, does not give me any purposes; it just offers me a legal tool to realize the purposes I have. This means it does not help me to conceptualize the normative presumptions or expectations I might have in regard to the collection of human tissue.

This can also be explained from a different angle. Property, we can say, is a difficult category. On the one side, there is the free circulation of property in our societies. In the case of human tissue, this concept can become problematic for several reasons: it abuses the altruism and the commitment of donors, and it may lead to pure market mechanisms. On the other side, we can imagine restrictions on property that appear as equally problematic: they might hamper research by granting donors too much influence on decisions that are necessary for research. Both alternatives are disappointing. Neither do we want an unlimited circulation of property in human tissue, nor do we want a limited access to property that might not be useful for anyone. What we do want instead is the appropriate balance between restriction and openness – a balance that would allow for the most beneficial development of research just by keeping ethical standards high. But it seems as if this balance cannot be reached through the regulation of property because each attempt to regulate has to choose one of the two alternatives: it is either too restrictive or too open, too conservative or too liberal. There seems to be no such thing as a fully satisfactory solution for the regulation of property.

A way to reach a solution for this dilemma is to differentiate – not so much between the different elements or 'sticks' of the property bundle but between the different frameworks in which property appears. Different discourses are used that very often are not recognized as such. We make ethical claims that very often are not translatable into a legal form. Or, the other way round: what we might obtain as a legal form of regulation might not be satisfactory from an ethical point of view. This is particularly true for all sorts of open regulations: a liberal approach to property is perfectly sound under a legal point of view, although from an ethical point of view, we might reject at least some of its consequences. Law and ethics do not necessarily harmonize in our case.

The same holds for anthropological considerations concerning the human body. A lot of problems we have with biomedical research cannot be solved on a general, regulatory level. Problems rather concern emotions or the symbolic meaning of body parts. Of course, bioethics tries to consider this emotional dimension. But the problem is that we never can find an appropriate expression for it in legal terms. All researchers can do is to ask donors for informed consent – without taking into account what their subjective attitude toward our practices is. From the perspective of regulation, subjective attitudes are relevant only insofar as they lead to a 'yes' or a 'no'.

One might be tempted to say that there is no problem with subjective attitudes as long as all legal requirements are met. But they become even more important if we look at the political or social dimension of tissue donation. Personal and subjective attitudes matter much more in this regard because they influence the decisions that are made. And again, the criteria do not always harmonize, as the legal form of regulation may not correspond to the political will or the social interests of a community.

This means we have to be aware of the specificity of discourses in bioethical debates. The attempt to establish a coherent form of regulation on the basis of property rights may not cover all our normative presumptions. Normative attitudes cannot always get translated into a legal form, and sometimes they should not even get translated. Property rights have to be accompanied by other provisions, based on political interests or ethical commitments. In this sense, a plurality of criteria should be respected. Bioethics has to be aware of the specificity of its own ethical discourse besides the legal dimension of the problem it tries to solve. The regulation of property rights in human tissue is one important aspect in regard to the autonomy of donors, but it is only *one* aspect of a broader image that also includes the ethical or social aspects of our use of human material. This does not mean that we need a normative standard in biobanking *instead* of a legal regulation; rather we need a normative and a legal standard *altogether*. One does not substitute or exclude the other. In this sense, it already has been said that speaking about duties toward our bodies is not meant to replace the discourse of autonomy or property, but rather to offer criteria we need whenever we have to make an autonomous decision or have to decide about the interest in our property.

But there are still some other questions that arise with the notion of property. The most important question has to do with property in our body. The claim that we own our body is not as evident as it may seem, at least not in its positive sense. Its negative meaning is clear: we own ourselves because no one else owns us. Self-ownership is a concept that allows us to defend ourselves against the claim of others. But what does it positively mean to own oneself? What does 'property' mean here? We can take this question as a starting point that will lead us to the notion of duties towards ourselves.

Owning Oneself – Caring for Oneself

Specifying discourses is all the more important when it comes to the question of self-ownership, or property, in regard to our body. Obviously, the idea of self-ownership is much more complicated than we can treat it here. Like property in general, it corresponds to individual autonomy. Self-ownership means the full right to control one's actions and decisions, and it plays a great role for the libertarian idea of the individual. We cannot explore this dimension here. Ownership of the body has been part of the focus of bioethics for quite a while; the growing interest in the 'Human Body and its Parts' brought up this question almost automatically (see Have et al. 1998). A particular focus has been laid on the interest in owning parts of the female body (see Dickenson 2002). But again, it is not the legal aspect of property we are interested in. The question of entitlements and rights, as much as issues of safety and data protection, do not belong to our focus here. The reason for this has already been named: the legal dimension of ownership basically concerns the negative function of property – property rights as defense against the influence of or the abuse by others. On the contrary, what we are interested in is the positive use of property rights, which can be identified with the ethical meaning of ownership. Questions that arise from the ethical point of view might not be relevant from the perspective of law, and vice versa. The main ethical questions are: In which sense am I allowed to treat my body as property? How far should this go, and is there a limit to my ownership? From a legal point of view, this question is simply not relevant because it belongs to my personal sphere of decision. Within the given legal frame the body *is* my property, and I can decide how much I want to make use of it. On the other side, the positive use of ownership has to do with the purpose of property. We have to ask whether property is a meaningful approach to what I am as an embodied self. In addition, we have to ask what we want to accept as common attitude towards our bodies (for example, in larger projects of biobanking). Only if we note this difference between the positive and the negative use of property rights (which corresponds to the notion of positive and negative autonomy), and subsequently between a legal and an ethical point of view, can the following remarks be fully understood.[8]

To begin with, I will quickly refer to some theories from the philosophical tradition. They are helpful insofar as they shed a critical light on the idea of ownership of our bodies. The idea that our bodies belong to the kinds of things we have rights to cannot be taken for granted, as these theories show. The first thinker we can cite for this is Plato.

In the *Phaedo*, the imprisoned Socrates states that killing oneself would not be legitimate in such a situation. The reason he gives is explained in a rather indirect way. According to a 'doctrine that is taught in secret about this matter', it can be believed 'that the gods are our guardians and that we men are one of the chattels of the gods'. A human being cannot decide about its own death but has to wait 'until god sends some necessity upon him' (Phaedo 62 b-c, in Plato 1914). This makes clear that there cannot be an ownership of oneself. A human being, for Plato, is not its own property but has to accept a higher will deciding how long and under what condition it shall stay alive. Obviously, the question about suicide that is raised here has a much higher weight than the question of tissue donation. And one could say that even if suicide is not allowed, the donation of body parts – as long as they are separable without the destruction of the body – could be. Nothing is said about the latter here. Therefore we do not seem to gain very much from this argument.

---

8   An example for the different views on property rights is expressed in the 'Ethics and Governance Framework' of UK Biobank, when it says: 'Participants will not have property rights in the samples. UK Biobank does not intend to exercise all of these rights; for example, it will not sell samples. Rather, UK Biobank will serve as the steward of the resource, maintaining and building it for the public good in accordance with its purpose' (UK Biobank 2007, 12). Following these ethical rules, the full use of property rights is limited by the purpose of the collection. Stewardship becomes the guiding standard when it is necessary to assess and to control the actions of UK Biobank.

However, it brings up two interesting points for our discussion. The first point is that Plato makes his claim within a discourse of ownership – humans as chattels – although he says that such ownership is not in the reach of human beings. We are forbidden to assume the ownership by ourselves, but it is possible to say that our life (or our body) belongs to someone. Methodologically, this means we do not have to exclude the idea of ownership completely from our discourse. The body might be owned by someone although it is not owned by us.

The other interesting point is that there is a rational argument why we should not kill ourselves. We have to wait for the 'necessity' that God, our owner, sends upon us. This does not mean that we have to wait until something inevitable happens. The idea is rather that all our dispositions in regard to ourselves need a reason to be legitimate. No action I might wish to perform in regard to the physical condition of my life shall be carried out without objective motivation. In our discussion, this means we are not allowed to give our body parts away unless there is a certain 'necessity' to do so, that is, a sufficient reason telling us that it is appropriate and meaningful to donate. In this sense Plato's argument can be easily translated into modern notions, albeit the somehow esoteric way in which it is introduced. Brought down to its rational nucleus, the argument about God as sending 'some necessity' means that we are obliged to make reasonable decisions – decisions that are legitimate according to the objective conditions of our life. A human being cannot despair with his or her life arbitrarily or by some subjective impulse. A human being has no ownership of itself, because ownership includes, among other things, the full entitlement to destroy whenever one thinks fit.

To illustrate this a little bit more, we can have a look at an argument from John Locke's *Second Treatise of Government* (Chapter II), where he says in regard to the state of nature:

> But though this be *a state of liberty,* yet *it is not a state of license:* though man in that state have an uncontrollable liberty to dispose of his person or possessions, yet he has not liberty to destroy himself, or so much as any creature in his possession, but where some nobler use than its bare preservation calls for it. (Locke 1980, 9)

Again, this argument concerns only suicide, and the formulation according to which humans have the 'uncontrollable' freedom to 'dispose' of their person could mean many things in regard to the donation of body parts. But still, and this is most important here, it speaks about a limit in regard to ourselves. Against the possibility of suicide, the preservation of oneself is explicitly stated as a duty: 'Every one, as he is *bound to preserve himself,* and not to quit his station willfully' (Locke 1980, 9). The primary relation to oneself includes the duty to act in the best interest of one's own physical condition. A voluntary decision against what is beneficial for our preservation would not be legitimate. This argument comes very close to what we have seen in Plato. Locke, however, underlines the moral aspects in the relation to our body which in Plato's discourse on God as owner have been referred to only implicitly. A human being has the obligation to care for himself and to act in favor of his best physical condition throughout the time span of his life.[9]

One might be tempted to ask what the justification for this duty is. Why, and by whom, should we feel obliged? Again the argument seems to be purely theological, depending on the conception of man as being created by a higher will. But like before, we can bring it down to a rational claim. Whenever the state of nature is no 'state of licence', we have to find a justification for what we do. We cannot arbitrarily decide for whatever we want. Now, as the will to self-preservation is something to which we are naturally 'bound', we need a reason to overrule it – a reason that tells us that for our life 'some nobler use than its bare preservation' can be identified. Obviously, this argument depends on many points. Most importantly, it has to be taken for granted that there is some sort of 'bond' to our life. But what matters most here is that we cannot feel indifferent toward our physical condition. In one sense or the other we have to think that it is *good* to preserve it or to destroy.

In fact, self-preservation is not carried out merely because some physical urgency might push us to react; it is not a momentary reaction to an impulse like hunger or pain. Preserving oneself does not only mean to eat several times a day and to visit a doctor every once in a while. It rather stems from a sense of care and responsibility for oneself. It means to lead one's life in a way that sustains and protects it in the long run. For a rational being, preservation is a purpose, and he/she lives life in order to fulfill this purpose as much as possible. This includes the striving for emotional satisfaction and a concern for psychological fulfillment in life. Even our happiness might appear as a form of duty to us, for example, in situations where we do not realize what is most beneficial for us (and not for the others). Especially in such cases, we see that the relation to our bodies or to ourselves seems much more of an obligation than an entitlement or right. We have to take care of ourselves, no matter what our external situation might be.

Obviously and undeniably, we *have* the ownership of ourselves, insofar as no other person has the right to decide for us. But besides this ownership and autonomy, we also have the responsibility to find out what is best for our preservation and to act accordingly. A rational being cannot deny this responsibility, unless he feels completely indifferent toward himself. Such responsibility needs a categorical framework of its own in order to be conceptualized, a framework that cannot be found if we rely on property as 'state of license' and free disposition.

---

9   Kant, in the *Metaphysics of Morals*, goes along with this normative aspect. According to him, suicide means to destroy 'the subject of morality', i.e., the ground on which morality exists and has to exist. Therefore it is a moral duty to preserve what is the necessary condition for a moral being. Obviously, this means that self-preservation is not a duty *per se*, but only insofar as it is necessary for the general 'humanity in one's person' (Kant 1996,177). But still, we simply have to exist in order to be human, and even selling parts of our bodies, like teeth or hair, means for Kant to disregard the entity in which our personality subsists. The necessary condition for moral worth also can be ascribed moral worth.

But what kind of duties are these in the case of self-preservation? Can we speak about a duty in the Kantian sense, that is, about an unconditioned obligation? Obviously not. It is not a strict duty to act in the interest of one's self-preservation, but rather a duty to act more in favor of it than not. Self-preservation is a rather open concept that allows for many exceptions or graduations, and it cannot be the ground for an unequivocal obligation. But whenever we ask what is best for our physical condition – and the fact that we ask we have to take for granted – good reasons tell us to care for ourselves. We might not always feel the duty to self-preservation, and we might not always be able to apply it to each given situation; however we can hardly avoid conceding that it would be better to preserve oneself than not, and that we should do what is necessary to act accordingly.

This notion of duty – we might call it a weak notion as opposed to a strong concept in the Kantian sense – does not contradict the idea of ownership as such. Even the commercial use of the body can be judged according to different criteria. We perhaps would accept the sale of body parts in the case of a parent who tries to provide money for the surgery of a child. Depending on the circumstances, this could be acceptable – we certainly cannot say that all types of commercial use have to be banned. The only reason why we think it should remain forbidden (if we think so) is the fact that we do not wish to make a general rule out of it. We presume that we should act more in favor of a restriction than not. All in all, a restrictive use of property corresponds more to our obligations towards the body than a liberal one, although the opposite might sometimes be true. In this sense, duties might coincide with acts of ownership, that is, with acts in which we dispose freely of our body as property. There seems to be no good reason why we should have a stronger notion than this.

Duties and the Phenomenology of the Body

The notion of duties, as we explained in the previous section, shows why we have normative presumptions with regard to our bodies – why we say that it is 'good' to do x or that y 'should not' be done. However, many ethicists might not agree with explaining these presumptions through the framework of 'duty'. This category might sound too strong, too much laden with moral implications. Being responsible, caring for oneself, etc. could appear as better, less demanding categories. In fact, what might seem disturbing in the notion of duties is the idea of an obligation coming from outside. Duties are in some way or another imposed on us. But how can we say that the relation to our own body has such an external dimension? The body is not separated from what I am: it is the medium through which I experience the world, through which I feel and express myself to others. How can this unity of me and my body be broken by an obligation that makes the body an object of my responsibility and care? How can I be identical with my body, for example, experience it from inside, and at the same time feel a duty towards my body imposed on me?

To put it formally, we have to ask about the link between the internal and the external relation to our body. As we will see, this question has two sides. The first point we have just raised concerns the problem of how there can be an external relation to what I intrinsically am. The second point we are going to address concerns the problem of how there can be an internal relation to something that has been externalized, that is, how we can relate to body parts that have been separated from the body. But let us begin with the first point.

At a first glance, we can find an easy answer to our question. The body can appear as an object of care, as something I have duties toward, because it can be seen as a thing in the world like any other thing. Just like my car or my dog, I see it; I have it in front of me. And just like I see that my car might need a wash, I see that my body might need some care. In addition, as an object in the world, it is also seen by others. This allows me to see it from an angle different from mine, to see it through the eyes of others, as much as this is possible. When we ask ourselves: 'How do I look?', we refer to our look and the look of others on us. In this sense, there is nothing surprising about the experience of one's body as something that is seen from an external point of view.

However, this does not explain why we feel an obligation to care for it. If the body were only a thing in the world, something we have to trim in order to make it look good in the eyes of others, we would have no duty toward it – or at least the duty would be nothing more than a function of social expectations and norms. But the duty to care is something different from this; it is an attitude I have towards my own body, independently of others. What we are looking for is a feeling of responsibility that is not reducible to social norms, like the duty of self-preservation that does not come from outside, but from our innermost experience. In this sense, the duty towards the body has a somewhat intermediate position. It is neither purely internal – because we do not only want to preserve ourselves but feel an obligation to do so – nor is it purely external – as a rule imposed by society. Rather it combines both internal and external points of view.

But still it seems unclear how such an attitude exists. How can we describe this mixed experience phenomenologically? Let us begin with our inclinations, the basic interests and feelings we have. We know what our body needs and usually we want to satisfy it. But what we feel and think is not only happening in a purely mental sphere. Hunger is a feeling and a thought but it is also something that exists within my body, which transforms my body from inside. We could even say that hunger *is* the body because a body that needs to eat is different from one that has been fed. What we feel and think about ourselves is at the same time what we are, what constitutes our physical being. The pain I feel determines my thoughts and at the same time it is 'there', as part of what my body is. In this sense, the body is my intentionality experienced in a bodily form. We can say that the body reflects my intentionality back onto me. We see such an experience, for example, when we forget to eat: the body reminds us of its need for food, but not as something that is purely physical and external, but as something that I want. *I* had forgotten that I wanted to eat. The external and the internal dimension are intermingled so that it is impossible to distinguish what is just the intentionality of my feelings and thoughts and what is given as a signal from the body. Feelings are reflected back as signals onto me, and signals are understood as transmitting what I feel.[10]

In this sense I care about my body, but I also have to care. My interest lives throughout my body, and it urges me to respond to it. Certainly I only respond to myself, but I am also bound to respond to my own interests as something that obliges me to be heard and taken care of. My body reminds me when I forget to give to it what it needs, and in this moment it appears as laying a responsibility on me. There are certainly many ways in which we make this mixed experience of the body, and there are extremes that are also possible. There is a purely internal and a purely external relationship to our body. But between these extremes, there is a continuum in which we feel the duty towards our body. The obligation might be stronger or weaker, but in any case something reflects my own intentionality back onto me and urges me to respond. This is the moment when my interest is transformed into a duty and a sense of obligation is being constituted.

One might be tempted to ask why this experience should have a normative dimension at all. That we are *obliged* to eat, and do not only *want* to eat, might not necessarily imply any ethical presumptions. It simply might be just a physical constraint. So again, why should our experience of the body contain any dimension of duty? The answer to this is simply because there is no necessity in our reaction. Even if we have to eat for physical reasons, we need to *decide* in order to eat. Physical necessities are not what bring us to act, as urgent as they might be. Even if something is simply necessary, like the amputation of a leg, what urges us to go to the hospital is our own will to take care of it. An amputation is not a reaction, like scratching one's head, but the result of a deliberate decision. The external necessity needs to be combined with an internal motivation. We also see this in the case of those who embark on a starvation diet. Here, people decide explicitly against their physical needs.

But in order to decide for something or another we need a reason telling us that it is good to do x. We need to give at least some kind of justification. And by doing so, normative questions are automatically at stake. Not only might we ask whether it is good to do x. We might also ask: do we want to do this repeatedly, does it correspond to what we ultimately want, will it be beneficial, etc.? The fact that we most often do not have to ask such questions when we sit down to eat or when we are planning a surgery does not mean that they could not arise. Even if our decisions very often are made by routine, there are presumptions underlying them.

In this sense, the very relationship to our body is a source of normativity. In responding to what the body reminds us to do, we take responsibility for it. Our body obliges us to care, and it urges us to decide, to think what would be the best way to care. Normativity enters in these two ways – in the obligation to respond

---

10   In his later thought, M. Merleau-Ponty also has underlined such an entanglement between the inside and outside experience of the body (Merleau-Ponty 1968).

and in the task to decide how to respond. Being responsible means, in our case, being obliged to react and being obliged to find a justified reason for what one does. The experience of the body is not that simple, unified experience of feeling and self-interest that it might seem. It is broken or, as we might say, reflective. There is an ethical attitude arising right out of the experience of my embodied self.

To conclude, let us briefly touch the other direction we mentioned above – the question why tissue, once it is separated from the body, should matter at all. Why do we have an internal relationship to something that has been externalized once and for all and that will never be reintegrated into the body? Why is there any interest in it beyond issues like biosafety and data protection?

Such questions are often raised in regard to tissue. And, in fact, the very size of such body parts or body liquids is such that they simply do not matter at all. 'It is just a tiny little piece like this' is often said, and there is no way to say that such a reaction is wrong. Do we concern ourselves about other body parts we constantly lose (hair, skin, urine, etc.)? The body is a dynamic unity; it constantly renews itself and separates what is no longer useful for it. But on the other side, how can we say that these parts are insignificant to us? Imagine someone who collects our hair, the cells we leave behind in the bathroom, on our toothbrush, towel, etc. Would we be indifferent toward this? Maybe yes, but maybe not, depending on the intentions of those who collect our cells and body parts. In any case it is not possible to decide *generally* whether the collection of such parts is insignificant or not – what is done to our parts *can* be seen as something that is done to us. There is no formal rule telling us when we should have no more interest in our body parts. The body, as mentioned before, is a dynamic unity. Its parts are not only what actually is connected to it. A part of my body is also what has been separated from it. And again, there is no general rule telling us where we should draw the line between those things that still belong to our personal sphere and those which are definitely outside of it.

In this sense, there is no clear answer as to why tissue stored in a biobank should matter to me or not. We simply have to leave this question open. All we can say is that there is no way to decide *a priori* that it should not matter any more. We have no way to simply overrule the mixed experience of body that brings inside and outside, intentionality and corporality, together. Even if something is separated from us, we still might feel the duty to care about it. The experience of our body is such that it allows for the intermingling of these dimensions. We cannot free ourselves from presumptions we have regarding our bodies. In this sense, dealing with the body requires us to develop an ethical standard in order to make explicit what we think or feel about it. As we have seen, there are many candidates for such a standard, most prominently 'altruism' and 'property'. 'Duty' however seems to be the most appropriate tool in order to state why we should care about our bodies and in order to conceptualize the sense of responsibility we so much need in the rapidly growing field of new technologies.[11]

---

11   Special thanks go to Lisa Dolling for her many helpful comments.

Bibliography

Batson, C.D. (1998), 'Is there genuine altruism?', in Nordgren, A. and Westrin, C.G. (eds), *Altruism, Society, Health Care* (Uppsala: Uppsala University), 21–36.

Björkman, B. (2005), *Ethical Aspects of Owning Human Biological Material. Licentiate Thesis in Philosophy* (Stockholm).

Bovenberg, J. (2005), 'Whose tissue is it anyway?', *Nature Biotechnology* 23, 929–33.

Christman, J. (1994), *The Myth of Property. Toward an Egalitarian Theory of Ownership* (Oxford: Oxford University Press).

Dickenson, D. (2002), 'Who owns embryonic and fetal tissue?' in Dickenson, D. (ed.), *Ethical Issues in Maternal-Fetal Medicine* (Cambridge: Cambridge University Press), 233–46.

—— (2004), 'Consent, commodification and benefit-sharing in genetic research', *Developing World Bioethics* 4, 109–124.

—— (2005), 'Human Tissue and Global Ethics', *Genomics, Society and Policy* 1, 41–53.

Furness, P. (2003), 'Consent to using human tissue. Implied consent should be enough', *BMJ* 327, 759–60, http://www.bmj.com/cgi/content/full/327/7418/759 (accessed 27 May 2009).

German Research Foundation (2003), *Predictive genetic diagnosis. Scientific background, practical and social implementation*http://www.dfg.de/aktuelles_presse/reden_stellungnahmen/2003/redstell/praed_genetische_diagnostik. html [original title: Deutsche Forschungsgemeinschaft, *Prädikative genetische Diagnose. Wissenschaftliche Grundlagen, praktische Umsetzung und soziale Implementierung*], accessed 27 May 2009.

Have, H.T. et al. (1998), *Ownership of the Human Body. Philosophical Considerations on the Use of the Human Body and its Parts in Healthcare* (Dordrecht/Boston/London: Kluwer).

Honoré, A.M. (1961), 'Ownership', in Guest, A.A. (ed.), *Oxford Essays in Jurisprudence* (Oxford: Oxford University Press).

Jack, A.L. and Womack, Ch. (2003), 'Why surgical patients do not donate tissue for commercial research: review of records', *BMJ* 327, 262.

Kant, I. (1996), *The Metaphysics of Morals*, translated and edited by M. Gregor (Cambridge: Cambridge University Press).

Locke, J. (1980), *Second Treatise on Government*, edited, with an Introduction, by C.B. Macpherson (Indianapolis: Hackett).

Merleau-Ponty, M. (1968), *The Visible and the Invisible*, followed by *Working Notes*, tr. A. Lingis (Evanston: Northwestern University Press) (Original: *Le visible et l'invisible, suivie de notes de travail*, C. Lefort [ed.]. Paris: Gallimard 1964).

Plato (1914), *Volume I. Euthyphro. Apology. Crito. Phaedo. Phaedrus.* Translated by H.N. Fowler. Loeb Classical Library (Cambridge: Harvard University Press).

Steinmann, M. (2008), 'Rechte oder Pflichten gegenüber dem menschlichen Körper? Normative Fragen im Umgang mit Biobanken', *Zeitschrift für medizinische Ethik* 54 (1), 61–72.

UK Biobank (2007), *UK Biobank Ethics and Governance Framework.* Version 3.0, http://www.ukbiobank.ac.uk/docs/EGF20082.pdf (accessed 27 May 2009).

Weir, F.R. and Olick, R.S. (2004), *The Stored Tissue Issue. Biomedical Research, Ethics, and Law in the Era of Genomic Medicine* (Oxford: Oxford University Press).

PART III
Towards a Richer Understanding of Property in Ethics and Law

Chapter 6

Property in Human Tissue: Triangulating the Issue

Roger Brownsword

Introduction

Ethicists and lawyers are unable to agree about a very basic question, namely: should regulators recognize that a person can have proprietary rights in relation to his or her own body, or in relation to body parts that have been removed (or, in some future world, in relation to personalized body parts that have not yet been fitted)? It is not so much that ethicists take one view and lawyers another; it is that ethicists dispute the question with fellow ethicists and lawyers with fellow lawyers.[1]

To be sure, some argumentation is wide of any possible mark. For example, as Harris (1996) highlights, it is clearly a non-sequitur to hold that, because A has a claim right to his bodily integrity, it follows that A has a *property* right in relation to his removed body parts. Even if B does wrong by lopping off A's arm (against A's will), it does not entail that A has proprietary rights over the removed arm. Equally, it is a poor and muddling argument (against property) to hold that, where A donates body parts to B, A has no property rights. Clearly, in a case of donation, A has no property rights *ex post* (otherwise this would not be a case of donation), but this says nothing about whether A has property rights in removed body parts *prior* to donation.[2] Indeed, one might wonder whether it is possible to 'donate' x without having *ex ante* property rights in relation to x. Again, it will not do to argue (against property) that, if we cannot have property in our own full bodies (because there is then no distance between me and my property), we cannot have property in our removed body parts; nor will it do to argue that, if we have no right to commercialize our body parts (which some advocates of property rights might concede), we can have no kind of property entitlements whatsoever (that is, claiming implicitly that property is an all-or-nothing matter).

---

1   See, e.g., Munzer 1990, esp. 37–58; and the most famous of legal cases, *Moore v. Regents of the University of California* (1988) 249 Cal. Rptr., 494; (1990) 271 Cal. Rptr., 146, (1990) 793 P2d, 479; cert. denied (1991) 111 S.Ct., 1388.

2   Compare the (unpersuasive) reasoning in *Greenberg v. Miami Children's Hospital Research Institute, Inc,* 2002 WL 1483266 (N.D. Ill); 264 F. Supp 2nd, 1064 (S.D. Fla. 2003) (02-22244-CIV-MORENO (Miami)).

Yet, if we eliminate the spurious and the specious arguments, why should this still be such a contested question? After all, when the question is modified to become whether a person can have proprietary rights over human tissue taken from another person, there is much less disagreement; apparently, it is widely accepted that such a person can have proprietary rights. Yet, if someone other than I can have proprietary rights over tissue of which I am the source – I am tempted to say, 'over tissue that is *mine*' – then is it not exceedingly odd that I cannot have proprietary rights over that tissue – again, I am tempted to say, 'over *my own* tissue'? How can it be rational for regulators to permit me to have property rights over your tissue and for you to have property rights over my tissue while not recognizing either of us as proprietors of our own tissue?

This chapter will suggest that our responses to the property question are driven by the particular ethical position that we presuppose. The first part will sketch what seem to be the three leading ethical constituencies (namely, utilitarian, rights-led and duty-driven dignitarian), each of these constituencies taking up one point of what I call the 'bioethical triangle'. The second part of the chapter will sketch how each of these constituencies arrives at very different views about the property question that we are considering. That question, it should be emphasized, is not whether the institution of private property can be justified, but whether, assuming such an institution, its rules should recognize that a person can have proprietary rights in relation to his or her own body or removed body parts. The third part will consider what each of the three ethical constituencies might say about proprietary rights over spare body parts. One thing that they surely cannot say is that the disconnected body parts have been 'abandoned' (thereby surrendering whatever proprietary claims might otherwise have been made); for these are body parts that are waiting to be connected.

The ambitions of the chapter are modest. The point is that, once we understand how the debate about property and bodies is triangulated, we can get fairly quickly to the crux of the protagonists' differences; but, alas, this is not to say that we can get so quickly to an incontrovertible answer to the question (compare Beyleveld and Brownsword 2000).

The Bioethical Triangle

Implicit within modern bioethical debates and within leading bioethical instruments, such as the UNESCO Universal Declaration on Bioethics and Human Rights,[3] we can detect three competing ethics –the three ethical views that make up the bioethical triangle. These are: the utilitarian view, advocating the pursuit of human welfare (human health, wealth, and happiness); the human rights view; and the view of a constituency that was previously termed 'the dignitarian alliance'

---

3   The Declaration was agreed by the General Conference in Paris on October 19, 2005.

(Brownsword 2003). Each of these constituencies has its own distinctive ethical perspective. Occasionally, the perspectives converge to invite regulators to act on a consensus (as is the case at present with human reproductive cloning); sometimes, a synthesis of utilitarian and human rights thinking will emerge (Brownsword 2004). However, all too often, these perspectives generate competing and conflicting views – as is the case, for instance, with therapeutic cloning and human embryonic stem cell research, and, more to the present point, as is the case with the question of property and bodies (or body parts).

Utilitarians count utility (encompassing individual pleasure and preference satisfaction, and the like, together with convenience and economy) the sum of utilities being aggregated in the credit column. They count disutility (encompassing individual pain, suffering, distress and the frustration of preferences and the like, together with cost, inconvenience and the general expenditure of resources) as totals in the debit column. For utilitarians, the maximization of utility and the minimization of disutility is all that counts; to do the right thing is to identify and adopt whichever option seems most likely to maximize utility or minimize disutility. Broadly speaking, Article 4 of the UNESCO Declaration – providing that '[i]n applying and advancing scientific knowledge, medical practice and associated technologies, direct and indirect benefits to patients, research participants and other affected individuals should be maximized and any possible harm to such individuals should be minimized' – speaks this kind of language.

Although utilitarians count the benefits/harms in relation to all those who are affected by an action, they restrict the calculation to those who are judged capable of experiencing pain or pleasure, having preferences and so on. Insofar as a human embryo is a pre-sentient life form, utilitarianism is not directly engaged: pre-sentient life fails to show interests in the relevant sense, and the logic of utilitarian thinking is that the same applies to post-sentient humans. As Lord Mustill famously remarked in the *Bland* case,[4] to talk about the 'best interests' of a human who is in a persistent or permanent vegetative state is to ignore the 'distressing truth' that they no longer have any interests in a material sense.[5] On the other hand, utilitarianism is directly engaged by sentient non-human life. Accordingly, in the *Harvard Onco-Mouse* case,[6] the utilitarian-minded examiners thought it perfectly sensible to weigh in the moral balance (that they took to be required by Article 53(a) of the European Patent Convention) the distress occasioned to a genetically engineered mouse.

For human rights theorists, the key is not positive or negative consequences so much as respect for individual human rights. Much of the history of bioethics hinges on ethical opposition to the idea that the interests of individuals may be legitimately sacrificed for the greater good. While Article 3(2) of the UNESCO Declaration emphatically confirms this opposition, insisting that '[t]he interests

---

4   *Airedale NHS Trust v. Bland* [1993] 1 All ER, 821.

5   Ibid., 894.

6   OJ EPO 10/1992, 590.

and welfare of the individual should have priority over the sole interest of science or society', which is to say that humans have rights and that they must be taken seriously, it remains moot who precisely qualifies for such protection. Like the utilitarians, human rights theorists do not usually recognize pre-sentient life as a bearer of rights.[7] Indeed, in the human rights tradition, an even more restrictive view is taken – even sentience does not suffice. Thus, in two recent decisions at Strasbourg, the European Court of Human Rights has declined to affirm that either a human embryo or a six month fetus is protected by the Convention right to life.[8] If the embryo has no *direct* protective entitlement, the only caveats that will be imposed by this ethical approach relate to the need for free and informed consent by relevant rights-holders, such as women who donate eggs or couples who donate embryos, or they reflect any *indirect* or precautionary considerations.

It should be said, of course, that the caveats relating to free and informed consent are by no means trivial, unproblematic or easily satisfied. Indeed, under pressure from proponents of human rights, these requirements have tended to become ever more demanding (particularly so in relation to the information to be supplied). For example, in Canada, there has been a lively debate concerning the adequacy of consent protocols where fresh embryos are sourced for stem cell research from IVF programs. At issue is the question of whether we can be satisfied that the donor's consent is adequate when there is inevitably an element of situational and relational pressure in play and when a donor might not fully comprehend the sacrifice being made in giving up an embryo that might be utilized for her own reproductive purposes (see Nisker and White 2005). Depending upon the stringency of our conception of free and informed consent, we will be more or less readily satisfied as to such matters. In principle, though, human rights theorists are willing to be satisfied that all is well, that the consent clearance is adequate and that embryonic stem cell research is ethically clean.

It should also be emphasized that the indirect or precautionary arguments carry some weight. Given that the human rights ethic is fundamentally committed to human freedom, the claim that certain acts should not be permitted lest they *indirectly* impact negatively on rights-holders, or that precaution should be exercised before excluding those life forms that might (for all we know) have the required characteristics, will not be accepted just like that. Nevertheless, any reflective proponent of the human rights ethic will recognize that claims of this kind do need to be taken seriously (Beyleveld and Brownsword 2006).

---

7 Compare, the position presupposed by Carl Cohen (Cohen and Regan 2001), 35: 'To be a moral agent is to be able to grasp the generality of moral restrictions on our will. Humans understand that some acts may be in our interest and yet must not be willed because they are simply wrong. This capacity for moral judgment does not arise in the animal world; rats can neither exercise nor respond to moral claims'.

8 *Vo v. France* (2005) 40 EHRR, 12 (a 6 month fetus); *Evans v. UK* [2006] ECHR 200 (7 March, 2006) (a human embryo).

By now, we are well versed in the tension between utilitarian promotion of the general good (where little or no attention is paid to the *distribution* of utility or disutility) and the constraints imposed if individual rights are to be respected.[9] Where human rights have made their mark, it is axiomatic, as was just said, that best practice demands careful attention to free and informed consent, that the capacity for autonomous decision-making should be respected, that privacy and confidentiality should be protected, and so on. However, if bioethics was once a two-way contest between utilitarians and human rights theorists, this is no longer the case.

Where a technology impacts on the human body, as is particularly the case with the human genetics applications of biotechnology, this is widely seen as raising concerns about human dignity. Even in the case of information and communication technology which largely raises questions within and between utilitarian and human rights thinking (issues of (Internet) content regulation apart), we find concerns about human dignity being expressed once a bio-application is proposed. Witness, for example, the discussion by the European Group on Ethics in Science and New Technologies with regard to ICT implants in the human body.[10] At all events, what we now have is a third ethical constituency, an alliance of dignitarian views, making up the plurality (Brownsword 2005a).

The dignitarian perspective condemns any practice, process or product – human reproductive cloning, therapeutic cloning and stem cell research using human embryos being prime examples (see, for example, Makdisi 2003) which it judges to compromise human dignity. Such condemnation (by reference to human dignity) operates as a 'conversation stopper' (Birnbacher 1998);[11] but the dignitarians are not troubled; to say that something violates human dignity is the ultimate condemnation. The emergence of the new dignitarian view creates a genuinely triangular contest, the dignitarians disagreeing as much with the utilitarians as they do with the human rights constituency – with the former because they do not think that consequences, even entirely 'beneficial' consequences (that is, 'beneficial' relative to a utilitarian standard), are determinative and with the latter because they do not think that informed consent cures the compromising of human dignity.

---

9 For some vivid examples of researchers putting their projects before their research participants, see Plomer 2005, Ch. 2 (US human radiation experiments), Ch. 3 (UK Porton Down experiments) and Ch. 6 (research trials in developing countries).

10 Opinion No 20 of the European Group on Ethics in Science and New Technologies to the European Commission, *Ethical Aspects of ICT Implants in the Human Body* (adopted 16.03.2005).

11 Compare Nuffield Council on Bioethics 1999, 96 (those who contend that genetic modification is intrinsically wrong or unnatural present views that 'have something of an "unarguable" quality, inasmuch as no amount of information, explanation or rationalisation would move a person with such views from their position').

Insofar as the dignitarian view expresses a religious or a Kantian approach, the duty to respect human dignity (or not to compromise human dignity) will be treated as cosmopolitan. Because the sharp end of dignitarian ethics is to identify which practices should be prohibited, it invites being regarded as imperialistic (Brownsword 2006). Insofar as it is communitarian, the dignitarian view might be of more limited range – for example, insisting on embryo protection at home but without arguing that all nations should do the same thing. Among its arguable cosmopolitan principles, dignitarianism decrees that human life should be protected and respected (from the point of conception onwards), that life should be recognized as having no price (hence, it should not be commercialized) and that life should not be instrumentalized (hence, it should not be commodified) (Caulfield and Brownsword 2006).

Finally, it should be understood that, while the third point of the bioethical triangle brings together a range of duty-driven approaches, each taking it as axiomatic that human dignity must not be compromised, the dignitarian alliance does not have a monopoly on the idea that human dignity should be respected. For, human rights thinking also subscribes (albeit in a rights-led way) to the fundamental importance of human dignity (Brownsword 2003, 2005b).

Property Entitlements and Bodies

What do each of the three ethical constituencies hold in relation to the question of property entitlements over our own bodies or our removed body parts? It is worth repeating that we are assuming that no one is arguing against the very idea of private property. The idea that an individual may hold property rights over, for example, their house or their clothes, is not at issue. The only issue is whether such property entitlements apply also to bodies and body parts. If we also make the standard assumption that the generic property right comprises a bundle of entitlements, then, for present purposes, the two critical claims concern: (1) the right to control access to and use of a particular body or body part; and (2) the right to exploit commercially a particular body or body part. Finally, to get the matter into focus, the burning question is whether an individual should have property claims of this kind in relation to his or her own body or removed body parts. What, then, does each of the ethical constituencies hold about this question?

First, for the utilitarian, there is no reason *a priori* to rule in or to rule out such property entitlements. If property rights are to be recognized, it will only be because, in the particular context, this makes good utilitarian sense. Generally, utilitarians will want to avoid two kinds of tragedy. One is the tragedy of the commons, where private property rights are insufficiently recognized as a result of which a particular resource is over-exploited and damaged. The other is the tragedy of the anti-commons, where too many private property rights are recognized; as a result of this a particular resource is under-exploited, again with a loss to the community. Hence, for utilitarians, the property puzzle is largely a matter of instating the profile of entitlements that promises to maximize the benefit obtained from the resource. In short, a (private) property-free zone will rarely be right, but neither will a zone that is dense with (private) property entitlements.

Characteristically, utilitarians will have no objection to individuals exploiting the commercial value that they have in their bodies. Utilitarians will not resolutely oppose prostitution or the sex trade; moreover, provided that there could be adequate assurances about safety and provenance, a market in human organs might be defensible according to utilitarian criteria. However, where it is proposed that the individual sources of human tissue for research should have proprietary rights over their removed body parts, that is another matter. What utilitarians tend to sense here is a tragedy of the anti-commons as too many proprietary stakeholders interfere with the progression of the research and delay the delivery of its benefits. On the other hand, of course, if prospective participants are reluctant to step forward to donate their body parts for research, then this might occasion rethinking; in some contexts, utilitarians might be persuaded that the recognition of property entitlements is the price that must be paid to procure cooperation.

In the light of these remarks, it will be apparent that utilitarians do not have a simple red light or green light approach to property: any particular property proposal will need to be audited for its projected utility and disutility. It also follows that, where the projections are unclear, there might even be disagreement within the utilitarian ranks (depending upon which projections are thought to be most reliable).

For both rights theorists and dignitarians alike, the consequentialist approach of the utilitarians is to be rejected. Property in our own bodies and body parts is either a matter of entitlement or not, and, whatever the position, it is categorically so. For the dignitarians, the position is pretty straightforward. At any rate, it is pretty straightforward in relation to any claimed right to exploit the commercial value of our bodies or body parts: quite simply, to recognize such a right would be to compromise our dignity as humans. In line with this view, Article 21 of the Convention on Human Rights and Biomedicine provides that: 'The human body and its parts shall not, as such, give rise to financial gain'. The partner claim, to have control over our own bodies and body parts, is less clear-cut. However, dignitarians will tend to see this kind of claim as involving the commodification of the human body, and, for this reason, they will condemn it again as compromising human dignity (Beyleveld and Brownsword 1998).

Although commercialization and commodification are closely related to one another, they should not be treated as identical; the difference between the two concepts bears a brief word of explanation. Where an object or resource is exploited for its commercial value, it is necessarily commodified; it is treated as a mere thing. Hence, commercialization presupposes commodification. However, this does not hold in reverse; for, we might commodify a resource without commercializing it. For example, if we have a market for the sale of human babies, babies are both commercialized and commodified. But, if we permit social sex selection of babies, it is arguable that babies are commodified (treated as mere products, like consumables coming off a production line) but they are not yet commercialized

(Brownsword 2005c). In the same way, dignitarians might object that, even if human body parts are not commercialized, to recognize the individual's right to control access to such parts as resources for research involves an element of commodification, and, hence, such property rights should be rejected.

This leaves the human rights constituency, the constituency from which there is most pressure for recognition of individual property rights in human bodies and body parts. Why should rights theorists so contend?

In relation to the commercialization of the human body or body parts, rights theorists see this as a matter of personal choice and lifestyle. Some rights theorists might put certain choices off limits (possibly selling oneself into slavery), but this goes against the grain of respect for individual autonomy. What rights theorists are most concerned about is that individuals who make risky choices should do so on the basis of a free and fully informed consent. If the consent is not in place or if we cannot confidently monitor the adequacy of consent, rights theorists might retreat to a more precautionary position. We see this move being made all the time, for example, in response to proposals put forward in test cases for the relaxation of prohibitions on physician-assisted suicide.[12]

The case of a market for human organs is an interesting one. In principle, a rights theorist will argue for an individual's freedom to sell, for example, a kidney or a cornea. However, where sellers typically come from economically disadvantaged circumstances and buyers come from economically advantaged circumstances, there are concerns about background duress and foreground inducement (Beyleveld and Brownsword 2007, Ch 5). If the baseline for fair dealing is given by a standard of global equity, it is quite likely that such transactions will fail to pass muster. The sellers might be under no foreground pressure, but their indigent circumstances involve a violation of basic rights standards and create an unacceptable situational pressure. It is less clear that inducements invalidate consent; even so, if the purchaser tempts the seller with an offer of big money, it is possible that the purchaser's intention is to divert the seller from addressing the risks.

As for property in removed body parts, rights theorists will think that sources are being exploited where researchers and others acquire property rights over the tissue downstream. Why should the sources, why should the many John Moores, not also share in the bounty? If the response takes a utilitarian shape, rights theorists will know that some irregularity is afoot.

It is clear, however, that for many rights-minded agents, the issue is not about sharing in commercial exploitation of the resource but about controlling its use.

---

12   In Europe, see *Regina on the Application of Mrs Dianne Pretty v DPP and Secretary of State for the Home Department* [2001] UKHL, 61; *Case of Pretty v. The United Kingdom* (2002) ECHR 2346/02, April 29; [2002] 35 Eur. H.R. Rep. 1. In North America, see *Washington v. Glucksberg* 117 S.Ct. 2258 (1997); 138 L Ed 2d 772, and *Re Rodriguez and Attorney-General of British Columbia* (1993) 107 DLR 4th 342.

We see this very clearly in the *Greenberg* case,[13] and it is fundamental also in the more recent *Catalona* case,[14] where the sources want the tissue to stay with a particular researcher rather than the institution at which the researcher is (or was) employed.

Quite how rights theorists might vindicate property rights for tissue sources is a moot point. If rights theorists major on the right to control, then one argument relies on the immanent logic of the secondary purpose provisions in Article 22 of the Convention on Human Rights and Biomedicine. According to Article 22: 'When in the course of an intervention any part of a human body is removed, it may be stored and used for a purpose other than that for which it was removed, only if this is done in conformity with appropriate information and consent procedures'. The obvious question is why the donor's consent is needed in such circumstances. And the obvious answer is that the donor retains a proprietary right to control the use of the tissue.

Another argument is that the essential idea of a property right is 'preclusionary'. What this picks up on is the idea that a property entitlement operates in a preclusionary way (in the sense of a right to control access to or use of some resource simply by asserting one's proprietorial stake and without further reason). If this is so, then the application of property rights to agents' body parts seems eminently appropriate (Beyleveld and Brownsword 2001, Chapter 8). We need not push this matter any further. The purpose here is not to rehearse arguments in support of the rights view so much as to indicate where it fits in the triangulation of property claims.

Property and Spare Body Parts

Imagine a future world in which each person's cord blood is stored at birth and then, using stem cell technology, a set of spare personalized body parts is cultivated and stored for each person. Arguably, the custodian of the facility at which these spare body parts are stored will have proprietary rights over them. However, the essence of the arrangement is that these are body parts for a particular person. It seems equally plausible, therefore, to view such dedicated body parts as already the property of that person. That person already seems to be in a position to complain if the body parts are allocated to some other person without the intended recipient's consent. But what would each of our three ethical constituencies say about this idea?

Utilitarians, as always, would want to weigh the options. First, of course, utilitarians would want to be satisfied that the consequences of holding spare parts are conducive to the welfare of the majority. That utilitarians would be so satisfied

---

13   Note 2 above.
14   *Washington University v. Catalona* 2006 US Dist LEXIS 22969 (N.D Mo. 2006).

is not a foregone conclusion. As Leon Kass (2002, 261), who has dignitarian reasons for rejecting such an option, has remarked:

> Even the most cursory examination of these matters suggests that the cumulative results of aggregated decisions for longer and more vigorous life could be highly disruptive and undesirable, even to the point that many individuals would be *worse off* through most of their lives, and enough to offset the benefits of better health afforded them near the end of life. Indeed, several people have predicted that retardation of aging will present a classic instance of the "Tragedy of the Commons", in which genuine and sought-for gains to individuals are nullified, or worse, by the social consequences of granting them to everyone.

If, however, utilitarians read the runes in a more positive way, then it becomes a matter of whether the appropriate covering framework is one in which individuals have proprietary rights over their own spare parts. On the face of it, this seems like a serious candidate, and, even if, in some contexts, it is not judged to be the optimal arrangement, utilitarians will certainly have it on their short-list.

For dignitarians, the very idea of a spare parts bank is almost certainly unacceptable. Once we hold spare body parts, it sounds as though we are commodifying humans; it sounds as though there is little difference between the way that we view our own bodies and body parts and the way that we view, for example, our motor cars and car parts. Essentially, in both cases, when the parts wear out, whether it is a human heart or a car battery, they need to be replaced. Accordingly, if we have a dignitarian concern to hang on to what is distinctively 'human' in our social and moral lives, we must resist any such banking proposal.

What about rights theorists? In this scenario, it is the right to control that seems to be fundamental. What the rights theorists will contend is that, applying preclusionary thinking, this is precisely the kind of case where the rights holder asserts pre-emption over the body part by simply asserting that 'It is mine'. Moreover, two arguments that might trouble the rights theorists in other contexts do not apply here. One is the argument that the right to personal (bodily) integrity does not equate to a proprietary right, and the other is the argument about abandonment. With regard to the former argument, where body parts are embedded within the person, the physical integrity right can be presented as doing the protective work. Where this is the case, no one can take possession of, for example, my heart or my kidney without violating my physical rights. However, where the body parts are detached from the body, they might be taken without any violation of a person's physical integrity. Hence, the right to physical integrity cannot do the protective work and we need a *proprietary* right for that purpose. As for the latter argument, concerning abandonment, that becomes an issue only where the body part has been discarded. However, as mentioned already, such an objection does not hold where the body part is destined for connection: in such a case, the body parts are spare (but committed to my future needs) rather than surplus to my future requirements.

All in all, even though the spare body parts scenario is futuristic, it looks like an attractive context for the rights theorists to push their claims.

Conclusion

This short chapter can be closed with an equally short conclusion. Ethicists and lawyers, we can be sure, will continue to debate the question of whether property rights should be recognized in relation to bodies and body parts. If we relate the positions taken up by disputants to the bioethical triangle that has been sketched in this chapter, we can at least see where the protagonists are coming from. Even if we can see where the disputants are coming from, it does not follow that we can see where the debate is going, nor (without a good deal more) where it ought to be going.

Bibliography

Beyleveld, D. and Brownsword, R. (1998), 'Articles 21 and 22 of the convention on human rights and biomedicine: Property and consent, commerce and dignity', in P. Kemp (ed.), *Research Projects on Basic Ethical Principles in Bioethics and Biolaw* (papers from the Utrecht meeting, November 1997) (Copenhagen: Centre for Ethics and Law), 33–67.

—— (2000), 'My body, my body parts, my property?', *Health Care Analysis* 8, 87–99.

—— (2001), *Human Dignity in Bioethics and Biolaw* (Oxford: Oxford University Press).

—— (2006), 'Principle, proceduralism and precaution in a community of rights', *Ratio Juris* 19, 141–68.

—— (2007), *Consent in the Law* (Oxford: Hart).

Birnbacher, D. (1998), 'Do modern reproductive technologies violate human dignity?' in E. Hildt and D. Mieth (eds), *In Vitro Fertilisation in the 1990s* (Aldershot: Ashgate) 325–33.

Brownsword, R. (2003), 'Bioethics today, bioethics tomorrow: Stem cell research and the "Dignitarian Alliance"', *Notre Dame Journal of Law, Ethics and Public Policy* 17, 15–51.

—— (2004), 'Regulating human genetics: new dilemmas for a new millennium', *Medical Law Review* 12, 14–39.

—— (2005a), 'Biotechnology and rights: Where are we coming from and where are we going?' in M. Klang and A. Murray (eds), *Human Rights in the Digital Age* (London: Cavendish Glasshouse) 219–34.

—— (2005b), 'Human rights – what hope? human dignity – what scope?' in J. Gunning and S. Holm (eds), *Ethics, Law and Society: Volume 1* (Aldershot: Ashgate) 189–209.

—— (2005c), 'Happy families, consenting couples, and children with dignity: Sex selection and saviour siblings', *Child and Family Law Quarterly* 17, 435–73.

—— (2006), 'Cloning, zoning, and the harm principle' in S. McLean (ed.), *First, Do No Harm* (Festschrift for Ken Mason) (Aldershot: Ashgate) 527–42.

Caulfield, T. and Brownsword, R. (2006), 'Human dignity: A guide to policy making in the biotechnology era', *Nature Reviews Genetics* 7, 72–6.

Cohen, C. and Regan, T. (2001), *The Animal Rights Debate* (Lanham: Rowman and Littlefield).

Harris, J.W. (1996), 'Who owns my body?', *Oxford Journal of Legal Studies* 16, 55–84

Kass, L.R. (2002), *Life, Liberty and the Defense of Dignity* (San Francisco: Encounter Books).

Makdisi, J.M.Z. (2003), 'The slide from human embryonic stem cell research to reproductive cloning: Ethical decision-making and the ban on federal funding', *Rutgers Law Journal* 34, 463–512.

Munzer, S.R. (1990), *A Theory of Property* (Cambridge: Cambridge University Press).

Nisker, J. and White, A. (2005), 'The CMA code of ethics and the donation of fresh embryos for stem cell research', *CMAJ* 173 (6), 621–2.

Nuffield Council on Bioethics (1999), *Genetically Modified Crops: the Ethical and Social Issues* (London).

Plomer A. (2005), *The Law and Ethics of Medical Research – International Bioethics and Human Rights* (London: Cavendish).

Chapter 7
Property Rights in the Body – A Philosophical Approach

Barbro Fröding[1]

Introduction

Many countries are currently experiencing an increasingly intense public debate regarding our rights to biological material, our own as well as that of our fellow man. Two current topics are: first, the commodification and commercialization of organs, cells and tissue and, second, national bio banks and DNA-records. Arguably, a contributing factor to the calls for commercialization stems from an increasing awareness of the organ and tissue shortage which is a reality in most countries today.[2] Indeed, for example, Iran, has opted for a legalization of a market in kidneys.[3]

This chapter addresses the question of property rights in biological material from a philosophical perspective. Who can be said to have which right to what? A brief example to highlight the urgency of this issue would be the case of *John Moore v. The Regents of the University of California*. Suffering from leukemia, the American John Moore agreed to have some tissue samples removed at UCLA Medical Center. Years later Mr. Moore found out that the doctors, without asking for his consent, had cultivated a cell line and then proceeded to take out a patent on it in collaboration with the University of California. As the example clearly indicates, this question is of great practical relevance and ought not to be underestimated (*Moore v. Regents of California*). What does our relationship to biological material really look like, and what are the relevant rights and obligations? A related issue is whether or not these relationships really ought to be labeled 'ownership', or if that only serves to create more confusion?[4] Many of us believe that we have a reasonably good understanding of what it means to own an object. When we use

---

1 Barbro Fröding (nee Björkman), since 2009.

2 See, e.g., a recent article in the Economist, 'Psst, wanna buy a kidney?' Anon., *The Economist*, November 18, 2006.

3 Although highly interesting, whether or not this step took take care of all the problems, ethical or otherwise, connected with kidney transplantations is not the topic of this contribution.

4 For the purposes of the present chapter, the words 'property' and 'ownership' will be treated as synonyms.

the word in an everyday sense, we often seek to describe the type of relationship I have with objects like my mobile phone or my jeans. But if we choose to define ownership in such a complete way, it becomes difficult to account for cases where there are several stakeholders, each holding a different set of rights as is the case with, for example, patents and copyrights. One such example is this text – the author owns the copyright, yet at the same time you as a reader might well own the physical copy of the book you are holding in your hands. Consequently, ownership needs to be divided up and then combined in bundles of rights and obligations which consequently can be attached to different agents.[5]

In a broad sense, the justification of property rights from a philosophical perspective has been expressed in two distinct versions. One of these two rivaling schools is generally referred to as the natural rights theory. The other, however, lacks an established name, but it can be called the social constructivist theory of property rights.

Property as a Natural Right

Today it is common to treat all biological material, ranging from hearts to stem cells, in a similar way from an ownership perspective. It is simply taken for granted that if we own our hearts we also, and in the same way, own stem cells which might be extracted from our bodies. Arguments supporting this view are often based on the conviction that property rights are natural rights. Very briefly, John Locke's version of natural rights (the most established one) as expressed in *Two Treatises of Government* holds that man is bound by a duty to God to preserve His creatures, which would include herself. In order to be successful in doing this, man must be able to acquire exclusive ownership rights to land and other objects. Without the possibility of private ownership our ability to provide for ourselves is jeopardized; we run a greater risk to starve and miss out on the good things in life. The actual privatization might take the following form: an agent who works on a previously unclaimed plot of land or a piece of wood mixes her labor with the object, thus adding value to it.[6] On Locke's view, this process makes her the legitimate and exclusive owner of that plot of land or piece of wood. It should be noted here that Locke, in stark contrast to, for example, Robert Nozick, argued that the riches of the earth were not initially unowned. Quite on the contrary, he stipulated that the earth was *res communis*, that is, owned by all of humanity, given to us by God.

This theory is based on the conviction that property rights precede the state and hence have legitimacy independently of the state and other cultural contexts.

---

5 Note the distinction between a legal and ethical perspective. Naturally a legal system ought to correlate with people's strong, considered moral intuitions, but we are still talking about two distinct issues.

6 It has been pointed out that it is perfectly possible to work on something without adding any extra value, see, e.g., Nozick's tomato juice example (Nozick 1974, 175).

Ownership occurs naturally and is indeed a prerequisite for the state. The creation of a state requires that the future citizens enter into a contract; they commit themselves to live their lives in a certain way, and this usually involves quite substantial curtailments of the personal freedom. According to Locke, the primary reason for any man to recognize a government and a state would be that such an entity has the power to create, and uphold, laws that protect private ownership.

A strength of Locke's natural rights theory is that it succeeds in providing a general account of property that gives some guidance as to when legitimate ownership is present or not. Indeed, although relatively rarely couched in theological terms, arguments based on the natural rights view of property are frequently used in the medical ethics debate, particularly in the USA (Reymond et al. 2002, Skene 2002, Swain and Marusyk 1990). However, the theory also contains certain inbuilt limitations which, arguably, make it less well suited as an analytical tool for immaterial rights where the property rights are split between several stakeholders. When faced with cases like, for example, John Moore's, it becomes clear that the theory presupposes an all-or-nothing view with respect to the contents of property rights. This inability to determine the exact nature of the property right in question is particularly unfortunate when discussing property in biological material. Such property can take very different forms, from patents and other types of intellectual property, to traditional ownership of material objects.

Let us very briefly turn to two practical cases where this problem becomes apparent as it seems that the authorities wish to grant the citizens *some but not all* property rights with regard to biological material. Both examples are from Sweden; the first is about blood plasma and the second about kidneys. In the case of plasma, it appears that the Swedish authorities have taken a natural rights position. Anybody who is successful in meeting the standards set by the National Board of Health and Welfare can become a blood donor. In return for being a good citizen, the donor receives some sort of remuneration, for example, a very small sum of money, coffee and a sandwich or a free vaccination. From the state side it is often said that this is not a payment for the plasma, that was a gift from the donor to someone in need, but rather a compensation for loss of income or some sort of reward for good behavior. However that may be, it is clear that a person is considered to be the owner of her plasma in such a way that she may give it up. This can then be compared to the case of kidney donations. In the last couple of years there have been a few Swedish examples of living organ donors who, for altruistic reasons, decide to help an unknown beneficiary. Again it appears that our relationship to certain biological material, for example, a kidney or a liver lobe, is such that we are free to dispose of it but only on certain conditions.[7]

It seems that if we want to grant people different types of rights with regard to different types of biological material, while maintaining the strong protection of the individual which private property gives, a theory of ownership which is more

---

7 For a discussion from a virtue ethics perspective, see Björkman 2006.

flexible than the Lockean natural rights is required. Social constructivism may provide a more suitable model.

Property as a Social Construction

This competing analytical tradition holds that legitimate ownership is a social construction. At the very heart of the theory lies the idea that ownership is the result of a series of social choices and events that could well have been different.[8] According to this view, society is free to choose the system of property rights that best promotes social goods, and one of the chief tasks of government is to create such a system. Property rights, taken in this sense, cannot exist independently of (some form of) government.

According to utilitarians like Jeremy Bentham and Henry Sidgwick (Bentham 1843, Sidgwick 1891), property rights are products of society designed to maximize utility, or perhaps the good. Sidgwick treated the choice of proper rules for property as a matter of 'expediency' to be determined by the balancing of different considerations. This approach to property was famously further developed by Felix Cohen (Cohen 1957). In the essay 'Dialogue on Private Property', he explained that property rights have their origin in the law, and historically laws express the interests of those who write and enforce them. Ethically, however, the merits of any legal arrangement should be judged according to how well it promotes the good life of those affected by it. Thus, property rights should be arranged to promote a proper combination of social goals such as welfare, justice and economic productivity. Naturally, a social constructivist theory of property rights can be attached to ethical theories other than utilitarianism; an example would be virtue ethics. Here the rights to be constructed would be those taken to promote virtuous behavior and the virtuous society.

Evidently the social constructivist view is quite different from the natural rights theory of ownership outlined above. Natural rights theorists tend to think of property as a relation between the owner and the owned object. This can then be contrasted with Cohen's view, namely, that for a detailed analysis of property rights it is more useful to see those rights as sets (bundles) of legal relations between the owner and the non-owners of an object. Which rights and obligations ought to be included in such a bundle depends on the object in question, and thus we can use the model to describe different kinds of ownership. In addition to this tailoring, there is also the possibility of attaching several bundles (each with a different mix of rights and obligations if necessary) to the one and same object.[9] Arguably, this

---

8   The social constructivist theory of ownership should not be confused with other theories that treat natural phenomena as social constructions. See, e.g., Hacking 1999.

9   Theoretically it would be possible both to have a multidimensional view of ownership and at the same time subscribe to a natural rights theory; in practice, however, such a combination is quite rare, and thus I have chosen the above outline.

flexibility is highly useful when discussing property rights in biological material. It can help explain why, as in the John Moore case, both the patient from whom a cell line was taken and the researchers who refined it seem to have (different types of) ownership rights to that cell line.

Honoré's List

A natural continuation of Cohen's analysis was to put together a detailed list of the various rights and obligations that might be included in the bundles. There are several such examples, but the most convincing one is Tony Honoré's.[10] His list includes 11 types of legal relations said to be the major components of the full liberal type of ownership manifesting itself in modern capitalism (Honoré 1961).

For all his focus on property rights and the various forms of ownership, Honoré admitted that we can have very strong interests in objects which we cannot own *per se*, for example, our bodies. We have a right to our own body, but it does not appear to take the form of ownership as we are not free to dispose of it as we see fit. Such inalienable rights, legally impossible to part with, are often called 'simple rights', and other examples would be the basic human rights as listed by the United Nations.[11]

Critics have said that Honoré's analysis is a better description of property rights as they were thought of in the nineteenth century, when the focus was on individual ownership. This critique is partly unfounded as it relies on a common misunderstanding as regards what Honoré intended when he spoke of Wittgensteinian family resemblance. Very briefly it can be said that the reference ought not to be interpreted as saying that there is a single criterion or combination of criteria that have to be met in order for ownership to be present. Quite to the contrary Honoré himself wrote: '[T]he listed incidents [the 11 components], though they may be together sufficient, are not individually necessary conditions for the person of inherence to be designated the owner of a particular thing' (Honoré 1961).[12]

---

10   Other examples are Sidgwick 1891, 70; Becker 1980, Snare 1972, Karlen 1986, Goodin 1991.

11   See, e.g., Immanuel Kant (1997, 127): 'a man is not entitled to sell his limbs for money, not even if he were to get 10,000 thalers for one finger for otherwise all the man's limbs might be sold off'.

12   On a general note, although the family resemblance approach may be adequate in cross-cultural studies of property rights, it does not seem to be a specific enough tool for analyzing ownership in modern capitalist societies. For the latter purpose, it appears to be more in line with actual linguistic usage to consider a person's right to sell an entity as the *core feature of ownership* to that entity. In the vast majority of cases, we are considered to 'own' those (material and immaterial) objects that we are allowed to sell, but only rarely is a bundle of rights that does not confer a permission to sell considered to constitute ownership of the entity in question.

Altruism Reconsidered

These are the 11 components as listed by Honoré;

1. *The right to possess*, namely 'to have exclusive physical control of a thing, or to have such control as the nature of the thing admits'.
2. *The right to use*, i.e. 'the owner's personal use and enjoyment of the thing owned'.
3. *The right to manage*, i.e. to 'decide how and by whom the thing owned shall be used'.
4. *The right to income*, i.e. to reap the benefits from 'foregoing the personal use of a thing and allowing others to use it for reward'.
5. *The right to the capital*, i.e. 'the power to alienate the thing, and the liberty to consume, waste, or destroy the whole or part of it'. This includes the power to transfer the holder's title to the object.
6. *The right to security*, meaning that the owner 'should be able to look forward to remaining owner indefinitely if he so chooses and if he remains solvent'. An exception is made for the power of the state to expropriate against adequate compensation.
7. *The incident of transmissibility*, meaning that 'the interest can be transmitted to the holder's successors, and so on ad infinitum'.
8. *The incident of absence of term*, meaning that ownership does not cease to be valid 'at a future date or on the occurrence of a future event which is itself certain to occur'.
9. *The duty to prevent harm*, meaning that the owner's liberty to use and manage the thing owned as he chooses is 'subject to the condition that not only may he not use it to harm others, but he must prevent others from using the thing to harm other members of society'.
10. *Liability to execution*, meaning that the owned thing can be 'taken away from him for debt, either by execution for a judgement debt or insolvency'.
11. *Residuary character*, meaning that 'either immediately or ultimately, the extinction of other interests would inure to [the owner's] benefit'. (Honoré 1961)

It is interesting to note that Honoré does not only include components which are positive for the owner but also restrictive factors such as liability to execution and the ruling out of certain types of usage. From the debate on patents on biological material, we recognize the argument that a patent is not really a property right and thus cannot be criticized on such grounds, as it is subject to a time constraint.

Applying Honoré

Regardless of which explanatory model for legitimate ownership one favors – be it a natural right or a social construction theory – the term in itself appears to create problems. A complicating factor is that most people believe that they have a relatively clear picture of what it means to own something. But as this brief introduction to the philosophical foundations of property rights has sought to show, this is not necessarily the case.

Arguably, an important lesson to be drawn from the current debate is that the issue of property rights to biological material should not be reduced to a simple binary issue of owning or not owning. A person's legal rights with respect to a biological material (from her own body or that of someone else) can be constructed in many different ways, depending on what types of legal relations are included in the bundle. The primary normative issue is what such a bundle of rights should contain.[13] It is only a secondary issue whether or not the chosen bundle of rights should be called a property right. To enable a constructive and nuanced debate on property rights in biological material, in particular material involving immaterial rights, Honoré's bundle model can be helpful. The possibility of assigning different types of property rights in an object to different people would be useful in, for example, cases like John Moore's. On this analysis one could imagine that John Moore might be assigned the rights to possess, use, manage and to draw income with regard to the tissue sample that was taken from his body. As for the cell line, such rights would be enjoyed by the doctors or, perhaps, the hospital. Yet another possibility would be shared property rights with regards to the cell line: the doctors could be assigned the right to possess, but the right to income might be shared with John Moore. Undoubtedly, some combinations are more promising than others, and 'the bundle approach' cannot be expected to solve all problems related to this complex issue. Therefore, a more open and constructive debate is needed on one of today's most pressing bioethical issues – what does it mean to own biological material?

Bibliography

Becker, L.C. (1980), 'The moral basis of property rights', in Pennock, J.R. (ed.), *Property* (New York: New York University Press), 187–220.

Bentham, J. (1843), *Principles of the Civil Code*. The Works, published under the superintendence of John Bowring (Edinburgh), Part 1, Chapter 8.

Björkman, B. (2006), 'Why we are not allowed to sell that which we are encouraged to donate', *Cambridge Quarterly of Healthcare Ethics* 15 (1).

— (2007), 'Different types – different rights', *Science and Engineering Ethics* 13 (2), 221-33.

Björkman, B. and Hansson, S.O. (2006), 'Bodily rights and property rights', *Journal of Medical Ethics* 32, 209–14.

Cohen, F.S. (1957), 'Dialogue on private property', *Rutgers Law Review* 9, 357–87.

---

13   For a discussion see Björkman and Hansson 2006, Björkman 2007.

Goodin, R. (1991), 'Property rights and preservationist duties', *Inquiry* 33, 401–32.

Hacking, I. (1999), *The Social Construction of What?* (Cambridge: Harvard University Press).

Hanson, M. (1999), 'Biotechnology and commodification within health', *Journal of Medicine and Philosophy* 24 (3), 267–87.

Honoré, T. (1961), 'Ownership', in Guest, A.G. (ed.), *Oxford Essays on Jurisprudence* (Oxford: Oxford University Press).

Kant, I. (1997), 'Lectures on ethics', in *The Cambridge Edition of the Works of Immanuel Kant*, Heath, P. and Schneewind, J.B. (eds) (Cambridge: Cambridge University Press).

Karlen, P. (1986), 'Worldmaking: Property rights in aesthetic creations', *Journal of Aesthetics and Art Criticism* 45, 183–92.

Locke, J. (1993), *Two Treatises of Government* (London: Orion publishing group).

Moore v. Regents of the University of California, Supreme Court of California, 51 cal. 3d 120, 793 P.2d 479, 271 Cal. Rptr. 146 (1990).

Nozick, R. (1974), *Anarchy, State and Utopia* (Oxford: Blackwell).

Reymond, M.A. et al. (2002), 'Ethical, legal and economical issues raised by the use of human tissue in postgenomic research', *Digestive Diseases* 20, 257–65.

Sidgwick, H. (1891), *The Elements of Politics* (London: Macmillan).

Skene, L. (2002), 'Ownership of human tissue and the law', *Nature Reviews Genetics* 3, 145–8.

Snare, F. (1972), 'The concept of property', *American Philosophical Quarterly* 9, 200–206.

Sowle, C.L. (2001), 'Genetics, commodification, and social justice in the globalization era', *Kennedy Institute of Ethics Journal* 11 (3), 221–38.

Swain, M.S. and Marusyk, W. (1990), 'An alternative to property rights in human tissue', *Hastings Centre Report* 1990, 12–15.

Chapter 8

Reflections on Entitlements in the Human Body from an Equity Perspective

Nils Hoppe[1]

[F]or the error is not in the law nor in the legislator but in the nature of the thing, since the matter of practical affairs is of this kind from the start ... For when the thing is indefinite the rule is also indefinite.[2]

Introduction

The juxtaposition of notions of property and the human body is fraught with difficulty and, more often than not, gives rise to heated, and regrettably often diffuse, debate. In many ways, these difficulties arise not from an actual problem in fact, but from one of terminology. Take the term *property*, for instance. Not only does it assume a variety of different meanings in an interdisciplinary setting, it also carries different definitions in everyday use depending on which context it is used in: from philosophical constructs of bundles of rights via a circumscription of a relationship, to inanimate things all the way to synonymous use as *thing*. The application of the term *propertization* conjures up negative images,[3] as does the term *commodification*[4] – both smacking distinctly of exploitation and debasement. The term *donor*, a favorite when attempting to justify the fact that remuneration for giving up part of oneself is frowned upon, and possibly the last remaining sheer veneer of altruism, is also mostly misapplied. It follows that when we speak of *the doctor taking the donor's gametes*, most people conjure up images of the healer gratefully accepting an altruistic philanthropist's gift for the purposes of fulfilling the greatest desire of a beautiful, loving couple who have been pining for an opportunity to raise children for years. In fact, we are in all likelihood talking about a technician overseeing the physical part of a commercial transaction for the purposes of creating multiple embryos, most of which will end up being

---

1   I am very grateful to the Center for Philosophy and Ethics of Science at the University of Hannover for their very generous support. The usual disclaimers do, of course, apply.

2   Aristotle, Nicomachean Ethics, Book V, §14 (1137b).

3   For a brief discussion, see Brownsword 2007, 16.

4   '[L]abourers, who must sell themselves piecemeal, are a *commodity*, like every other article of commerce, and are consequently exposed to all the vicissitudes of competition, to all the fluctuations of the market' (my emphasis). K. Marx and F. Engels (1848), *Manifesto of the Communist Party*.

used for research, be discarded or will miscarry.[5] Either things have changed and years ago the situation was indeed different, or we are putting up a smoke screen of insufficient words to make medical reality look nicer than it is. The woes of language continue – to speak of *ownership* in human body products seems, at first glance, uncomfortably close to speaking of ownership in humans.[6] Ownership, as a concept, compels us to ask at which stage such ownership rights come into existence, and to whom. The inevitable answer (to keep up that veneer of altruism) is to disenfranchise the *donor* (sic) in order to keep medical reality going strong and looking nice.

The linguistic hand we have been dealt is something we need to live with; it may aid the debate, however, if we are at least aware of its restraints or even able to define a number of terms we can dispassionately use to argue this issue. I would submit that the word *donor* is to be avoided at all costs in this context and *source* to be used in its place. Terms such as *commodification* and *propertization* are unsuitable for the purposes of unemotionally assessing the applicability and admissibility of proprietal appraisals of the human body. As the term *ownership* denotes, in the view of this contributor, the quality of an entitlement rather than the question of the entitlement per se, it is also less suitable in this context. It is suggested that (a) more can be achieved by looking at the idea of *possession*, and (b) possession is a stronger legal concept than ownership. The issue may well turn out to hinge on the question of control rights, actual possession and the proportionality of enforcing the realization of conflicting entitlements against possessors. *Possession*, as a concept and term is also considerably less contentious than *ownership* in the context of human cells and genetic data.

This chapter will therefore concentrate briefly on the question of possession and control rights before turning to the applicability of these concepts to the human body and then will examine the notion of making profit from the commercialization of the human body before looking at the case of John Moore. The case has been discussed in this context ad nauseam, and fresher case law, such as Catalona[7] and Greenberg[8] is available for illustration purposes. Nonetheless, the case of Moore has yet to be surpassed in terms of clarity of fact and outrageousness of content and lends itself as a perfect illustration. For these reasons the chapter will use it to lead into the suggestion of using the concept of Equity in order to weight entitlements in human tissue and cells ('Bioequity'). After a brief introduction

---

5   A quick Internet search reveals this gem: *'free sperm donors? no way!!! Make a bunch of money, sell sperm. You get between $60-$80 per visit by doing sperm donation for money!'*. http://www.spermbanker.com/bank/info/top-5-reasons-to-donate-sperm (accessed 21.05.2009). Amounts of $25 for sperm and between $2,000 and $20,000 for oocytes are discussed in more serious publications. See Daniels 2000, 208 and 210.

6   See Mason and Laurie 2006, 516, in relation to the fetus in vivo.

7   *Washington University v. Catalona*, 437 F. Supp. 2d 985 (E.D. Mo. 2006).

8   *Greenberg v. Miami Children's Hospital Research Institute, Inc.* 2002 WL 1483266 (N.D.Ill.), 2003, 264 F. Supp 2 1064 (S.D.Fla.).

into the nature and history of Equity, the chapter will briefly highlight its possible uses in the life sciences and finish off by revisiting Moore with the new old tools of Equity. A complete solution will not be provided, but the possibility of an alternative property regime will be raised, which may come closer to what we have in mind when speaking of entitlements to our bodies. The chapter will also show the flexibility and self-healing capacities the law has shown in the past when rigidity in the Common Law has led to unfair results and will plead for a similar process now in order to legally envelop medical reality and ethical considerations rather than force inappropriate law on rapidly developing science.

Law's Darling is the (Bona Fide or Not So Bona Fide) Possessor of Value (With or Without Notice)

One of the first (of many) wisdoms instilled in budding law students is that of possession being nine tenths of the law. Optionally attributed either to ancient Roman or Persian law, a strikingly similar phrase can be attributed with certainty to William Murray, Earl of Mansfield, in the mid-eighteenth century.

> 'Possession is very strong: rather more than nine points of the law'.[9]

The intention behind this maxim, and no doubt the reason for its continued deployment in legal education, is to get across the importance of control rights over property. It does not intend to convey an accurate representation of the proportion of the law (possibly adversely) occupied by the notion of possession, but a point is being made. He who has control over property[10] is in a strong position against the world save for the owner; he who has possession and legal ownership simultaneously has an almost unconquerable entitlement, footed in fundamental right to own property and the premise that to remove something from someone else's possession will ordinarily require some degree of force. The use of such force to wring something from someone else's possession is *prima facie* unacceptable, unless there is an appropriate mandate and adequate proportionality for the use of such force – that is to say, even where the entitlement is better than the possessor's, the sequestration cannot ordinarily take place where it is disproportionate.[11] The individual who is in possession, therefore, in many cases, has the strongest entitlement to the item in question.

---

9   *Corporation of Kingston Upon Hull v. Horner* (1774); Lofft, 576, 591; 98 ER 807, 815.

10   Intended in this chapter to mean property in terms of 'tangible and intangible property', synonymous with thing, item, object.

11   See, for example, *Winston v. Lee* 470 U.S. 753 (1985) (US Supreme Court): 'A shopkeeper was wounded by gunshot during an attempted robbery but, also being armed with a gun, apparently wounded his assailant in his left side, and the assailant then ran from

It might be argued that it is not the comfortable legal idea of outright ownership that provides the softest cushion for our entitlement but rather having physical control. Many years ago a favorite tutor suggested that the simple answer to the question of how to obtain land is simply to lay claim to its possession: build a fence around it and put a sign on the gate saying that you are in possession of the land, wait 12 years[12] and it's yours.[13] Indeed, the German word for possession – *Besitz* (n.) – literally means 'to sit on'.[14] Possession is thus perfectly sufficient where no one contests it. And – as in the case of adverse possession – the occupation of the property may mature into outright ownership with time. The principle of transferring adverse possession to outright ownership mirrors society's interest in an efficient economic utilization of property. In much the same way, abandoned ships at sea can be taken possession of by the salvager, and the state reserves the right to decide whether it can make better use of your land than you.[15]

Possession, and the rights and duties that attach to this status, are among some of the most important aspects of the interrelationship between people and entities. Fundamental rights and freedoms regularly include the right to own (and, clearly, possess) property. Society, states and much of our individual existence is based on what, and how much, we have. The accumulation of wealth and property represents one of the nucleic features of life, and it is of little surprise value that the sets of rules governing property are finely tuned and have been expertly chiseled over the centuries. Entitlements to property permeate all facets of life; specific and narrowly defined regimes are in force for all kinds of property, real and personal. Every aspect of possession, ownership, conflict of title and simultaneous entitlements has been covered; every exception has been defined. The law knows exhaustive, and sometimes complex, rules on how ownership and possession of our assets

---

the scene. Shortly after the victim was taken to a hospital, police officers found respondent, who was suffering from a gunshot wound to his left chest area, eight blocks away from the shooting … [T]he Commonwealth of Virginia moved in state court for an order directing respondent to undergo surgery to remove a bullet lodged under his left collarbone, asserting that the bullet would provide evidence of respondent's guilt or innocence'. After the procedure was deemed to require a general anesthetic, the US Supreme Court held that 'The proposed surgery would violate respondent's right to be secure in his person and the search would be "unreasonable" under the Fourth Amendment'.

12   Do trim the hedges and mow the lawn occasionally.

13   In the case of unregistered land; *section 15, Limitation Act 1980*. In the case of registered land, the adverse possessor can register his interest after ten years, at which point the registrar gives notice to the registered proprietor, who may then contest the registration; *paras. 1, 2, Schedule 6, Land Registration Act 2002*. Gary Watt (Warwick) and Roger Sexton (Nottingham Trent) will be pleased to note that I have finally grasped the difference between registered and unregistered land. It just took ten years.

14   Also see Pipes 1999, 68, cited in Smith and Zaibert 2001.

15   *Dominium eminens*; see, e.g., the *Compulsory Purchase Act 1965*, the *Planning and Compulsory Purchase Act 2004*.

are to be dealt with when we die.[16] The law has defined entitlements in land, in chattels, in treasure trove and abandoned ships, in oil and gold found under our front lawns, in escaped swarms of bees, as well as other pets less likely to make off in mid-air. The law has taken pains to capture the complex character and special requirements of living property: *ferae naturae*, animals wild by nature, can be owned by me as long as I have them under control. Once they escape and show no inclination to return to me, they are rendered *res nullius* – no-one's thing.[17] This principle extends to other physical phenomena: water under my control is mine until it escapes;[18] combusted chattels are rendered *res nullius* when the fumes escape (Baker 2002, 387).

The most desirable scenario seems to be the achievement of best possible economic use for all things ownable. If something is rendered *res nullius*, there must be some way to regain possession and thus possibly ownership. Within this cover of rules we try to envelop all tangible and intangible things the world is made of, and quite rightly, too; for without these rules, the interaction between individuals and the things they make and use is impossible. This extends to human bodies, of course. From mundane questions of who is lawfully in possession of bodies for the purposes of interment all the way to Benthamian[19] and Aveburian[20] ex ante provisions for the useful exploitation of bodies ex post.

This is usually the moment where the point is made that life has changed, and the human body has entered the realm of the 'ownable', 'purchaseable' and of the 'commodity'. That, however, is plainly not true. Life has not changed – the human

---

16   And where we have failed to make provisions and have carelessly departed without leaving statutory beneficiaries, the property ends up in the coffers of the Crown, the Duchy of Lancaster or the Duke of Cornwall, respectively. *Section 46, Administration of Estates Act 1925.*

17   The German Civil Code, as an example, contains a specific provision stating '[A]nimals are not property. They are protected by specific legislation. The law of property is applicable to animals as long as no other provisions exist'. §90a BGB (my translation).

18   And, presumably, fails to show inclination to return to me.

19   Jeremy Bentham bequeathed his hastily preserved body to University College London where his *auto-icon* is known to have been brought in to attend College Council meetings some considerable time after his death, being recorded as 'present but not voting', http://www.chem.ucl.ac.uk/resources/history/chemhistucl/hist03.html (accessed 21.05.2009). Also see Andrews and. Nelkin 2001, 6.

20   Lord Avebury, a liberal democrat peer, has offered his body to Battersea dog's home for the purposes of feeding the lucky hounds after his demise (his offer was turned down, possibly because it would have been in bad taste one way or the other). http://specials. ft.com/election2001/FT3T5K63MNC.html (accessed 14.08.2007). It is reported that he has made similar alternative arrangements but, given the sensitive and private nature of the matter as well as the somewhat perfunctory press response to the inadvertent revelation of his first idea, Lord Avebury was quite understandably unwilling to comment when I contacted him.

body has always been within this realm. It is our perception of the human body that has changed, and that has shifted the scope of the realm.

Changing Notions of Usufructuary Rights to the Human Body

Possibly as good a starting point as any in addressing the question of how the human body has been, and will continue to be, the subject of usufructuary interests is how the body of an individual can be of interest to third parties. The validity of those third parties' motives is, I would submit, inconsequential to this contemplation.

The social usefulness of adorning oneself with severed constituents of an enemy's body has been widely discussed.[21] Though the premise of routine tribal anthropophagy in the past has been somewhat contentious (see Arens 1980), it is also fairly certain that sporadic cultural anthropophagic use of executed prisoners' bodies has taken place.[22] Quite apart from the use of parts or products of an individual's body (such as blood or adipose) for supposedly curative purposes, entire bodies have been the subject of desire of anatomical laboratories from antiquity (see Edelstein 1932) to 'modern' nineteenth century anatomical colleges in Scotland.[23]

The fact that human bodies were to be at the disposal of British medical colleges was enshrined in legislation, first by the *Murder Act 1752* and then by the *Anatomy Act 1832*. While the Murder Act saw the option 'hanging followed by dissection' as a form of penal upgrade of the death penalty,[24] the Anatomy Act was more on the track of economics, recognizing a need for authentic medical training in the medical colleges and thus a high demand for cadavers with an unfortunate low supply. Interestingly, the Anatomy Act used similar language as was used in the Human Tissue Act 2004 – now in force to regulate the use of human tissue – in terms of having to be licensed to perform certain acts with human bodies and tissues. The former aimed at increasing the output of bodies in the best interest of medical research; what about the latter?

What is certain is that access to the human body continues to be eminently necessary both for medical science and for industry. Bodies are still needed for anatomical training in medical colleges.[25] Bodies are also required by privately

---

21 For a recent discussion, see Chacon and Dye 2007.

22 Herzog 1994, cited in Bergmann 2004, 171.

23 Most notably the astounding case of Burke and Hare who supplied fresh bodies to the Edinburgh Medical College in the first half of the nineteenth century, first by appropriating the bodies of the freshly buried of Edinburgh from graveyards, then by helping victims along on their way to the graveyard.

24 Arguably as a deterrent, playing on religious discomfort felt at the thought of interference with one's body after one's demise.

25 See http://www.pdn.cam.ac.uk/doc/donate.html (accessed 21.05.2009) for an example of body donation to academia, in this case the Department of Physiology,

owned companies providing continuing education for surgeons and other customers in order to practice complex (and possibly not quite so complex) medical procedures.[26] While the demand for blood and blood products is decreasing (by some 15 percent in the last six years), so is the amount of 'donations' (currently at approximately 20 million 'donations' each year).[27] Nonetheless, blood and blood product 'donations' are needed worldwide. Cosmetic and therapeutic products are manufactured from products of the human body, such as human growth hormone or the use of (admittedly the patient's own) collagen. Implants are manufactured from bones taken from post-mortem 'donors' and commercially marketed; the use of human cells for therapeutic interventions (such as in arthroplasty) is indispensable.

What has changed is thus not the usefulness of the human body. It is clearly the marketability of the human body – the economic charge human tissue has acquired. The incredible sums associated with scientific discoveries using human tissue and cells will become clear when the case of John Moore is briefly discussed again at a later stage. Another prime example is that of the identification of individual genetic disease features, which would be impossible without the acquisition of material from closed groups of individuals.[28] The subsequent production of pharmaceutical products to combat such diseases (particularly widespread diseases such as, in our example, asthma) produces considerable revenue.[29] Additionally, even in areas where the legislator has successfully prevented a commercialization, such as organ transplantation, we have all the characteristics of a market with a considerably higher demand than supply: the UK Transplant activity report reveals 3,087 transplantations in 2006/2007 (up by 293 from 2005/2006) with some 7,234 patients waiting for a transplant (up by 536 from 2005/2006).[30]

Development and Neuroscience of the University of Cambridge. Also see http://www. bodymobil.de/en/home.html (accessed 21.05.2009) for Gunther von Hagens' extraordinary 'Bodymobil' for the purposes of body donation to his collection.

26 For an enormously entertaining, but not very academic, exploration of this issue, see Roach 2003, 19–33.

27 Both statistical items from paragraph 3.1.1., 'Modernising Blood Collection', in NHS Blood and Transplant Service Strategy 2006–10, 28 November 2006, available at http:// www.nhsbt.nhs.uk/downloads/nhsbt_service_strategy_dfd.pdf (accessed 21.05.2009).

28 Such as the identification of the asthma gene by a Canadian company following detailed assessment of a closed population group on the remote Atlantic island of Tristan da Cunha. See Zamel et al. 1996.

29 Sequana Therapeutics bankrolled the expedition to Tristan da Cunha. The patent rights were subsequently sold to Boehringer Ingelheim for $70 million. Andrews and Nelkin 2001, 65.

30 NHS Blood and Transplant (2007) 'Transplant Activity in the UK', available at http://www.uktransplant.org.uk/ukt/statistics/transplant_activity_report/current_activity_ reports/ukt/transplant_activity_uk_2006-2007.pdf (accessed 21.05.2009); NHS Blood and Transplant (2006) 'Transplant Activity in the UK', available at http://www.uktransplant.

Given that we ostensibly have a seller's market for organs, the price of the organ is dictated by the investment required to carry out the transplant plus whatever the purchaser is willing to pay. Numerous studies have been carried out in relation to how much a transplantation costs and countless figures have been suggested.[31] To recite them here would be quite useless as they very much depend on which kind of health system they were calculated for and which collateral factors, if any, they take into account (such as comorbidity, transport costs, costs to the patient). Once the entity carrying out the explantation and the transport decides to charge the health insurance, if any, more than the real expenditure it incurs (for practical purposes, such as a flat rate for certain activities), the problem is reduced to an unwillingness to make too much profit, not an unwillingness to make profit per se. The problem lies in the question of how much extra we are willing to pay on top of the expenditure incurred in explanting, transporting and implanting the organ. It is certainly not within the ambit of this chapter to look at the ethical admissibility of opening up the market for organs to the idea of profit margins, but the threshold we seem to be loathe to cross appears to lie just here.[32]

The point is this: material derived from the human body – be it cells for research and analysis for the development of pharmaceutical agents or complete or part organs for transplantation – are potentially commercially valuable, scarce and scientifically indispensable. Regardless of where the threshold which we dare not cross lies, the issue should be addressed and the law has a duty to encompass the established practice to utilize the human body and its products adequately nonetheless. As with most medico-legal issues, the law is merely the understudy of an ethically acceptable framework within which we may act: it cannot and must not attempt to normalize criteria which go against current moral considerations.

Interests, Entitlements and Problems of Sublimation

Questions of the quality of one's entitlement only become interesting once a conflict arises: I need not justify my possession of a certain thing unless someone else suggests that she has a better entitlement to it. Without wishing to encroach on the debate of whether we can own ourselves[33] or to outline the idea of various combinations of sticks making up bundles of rights amounting to property,[34]

---

org.uk/ukt/statistics/transplant_activity_report/current_activity_reports/ukt/transplant_activity_uk_2005-2006.pdf (accessed 21.05.2009).

31   See, e.g., Mathew and Chapman 2006, Kontodimopoulos and Niakas 2006, Best and Sullivan 1998.

32   For a more elaborate debate, see Radcliffe-Richards et al. 1998, Brownsword and Beyleveld 2001, chapter 8.

33   See, e.g., Smith and Zaibert 2001, 162.

34   For a comprehensive overview of the different bundle theories, see Björkman and Hansson 2006, though I am unconvinced by the legal utility of Björkman's and

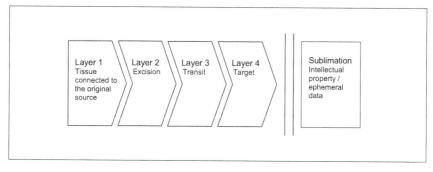

Figure 8.1   The layers model

I would like to look at some of the pragmatic issues in relation to possession of human biological material. These depend largely on the exact circumstances in which the material finds itself.. A graphic representation of the circumstances could be as seen in Figure 8.1.[35]

Layer 1 – Source

In Layer 1, the tissue is part of the original organism. To remove the tissue from the possessor requires some degree of force. An illustration of this is the fact that any medical intervention – such as the taking of cells – is prima facie a battery. The illegality of the excision can in most cases only be nullified by the patient's full informed consent and the therapeutic telos of the procedure. It is without doubt the easiest layer to look at and evaluate. The best entitlement to the material clearly rests with the individual to whom it is attached. The decision to take material from this individual against his wishes has to be legitimated appropriately[36] and be proportionate.[37]

Layer 2 – Excision

This is arguably the most exciting point in time in relation to entitlements in the material and a pivotal point in the discussion. If we follow the reasoning in Moore (see below), this is the point in time when property capable of ownership actually comes into existence – and accrues to the individual who does the excising.

Hansson's suggestion.

35   I suggested a similar model earlier. See Hoppe 2006. Ryan Morgan (Cork) developed a similar and much more detailed model, using the idea of *watersheds*, some time before me as part of his unpublished postgraduate work.

36   Such as the taking of blood, for example, subsequent to a charge of driving under the influence.

37   See *Winston v. Lee*, op cit.

This appears to be the current judicial approach to the question of proprietary entitlements in the human body.[38]

Layer 3 – Transit

This layer describes the material in transit. The material will be in the possession of the person or entity performing the transport (for example, from donor to recipient in the case of an organ transplantation). If we hold possession to be key in instances where there is potentially no right to own, the transfer of possession takes on considerable importance. Further, during transport the material attracts status akin to a commercial status. It is often insured against loss, transport charges are incurred which add to the cost of the material and it is usually the subject of a transport or material transfer agreement.

Layer 4 – Target or Use

Once implanted – in the case of an organ or a graft – or depleted for research, the material has passed a 'point of no return' and can no longer be described as the original material. In particular, it would be unthinkable and quite absurd if, for example, a kidney was to be repossessed in cases where the recipient's health insurance failed to pay for the transplantation. Again, the dispossession of the possessor would require force and be disproportionate in any circumstances. As far as depletion for research is concerned, the material is simply destroyed, mixed or converted beyond recovery.

The idea of these layers becomes relevant when we look at the legal and ethical consequences of proprietal dealings with human tissue. It would be unhelpful, but regrettably it does happen in literature, if we were to speak broadly of 'ownership in the human body' and make no distinction between layer 1 and layer 3. Kelly, for example, is law which applies only to layer 3 and arguably occurs at some stage in layer 2 (layer 4 does not come into the equation because once made into anatomical specimens, the material is not depleted or implanted). When considering questions of entitlements in such material, we ought to bear in mind the state (or layer) which the material is in at that stage.

---

38   Also see *R v. Kelly* [1998] 3 All ER 741. Kelly and an accomplice had misappropriated a number of anatomical specimens from a collection and were charged with their theft. The question of whether body parts generally satisfy the 'someone else's *property*' requirement of the statutory definition of theft was elegantly circumnavigated by the court in favor of a Lockean 'fruits of labor' solution – the artful work invested in changing parts of a cadaver into anatomical specimens was sufficient to make them property capable of ownership: '[P]arts of a corpse are capable of being property within section 4 of the Theft Act, if they have acquired different attributes by virtue of the application of skill, such as dissection or preservation techniques, for exhibition or teaching purposes', per Rose, L.J., 749. Also see *Doodeward v. Spence* (1908) 6 CLR 406.

Moore Revisited (Again)

'[B]ut how actions must be done and distributions effected in order to be just, to know this is a greater achievement than knowing what is good for the health'.[39] This is an opportune moment to outline the case of John Moore[40] in all brevity. Moore was being treated for a rare form of leukemia[41] at the University of California, Los Angeles. The doctor treating him, Dr Golde, said that he 'had reason to fear for his life, and that the proposed splenectomy operation ... was necessary to slow down the progress of his disease'.[42]

The operation not only slowed down the progress of the disease, but also yielded highly valuable material. Moore's spleen possessed characteristics which would, together with further samples, lead to a patent estimated by some to be worth up to 3.01 billion US dollars (USD).[43] What is certain is that Moore was coaxed back from his home town of Seattle to the University of California's Medical Center[44] regularly for some seven years (between November 1976 and September 1983). Golde, and his researcher Quan, extracted blood, blood serum, skin, bone marrow aspirate and sperm,[45] making Moore believe that he was in fact enjoying aftercare for his condition as opposed to being the unwitting participant of cutting-edge cancer research. Regardless of whether we subscribe to the fantastic figure of $3 billion above, it is certain that Quan and Golde benefited financially – personally and substantially – from the development of the patent[46] which was the result of the sustained and unlawful extraction of cells from Moore.

Moore attempted to gain access to some of the pecuniary benefits paid to Golde, Quan and the Regents of the University of California through the courts; the obvious illegality of the acquisition of his cells, he believed, morally entitled him to a share of the substantial commercial value of the end product. This contributor would agree with him on this point – and so did the court: it was morally on his side and suggested he retry by claiming a breach of fiduciary duty on the part of the doctors treating him. Legally, unfortunately, they were not on his side and, in order not to shackle the progress of science, dismissed his claim for conversion, leaving him without the windfall he had hoped for.

---

39   Aristotle, Nicomachean Ethics, Bk V, §13 (1137a).
40   *Moore v. Regents of the University of California*,793 P 2d 479 (Cal, 1990).
41   Hairy cell leukemia. The Leukemia and Lymphoma Society estimates that only between 500 and 800 people in the US develop hairy cell leukemia out of an expected 40,440 people developing leukemia in 2007 (only 1.2–2 percent). See http://www.leukemia-lymphoma.org/ (accessed 21.05.2009).
42   *Moore v. Regents of the University of California*, 481.
43   *Moore v. Regents of the University of California*, 482; also see Merz 1990.
44   Well over 1,000 miles.
45   *Moore v. Regents of the University of California*, 481.
46   U.S. Patent No. 4,438,032 (March 20, 1984).

The question of the conversion of property and the act of mixing or converting the material beyond recognition or recovery is one which leads to what has in the past been described as the *sublimation of the entitlement* (Hoppe 2007). Following this theorem, an entitlement in tangible property should sublimate to an entitlement in intangible property when, as in the Moore case, the downstream profit and the aim of the entire exercise lies not on the sustained storage and work with the tangible material, but the intangible information it contains as a type of medium. This is made necessary by the particular characteristics of the genetic information stored within our cells; the cells merely function as a medium for transport and the aim of the procurement of the cells is in some cases only to obtain access to that information. Much like the value of a check is not the value of the paper it is printed on but of the *chose in action* it represents. Where, as in the Moore case, the appropriation is illegal, we need to ask whether the source can legitimately be said to have waived his entitlement in the cells or – by sublimation – the information contained therein.

This, to some extent, follows the notion of the tort of conversion, which Moore pleaded as part of his claim:

> The tort of wrongfully dealing with a person's goods in a way that constitutes a denial of the owner's rights or an assertion of rights inconsistent with the owner's. Wrongfully taking possession of goods, disposing of them, destroying them, or refusing to give them back are acts of conversion.[47]

Moore was quite right in that there was certainly a wrongful interference on the part of Golde and Quan. The acquisition of samples from Moore for the purposes of research, outside the ambit of his consent, certainly constituted a tortious interference with the person, so why not a tortious interference with property? Interestingly, Moore need not be the outright owner to bring his claim for conversion but merely be in lawful possession of the converted chattel. This fits in neatly with the notion of ignoring ownership for the purposes of this chapter and concentrating on possession instead. Regrettably, the claimant needs to show that what was converted was a chattel and establish a reasonable market value for it; it is a steep order to ask the court to follow a line of reasoning resulting in a quantification of the value the human body.[48] Even if the value of his cells was to be established, did the value he was after not relate to the genetic information encoded in the cells (locked away for him prior to the artful intervention of Golde and Quan)? Moore's claim for conversion capsized, foreseeably, because the law he chose was unsuitable for the ethical and medical realities he tried to encompass, and the court was afraid of stopping medical progress in its tracks.

---

47   Extract of the entry for 'conversion' in the *Oxford Dictionary of Law*, 4th Edition (Oxford: Oxford University Press, 1997), 107.

48   Even if such quantification routinely takes place where the result of an accident is the loss of a limb. See, e.g., Kemp 2000.

Epikeia, Aequitas, Equity, Bioequity

Before this chapter returns to Moore's dilemma, a quick look at the different available legal mechanisms of property is useful. It will, in particular, draw attention to the tools and ideas provided by Equity, as opposed to Common Law proprietary notions. Approaches to property cushioned in principles of Equity are eminently useful in relation to question of entitlements in the human body and its products. Equity is far too complex to do it justice in the context of this chapter. Discussion will have to be limited to superficially illustrating some of the elements of Equity which appear relevant and interesting in relation to our question. First, we need to again look at a problem of terminology.

The term *Common Law* attracts two different meanings. On the one hand, we use the expression as an umbrella term for the common law class of legal systems. In the context of Equity, the English and Welsh legal system is subdivided into the Common Law system and Equity. Both systems coexist, generally peacefully, until a conflict arises.

> Subject to the provisions of this or any other Act, every court exercising jurisdiction in England or Wales in any civil cause or matter shall continue to administer law and equity on the basis that, wherever there is any conflict or variance between the rules of equity and the rules of the Common Law with reference to the same matter, the rules of equity shall prevail.[49]

Where there is a conflict between the Common Law and Equity, Equity therefore prevails. The idea of Equity is this: where the rigid application of the Common Law would lead to a manifestly unfair result, Equity attempts to redress this imbalance, acknowledging that the law is not perfect. The notion that the law can, by definition, not cover all eventualities and may need to be second-guessed by a morally oriented instance is an ancient one. Consider the idea of *epikeia*, which we can find in Aristotle:

> Hence whenever the law makes a universal rule, but in this particular case what happens violates the [intended scope of] the universal rule, here the legislator falls short, and has made an error by making an unconditional rule. Then it is correct to rectify the deficiency; this is what the legislator would have said himself if he had been present there and what he would have prescribed, had he known, in his legislation.[50]

and the translation of the principle by Thomas Aquinas in his *Summa Theologiae*:

---

49 Supreme Court Act 1981, 49.
50 Aristotle, Nicomachean Ethics, Book V (1138a).

Legislators in framing laws attend to what commonly happens: although if the law be applied to certain cases it will frustrate the equality of justice and be injurious to the common good, which the law has in view. Thus the law requires deposits to be restored, because in the majority of cases this is just. Yet it happens sometimes to be injurious – for instance, if a madman were to put his sword in deposit, and demand its delivery while in a state of madness, or if a man were to seek the return of his deposit in order to fight against his country. On these and like cases it is bad to follow the law, and it is good to set aside the letter of the law and to follow the dictates of justice and the common good. This is the object of 'epikeia ' which we call equity. Therefore it is evident that 'epikeia ' is a virtue.[51]

Equity is thus a means by which we can redress the negative side effects of a system based on abstract rules.

The Nature of Equity

The idea of Equity, as a legal system alongside (not within) the common law system, escapes many English and Welsh lawyers when first contact is made with the concept.[52] It is thus overly optimistic to assume that in an interdisciplinary setting, such as medical and health law, readers can gain easy access to its workings. Whilst the rules of Equity fill many volumes and tell the tale of many cases, the genesis of Equity can be summarized as follows.[53]

In medieval England, the law was adjudicated by the king's judges,[54] whose decision-making was influenced heavily by social, political and bureaucratic aspects. In particular, the rigidity applied by the system of writs,[55] which provided that claims had to be brought in a particular formal style increasingly led to a manifestation of unfair results in the courts. The Common Law solidified in a way which led to a considerable number of actions, which in terms of justice were appropriate, failing due to the strict application of Common Law rules and a restrictive interpretation of the writs system. This had political reasons,

---

51   Thomas Aquinas, *Summa Theologiae*, 2,2, Question 120, Art. 1.

52   This may be a good opportunity to underline the necessity of teaching foundation subjects, such as the history of law and philosophy of law at undergraduate level.

53   I borrow considerably from Worthington 2006 (part 1) for this portion of the chapter.

54   For ease of reference, I shall refer only to 'king's judges' and 'King', which is factually not entirely correct as there was one queen, though she did not call herself so and was only monarch for a few weeks. For more details on this very interesting period of English history, see Chibnall 1993.

55   Forms of action – the right one had to be picked to bring a claim; failure to do so would result in an irrecoverable failure of the claim. If a writ and thus a remedy were not already in existence, the court would refuse to evolve the law to encompass potentially new developments.

falling within a period of considerable power struggles between courts, king and Parliament (Worthington 2006, 10). In order to limit the power of the king and his government official in charge of writs (the Lord Chancellor), the courts refused a wide interpretation of writs. This led to a non-evolving, rigid and, more often than not, an unfair legal system. Just like most other systems, however, the English system provided for a monarch's bounty – the head of state, being in the position of the ultimate instance of appeal, is able to overturn court decisions in the interests of justice. Having been failed by the Common Law, petitioners could ask the king to re-decide the action on his mercy and conscience and overturn the judgment of the Common Law judges.

Ironically, the inflexible attitude of the courts, aimed at limiting the power of the Crown and its agents to issue new writs and develop the law, achieved quite the opposite: the king delegated the decision-making in relation to petitions in Equity to his chief advisor, mostly a cleric – the Lord Chancellor (the very man the courts had tried to factor out in the first place). A variety of chancellors developed Equity and applied the same decisions in similar cases through the Court of Chancery. In this way, a comprehensive body of law developed alongside the Common Law: based on justice, morality and the appropriate appraisal of individual cases, Equity continued to unhinge the Common Law where the Common Law was found wanting. '[T]he result is a constant tension between the desire for universal, generalized rules and the need for individualized, context-specific, fact-sensitive justice (Worthington 2006, 3).

Since the beginning of this chapter noted that rules pertaining to possession represent a considerable proportion of the law, it is hardly surprising that Equity busies itself in principle with entitlements and – in particular – the satisfaction of moral entitlements where the law sees none. Equity went on to develop a different conceptualization of property to the Common Law (Worthington 2006, 58). In particular, the adaptability of equitable property concepts is its major asset: equity was as quick to embrace the notion of slavery as it was to reject it when it was no longer socially acceptable. Well before the Common Law, Equity had recognized the need for a property regime for intangible assets. This contributor believes that intellectual property regimes worldwide would not be where they are today had it not been for Equity. *Choses in action* could be transferred in Equity when the Common Law did not yet recognize such a mechanism.[56] Can the flexible evolutionary characteristics of Equity be used to develop a suitable proprietary regime which we can apply to the human body?

Anything that could be described as usable and transferable wealth rests within the envelope of equitable property notions; this idea brings us full circle to our original contemplation: possession and the factual reality of transferability are the decisive elements in considering entitlements to the human body and its products. The fact is that in reality we have possession of our cells as long as they are attached to us, and the assertion that we have (a moral) entitlement to these cells should not

---

56   It does now. S. 136, Law of Property Act 1925.

be overly contentious. Upon excision or excretion they become transferable and, as in the case of Moore, potentially attract the status of wealth.

Equity's Darling is the Bona Fide Purchaser of Value Without Notice

This chapter will now revisit Moore to finish off: Equity recognizes concurrent entitlements, one enjoys stronger protection while the other one enjoys the, prima facie less complicated, texture of legal ownership. This means that a certain thing can be legally owned by one party while the equitable entitlement rests with another. Equity recognizes that the legal owner can use the semblance of outright entitlement to dishonestly divest the property and has developed strategies to protect the person with the equitable entitlement. Applying the ailing legal concept of proprietary interests arising ex post (as in the cases of *Moore v. the Regents of the University of California*, *R v. Kelly* and *Doodeward v. Spence*), we acknowledge that Golde and Quan have acquired a legal entitlement in Moore's biological material. Let us assume that Moore retains the equitable entitlement: Golde and Quan have obtained the material on the condition that they use it to further his health and well-being. They are quasi-trustees of his cells and the information they contain. If they go ahead and sell the material or the information derived from investing the material in research, Sandoz Pharmaceuticals, a co-defendant in the case, can only be protected from Moore's claim if they were bona fide purchasers for value without notice.[57] In the case of intellectual property derived clearly from genetic information, it is prudent and reasonable to expect Sandoz to realize that there is a source involved, whose equitable entitlement has to be waived before the property is free to be used commercially. Had Golde and Quan been straightforward and honest with Moore, he may have waived his entitlement. The illegality of the acquisition results in a number of possible remedies in Equity for Moore.[58] In particular, he may be able to trace his entitlement in Equity, resulting in a full recovery of the unlawful profit accumulated by Golde Quan, the University of California and Sandoz. It is therefore the illegality of the act which prejudices the accrual of financial benefits to the researchers, not the notion of medical research: the progress of science would continue unshackled if the protagonists only obtain sufficient consent for their actions. This, is more than in line with current standards of informed consent in relation to patient autonomy and research subjects' rights.[59]

---

57   Even Worthington suggests that these are 'rare people' (2006, 65).

58   For the avoidance of doubt I should point out that Equity would not have worked for Moore in California. I am referring to the jurisdiction of England and Wales and am hypothesizing on what Moore would have achieved in this jurisdiction.

59   Even if we are to hold that Moore was a research subject as opposed to a patient, which – I would argue – is difficult.

Concluding Thoughts

This exploration can be one of two things: mildly interesting but too far removed from legal reality to be taken seriously or a serious impetus for thought on how to develop rules which apply to reality rather than developing reality to fit in with the rules we have already. The intention of this chapter is to show that the law – many years ago – faced similar stagnation for different reasons. Rules were no longer developed and morally refutable results were manifested in the courts. The implementation of positive law to catch all possible permutations of the expeditious developments of the life sciences seems arrogant. Equity may not provide ready-to-use solutions but rather a number of exciting entry points into developing alternative proprietary notions: equitable/moral entitlements, possession and control rights rather than ownership, requirements of honesty and fiduciary duties between researchers and patients; and thus a system which encourages honest research and underpins the rights of patients and research subjects.

Bibliography

Andrews, L. and Nelkin, D. (2001), *Body Bazaar – The Market for Human Tissue in the Biotechnology Age* (New York: Random House).

Arens, W. (1980), *The Man-Eating Myth: Anthropology and Anthropophagy* (Oxford: Oxford University Press).

Baker, J.H. (2002), *An Introduction to English Legal History* (London: Butterworths LexisNexis).

Bergmann, A. (2004), *Der entseelte Patient* (Berlin: Aufbau Verlag).

Best, J.H. and Sullivan, S.D. (1998), 'The changing cost-effectiveness of renal transplantation: The impact of improvements in immunosuppressive therapy', *Transplantation Reviews* 12 (1), 34–41.

Björkman, B. and Hansson, S.O. (2006), 'Bodily rights and property rights', *Journal of Medical Ethics* 32, 209–214.

Brownsword, R. (2007), 'Biobank governance: Property, privacy and consent', in Lenk, C., Hoppe, N. and Andorno, R. (eds), *Ethics and Law of Intellectual Property – Current Problems in Politics, Science and Technology* (Aldershot: Ashgate), 11–25.

Brownsword, R. and Beyleveld, D (2001), *Human Dignity in Bioethics and Biolaw* (Oxford: Oxford University Press).

Chacon, R.J. and Dye, D.H. (eds) (2007), *The Taking and Displaying of Human Body Parts as Trophies by Amerindians* (Heidelberg: Springer).

Chibnall, M. (1993), *The Empress Matilda – Queen Consort, Queen Mother and Lady of the English* (Oxford: Blackwell Publishers).

Daniels, K.R. (2000), 'To give or sell human gametes – the interplay between pragmatics, policy and ethics', *Journal for Medical Ethics* 26, 206–11.

Edelstein, L. (1932), '*Die Geschichte der Sektion in der Antike*', translated and reprinted as 'The History of Anatomy in Antiquity' in Temkin, O. and Temkin, C.L. (eds) (1967), *Ancient Medicine* (Baltimore: Johns Hopkins Press), 247–301.

Herzog, M. (1994), 'Scharfrichterliche medizin. Zu den beziehungen zwischen henker und arzt, schafott und medizin', *Medizinhistorisches Journal* 29, 309–32.

Hoppe, N. (2006), 'A systematic approach to discussing commodification', *PropEur Newsletter* 2, 4. Available at: http://www.propeur.bham.ac.uk/newsletter.htm (accessed 21.05.2009).

—— (2007), 'Bioequity: applying the principles of Equity to resolve conflicting interests in human tissue'. Paper presented at the PropEur Final Conference, University of Birmingham, 22 September 2007.

Kemp, D.A. (ed.) (2000), *Kemp and Kemp: The Quantum of Damages* (London: Sweet & Maxwell).

Kontodimopoulos, N. and Niakas, D. (2006), 'Overcoming inherent problems of preference-based techniques for measuring health benefits: An empirical study in the context of kidney transplantation', *BMC Health Services Research* 6(3). Available at http://www.biomedcentral.com/1472-6963/6/3 (accessed 22.05.2009).

Martin, E.A. (ed.) (1997), *Oxford Dictionary of Law, 4th Edition* (Oxford: Oxford University Press).

Mason, J.K. and Laurie, G.T. (2006), *Law and Medical Ethics* (Oxford: Oxford University Press).

Mathew, T.H. and Chapman, J.R. (2006), 'Organ donation: a chance for Australia to do better', *MJA* 185 (5), 245–6.

Merz, B. (1990), 'Biotechnology: Spleen Rights', *The Economist*, 11 August 1990, 30.

Pipes, R. (1999), *Property and Freedom* (New York: Vintage).

Radcliffe-Richards, J. et al. (1998), 'The case for allowing kidney sales', *Lancet* 352, 1950–52.

Roach, M. (2003), *Stiff: The Curious Lives of Human Cadavers* (New York: Norton).

Smith, B. and Zaibert, L. (2001), 'The metaphysics of real estate', *Topoi* 20, 161–72.

Worthington, S. (2006), *Equity* (Oxford: Oxford University Press).

Zamel, N., et al. (1996), 'Asthma on Tristan da Cunha: looking for the genetic link. The University of Toronto Genetics of Asthma Research Group', *American Journal of Respiratory Critical Care Medicine* 153 (6), 1902–06.

PART IV
Models of Governance: Pitfalls and Possibilities

Chapter 9

Using Tissue and Material from the Human Body for Biomedical Research: Proposals for a Normative Model[1]

Christian Lenk and Nils Hoppe

The continuing progress of biomedical research results in a changing perception of the human body. Material and tissue from the body, which were formerly classified as 'waste' after an operation, giving birth or diagnostic measures are now – at least in some fields of medicine – valuable raw material for possible future discoveries (Annas 1999, Weiss 2006, Check 2006). At the same time a normative vacuum exists, and the problem very much appears to be how to regulate property issues and usufructuary rights for biomedical research. Usufructuary and control rights for things are but one aspect of property. Generally, property is characterized as a twofold relationship between a thing and its owner. Further, ownership has to be recognized by society, if the owner wants to achieve complete usufructurary and control rights for such a thing. The human body is an exceptional case, because it is neither personal nor real property but the substratum of personhood, and therefore enjoys special protection. The occidental tradition of enlightenment stipulated the human body's integrity and dignity pursuant to religious traditions which interpreted the human body as being in the image of and a gift from God. As an illustration, the German philosopher Immanuel Kant wrote:

> But a man is not a thing, that is to say, something which can be used merely as means, but must in all his actions be always considered as an end in himself. I cannot, therefore, dispose in any way of a man in my own person so as to mutilate him, to damage or kill him.[2]

Nobody is going to seriously cast doubt on the assertion that removed organs or tissue parts are not parts of the person, but parts of that person's body. Two problems result from this state of affairs: first, it is not clear what the normative

1   This study was funded as a part of the PropEur-project (www.propeur.bham.ac.uk) in the 6th Framework Programme of the European Commission (contract nr. PL510239). An earlier version of this text in German language was published in Taupitz (2007).
2   *Metaphysics of Morals, Second Section: Transition from Popular Moral Philosophy to the Metaphysics of Morals*. BA 67, translated by Thomas Kingsmill Abbott.

status of materials which have been removed from the human body really is. Second, it is questionable how and on what terms other individuals can obtain a usufructuary right to body materials as would be the case in biomedical research. These questions have to be resolved with the involvement of three parties: patient, researcher and society. The normative model which will be discussed below rests on three important presuppositions:

1. The use of body tissue and material for biomedical research is only acceptable with valid consent of the person concerned.
2. The patient or research subject has to be informed about the aims and objectives of the research undertaken, and a contract or an agreement of some sort on the use of the material is concluded.
3. Society has to regulate the extent of such agreements regarding the sort of material, the type of use and the extent of usufructuary rights.

The Use of Body Material and Consent

The view that 'superfluous' material, for example after an operation, is 'waste' seems to stem from past times when these materials were indeed 'waste' – in other words worthless – for patient and physician. Nonetheless, the fact that something is worthless for a patient or for a medical layman does not imply that these materials have no value at all. Something can be of very little or no value to the owner but can be very important to other individuals without an onus on the owner to abandon them in favor of these others for their own use. It is perfectly possible to achieve a high price in return for something which is completely devoid of value for oneself but is of high value for others. As Marx argued, this is one of the reasons why people take things to the marketplace to sell them:

> The owner makes up for his lack in the commodity of a sense of the concrete, by his own five and more senses. His commodity possesses for himself no immediate use-value. Otherwise, he would not bring it to the market. It has use-value for others; but for himself its only direct use-value is that of being a depository of exchange-value, and, consequently, a means of exchange (Marx 1995, 51).

Equally, the mere therapeutic intervention of a physician does not give rise to any rights over the patient's bodily material because the physician has already been paid for his work by the patient himself or the patient's insurance. The patient is not indebted (in the two senses of the word) to the physician after a surgical intervention because the work of the surgeon is reimbursed via other mechanisms. Both undertakings, the therapeutic and the scientific, should be distinguished, and the patient's willingness to participate in a scientific study should not, as in all other cases, be a precondition for therapeutic treatment. Medical interventions and medical research require the patient's consent, and it is therefore also necessary to obtain the patient's consent for the removal or use of excised material:

> Hospitals have the right to dispose of human tissue (such as blood and placentas) in a manner consistent with good hospital practice. When placental blood was seen as a useless waste product of childbirth, disposing of it in the same manner as other human tissue that is considered waste was reasonable. But once placental blood is identified as valuable, that value must be explained to the mother and her permission obtained to use the placental blood in the manner desired by the physician or the hospital (Annas 1999, 1522).

Valid consent and comprehensive information of the patient also lead to the desirable result that the physician or researcher has to disclose a possible conflict of interests. Most patients would probably consent to the use of their tissue for medical research, in particular where this research is in relation to their own disease. From the legal point of view, the removal of body material without the patient's valid consent is considered to constitute an assault occasioning bodily harm.

Augmenting the reasoning behind this consequence is the fact that medical research – especially in the field of genetics – can touch upon personality and privacy rights (see Widdows 2007) and that additional work by medical researchers can lead to high value products from the original 'raw material' – the patient's tissue. The anonymization of tissue samples for the purpose of biobanking solves the problem of privacy, but with the awkward consequence that it is no longer possible to contact the patient and inform him about possibly vital research results. Further to this ethical problem, it is still a fact that population biobanks need to gather additional personal morbidity data to achieve their scientific goals (Shickle 2006, 504-5). This is due to their aim of identifying genetic disease dispositions – which have to be compared with a person's actual health condition. Therefore, some of the projects in the field cannot anonymize data because of scientific reasons. A mere pseudonymization of samples, where only the operator of the biobank has access to personal data, does not solve the first problem entirely, at the same time opening up new problems. For example, it could be possible to re-identify somebody's sample in a biobank or to demand the disclosure of somebody's identity through a biobank for the purposes of criminal proceedings:

> It has been suggested that 'linkability' in research projects involving placental blood be maintained but that 'appropriate firewalls' be constructed to protect the donor's identity and privacy. But I believe that the best policy for the storage of nonautologous placental blood, from the standpoint of privacy, is to remove all identifiers from the sample so that the blood can be freely tested without simultaneously testing the child or the mother. This policy would also prevent recipients or their families from trying to contact the donor for another donation if the initial donation is not successful. Physicians who want to maximize the

protection of their patients' privacy should advise them against donating placental blood to a blood bank that retains patient identifiers (Annas 1999, 1523).

Information and Disclosure of Research Objectives

The patient has the power of decision-making regarding the use of tissue and material from his body and, therefore, has a right to receive appropriate information about the objectives and the method of the research which will be undertaken on his tissue. Patients will often support biomedical research, especially if it may prove to be useful in relation to the development of a future therapeutic option for their disease. Cases of extensive cooperation between patient or population groups and medical researchers are known in international discussion (Berg 2001, Dickenson 2004, 112 et seq., Pullman and Latus 2003, Sheremata 2003). Advantages for patients participating in these research projects include often privileged access to newly developed therapies. This is an example of how patients can participate in the non-pecuniary profit generated in research projects. But it is also possible that patients will disapprove of the use of their tissue or body material for some objectives of research, for example, on ethical grounds in the case of stem cell research or when research findings may have an influence on other individuals, such as relatives or members of an ethnic group (see Widdows 2007). Both instances show the importance of appropriate disclosure of information for possible tissue donors.

From the perspective of medical research, the most comfortable solution would without doubt be a general (or 'blanket') consent from the patient. It is highly questionable whether such a general consent for tissue research is either legally permitted or even in the patient's interest (Cassell and Young 2002, Trouet 2004). A similar position is enshrined in Article 22 of the European Council's *Convention on Human Rights and Biomedicine*:

> When in the course of an intervention any part of a human body is removed, it may be stored and used for a purpose other than that for which it was removed, only if this is done in conformity with appropriate information and consent procedures.

The 'appropriate information and consent' certainly has to be like that in other fields of biomedical research. The structured organization of research, for example in biobanks, does not diminish the need for protection of patients but makes it rather more important. Further, it is submitted that 'blanket consent' can never be a valid form of informed consent. Hansson et al. (2006) discuss the possibility of a 'broad consent', which may be practicable in some cases. But the problem of the authors' line of reasoning is that they focus too strongly on the additional risk to patients connected with the excision of their tissue – which will usually be negligible in the case of body material for the purposes of biobanking. This does not solve the problem of personal rights which can, in this case, be far more important than risk control. It may be a practicable solution in this context to give the patient a sufficient description of a specific research project which is connected with one specific biobank that is not used by other researchers and obtain proper informed consent in this way. This constellation, it seems, could be applied to a number of research projects. Nonetheless, this solution would not be applicable to publicly accessible biobanks, which are intended to cater to all kinds of research projects without limitation.

Society Has to Regulate the Extent of Such Agreements

(1) For the Type of Tissue

A number of distinctions exist regarding the type of material which is suited for biomedical research. Insofar as these distinctions stem from other fields of application, such as transplantation medicine, they are not particularly appropriate for the regulation of research on tissue. The distinction, for example, between tissue which has the ability to regenerate and tissue which does not is pointless for research using human tissue, which is almost always removed in the course of a therapeutically-surgical intervention. In most cases it is the therapeutic objective of the intervention to remove the tissue from the patient's body. In the case of a non-therapeutic removal of tissue on scientific grounds, which is additional to a therapeutic intervention, the case becomes infinitely more problematic. The patient should be informed that the entire intervention is not necessary from a therapeutic point of view, and the researcher clearly needs the consent of the patient for additional tissue removal, if any. This applies especially to cases of the removal of tissue from functioning body parts, such as the heart muscle. In the end it is the researcher's responsibility to ensure that the removal of additional tissue on the grounds of research definitely does not harm the proper functioning of the organ concerned.

It is society that has to define the line between acceptable and unacceptable, ethically controversial research projects. Patients may have qualms about legally permissible, but ideologically controversial, research projects, such as, for example, therapeutic cloning, which should be respected by the researcher. It is interesting to note that ethical problems arising from the use of tissue for biomedical research do not seem to result from a special moral status of this tissue, but from the patient's disagreement with the objectives of controversial research. Finally, there is research using tissue from deceased or aborted embryos. It appears prima facie appropriate to apply regulation in relation to organ removal from deceased relatives to this latter case to ensure a maximum of control for the parents affected. In any case, excising tissue from deceased infants or aborted embryos seems to only be acceptable with particular consideration being given to the parent's grueling situation and with the utmost respect for their worries and their perspective, however emotional it may be.

(2) For the Type of Use

It is a common distinction in medical research ethics to differentiate between therapeutic and non-therapeutic, that is, merely scientific, research. Although some critics doubt the practicability of this distinction, it appears to be anchored far too strongly in medical practice to ignore it. The relevance of the distinction between therapeutic and non-therapeutic research arises from the notion of risk. From the patient's point of view, it is rather more rational to accept treatment risks for therapeutic interventions but not for non-therapeutic interventions, due to the possible benefit which arises from the therapeutic intervention. Non-therapeutic interventions produce by definition no direct benefit for the patient's health, and therefore it seems inappropriate to accept major risks for this kind of research. The sum that remains when the patient subtracts potential risk from potential benefit is what primarily guides the decision-making process. When he subtracts the risk from zero benefit, the result is likely to be negative. This distinction can also be transferred to the removal of body tissue and material when there is any risk to or burden for the patient. It follows that the removal of tissue for non-therapeutic research should only produce minor risk or discomfort for the patients concerned.

One of the ethical objectives of biomedical research is a possible participation of patients in the therapeutic success of a research project. In therapeutic studies this goal is realized through the possibility for all patients (including those in control groups, etc.) to achieve the best possible medical treatment. The research on tissue can also produce therapeutically relevant data for the individual patient in question. Therefore, from an ethical point of view, it is worth striving for the possibility to let tissue donors participate in scientific findings of a biobank project insofar as these findings have therapeutic relevance for this patient. The question of the participation of the patients also has some relevance in the case of commercial research. Even though pecuniary incentives are problematic in the field of organ transplantation, there are some arguments in the field of biomedical research with tissue which point to – at least indirect – participation of patients also in the economic success of commercial research projects (see Lenk and Hoppe 2007, especially the arguments concerning the *Moore* case).

(3) For the Extent of Transferable Rights

The extent of transferable usufructuary rights has direct implications for a possible commercialization of tissue and the question whether commercial trade with tissue is at all possible. Analytic examination of property rights shows that property consists of a bundle of individual rights which should not be granted in whole in the case of human tissue (for an overview of the several 'bundle-theories' of property, see Björkman and Hansson 2006). Normally, property means a right to freely dispose of a thing, the right to destroy, to keep, to sell and to use a thing in an unrestricted manner. In many countries, property rights in relation to animals is restricted – that is, the bundle is thinner – insofar as the owner of an animal has extensive duties to treat the animal not as a mere thing, but to ensure the animal's welfare. 'Animals are not chattels. They are protected by means of specific legislation. Notwithstanding legislation to the contrary, the law in relation to chattels is to be applied to them'.[3]

In this sense, restricted property rights apply to animals because the animal's owner cannot claim the right to exploit the animal and treat it in any way he may wish to as there is specific legislation protecting animals from maltreatment.

This notion can be transferred to the field of property rights for human tissue: the decisive aim for biomedical research is the right to use such tissue. In contrast, the right to buy or sell such tissue is not necessary for carrying out research projects as such. It is therefore possible and appropriate to define made-to-measure rights for the storage of tissue in biobanks. Patients could, for example, transfer usufructuary rights in tissue to a biobank and impose the condition to make the tissue accessible for trustworthy and non-commercial scientific projects and not to sell the tissue. An important question in this context is the transition from the public to the private sphere. From the point of view of justice, it seems to be appropriate that tissue, which is stored with public resources, should be accessible for non-commercial research; the privatization of research findings should therefore be prevented.

Concluding Thoughts

The model discussed above for the use of tissue and bodily material for biomedical research has the following qualities, which we submit would aid adequate regulation of this ethically highly charged sphere:

- A valid usufructuary right with sufficient property aspects is constituted through a contract or a mutual agreement between the person who gives material and the person or entity which excises/obtains the material for scientific research.
- Society has to determine the ethical and legal framework within which such contracts or agreements can be valid.
- The normative objective is cooperation between researcher and patient for the benefit of scientific research and, in particular, the participating patient or group of patients.
- The foundation for such an agreement is the voluntary and informed consent of the patient, who has the right to be informed about the research purpose.

---

3   Para. 90a, Bürgerliches Gesetzbuch (German Civil Code), authors' translation.

- It should be ensured that patients can profit from therapeutically relevant findings of the research using biobanks they contributed to.
- It is necessary to develop models for benefit-sharing and the transition from the public to the private sphere. Private actors' unilateral commercial benefit from publicly founded biobanks ought to be prevented.

Bibliography

Annas, G.J. (1999), 'Waste and longing – the legal status of placental-blood banking', *Legal Issues in Medicine* 340 (19), 1521–4.

Berg, K. (2001), 'The ethics of benefit-sharing', *Clin Genet* 59, 240–43.

Björkman, B. and Hansson, S.O. (2006), 'Bodily rights and property rights', *Journal of Medical Ethics* 32, 209–14.

Cassell, J. and Young, A. (2002), 'Why we should not seek individual informed consent for participation in health services research', *Journal of Medical Ethics* 28, 313–17.

Check, E. (2006), 'Tissue-sample payments anger lawmakers', *Nature* 441, 912–13.

Dickenson, D. (2004), 'Consent, commodification and benefit-sharing in genetic research', *Developing World Bioethics* 4 (2), 109–24.

European Council (1997), *Convention on Human Rights and Biomedicine*. Oviedo, 1997. http://conventions.coe.int/Treaty/EN/Treaties/Html/164.htm (accessed on 19 May 2009).

Hansson, M.G.,et al. (2006), 'Should donors be allowed to give broad consent to future biobank research?' *Lancet Oncology* 7, 266–9.

Lenk, C. and Hoppe, N. (2007), '*Ein Modell zur Konstitution von Nutzungsrechten an menschlichem Gewebe und Körpermaterialien*', in Taupitz (ed.), 199–211.

Marx, K. (1995), *Capital* (Oxford: Oxford University Press).

Pullman, D. and Latus, A. (2003), 'Clinical trials, genetic add-ons, and the question of benefit-sharing', *Lancet* 362, 242–4.

Sheremata, L. (2003), 'Population genetic studies: Is there an emerging legal obligation to share benefits?', *Health Law Review* 12 (1), 36–8.

Shickle, D. (2006), 'The consent problem within DNA biobanks', *Studies in History and Philosophy of Biological and Biomedical Sciences* 37, 503–19.

Taupitz, J. (ed.) (2007), *Kommerzialisierung des menschlichen Körpers* [Commercialization of the Human Body.] (Berlin, Heidelberg, New York: Springer).

Trouet, C. (2004), 'New European guidelines for the use of stored human biological materials in biomedical research', *Journal of Medical Ethics* 30, 99–103.

Weiss, R. (2006), '"Serious misconduct" by NIH expert found. Scientist did not report sending tissues to drug firm and getting paid, report says', *Washington Post*, June 14.

Widdows, H. (2007), 'Reconceptualizing genetics: Challenges to traditional medical ethics', in Lenk, C., Hoppe, N. and Andorno, R. (eds), *Ethics and Law of Intellectual Property. Current Problems in Politics, Science and Technology* (Aldershot: Ashgate), 159-74.

Chapter 10
Preventing Conflicts of Interests in the Field of Human Biological Materials: the 'Contractual Model' as an Avant-garde

Christine Noiville

The argument being defended in this chapter is that in order to prevent conflicts of interest provoked by the use and exploitation of human biological material, the contractual model may be useful, perhaps more useful than the traditional property or consent models within which the debate has been confined until now.[1] Before explaining the reasons for such an argument (which may seem quite surprising at first glance), the chapter will recall rapidly why it has become essential to look for new solutions capable of preventing conflicts of interest and why French law, in its current status, does not appear to be up to it.

Conflicts of Interests in the Field of Human Biological Materials

Why has it become necessary to anticipate and prevent what qualify as potential 'conflicts of interests', and first and foremost, what 'conflicts' are we talking about? It will not be necessary to talk too much about these issues as there is already a great awareness of them. The potential conflicts this chapter is referring to, of course, are between, on the one hand, those who give biological materials from their body, and, on the other hand, those who use and exploit such materials. Why should there be some conflicts between them when it has been a very long time since doctors have taken biological material from the human body (blood, organs or other samples) without any problem? As everybody knows, things have changed dramatically with the development of biotechnology, from two points of view at least.

From a scientific and technical point of view, biotechnology has led to an unprecedented control of living matter and given rise to very new uses of biological materials where cognitive purposes, therapeutic hopes but also industrial competitivity and the prospect of big profits are at stake.

---

1 This chapter is part of the research I started with my colleague F. Bellivier, which focuses on 'conflicts of interests in the field of human biological materials'. See Bellivier and Noiville 2004, 2005, 2006 and 2007.

From a legal point of view, this scientific revolution has directly led to a dramatic legal change, particularly the possibility to patent biological materials and the products derived from them, as soon as they have been isolated, purified, analyzed, transformed and applied in industry. Doctors, researchers and firms can then get intellectual property rights – that is, exclusive rights – on body parts.[2]

And here lies the potential conflicts of interests between donors and users of biological materials. Researchers and industry now get property rights – at least exclusive rights – on materials that donors have given as a gratuitous act since, according to French bioethics law – namely, Article 16 of the *Code Civil* – donors have no ownership on their body parts and elements.

Is there not a power imbalance at this point, a distortion between, on the one hand, a free gift, altruistic and unconditional, and on the other hand, a commercial exploitation of this gift? Of course, well known counter-arguments come to mind: what donors give has no value as such; if information and products derived from the samples may be patented, it is because research and industry have invested much time and money, etc.

But the fact remains that without donors, there would be no material; in these conditions, it would be fair that donors benefit in one way or another from the research, or at least that they do not suffer from the research.

As a matter of fact, patients sometimes have to face quite detrimental situations where they gave biomaterials to a researcher or a doctor who identifies an interesting gene, develops a genetic test and asks for such a broad patent that no other research (to develop a better test for instance) is really possible in this field, or the patentee licenses the test at such a high price that donors cannot afford it. The possibility of a conflict regarding benefits from research indeed exists and needs to be prevented; otherwise there cannot be any sustainable exploitation of human biological materials.

Limits of French Bioethics Law

Does French bioethics law, recently modified,[3] meet this requirement? One may doubt this. The French legislator has sought to reinforce donors' consent in order to balance the relationship between donors and users. Consent then appears as the milestone of new French regulation.

First of all, it is now *systematically required* that no removal of any biomaterials will be allowed without the patient's knowledge, and even in case of surgical operations undertaken in the interest of patients themselves, it is now necessary to inform them (*parts removed during a surgical operation are no longer considered to be waste products – res derelictae*).

---

2 Loi 'no 2004-800 du 6 août 2004 relative à la bioéthique', Official Journal no 182, 7 août 2004, page 14040 ; art. L. 613-16 du Code de la propriété intellectuelle.

3 Loi no 2004-800 du 6 août 2004 relative à la bioéthique.

Second, there is no more blanket consent (*for all future unspecified genetic research*):[4] the donor should now consent on each new use of the material. That means that the uses of material by research or industry must coincide with the use to which the donor consented;[5] this also means that consent will have to be regularly requested as long as the research changes: in this case, the scientists must re-contact the donor so that he may, if he wishes, object to the new uses planned.

What is the result of this? Certainly a more active donor who should not be a passive agent any more, who should be able to better control the destiny of parts and products of his body. But, what precisely is the extent of that control? In fact, it is fairly limited. The donor is informed of the types of use to which his materials will be put, and he can object, but that is all. He cannot retain control of the increasing industrial and commercial uses of his biological material. He cannot negotiate commercialization. He cannot exclude or limit patentability. In a word, the best he can do is object to a research, but he cannot set conditions on the use of his samples, even though he has a direct interest in the matter. While reinforcing consent is of course necessary, it also turns out to be insufficient.[6]

In such a context, it is interesting to see how some donors, some patient organizations to be precise, seek an alternative solution in the contractual model: the property model does not fit, the consent model is not sufficient, why not a contractual model?

The 'Contractual Model' Contribution

The argument that the contract may be an adequate tool for preventing conflicts of interest in the field of human biomaterials may seem very shattering at least to most lawyers. As a matter of fact, European legislators have always been on their guard against contractual agreements as far as the human body is concerned. The

---

4   Ibid. The new article L. 1211-2 of the Code de la santé publique states: 'The use of parts of the human body for medical or scientific purposes, other than the purpose for which they were removed or collected, is possible, unless opposition is expressed by the person from whom this sample or part was taken, who was duly informed beforehand of this other purpose'. In the event that the living person is a minor or has a legal guardian, the potential objection will be 'exercised by the person with parental authority or the guardian. This obligation to inform may however be derogated if it comes up against the impossibility of finding the person concerned'. The article remains unclear on several critical points (control of research by the donor, meaning of the terms 'medical or scientific purposes other than', possibility to oppose industrial or commercial use of biomaterials, etc.).

5   It is not clear, nevertheless, whether the donor may exclude a type of use – for example, the development of cosmetics – but not another – for example, cancer research.

6   For a strong position in that sense, see J.C. Ameisen's diverging opinion in the very recent advice no 93 given by the French Ethical Committee (2006). Ameisen holds that participants to a research project should be able to set conditions on the use but also on patentability of their individual samples, as part of the consent.

contract is a favorite tool of the market and means most of the time unrestrained freedom and too little protection of the weak. That is the reason why the debate on biomaterials has been confined to the alternatives of 'consent or property'.

But here, the contractual model may be another option to rebalance the relationship between donors and users of biological materials (see Noiville 2005). This is quite clearly highlighted by the *Greenberg* case which was recently judged by the Court of Florida.[7] In this case, an association of parents requested the development of research concerning *Canavan disease*, a rare genetic disease affecting their children. To this effect, the association had both contributed financially to this task and also provided doctors with a quantity of biological samples. Some years later, one of the doctors identified the gene, isolated it and, without the authorization of the donors, applied for a patent covering the gene, a genetic test and gene therapy methods. While the patent was not exploited in an abusive way, its very existence could run against the interest of patients as the monopoly conferred was broad and could reduce the possibility of other research for more efficient tests.

The judge observed that for the main part, the arguments of the plaintiffs were not admissible under American law.[8] According to US law, they cannot say they were stolen because they have no property rights on their samples, nor can they say that the doctor had no right to patent the gene and the test without their authorization because it was not part of the consent as organized by the legislator. Nevertheless, the judge added that if donors had known that the defendant intended to commercialize the genetic material through a policy of intellectual property, they would not have made their blood and tissues available under those terms; previously, by contract, they could have organized things (confidentiality, patentability conditions, etc.) and very precisely anticipated the conditions for the circulation of material removed and the conditions for exploiting any resulting innovation. Hence, what the judge meant here is that the contract offers them the possibility to attach more precise and more protective conditions to their consent than the prevailing legal conditions (within the limits of public order, of course).

Indeed, more and more patient associations have recourse to the contract and invent new dispositions to protect their interests. The example of an agreement between the US association *PXE International* (which brings together patients who have a rare genetic disease) and the University of Hawaï is a good example of this

---

7   *Greenberg et al. v. Miami Children's Hospital Research Institute*, no 00 C 6779, D.C. for the Southern District of Florida, 29 May 2003.

8   The arguments were: breach of informed consent (the doctor having obtained the patent without donors' consent), breach of fiduciary duty (resulting from the doctor's silence on his commercial pretentions), unjust enrichment (the association having funded part of the research), fraudulent concealment (the doctor having hidden his intention to patent), conversion (defendants arguing that they have a 'property interest' on their samples and the related genetic information) and misappropriation of trade secrets (the Canavan registry being confidential according to defendants).

trend. The contract stipulates that the patients' organization will become co-owner of any patent granted; then, as a co-owner, not only the association can obtain royalties but also it gains a power to control the commercial developments.

Other quite innovative examples exist like this one, where associations that have created their own biobanks make their samples available to research scientists according to conditions like fiduciary relationship, trade secret, preferential access to future therapeutic products and so on. In short, associations see in the contract a very flexible tool, which can both organize the circulation of their materials and correct legislative mechanisms which they consider insufficient.

Certainly, the aim is not to abandon the field of human biomaterials to contractual freedom; the legislature should support as well as regulate the use of such agreements. One must also beware of any idealism for several reasons. In the first place, the concrete effectiveness of such contracts remains to be seen. Secondly, though examples given above are very innovative and interesting, they are what we could call 'context-specific'. What holds for such or such patient association will not be valid in other cases. So one cannot see in the contractual model a universal solution to the problem we are dealing with, that is, prevention of conflicts of interests. A more general solution, be it legal or regulatory, is certainly necessary.

A fact remains nevertheless. Whereas the legal debate on biomaterials has been imprisoned within the property model and the consent model, it is interesting to see how the 'contractual model' emerges as an interesting alternative. Though it is generally seen as quite dangerous in our field, donors find in the contract an instrument for exchanging their material in a very flexible way but also with social justice; they conceive the contract as a powerful means for redressing the power imbalance that currently beleaguers the relationship between researchers and them. It certainly does not provide a complete answer to problems encountered in this area, but it might be part of the answer. Legislators should even find in this practice some good ideas for the future.

Bibliography

Bellivier, F. and Noiville, C. (2004),'The commercialisation of human biomaterials: what are the rights of donors of biological material?', *Journal of International Biotechnolgy Law* 3 (1), 89 et seq.

— (2005), 'La circulation du vivant humain: modèle de la propriété ou modèle du contrat?', in Revet, T. (ed.), *Code civil et modèles. Des modèles du Code au Code comme modèle. Bibliothèque de l'Institut André Tunc* (Paris: Presses de la Sorbonne), 101 et seq.

— (2006), *Contrats et vivant. Le droit de la circulation des ressources biologiques* (Paris: LGDJ).

— (2007), 'Contribution des associations de patients à l'organisation, au fonctionnement et à la réglementation des collections d'échantillons biologiques', *Revue d'économie industrielle*, no 120, 175 et seq.

Bellivier, F. and Noiville, C. (Dir.) (2009a), *La bioéquité*, batailles autour du partage du vivant, *Autrement*, série Frontières (Paris).

Bellivier, F. and Noiville, C. (2009b), *Les biobanques, Que sais-je ?* (Paris: PUF).

French Ethical Committee (CCNE) (2006), Commercialisation des cellules souches humaines et autres lignées cellulaires. No. 93 (Paris).

Noiville, C. (2005), 'Partage des biotechnologies: le contrat comme avant-garde', *Médecine-Sciences* 11, 21–5.

Chapter 11

The Model of Trust

Caroline Mullen

Charitable trust is gaining attention as a model for the control and management of collections of human tissue and associated information, for use in biomedical research. The case for charitable trust has been made by Winickoff and Winickoff (2003), who raise concerns about the practice of academic medical centers supplying donated tissue samples to biobanks managed on a for-profit commercial basis. Further the model has been implemented by UK Biobank, which is a charitable company intending to create a research resource involving samples, along with information on lifestyle, environmental and medical history, from 500,000 people (see UK Biobank and UK Biobank Ethics and Governance Council 2006, 3). Briefly, the trust model involves people donating samples and information, along with property rights over the donation, to the trust organization (UK Biobank Ethics and Governance Council 2006, 6). The trust will control the donations, and the use of the donations, in accordance with principles which are designed to be in the interests of the public (see Winickoff and Winickoff 2003, 1182). This chapter assesses the plausibility of the trust model as a means of adequately responding to ethical considerations associated with biobanks. I argue that the structure of the trust model means that it has the capacity to address ethical issues which could not be sufficiently accommodated by for-profit commercial management of biobanks. However, the trust model is not the only approach with the potential to overcome problems faced by such commercial control, and public control of biobanks might offer a similar capacity to resolve ethical concerns. Moreover, while a model of trust has the capacity to meet ethical standards, there is a further question of whether any given trust will do so in practice. Given this uncertainty, there is a societal responsibility to check the practice of trusts, and, if necessary, to take on the burden of ensuring that biobanks meet ethical requirements.

Biobank Ethics

Biobanks face ethical questions from a number of directions, and the system by which a biobank is controlled will be a major factor influencing its ability to adequately address those questions. Winickoff and Winickoff (2003, 1180) describe their increasing value in biomedical research; for instance, biobanks are being created within the UK with aims of facilitating research on multiple sclerosis[1] and on cancer.[2] UK Biobank is especially ambitious, as is shown in the description by the UK Biobank Ethics and Governance Council:

> Scientists have known for many years that our risks of developing different diseases are due to the complex combination of different factors: our lifestyle and environment; our personal susceptibility (genes); and the play of chance (luck). Because UK Biobank will involve thousands of people who develop any particular disease, it will be able to show more reliably than ever before why some people develop that disease while others do not. This should help to find new ways to prevent death and disability from many different conditions. (2006, 3)

Biobanks have value in their potential for helping in the development of treatment for serious and life threatening illness and disease; however, as Levitt (2005, 79) has argued, they will be subject to ethical questions on whether the research that they do facilitate is research that should be given priority given other demands on resources for health. These questions will concern the research that is conducted using the resource in the biobank, and the opportunity cost of developing the biobank itself. Biobanks also face particular ethical questions regarding concern for the interests and respect for the autonomy of donors. One concern, noted by the UK Biobank Ethics and Governance Council (2006, 6), is that the function of biobanks, as a resource for future research, makes it difficult to define the use to which samples and information may be put, so effectively ruling out the possibility of gaining donor consent for specific use. A further issue is described by Laurie et al.: 'The value of databases derives from the collective nature of their data. Often, the prospect of direct individual benefit is minimal. Thus, the justification for a database is more likely to be grounded in communal value, and less on individual gain' (2003, 7).

People donating samples and providing information to biobanks should not expect to receive direct personal gain from their donation, and this fact will impact on considerations of the defensibility of asking people to accept what is, at best, inconvenience and, at worst, personal risk associated with participation in the biobank. Moreover, the personal risks may not be insignificant; both the WHO Advisory Committee on World Health (2002, 124) and the (UK) Parliamentary Office of Science and Technology (2002, 3) note that samples which include genetic or other personal information which is not irreversibly anonymized,[3] create the potential for later discriminatory treatment from insurers or employers and might have value for the police.

---

1   UK Multiple Sclerosis Tissue Bank (webpage), accessed 24 May 2009.
2   See Cancer Research UK (webpage), accessed 24 May 2009.
3   As will be the case with UK Biobank (see UK Biobank Ethics and Governance Council 2006, 6).

The questions for this chapter concern the extent to which the trust model can adequately address the ethical issues surrounding research priorities and resource use, while defensibly protecting the interests and autonomy of donors to the biobank. Does trust have ethical potential which makes it preferable to profit driven commercial approaches to control and management of biobanks? These questions cannot be separated from the ethical questions of how the value of different research priorities should be judged, how limited resources for health should be used, and what protection of interests and autonomy donors should receive.

Donor Interests and the Tendency Case for Trust

In making the case for the trust model, Winickoff and Winickoff (2003) argue that this approach is better placed than for-profit commercial control in avoiding what they maintain to be indefensible ethical practices and meeting ethical requirements for biobanks. They point to the fact that uncertainty about future research involving biobank samples means that it is not feasible (or perhaps even possible) to obtain donor consent for specific uses of a sample, and this, they argue, presents difficulty in meeting ethical requirements for informed consent. However they suggest this difficulty might be sufficiently addressed if there is an ethics review of any research involving biobank samples, and if there are 'clearly stated time limits for the project, an absolute right of withdrawal, disclosure of details about commercial arrangements, and provision of information about subsequent contact' (2003, 1180).

In this respect it is observation from current practice that prompts Winickoff and Winickoff's objection to profit-driven commercial control of biobanks which have been supplied with samples collected by academic medical centers. They note that in some cases, commercial biobanks have failed to implement sufficiently rigorous ethical review (2003, 1181), that the information provided on donor consent forms has been misleading (falsely suggesting that samples have no market value [2003, 1180]), and that commercial biobanks have been given permission to use samples without time limits (2003, 1181). However, it is not clear that these observations make a strong case for trust even if we accept the ethical indefensibility of these practices and further accept that protection for donor interests requires ethical review of research, right of withdrawal, time limits and supply of information. There is no apparent reason to suggest that a trust could not meet these ethical requirements, but similarly it is not clear that strong (and well enforced), regulation for all commercial biobanks could not also overcome ethical problems described by Winickoff and Winickoff. The advantage for trust in this case is simply that it will not be subject to the commercial pressures to make profit which might motivate disregard for ethical standards.

Issues of consent are complicated by the fact that donors cannot expect that research facilitated by the biobank will be of direct benefit to them. The UK

Biobank Ethics and Governance Council describe donation as '[a]n opportunity to contribute to a resource that may, in the long term, help enhance other people's health' (2006, 6).

Since donation involves inconvenience and possibly risk to the donor, there is some question about the legitimacy of asking for donations. The HUGO Ethics Committee has stated the relevance of considering '[c]ompensatory justice: meaning that the individual, group, or community, should receive recompense in return for contribution' (2000, Section E. Justice).

A controversial response to this consideration, and one that might sit more easily with for-profit commercial approaches than with charitable trusts, is the suggestion of direct payment to donors.[4] If it is argued that direct payment is unacceptable, then arrangements to provide the donor group with other benefits might satisfy requirements for compensatory justice. The HUGO Ethics Committee suggest benefits 'such as medical care, technology transfer, or contribution to the local community infrastructure (e.g., schools, libraries, sports, clean water, ...) could be provided' (2000, Section G. Benefit-Sharing).

Winickoff and Winickoff (2003, 1182) raise further doubts about some commercial practice with respect to compensatory justice, citing instances of community discontent with benefits offered by companies wishing to set up biobanks using donations from that community. Again it may be possible to point to cases where companies have acted in an overtly ungenerous manner, and it is plausible to suggest that for companies whose purpose is profit, there are tensions which pull against fair provision of benefits to the donating community. On the other hand, a trust is not subject to commercial considerations in the same way, and as Winickoff and Winickoff (2003, 1183) suggest, its responsibility to determine how the collection is used could include responsibility to assess benefits to the public.

The legitimacy of asking people to donate to biobanks and the motivation that people have in donating need not solely rely on forms of direct compensation. If biobanks facilitate biomedical research which could 'enhance other people's health' (UK Biobank Ethics and Governance Council 2006, 6), then they are contributing to a development which has the moral value of promoting people's interests in good health. It might be argued that people would be motivated to donate to biobanks because they recognize the moral value of their actions.[5] However, the force of the moral reason to donate will depend on moral assessment of the value of the biobank: in other words, are people asked to donate to something that is not only morally valuable (in virtue of its part in providing means for protecting people's

---

4   For instance, the HUGO Ethics Committee states that there should not be any financial gain from participation in genetic research. This does not exclude, however, the possibility of reimbursement for an individual's time, inconvenience and expenses (if any) (2000, Section G. Benefit-Sharing).

5   Harris (2005) has argued that participation in medical research could be understood in a stronger sense as an obligation.

health), but is as morally valuable as it could be? As has been mentioned above, substantial ethical questions surround the priorities of research using samples stored in biobanks and the relative (ethical) value of the research facilitated by the biobank when compared to the opportunity cost of the resources devoted to the biobank. This raises questions of what constitutes defensible research priorities, how should these priorities be determined and how we should assess the opportunity cost of a biobank.

The Good of Biobanks

On questions of the good of biobanks, profit-motivated commercial approaches might claim what seems, initially, at least, to be an ethically plausible response. With a for-profit commercial approach, the idea is that it is potential research beneficiaries (that is, people who would benefit from development of treatments) who decide what research should be conducted. In deciding how much they are willing to pay for research (or more probably for treatment resulting from research), the beneficiaries determine for themselves the value of research or treatment in comparison to the other benefits that they could have obtained for the price of the treatment.[6] However, while this approach has the attraction of apparently showing respect for people's own judgments of value of research, it faces the (perhaps obvious) objection that people would only be able to benefit from research if they happen to be wealthy enough to pay. It cannot reasonably be maintained that people without wealth value treatment (and so their health or life) any less than those who are wealthy.[7] As Dworkin (2000, Chapters 2 and 8) argues, under conditions where some people are less able to pay, leaving questions of research priorities and determination of opportunity cost to a profit-driven commercial system is to accept – and sustain – a system which fails to show equal concern for each person. Thus it fails to treat them 'as people who matter and hence matter equally' (Harris 1997). It is possible that a commercial biobank would happen to facilitate research likely to result in treatment meeting health needs and being affordable for those who need it; however, such an outcome would be a matter of luck rather than design. Where there are significant inequalities in wealth, or in need for treatment, it is doubtful that this outcome would occur.

Responsibility and Purpose

Perhaps there could be an attempt to save the profit-motivated commercial approach from this objection by looking to the moral sensitivity of companies.

---

6 This description is adapted from the account of the market given by Anderson (1988, 55).

7 An argument made by Dworkin (2000, Chapter 8) and Williams (1988, 111).

Realizing that people were suffering from conditions for which they could not afford to cover costs for treatment, companies might beneficently decide to reduce their costs. While it could be supposed that companies might take this sort of generous decision, it is not clear that a profit-driven commercial approach can be justified on the basis that it provides this possibility. The problem is that companies may decide not to reduce their costs, and if that happens, then people who need, but can not afford treatment, will remain untreated; therefore, it would appear that the objection remains. Nevertheless, it might be argued that if companies do not reduce their costs, then the relevant moral judgment would be a judgment of their particular actions; it would not amount to a reason to judge the commercial approach in principle. The first difficulty for this suggestion is that it may not be reasonable to expect profit-motivated commercial companies to take on the burden of reducing research costs. They may fail to reduce their costs either because they simply choose not to, or because to do so would place a significant burden on them; for instance a company may not have the finances to cover research costs itself. Perhaps it could be argued that in this case, no one has responsibility to help, and that while it is unfortunate that people will not receive treatment that they need, there is no wrong committed by their not receiving treatment. However, this argument would only be plausible if there were no means to provide the treatment other than for the companies to reduce their costs. Similarly, even where it is reasonable to hold a company responsible, any claim that it is *only* the company who has responsibility for developing treatment is implausible, given the existence of alternatives to the profit-motivated commercial system.

In assisting with research prioritized on the basis of people's needs rather than on what they can afford to pay, the model of trust offers some promise. Unlike for-profit commercial companies, the trust has a primary purpose in using its resources for the public interest – so it can aim to show equal concern. The trust has the possibility of considering what research priorities would help to meet the health needs of all who require treatment and of working out how, given the possibilities available, the samples donated can best be used to meet those needs. The trust only manages samples and does not actually conduct research and development; however it is a resource which can contribute to providing healthcare according to need. As Winickoff and Winickoff (2003, 1183) suggest, it has the capacity to make its resource available (perhaps at minimal or no cost)[8] for research which holds the prospect of meeting public need. It can insist on data sharing, when and if there are reasons to suggest that this will help in the development of necessary and affordable treatments.[9] Therefore, in the sense that it can plan according to

---

8   UK Biobank Ethics and Governance Council (2006, 15) suggest the possibility of varying fees according to expected financial gains from research using the biobank resource.

9   Chokshi et al. (2006) make the point that consideration needs to be given to the question of whether or how data sharing will increase the availability of treatment for those who require it most.

need, and in the extent to which it has power to provide for people's needs, the trust has the potential to help to prevent conditions in which some people are unable to receive treatment simply because they cannot afford to pay for it.

Funds

As the aim and responsibility of a trust can be focused on protection of donor interests and facilitating research that meets health need regardless of ability to pay, the trust has an appeal over a commercial approach that will tend (not unreasonably) to have interests which conflict with ethical requirements. However, the non-profit aims of a trust, in turn raises questions about the viability of this approach. Winickoff and Winickoff suggest '[a] clear advantage of private biobanks is that they can quickly attract large amounts of venture capital. Raising the necessary finds for proper administration of a charitable trust would be a great but surmountable challenge' (2003, 1183).

Private donations, charities and public bodies are all candidate sources of funding for a trust.[10] The difficulty for a trust is that it cannot appeal to the self-interest of funders in the way that is open to a commercial enterprise although it can appeal to funders' moral sense – perhaps framed in terms of corporate social responsibility (if it seeks donations from companies) or shared aims (if appealing to charity or public bodies). However, the concern is that a trust will be constantly competing with other (potentially) morally valuable works for limited funds.

In light of this concern, there is temptation to suggest that while, other things being equal, trust might be preferred to a commercial approach; in practice it should be accepted that commercial approaches will have greater success in creating biobanks. The argument would be that while the research resource provided by profit-motivated biobanks is less ethically adequate than would be the case with biobanks run on a model of trust, they would be more ethically defensible than simply having fewer or smaller biobanks. Even though profit-motivated commercial biobanks might not contribute to health research that shows equal concern (to that of a trust), if they facilitate any research which results in treatment, then they have achieved something valuable. However, there are a number of objections to this suggestion. First, it might be argued that concerns about inadequate protection of donor autonomy and interests by profit-motivated biobanks are so significant as to outweigh the moral value of the research made possible by the biobanks. Accepting this argument would provide reason to pursue strong and enforced regulation of profit-motivated commercial biobanks; however, it would count against all such commercial biobanks only if regulation could not protect donors. The second objection is similar to the argument of the previous section of this chapter, which claims that it is not sufficient to accept a system that

----

10   For instance, UK Biobank is funded by both charity and public bodies (see UK Biobank Ethics and Governance Council 2006, 3).

does not show equal concern. If too little funding is offered to biobanks which operate on a system that has an aim of facilitating research which will respond to health needs rather than ability to pay, then the case should be made for greater funding rather than for giving up the aim of equal concern. This case is not a matter of asking, and hoping that funders might wish to provide more, but rather is a moral obligation on society to ensure that its systems and institutions do not fail to show equal concern,[11] and if necessary take on the cost of this provision.[12]

Open Questions

The arguments of the previous sections of this chapter maintain that biobanks should be managed in a way that adequately protects donor autonomy and interests and contributes to provision of treatment that shows equal concern for each person. The claim has been that it is probable that commercial biobanks will fail in this provision, and that an approach with a dedicated aim of fulfilling these ethical requirements is better placed to succeed. Charitable trust is an approach that has the capability of taking on this dedicated aim; however it is not the only one. Public management of biobanks also has the potential for the direct focus on fulfilling ethical requirements that appears to be necessary, and this raises the question of whether there is reason to prefer charitable trust to public management. Facts of funding might again seem a relevant aspect in answering this question; in some circumstances necessary funds might be more easily made available to a charitable trust,[13] and in other circumstances it could be a publicly managed biobank that is better able to secure money. If either approach is capable of a focus on meeting ethical requirements, should we chose between a trust or public management simply on the basis of which is more likely to secure funding?

Two related considerations present grounds for caution on the approach of a trust and could lead to preference for public management. The first issue concerns the degree to which any given trust is able to determine its own ethos. In this chapter the model of trust has been assessed according to its capacity to manage biobanks in a way that shows equal concern. Nevertheless, while a trust may have the capacity to aim at equal concern, if it also has independence which allows it to determine its own ethos, then there is a question about whether it will decide to aim at (what could plausibly be described as) equal concern. The model of trust discussed in this chapter has included the provision that the biobank will be run in the interests of the public, and this might reasonably be assumed to

---

11   A point made by Dworkin (2000, 1).

12   Harris (1997) also makes the argument that there is a responsibility on government to provide funds to meet health needs.

13   As has been noted, this could include public money made available to a charitable trust, as in the case of UK Biobank bodies (see UK Biobank Ethics and Governance Council 2006, 3).

rule out management which exhibits stark partiality or prejudice (for instance, management which aims primarily to meet the interests only of a sub-section of the public). However, the 'interests of the public' is a notion which could be interpreted according to a number of value systems, some of which would be in tension with conceptions of equal concern. Therefore, we could imagine a charitable trust having a value system which makes it unwilling to facilitate certain types of research (for instance, research aimed at providing safer contraception) but which can still make the (disputable) claim that it is serving the interests of the public. If equal concern is an aim that biobanks should adopt, then there is reason to be careful about the idea of relying on charitable trusts which have independence in their interpretation of the interests of the public. This would not amount to an objection in conditions where a charitable trust does operate with an aim of equal concern. However, where these conditions are not met by a trust, then, as would be the case if a profit-motivated commercial approach failed to show equal concern – there will be a societal responsibility to provide a system which shows equal concern for the health needs of each person.

The second consideration stems from the recognition that even if there is agreement on an aim of operating in a way that shows equal concern, there remain substantial questions about practice. The difficulty is that equal concern is a concept open not only to theoretical argument,[14] but also to debate on what it would mean for a given theoretical interpretation to be reflected in practice. For instance, there may be questions about how risks to donors (perhaps risks of discrimination) should be compared to what may be only potential benefits to others from research. Moreover, there is likely to be uncertainty over what sorts of research should be facilitated, where it is not possible to conduct all research which would potentially be of benefit (UK Biobank Ethics and Governance Council notes that 'biological samples … are limited and depleteable' [2006, 3]). Similarly, Levitt (2005, 79) has noted that there is potential for debate on whether the resources taken up in a biobank should be used for other purposes. In short, an aim of equal concern can show what is not acceptable practice is; however, it does not give a complete account of what should be done. Uncertainty on how an aim of equal concern should be applied is as much an issue for a biobank run under public management as it is for one run by charitable trust. Given this uncertainty, the justification of the management of any given biobank may depend not only on its accepting an aim of equal concern, but also on its having reasonable arrangements for deliberations resulting in decisions which are defensible interpretation of the aim of equal concern (albeit that they may be decisions which remain open to debate). Again, if the management of a given biobank is unable to come to defensible decisions, then there is a societal responsibility to intervene to and provide for people's needs.

---

14   For instance, see Dworkin's own discussion on whether equal concern should be understood as equality of welfare or equality of resources (2000, Chapters 1 and 2) and the difference between Dworkin and Cohen (1989).

Conclusion

The discussion of this chapter suggests greater confidence in the model of trust rather than a profit-motivated commercial approach as a form of management with the capacity to meet ethical standards for biobanks. However, there remains a societal responsibility to check that aims of equal concern are adopted, and defensibly interpreted, by trusts that manage biobanks. If these aims are not met by a trust, then there is societal responsibility to provide a system which does show equal concern.

Bibliography

Anderson, E.S. (1988), 'Values, Risks, and Market Norms', *Philosophy and Public Affairs* 17 (1), 54–65.

Cancer Research UK, 'Hertfordshire set to house world-class cancer tissue bank', *News Archive 04 June 2007,* http://info.cancerresearchuk.org/news/newsarchive/2007/june/18167883, accessed 24 May 2009.

Chokshi, D.A., Parker, M. and Kwiatkowski, P.K. (2006), 'Data sharing and intellectual property in a genomic epidemiology network: policies for large-scale research collaboration', *Bulletin of the World Health Organization* 84 (5). http://www.scielosp.org/scielo.php?script=sci_arttext&pid=S0042-862006000500018, accessed 24 May 2009.

Cohen, G.A. (1989), 'On the currency of egalitarian justice', *Ethics* 99, 906–44.

Dworkin, R. (2000), *Sovereign Virtue: the Theory and Practice of Equality* (Cambridge: Harvard University Press) .

Harris, J. (1997), 'The rationing debate: maximising the health of the whole community. The case against: what the principal objective of the NHS should really be', *British Medical Journal* 314, 669. http://www.bmj.com/cgi/content/full/314/7081/669?ijkey=f62f7dd8e55161247d6dbf62f91d7abf6d96e7a1&keytype2=tf_ipsecsha, accessed 24 May 2009.

—— (2005), 'Scientific Research is a Moral Duty', *Journal of Medical Ethics* 31, 242–8.

Human Genome Organisation (HUGO) Ethics Committee (2000), *Statement on Benefit Sharing,* http://www.eubios.info/BENSHARE.htm, accessed 24 May 2009.

Knoppers, B.M. and Chadwick, R. (2005), 'Human genetic research: emerging trends in ethics', *Nature Reviews Genetics* 6, 75–9.

Laurie, G. et al. (2003), *Genetic databases. Assessing the benefits and the impact on human and patient rights* (European Partnership on Patients' Rights and Citizens' Empowerment, A network of the World Health Organisation Regional Office for Europe).

Levitt, M. (2005), 'UK Biobank: a model for public engagement?', *Genomics, Policy and Society* 1 (3), 70–81.

Parliamentary Office of Science and Technology (2002), 'The UK Biobank', *Postnote* 2 http://www.parliament.uk/documents/upload/POSTpn235.pdf , accessed 24 May 2009.

UK Biobank, http://www.ukbiobank.ac.uk/about/what.php, accessed 24 May 2009.

UK Biobank Ethics and Governance Council (2006), *UK Biobank Ethics and Governance Framework.* Version 2.0 July 2006, www.ukbiobank.ac.uk/docs/ EGF_Version2_July%2006%20most%20uptodate.pdf, accessed 24May 2009.

UK Multiple Sclerosis Tissue Bank http://www.ukmstissuebank.imperial.ac.uk, accessed 24 May 2009.

WHO Advisory Committee on World Health (2002), *Genomics and World Health* (World Health Organization).

Williams, A. (1988), 'Ethics and efficiency in the provision of health care', in Bell, J.M. and Mendus, S. (eds) (1988), *Philosophy and Medical Welfare* (Cambridge: Cambridge University Press), 111–26.

Winickoff, D.E. and Winickoff, R.N. (2003), 'The charitable trust as a model for genomic biobanks', *The New England Journal of Medicine* 349 (12), 1180–84.

Chapter 12

Moore's Law and the Taxman: Some Theses on the Regulation of Property in Human Tissue

Jasper A. Bovenberg

'All precious matter is priceless'

The Double Standard

The case of *Moore v. the Regents of the University of California.* The researcher Dr Golde excised cells from one of his patients (John Moore). He developed and patented a cell line out of them (the 'Mo cell-line'). John Moore found this out (after ten years of repeat visits). He sued Dr Golde (et al.) and claimed a property right in his excised cells to share in the profits.

The California Supreme Court denied Moore a property right in his excised cells. He argued as follows: the goal and the result of the research were to produce lymphokines, a group of proteins which, unlike a name or a face, has the same molecular structure and function in every human being. The particular genetic material which is responsible for the natural production of lymphokines is:

- also the same in every person
- is no more unique to Moore than the number of vertebrae in the spine or the chemical formula of haemoglobin.

Moore's cells only were unique insofar as they overproduced lymphokines because of an infection with the human T-cell leukemia virus type II (HTLV-II).

Thirteen years later *Moore* was revisited. Dan and Debbie Greenberg had a son with a fatal disorder (Canavan disease). They collected worldwide body tissue and genetic data, and they provided the tissue collection, data and funding to Dr Rueben Matalon, who isolated the Canavan gene. He then moved to the Miami Children's Hospital. The hospital filed for a patent for the genetic sequence and related applications. It began negotiating exclusive licensing agreements and charging royalty fees. Dan and Debbie Greenberg filed suit.

The Florida court upheld *Moore (Greenberg v. Miami Children's Hospital)* with the following arguments:

- There is no property interest in body tissue and genetic information voluntarily given to the researchers.
- Donations were made for research without any contemporaneous expectations of return.
- The researchers had invested significant amounts of time and money in research with no guarantee of success and were thus entitled to seek reimbursement.

However, the same could be said of patients and tissue donors. A claim for *unjust enrichment* was upheld.

Another recent case is *The Washington University v. Dr W. Catalona et al.* (March 31, 2006). Catalona was a prostate surgeon employed by WU. He built up a biorepositroy for prostate cancer tissue and then moved to Northwestern. Catalona asked research participants to direct their material to him. WU filed an action for a declaratory judgment to establish ownership in the tissue contained in the biorepository. The Missouri district court said WU had possession and asserted ownership because the donation was a gift *inter vivos*. The court followed *Moore* and *Greenberg*.

The *Catalona* court policy arguments can be summarized as following:

- The use of tissue in research collections cannot be left to the whims of a research participant.
- Allowing a donor to choose who can have his sample is tantamount to a blood donor dictating that his blood can only be transfused into a person of a certain ethnic group.
- Selling excised tissue on eBay would become just as commonplace as selling your old TV on eBay.

From this logic, law allows researchers to capitalize their efforts; but law denies donors of biological materials the right to compensation for their contributions.

Criticism of the Double Standard

Moore, Canavan and *Catalona* have/will me(e)t with extensive criticism. Principles of fairness, equity and distributive justice can be named:

- For all his expertise, Dr Golde could not have produced the 'Mo cell-line' out of thin air.
- Patients contribute to the research enterprise.
- Their investments are wholly appropriated by firms or universities.
- They are appropriated with no commitment to share profits equitably or to return to those patients something of value that they can both access and afford.

But patients' contributions are no longer minimal, let alone undetectable. Patient groups have become key players in the promotion, facilitation and acceleration of studies of the causal role of genetics in diseases. The Greenbergs had located other Canavan families and convinced them to provide tissue (for example, blood, urine and autopsy samples) and financial support. Research participants make substantive contributions to the direction and performance of research. Sharon Terry, mother of two children with connective tissue disease (pseudoxanthoma elasticum, PXE), became the first lay person mentioned as a co-inventor on a gene patent.

The argument that benefits may become available in the long run ignores the fact that:

- In the long run we are all dead.
- These benefits may not be accessible or affordable to those who contributed time and cells and/or tissue (IVF-treatment).
- Legislatures and funding agencies order academic institutions to maximize valorization.
- The resultant IP (intellectual property) rights may diminish public access to diagnostics and therapeutics
- …without imposing legal obligations to share profits.

Biomedical researchers depend heavily on the long-term participation and cooperation of cell and tissue donors. The tension over property rights to donated biological materials compromises this relationship. The double standard is a possible source of public *mistrust* in the biomedical research enterprise. As they become more aware of their position as stakeholders in the collaborative research enterprise, donors of cells and tissues are increasingly abandoning altruistic participation and claiming a benefit-share in exchange for their contributions.

Alternative Models

The double standard of Moore's law demands the creation of an alternative *benefit-sharing* model. Four models shall be discussed:

- Contract model.
- Charitable trust model.
- Non-market compensation model.
- Global public good model.

Contract Model

This model is rooted in the notion of autonomy and the related requirement that a person's tissue cannot be removed and subsequently used unless he has given his prior, free and informed consent. The requirement of informed consent provides the tissue source with a trump card to negotiate acceptable benefit terms on which researchers may use the tissue concerned. But the model is problematic insofar as:

- It is unlikely to work for individual patients.
- There is a lack of collective bargaining power.
- Patients may have no energy or knowledge to negotiate with their physician at their bedside over a share in any benefits accruing from the use of their excised tissue.
- It may not work either for large groups, such as those represented in a national collection of newborn screening cards. Although the size of these groups suggests significant collective bargaining power, their genetic and phenotypic heterogeneity is likely to trigger many conflicts of interest and may be prohibitive to effective bargaining.

The model is reduced to practice by disease-communities, such as PXE International. Under the PXE contract the foundation retains:

- ownership rights in any patent application arising from the research, including a profit share in any revenue generated by such invention;
- a right of control ensuring broad and affordable availability of genetic tests;
- and a right to influence future licensing of the IP.

There is a devil's dilemma: IP rights retained by one group may put it in a position to abuse its monopoly by furthering its own interests at the expense of patients suffering from other diseases. For instance, there is evidence that the gene associated with PXE might also play a role in the development of hypertension. PXE has a conflict of interest: should it negotiate the most lucrative license possible to further research on PXE? Or should it worry about the speed of development of treatments for hypertension patients? As PXE put it, PXE International could 'make a killing because who cares if we're making the costs of cardiovascular treatment huge'.

Charitable Trust Model

According to this model, the donor would transfer his property interest to a charitable trust. Tissue donors would collectively appoint a trustee, who would have legal fiduciary duties to keep or use the property for the benefit of the general public. The terms of the trust agreement could allow the donor group to participate in the governance of the trust and thus have a say in the sharing of the benefits. Applications for permission to do research on the collection could be evaluated by the trustees according to a set of criteria that would ensure benefits to the public. The charitable trust model could apply trans-nationally or even globally. Its drawbacks are

- Human body part commoditization is constituted.
- The model works only if the trust is entirely funded on a public basis.
- In the case of the public-private partnership set up to establish the Estonian Gene Bank, for example, the insistence of the original private investors on making additional funding conditional on limiting the scope of the biobank to focus on research into two specific diseases presented a serious problem.

Notably, one of the few publicly funded initiatives worldwide, the UK Biobank, has explicitly renounced the idea of rewarding participants with a financial benefit share, as the benefit is deemed to lie in the bank itself. Any financial income will simply be reinvested in the resource.

Non-market Compensation Model

Following this model, the compensation of tissue donors should only be due in rare cases where their tissue has actually been commercially valuable. Researchers and institutions can freely use any tissue without the obligation to obtain any property rights or to negotiate in advance over a share in future benefits, provided the tissue has been obtained with adequate informed consent. If their research activities result in the sale of marketable products, they are under a legal obligation to report and pay for significant uses. In this case, the fair market value of the tissue is to be determined by a compensation tribunal, using statutory evaluation standards. The original tissue contributor could be traced by obliging patent applicants or those applying for marketing authorization to identify any tissue sample that bears a significant relationship to the claimed invention or the product concerned. If tracking fails or the contributor does not claim his share, the company would be required to pay the adjudicated sum into a charity fund.

This model is still hypothetical. Its obvious drawback is that it is complicated and needs costly implementation. It requires detailed statutory provisions and the establishment of a new administrative agency. Finally, its outcome seems rather unpredictable, and potentially it may hamper research and commercial development.

Global Public Good Model

Here the underlying premise is that we all share the same genome, a common heritage of humankind. Health benefits arising from research advances associated with the human genome should be available to all, although researchers, institutions and commercial entities have a right to a fair return for intellectual and financial contributions to databases.

Forms of benefit-sharing could be:

- special assistance to the persons and groups that took part in the research;
- access to medical care;
- provision of new diagnostics and facilities for new treatments or drugs stemming from the research;
- the development and strengthening of the capacity of developing countries.

For instance, the Human Genome Organisation (HUGO) has recommended that profit-making entities dedicate a percentage (that is, 1–3 percent) of their annual net profit to healthcare infrastructure and/or to humanitarian efforts

Problems associated with the global public good model are that it fails to indicate to whom the proposed benefits, such as access to medicines and the building of healthcare infrastructure, will be distributed, how they will be realized and how the associated costs are to be apportioned between researchers and tissue sources. The HUGO 3 percent proposal bears an arbitrary element as

- the dedication of profits may be self-serving;
- it is not subject to the tissue source, so that there is much less democratic control;
- compliance seems hard to monitor.

Drawbacks of All Models

A central feature of most benefit-sharing models is that they seek to secure for the individual (for example, John Moore) or the disease group concerned (for example, PXE International) a portion of the financial benefits of an invention based on tissues originating from these sources. Is it truly equitable, however, for an individual or a group to enjoy a windfall simply because he/she/it happens to have tissue that is valuable to researchers? The counter-argument is that the individuals/groups concerned can hardly be called lucky and are more deserving of an appropriate reward for their hardship and valuable contributions than those who would otherwise have a free ride on their genetic bad luck. Moreover, if people can freely exploit their natural endowments, such as natural beauty, talent or scientific genius, then why not their genes and tissues?

On the other hand, the global public good model implies that any benefits from mining the human genome should be shared equally with all. Limiting returns to only those who have specific mutations or participated in the research could create divisiveness within groups and is inconsistent with the principle of solidarity implied in the common heritage principle. In addition, as the court in *Moore* considered, the particular genetic material that is responsible for the natural production of certain valuable biological products 'is also the same in every person; it is no more unique to Moore than the number of vertebrae in the spine or the chemical formula of hemoglobin'.

The Taxman

There is an alternative solution to remedy the double standard: the Taxman. Taxation is an effective, if indirect, mechanism for letting a community share in the benefits resulting from the efforts of the taxpayer concerned. Compared with most of the other benefit-sharing models, the advantages of using the tax system to return benefits to donors are numerous:

- It is enforceable and collectible in many countries.
- It applies regardless of whether people have specific genes and whether or not their tissue was involved in the R&D leading to the diagnostics or therapeutics concerned.
- It preserves existing incentives, such as patents, to move basic research from the bench to the market place.
- It does not involve endless negotiations over the sharing of uncertain future benefits.
- It avoids speculation over relative contributions of specific tissue to the end-product.
- It is only due when an actual profit is made, implying that the underlying invention has actually been patented and an actual product was made and sold, at a profit.
- Unlike direct compensation schemes, it does not exert undue influence on individuals or groups to donate or sell tissue or to participate in research.
- Instead of being arbitrary, the levy of a tax, the tax base, the tax rate and its collection and redistribution are subject to democratic control; there is no taxation without representation.
- The proceeds could be earmarked to sustain, for example, government subsidies of affordable healthcare insurance.

Taxation could take many forms:

- Current corporate income tax already acts to redistribute the corporate fortunes resulting from investments in biomedical research.
- The sale of the 'Mo cell-line' may be subject to a sales tax. Notably, this fact is almost always overlooked in the debate over the inequity of the double standard.
- These types of taxation do not, by definition, constitute payment for the taking of freely donated human tissues or cells.

Thus, it may be appropriate to design a special tax specific for tissue and cell products that have been directly developed from human sources.

The global public good model suggests an analogy with the special taxation of other natural resources. Various states have imposed a tax on the removal of deep seabed minerals, which have been declared the common heritage of mankind under the United Nations Convention on the Law of the Seas. The US Deep Seabed Hard Mineral Resources Act of 1980 imposed a tax on any removal of a hard mineral resource from the deep seabed pursuant to a deep seabed permit. The tax would be in addition to normal corporate taxes. The act also established a Trust Fund in the US Treasury. The amounts in the Trust Fund were to be available for purposes of the sharing among nations of the revenues from deep seabed mining.

A similar tax has also been adopted for the mining of minerals on national territory. The Dutch state levies a 'state-profit-share' on anyone who has been granted a license to mine minerals, oil or natural gas on Netherlands territory, onshore or offshore. The state-profit-share rests on the logic that:

- the natural resources concerned are state property and thus belong to the Dutch people;
- in exchange for receiving an exclusive license to mine those resources, the licensee must pay an appropriate fee to the state.

The state-profit-share applies only to the net annual profit that is generated by the licensed activities. The proceeds go to the Treasury and can be used for public expenditures, subject to democratic control.

A tissue tax would rest on the logic that the human genome, and, by extension human tissues and cells, constitute a natural resource. It could be levied on profits made on the basis of an exclusive license to mine a specific part of the human genome (for example, a gene patent), that is, on profits from a biological product directly developed from human sources. To avoid any difficulties in its implementation, the precise tax base, the proper tax rate and the design of possible exemptions clearly need further exploration.

If the direct compensation for donation is undesirable or impracticable, and if today's biomedical research is indeed a collaborative research enterprise, then taxation of the use of raw materials by this approach should be investigated.

Chapter 13

An Investigation of the Conception, Management and Regulation of Tangible and Intangible Property in Human Tissue: the PropEur Project

Caroline Mullen and Heather Widdows

This chapter outlines and analyzes the key issues of ethics and governance which arise in the context of conceptualizing and regulating human tissue. The chapter draws on the findings of the PropEur Project (Property Regulation in Science, Ethics and Law), a three-year, EC-funded project that finished in February 2007, which examined the political and ethical issues involved in conceiving, managing and regulating tangible and intangible property in four themes, of which human tissue was one. The project addressed the issue by considering the ethical and political implications of a number of differing approaches or models of governance of human tissue, drawn from current practice and from models emerging in the literature and policy debates. This paper describes the models studied in the project, outlining the key ethical issues which arose in the 'human tissue' theme, such as debates on commodification and commercialization, and questions concerning the balancing of the rights of individuals with those of communities and companies. The paper analyzes the political and ethical issues which arose in the project, and considers the emerging trend towards more communal models of governance and the difficulty in implementing such models, with particular reference to the new political and ethical implications arising in the context of governing intangible property.

This chapter is divided into three sections: the first describes the conceptual and scientific questions of the PropEur project, the second the methodology of the project and the processes by which we attempted our task, and the third considers the key political and ethical issues which arose across themes and models.

The Appropriateness and Usefulness of the Concept of Property

The PropEur project addressed cutting edge questions about the ways in which tangible and intangible property in human tissue could and should be managed. These are questions which are pertinent and timely. In a context where actual and potential uses of human tissue in research and medical care continue to generate complex ethical questions, governance decisions are being made which will set the precedents according to which future governance will comply. For instance, the project considered issues of egg donation for use in *in vitro* fertilization (IVF); conditions governing use of tissue, including embryos, in research; requirements of consent in giving tissue for transplant; and governance of the increasing number of both small and large scale biobanks.[1] Despite the fact that in each of these areas governance mechanisms are currently being established, there is little consensus regarding the principles by which tangible and intangible property in human tissue should be owned and managed. A glimpse of this controversy can be seen by sketching just a few examples. There is controversy over the acceptability or defensibility of offering financial benefits to women who provide ova for use either in research or by others in IVF. Areas of contestation include whether or not financial benefits amount to commodification of ova, and, if so, whether commodification is indefensible per se or whether is it only unacceptable if it leads to unacceptable consequences, such as a black market in provision of ova or exploitation of those involved in the exchange.[2] Biobanks have raised numerous issues. For instance, the difficulties of anticipating all future uses of tissue samples given to biobanks have challenged ideas that full information can be provided to donors prior to giving tissue samples, thus promoting reassessment of conceptions of informed consent.[3] Further issues surround the treatment of donors to biobanks run on a commercial basis, including concerns that commercial pressures may lead to donors being given poor information on the value of their donations and concerns about the acceptability of commercial entities asking donors to provide tissue samples for no payment.[4] Broader questions have followed from the consideration that:

> The value of databases derives from the collective nature of their data. Often, the prospect of direct individual benefit is minimal. Thus, the justification for a database is more likely to be grounded in communal value, and less on individual gain. (Laurie et. al. 2003, 7)

---

1 For instance, UK Biobank (webpage), accessed 08 February 2008; Generation Scotland (webpage), accessed 08 February 2008; CARTaGENE (webpage), accessed 08 February 2008; UK Multiple Sclerosis Tissue Bank (webpage), accessed 08 February 2008.

2 See, for instance, Roberts and Throsby 2008, Dickenson 2004, Storrow 2005 and news items such as BBC News Online, 13 September 2007 (webpage), accessed 08 February 2008; Braid, 26 March 2006, Brice, 16 February 2006 (webpage), accessed 08 February 2008.

3 See Knoppers and Chadwick 2005, 75–6.

4 See Winickoff, and Winickoff 2003, Doukas and Berg 2001, Parker and Lucassen 2003.

This understanding has motivated debate on the sufficiency of ethical standards which focus on the interests and autonomy of the individual and on how concern should be shown for interests and needs of wider groups.[5]

These brief examples provide some insight into the confusion surrounding the governance of human tissue. There is little agreement on the nature of property per se, before reaching questions of whether such material and information should be understood as property, and if it is, to whom it belongs. The lack of consensus at the conceptual level became increasingly pronounced through the course of the project as we attempted to address not only conceptual issues but also issues of policy and practice. The project aim then was to confront this uncertainty about how to conceive of, manage, regulate and govern property.

The project focused on two overarching questions – or more accurately groups of questions – the first about the nature of the property (or not) in question and the second about how this property (if this is an appropriate concept) should be governed.

The first questions concerned what property could and should mean in the four areas of the project. Here, the pertinent questions ask whether or not concepts of property are able to accommodate either the physical or the informational nature of human tissue. For example, is property an appropriate concept for governance when considering how to manage and legislate for tissue samples and related information held in a biobank? Or is ownership an applicable concept in relation to the use of embryos for research purposes? Or are ownership rights ascribable – and if so, should this be to groups, individuals or wider society – in such contexts? Such conceptual issues of definition and applicability regarding property, ownership, control and commodification were core themes which ran throughout the project.

The second question, or group of questions, concerned the policy and practical arenas and sought to answer how such intangible and tangible 'property' should be managed and regulated. In order to examine and compare different possible approaches, we used what we loosely termed 'models of governance' as a theoretical tool. By this we meant approaches to governance such as donation, trust, benefit-sharing, commodification, conditional gift and compulsory licensing. This focus on models was not based on any idea that a single model, or combination of models, would embody ideal governance. Rather the approach was taken because the models served as a useful research tool for ethical analysis and because they provided examples of possible structures of governance which could be drawn on in recommendations for policy development. In other words, we were not concerned with what constituted a model – in theory or practice – but rather how we should conceive of, manage and regulate the tangible and intangible property in the four project themes. This broad understanding of the nature of models allowed us to consider the advantages and disadvantages not only of current or easily applicable models (although in fact most of the models we considered were

5   See, for instance, Knoppers and Chadwick 2005.

currently practiced to some extent or were very real possible options) but also more unusual models as they too might have insights or elements that could be adopted in policy and practice.

Project Methodology

The approach PropEur adopted in examining these questions about the nature of property and governance of such property was fundamentally multidisciplinary. The multidisciplinary approach was facilitated by workshops to encourage wide participation. We will now consider this approach – the means by which the questions were considered – looking first at the multidisciplinary approach, then at the project organization and finally at the outcomes of the project.

The project adopted a multidisciplinary approach not as a matter of convenience but as a foundational methodological commitment. This commitment derived from the premise that the types of questions being addressed by the PropEur project encompass areas of ethics, politics, science and law, raising issues of theory, policy and practice. Questions of this scope could not be adequately addressed within one disciplinary framework, nor could useful outcomes be achieved if issues of policy and practical applicability were not taken into account. In short, these questions of the nature and governance of tangible and intangible property were simply too broad for narrow responses. In addition, as discussed elsewhere, national and regional solutions are inadequate for global problems: global problems need global solutions.[6] In order to fulfill this methodological commitment, many disciplines have been represented in the project, including, philosophers, lawyers, social scientists, anthropologists, medics and research scientists. In addition, we included representatives from policy and practice, including members of non-governmental organizations, policy makers from the World Intellectual Property Organization (WIPO), journalists, librarians, judges and representatives from the UK Biobank Ethics and Governance Council.

To affect this multidisciplinary approach we organized the project around workshops as the most effective way of encouraging debate and communication between those from different perspectives. Accordingly, the project was organized around a series of workshops which brought together those from practice, policy and academia in each of the four themes in order to have a representative and multidisciplinary meeting. Workshops took place in all the countries of the project partners. The human genome workshops were held in Cardiff, UK (July 2004) and Bilbao, Spain (December 2005); copyright and the information society were held in Goettingen, Germany (September 2004) and Sofia, Bulgaria (March 2006); plant and animal genomes in relation to biodiversity in Lund, Sweden (December 2004) and Paris, France (May 2006); and human tissue in Tübingen, Germany (January 2005) and Bratislava, Slovakia (June 2006).

---

6   See Widdows 2007.

Models were chosen according to each project theme and with the intention of being the most useful in practice. In relation to the theme of human tissue, the relevant models the project considered were donation, conditional gift, charitable trust, commodification and benefit-sharing. These models have the advantage of being obvious and relatively defined in the literature and used to a greater or lesser extent in practice. For instance, charitable trust has been advocated as a model of governance[7] and is now being implemented in the governance of the UK Biobank.[8] Benefit-sharing also has prominence in relation to biobanks; for instance, The Human Genome Organisation (HUGO) Ethics Committee has made recommendations that benefit-sharing should be considered in genetic research.[9] Further, in relation to transplants and to use of human ova, conceptions of donation and gift are contrasted with commodification.[10]

The project brought these findings together in accessible and useful forms, through the creation of two main documents: a database and a 'guidelines for guidelines' document. The database, which was made widely available as a CD-ROM, includes descriptions of the laws, regulations, guidelines and practices as well as lists of the papers and NGO positions in each of the four project themes. The guidelines for guidelines document is a policy document providing an analysis which can act as a basis for developing policy on property governance in the four areas of the PropEur Project. It describes the models considered by the project and analyzes the key ethical, social and political issues relating to each. In this way it provides a commentary on the current state of play as well as pointing to possible alternative models or additions from these models. The next part of this chapter will draw on the guidelines for guidelines document in presenting an analysis of the ethical and political considerations raised by governance of property in human tissue.

Analysis: Individual and Collective Approaches

As was described earlier, the PropEur project considered the models of donation, conditional gift, commodification, charitable trust and benefit-sharing as approaches to the governance of human tissue. This section briefly summarizes descriptions of the models, setting out the key ethical and political issues and concluding with a few comments on broad themes and ideas that emerged from the research.

---

7   For instance, by Winickoff and Winickoff 2003.

8   UK Biobank (webpage), accessed 8 February 2008, and UK Biobank Ethics and Governance Council 2006, 3.

9   Human Genome Organisation (HUGO) Ethics Committee 2000.

10   On payment for organs, see, for instance, Erin and Harris 2003; on use of ova, see, for instance, Brice (16 February 2006) (webpage) accessed 08 February 2008, Dickenson 2004.

Donation is described as consent to give tissue to be used by another person, without asking for (at least direct) payment in return. The related notion of conditional gift shares the characteristic of consenting to give tissue without asking for payment; however, it allows the donor to attach conditions on its use. These models raise issues relating to the nature and role of consent, dignity, protection of the donor's interests and fairness. One aspect of the issue of consent is the ethical commitment to the donor having the power to decide the use to which their donation is put. Conditional gift appears to privilege the importance of respect for the preferences of the individual over any communal good (including perhaps the health needs of others) that could be gained through use of the tissue. This raises questions of the relative weight that should be given to individual preferences and against the interests of others. The notion of dignity also bears on the question of 'donor' control, albeit in a different sense. For example, some argue that people should not have a property right in their own bodies which would allow them to sell parts of their bodies, since such a property right would amount to treating the body (and by inference, the person) as an object and thus contravene human dignity.[11] This view is in tension with the accepted view that once tissue is donated – that is, separated from the body – it is permissible for researchers (or companies) to benefit commercially from the use of the tissue in research and thus in essence to hold property rights in it.[12] A further consideration concerns how non-payment relates to fairness. Since donation is something that is given without requirement for payment in return, it has been held to be an altruistic act by the donor. However, such altruistic assumptions are being questioned and increasingly the context in which it is reasonable to ask people to behave altruistically is being problematized. For instance, while it might be considered good if people are willing to donate regardless of their own situation, or self-interest, such selflessness might also be thought to be more than it is reasonable to expect. However, in a society where potential donors are themselves shown concern (for instance by protection of a health service which would treat them if necessary), then donation might be understood as showing fair concern to others, in view of the fair concern that the donor receives (cf. Harris 2005; Mullen forthcoming 2009).

Many of the issues relating to commodification correspond to those associated with donation. As mentioned above, there is an argument that to allow people to buy and sell human tissue violates human dignity. Against this is the argument that individuals should be able to make informed decisions about their own lives, which entails the freedom for informed and consenting adults to decide to buy or sell tissue. One objection to this is concern that when tissue is sold, there are often reasons to doubt that the information or consent is adequate.[13] A further concern is

---

11   Wilkinson 2003, 45–7 describes a version of this argument.

12   A point made by Erin and Harris 2003.

13   This point is made by Winickoff and Winickoff 2003 and also by Beauchamp 2003, 272, who notes that where people are in economically weak situations they might

that a market approach would meet only the needs of those who can afford to pay. If moral weight is given to people's health, rather than simply their ability to pay, then the full market model becomes increasingly less ethically acceptable.[14]

There are senses in which the models of benefit-sharing and charitable trust can be understood as responding to these concerns raised in relation to donation, conditional gift and commodification.[15] Charitable trust, in the context of property in human tissue, involves people donating tissue, either for research or for transplant, to an organization which has responsibility to look after and to use that tissue for agreed purposes. Those purposes might be distribution of tissue for transplant according to need, medical research aimed at meeting particular health needs or as yet undefined research which will be judged as acceptable by the charitable trust body. Benefit-sharing involves a company, or organization, concerned with research and development which involves a wider community (perhaps by using human tissue samples or associated information in research), agreeing to provide the community with some benefit, such as 'medical care, technology transfer, or contribution to the local community infrastructure (e.g., schools, libraries, sports, clean water)' (HUGO Ethics Committee 2000, Section G).

The HUGO Ethics Committee adds a further requirement that 'consultation with individuals and communities and their involvement and participation in the research design is a preliminary basis for the future distribution of benefit and may be considered a benefit in itself' (2000, Section G).

It should be noted that benefit-sharing can work along side the model of charitable trust; that is, there may be provision for benefit-sharing coupled with the use of the donated tissue. However, benefit-sharing may also operate within other approaches to governance, such as commercial approaches.

The model of charitable trust has been promoted by Winickoff and Winickoff (2003) in large part as a direct response to concerns about research involving human tissue which is conducted within a market system. In particular, they express the concern that commercial pressures contribute to conditions in which potential donors are given misleading information, and in which donor interests are not adequately protected (2003, 1180–81). They argue that these concerns would tend to be avoided by a charitable trust, which is less constrained by commercial pressure.

---

make decisions which they later regret. There is a further argument that even if people give well-informed consent to sell tissue, their choice may be one that they should not have to make. This argument applies forcibly in the Third World where organs may be the only economically valuable asset a person has. See Scheper-Hughes 2003.

14   So, for instance while Erin and Harris 2003 argue in favor of some sale of organs, they also argue that the distribution of the organs should be conducted 'according to some fair conception of medical priority'.

15   Issues relating to charitable trust, and to benefit-sharing are discussed in more detail in the later chapter 'The Model of Trust'.

Benefit-sharing might be understood as addressing concerns over the defensibility of asking donors to act selflessly in circumstances where they themselves do not live in a society that shows concern for their needs. In a narrow sense, it might be argued that benefit-sharing would address such concerns in relation to the individual donors, by offering compensation for their donation. However, the HUGO Ethics Committee (2000, Section G. Benefit-Sharing, and Recommendation No. 2) has advocated a broader use for benefit-sharing, in which benefits are provided to the wider community and not solely to those individuals who donate. This understanding of benefit-sharing not only attempts to redress the concerns about individual donors but further asserts the ethical of the needs of all the community's members.[16]

Both charitable trust and benefit-sharing allow the possibility that decisions concerning the use of tissue, that is decisions on research or treatment priorities, can give greater emphasis to meeting need rather than giving emphasis to provision on the basis of ability to pay. In this way, both may be seen as addressing one of the significant objections to commodification and the market model. If such models are to be endorsed, then attention will need to be given as to how to finance research and treatment as critics maintain that the extent of research and treatment will be greater if the incentives of commodification and the market are allowed to operate.

Further trust and benefit-sharing also involve the possibility of collective and public deliberation in making decisions how donations should be used: as is noted above, community consultation has been advocated as a necessary aspect of benefit-sharing, and the trust model offers (at least the possibility of decisions) being considered and justified by the members of the trust. This contrasts with the model of conditional gift in which decisions on how tissue should be used are primarily determined by the donor. In this way, trust and benefit may answer concerns about too great a weight being placed on the preferences of individuals. However, they in turn stand open to objections that the individual should decide what becomes of their tissue.

Concluding Comments

The analysis of the approaches to governance reveals a broad division between approaches which emphasize the decisions and choices of the individual – including conditional gift, some approaches to donation and commodification – and those models which take account of the interests and the reasoning of wider groups – including benefit-sharing and trust. As outlined in the previous discussion, criticisms can be leveled at either group of approaches. In some cases the questions

---

16   This interpretation gains some weight from the statement that 'limiting the returns to only those who participated could create divisiveness within a group and is inconsistent with solidarity' (HUGO Ethics Committee 2000, Section G).

of how these criticisms can be answered will depend on empirical issues – such as whether commodification really does create conditions in which donor interests are not adequately protected. In other cases the answer will depend on an ethical argument, such as the weight that should be given to individual preferences. What the PropEur project did was to clarify and explore the issues of property in the context of the governance of human tissue, revealing the tensions in the theory and practice of current mechanisms of tissue management. In so doing the project contributes to understanding and debate on policy in governance of property in human tissue and thus informs future decision-making.

List of Project Participants

Lead Partner

Dr Heather Widdows, Centre for the Study of Global Ethics, University of Birmingham
Dr Caroline Mullen, Centre for the Study of Global Ethics, University of Birmingham
Dr Dita Wickins-Drazilova, Centre for the Study of Global Ethics, University of Birmingham

Partners

Prof. Urban Wiesing and Dr Michael Steinmann, Tübingen University, Germany
Dr Peter Sýkora, S. Cyril and Methodius University, Slovakia
Dr Paul Oldham, Lancaster University, UK
Dr Aitziber Emaldi Cirion, Universidad de Deusto, Spain
Dr Itziar Alkorta Idiakez, University of the Basque Country, Spain
Dr Christian Lenk, University of Göttingen, Germany
Dr Krassimir Petkov, University of Sofia, Bulgaria
Prof. Göran Hermerén, Lund University, Sweden
Prof. Christian Byk, International Association of Law, Ethics and Science, France

Bibliography

BBC News Online (13 September 2007), 'Half-price IVF offered for eggs: Women in the north of England are being offered half-price fertility treatment if they donate some of their eggs to medical research' http://news.bbc.co.uk/1/hi/england/6992642.stm, accessed 24 May 2009.
Beauchamp, T.L. (2003), 'Methods and principles in biomedical ethics', *Journal of Medical Ethics* 29, 269–74.

Braid, M. (26 March 2006), 'The donor business: The price of eggs', *Independent*. http://www.independent.co.uk/life-style/health-and-wellbeing/health-news/ the-donor-business-the-price-of-eggs-471426.html, accessed 24 May 2009.

Brice, P. (16 February 2006), 'HFEA favours altruistic egg donation for cloning research', *PHG Foundation.* http://www.phgfoundation.org/news/2291, accessed 24 May 2009.

CARTaGENE, http://www.cartagene.qc.ca/cartagene/index.php?lang=english, accessed 24 May 2009.

Dickenson, D. (2004), 'The threatened trade in human ova', *Nature Reviews Genetics* 5, 167.

Doukas, D.J. and Berg, J.W. (2001), 'The family covenant and genetic testing', *The American Journal of Bioethics* 1(3), 2–16.

Erin, C.A. and Harris, J. (2003), 'An ethical market in human organs', *Journal of Medical Ethics* 29, 137–8.

Generation Scotland, http://129.215.140.49/gs/gindex.html, accessed 24 May 2009.

Harris, J. (2005) 'Scientific research is a moral duty' *Journal of Medical Ethics* 31, 242-8.

Human Genome Organisation (HUGO) Ethics Committee (2000), 'Statement on Benefit Sharing', http://www.eubios.info/BENSHARE.htm, accessed 24 May 2009.

Knoppers, B.M. and Chadwick, R. (2005), 'Human genetic research: emerging trends in ethics', *Nature Reviews Genetics* 6, 75–9.

Laurie, G. et al. (2003), *Genetic databases. Assessing the benefits and the impact on human and patient rights* (European Partnership on Patients' Rights and Citizens' Empowerment, a network of the World Health Organization Regional Office for Europe).

Mullen, C. (2009) 'Decisions, consent and expectations of the individual' in Widdows, H. and Mullen, C. (eds) (forthcoming) *The Governance of Genetic Information: Who Decides?* (Cambridge: Cambridge University Press).

Parker, M. and Lucassen, A. (2003), 'Concern for families and individuals in clinical genetics', *Journal of Medical Ethics* 29, 70–73.

Roberts, C. and Throsby, K. (2008), 'Paid to share: IVF patients, eggs and stem cell research', *Social Science and Medicine* 66 (1), 159–69.

Scheper-Hughes, N. (2003), 'Keeping an eye on the global traffic in human organs', *The Lancet* 361 (9369), 1645–8.

Storrow, R.F. (2005), 'Quests for conception: Fertility tourists, globalization and feminist legal theory', *Hastings Law Journal* 57 (2), 295.

UK Biobank, http://www.ukbiobank.ac.uk/about/what.php, accessed 24 May 2009.

UK Biobank Ethics and Governance Council (2006), *'UK Biobank Ethics and Governance Framework,*Version 2.0, July 2006'. www.ukbiobank.ac.uk/ docs/EGF_Version2_July%2006%20most%20uptodate.pdf, accessed 24 May 2009.

UK Multiple Sclerosis Tissue Bank, http://www.ukmstissuebank.imperial.ac.uk/, accessed 24 May 2009.

Widdows, H. (2007), 'Moral neocolonialism and global ethics', *Bioethics* 21 (6), 305-15.

Widdows, H. (2008), 'Why and what global ethics?', in Wim, M.S. et al. (eds), *Ethics in an Era of Globalisation* (Aldershot: Ashgate).

Wilkinson, S. (2003), *Bodies for Sale: Ethics and Exploitation in the Human Body Trade* (London: Routledge).

Winickoff, D.E. and Winickoff, R.N. (2003), 'The charitable trust as a model for genomic biobanks', *The New England Journal of Medicine* 349 (12), 1180–84.

PART V
The Persisting Challenges of Regulation

Chapter 14

Personal Rights over an Individual's Biological Sample Stored for Research

Aitziber Emaldi-Cirión

Introduction

Genetic research requires the use of biological samples, either from the subjects who undergo the experimentation or from other people who are not part of the experimentation.

The biological samples, which are of human origin and whose use can be relevant, come from the most diverse sources, but a great part come from the everyday acts of ordinary health assistance: surgical remains, birth, abortion and death related products. These materials can either be the result of donations that have been purposely directed to be destined for research or can be the result of any of the aforementioned situations if there has been consent for this purpose.

The fact of having these biological samples available is of the utmost importance as it allows the carrying out of different types of studies, such as clinical or genetic research.

This situation has led to the need to create banks of biological samples in order to carry out new studies.[1] Therefore, urgent measures must be taken in order to store and use the biological sample that has been extracted from the person affected in order to respect the rights that this person has over such sample. Nonetheless, several problems can arise that are usually not foreseen by the regulation on the research and experimentation with human beings or with biological samples of human origin.

Definition of Biological Sample and Biobank

A s*ample* is a 'part or portion extracted from a whole by methods which allow us to consider it as representative of such'.[2]

---

1 Spain. According to Article 2 of Royal Decree 411/1996 of 1 March on the regulation of the activities related to the use of human tissues, a bank of tissues is the technical unit whose mission is to guarantee the quality of the tissue from the moment of obtaining it until its clinical use as autologous or allogeneic grafts.

2 *Spanish Royal Academy Dictionary*, fifth meaning.

Biological sample   In accordance with the International Declaration on Genetic Data of UNESCO of October 2003, *biological sample* is 'any sample of biological material (for example blood, skin and bone cells or blood plasma) in which nucleic acids are present and which contains the characteristic genetic make-up of an individual' (Article 2, Section iv).

Biobanks   A bank (of organs, tumors, cell lines, tissue, gametes, embryos, etc.) is a collection of biological samples that are organized as technical units based on criteria of quality, order and purpose.

One can notice that these banks or biobanks are being established, as the biological samples are being collected and stored in laboratories and hospitals in order to use them in donation, therapy, diagnosis and research.[3] Some of these collections have been the object of legal regulation[4] with the fundamental purpose to guarantee the protection of human health. These set of samples can be of enormous value to the researcher (especially to the geneticist) as they represent the genetic diversity that is the basis of their research.

---

3   The number of stored samples is really high, and that situation is increasing each year. These samples are for the greater part stored in the section of pathologic anatomy, but the most spectacular increase was in the number of samples produced in the ambit of the screening of newborns (National Bioethics Advisory Commission 2000). See Sánchez-Ventura 2003. The author reviews the magnitude of the problem, the diagnostic method and other matters related to the congenital hypothyroidism in neonatal screening, phenylketonuria and cystic fibrosis of the pancreas, in which a high number of blood samples of newborns are stored. In the United Kingdom, 3 million samples are stored annually in the laboratories of pathologic anatomy (Furness 2003). See also other examples in VVAA 1990.

4   Spain. According to Article 2 of Royal Decree 411/1996 of 1 March on the regulation of the activities related to the use of human tissues, a bank of tissues is the technical unit whose mission is to guarantee the quality of the tissue from the moment of obtaining it until its clinical use as autologous or allogeneic grafts. Semen banks shall be established in health centers or health services providers that have as their finality the obtaining, evaluation, conservation and distribution of human semen for its use in the Assisted Reproduction Techniques (Article 3 of the Royal Decree 413/1996 of 1 March, whereby the precise technical and functional requisites are established for the authorization and homologation of the health centers and health services providers related to the techniques of human- assisted reproduction). This Decree establishes the requisites that must be followed as well as those established for embryo banks. Spain. Royal Decree 2070/1999 of 30 December regulated the clinical obtaining and use of human organs for donation and transplantation.Spain. Royal Decree 1854/1993 of 22 October establishes the technical requirements and the minimal conditions for blood donation and blood banks.

Personal Rights over an Individual's Biological Samples Stored in a Biobank for Research

Once the information that can be obtained from a sample is associated with an identifiable person, we shall have to mention the rights available to such person (see Nicolás 2006).

The Right to the Protection of Data

Protection of genetic data Discussion has focused on whether genetic data is different from other health data. Therefore, it requires a specific ethical and legal reflection (this position is known as genetic exceptionalism; see Green and Botkin 2003). As has been said, some characteristics of genetic data are shared by other health data, but what is peculiar is the presence of all of the special notes. This circumstance around the genetic data creates an environment where several different interests are involved. This has real effects, as the need of recommendations in these fields is required. In 2004, the European Commission published a document with 25 recommendations on ethical, legal and social implications of genetic testing, which said that 'genetic exceptionalism' should be avoided, internationally, in the context of the European Union and at the level of its Member States. However, the public perception that genetic testing is different needs to be acknowledged and addressed. All medical data, including genetic data, must satisfy equally high standards of quality and confidentiality'.[5] It is true that the principles seem to be applicable to the conflicts in the field of health information in general (in this sense the ethical and juridical basis of the protection is the same), but those conflicts are different; therefore, a particular projection of the general principles to the problems raised in genetic testing was needed.

This is reflected in the UNESCO International Declaration on Human Genetic Data (2003), which pointed out that human genetic data have a special status because:

1. they can be predictive of genetic predispositions concerning individuals;[6]
2. they may have a significant impact on the family, including offspring;[7]

---

5 Recommendations: http://europa.eu.int/comm/researc/conferences/2004/genetic/pdf/recommendations_en.pdf.

6 In this sense, depending on the disease, this information would allow us to predict the future of the patient. In some instances, the diagnosis can even make reference to mere predispositions to suffer a disease, that may not really develop in the future but that nonetheless will be taken into account as if they were truly going to suffer them, with all that this entails.

7 I mean that genetic testing undertaken on a person will not only provide data of the person affected but also of the rest of the members of his or her biological family. The latter, in turn, have a high probability of having a similar genetic profile and, therefore, of

3. they may contain information the significance of which is not necessarily known at the time of the collection of the biological samples;
4. they may have cultural significance for persons and groups;
5. genetic data remain the same all life long (and after death);
6. they can be obtained from all the cells of the human body (so the parts separated from the body support the information);
7. they can be found unexpectedly;
8. there is a great scientific interest in the study of an individual's genome.

These principles of the UNESCO Declaration are applied to the genetic data, as well as to the proteomic data and to the biological samples. The Declaration encompasses a wide frame of applications, which is suitable to gain an adequate protection of the rights of the subjects. Let us remember that biological samples are a physical documentation of all the genetic information of an individual, which material is not an object of data protection law. Nevertheless, since it is known, the accumulation of biological samples in hospitals and research centers increases dizzily, as well as the scientific interest to accede to that material. The protection that is granted to the genetic information must be spread to the biological samples as a physical document of information.

Secondly, another question that has been debated in different forums is the concept of genetic information regarding its specific protection. In this matter, there are two options. The first one is to restrict the concept to the information obtained from the analysis of nucleid acids. The second one is wider and includes any genetic information obtained from any scientific analysis.

The Declaration has chosen correctly this second notion of protection. Another possibility would be to establish two categories for what in fact is the same information. By using other methods it is possible to come on occasion to the same conclusions as using the analysis of nucleid acids.

As seen from the matters that have been analyzed, genetic information must be regulated under some specific norms of protection in order to avoid abuses and discriminations based on the genetic heritage.

Protection of personal data   Genetic information or biological samples from which information can be taken have to be protected because they are linked to an identifiable person or to recovery unlinked to an identifiable person. (For example, when all identifying information about that person is replaced by a code, that identity could be known by some procedures). The danger for the privacy or for the right to non-discrimination disappears only when the data cannot be linked to an identifiable person through the destruction of the link to any identifying information.

According to Directive on Data Protection:

---

having the same limitations and thereby even be subject to the same type of discrimination (within the work place, with insurance policies, etc.).

[P]ersonal data, are any information relating to an identified or identifiable natural person (data subject); an identifiable person is one who can be identified, directly or indirectly, in particular by reference to an identification number or to one or more factors specific to his physical, physiological, mental, economic, cultural or social identity. (Article 2)

Recital 26 says:

[T]o determine whether a person is identifiable, account should be taken of all the means likely reasonable to be used either by the controller or by any other person to identify the said person: whereas the principles of protection shall not apply to data rendered anonymous in such a way that the data subject is no longer identifiable.

The world 'reasonably' means that 'the level of impossibility of identification is limited to certain degree (the reasonable), although by extraordinary, complex, expensive and other non-reasonable procedures that person could be identified' (Romeo-Casabona 2004).

Following this reasoning, according to the UNESCO Declaration on Human Genetic Data, these categories of data can be distinguished:

* *Data linked to an identifiable person*: data that contain information, such as name, birth data and address, by which the person from whom the data were derived can be identified.
* *Data unlinked to an identifiable person*: data that cannot be linked to an identifiable person, through destruction of the link to any identifying information about the person who provided the sample.
* *Data irretrievably unlinked to an identifiable person*: data that cannot be linked to an identifiable person, through destruction of the link to any identifying information about the person who provided the sample.

A practical consequences of what has been said is, for example, that if a researcher requests genetic data from several clinical records or biological samples and the request is attended after the identities are deleted, the information will turn anonymous for this researcher. But it cannot be assured that the data is not going to be associated with the patient's identities, since the identities are kept in other files. It does not matter who could establish the link between information and individual to consider these data as object of this special protection.

Privacy and Confidentiality

The subject has a right to privacy which is embodied in the duty of confidentiality. Any health professional who has legitimate access to the information must keep it a secret. This right is recognized in domestic laws.[8] Furthermore, the breach of the right to privacy may entail an offence in some countries.[9]

On the one hand, some believe that the subject of the genetic information is not of the individual but the biological family, and that, therefore, the duty of secrecy of genetic information does not apply in relation to the biological family of the patient (Knoppers 1998). According to this position, the biological family is the juridical subject of the genetic information because the genetic characteristics are shared between its members. Following this, the traditional model of privacy in the healthcare system that is based on the extreme individualism of the Western cultures has to be changed (Kegly 1996).

Non-directive genetic counseling is the situation where the physician does not interfere in the individual decisions of the patient and his freedom to make individual decisions. According to the aforementioned position, non-directive genetic counseling is neither ethical nor effective. This is because a family is no purely biological entity, and it is neither a set of separated individuals. To the contrary, the 'genetic family' has to be taken into account in the legal framework. The decisions to be taken in relation to the genetic information correspond to more than one individual. In conclusion, with genetic information there has arisen a new legally relevant group, the biological group. All its members have a right to access the genetic information of the other members. This is because it is not information of a third member but rather information that personally belongs to each individual member.

On the other hand, we have to bear in mind that at least from the biological perspective, there is not a defensible way for total identification of the members of the family as the same subject. This is because genetic information shared among relatives is a probability that depends on the inheritance mechanisms. Furthermore, the gene expression depends also on other non-genetic factors.

In general, national legislation has considered the individual from whom the information has been obtained as the subject of the information. This criterion is also followed by international regulations, such as the Convention of Biomedicine of the Council of Europe (Council of Europe 1997) and the UNESCO Declaration, which stipulates that human genetic data should not be disclosed or made accessible to third parties, in particular, employers, insurance companies, educational institutions and the family, except in two cases:

1. for an important public interest reason in cases restrictively provided for by domestic law consistent with international law of human rights or
2. when the prior, free, informed and express consent of the person concerned has been obtained, provided that such consent is in accordance with

---

8   Spain: (*General Health Law*) Ley General de Sanidad (Article 10); Data Protection Law / Ley 41/2002 básica reguladora de la automía del paciente en materia de información y documentación clínica (Article 7.1).

9   Spain. *Criminal Code* (Article 199).

domestic law and the international law of human rights.

To sum up, the general rule is the duty of secrecy, and only if the patient consents, the physicians would reveal this information to others. However, there are specific situations in which there is a conflict between this duty and the possibility of informing third persons relatives with the aim of providing them a benefit or avoiding damage. In those cases, it would be interesting to convince the patient to inform his / her family.

The Right Not to Know

The recognition of the right not to know arises in order to face situations where unexpected findings could occur. This hypothesis is frequent in biomedical research. The right acquires a special importance in the use of biological samples for research. It is recognized in the Convention on Biomedicine (Article 10.2) and in the International Declaration of UNESCO on Human Genetic Data (Article 10), which states that when human genetic data or biological samples are collected for medical or scientific research purposes, the information provided at the time of consent should indicate that the person concerned has the right to decide whether to be or not to be informed of the results. In reference to the domestic Spanish law,[10] the waiver to receive the information is limited by: (a) the health interest of the patient, (b) that of third parties and (c) the interest of the collective.

Therefore, in the event of the solicitation for the consent to participate in research that involves the analysis of biological samples, the most proper method would be to ask the person concerned on his right to be informed or not about the unexpected findings about his or her health as well as the repercussions on his or her family members.

The Recommendation R(92)3 of the Council of Europe on genetic testing and screening for health care purposes[11] establishes that:

> In conformity with national legislation, unexpected findings may be communicated to the person tested only if they are of direct clinical importance to the person or the family. Communication of unexpected findings to family members of the person tested should only be authorised by national law if the person tested expressly refuses to be informed even though their lives are in danger (principle 11).

---

10   Spain. Patient's Right Law (Ley 41/2002 báscia reguladora de la autonomía del paciente y de derechos y obigaciones en materia de información y documentación clínica (Article 9.1). See also the Spanish Law on Biomedical Research 2007 (Ley 14/2007, de 3 de Julio, de Investigación Biomédica).

11   R(92)3 of the Council of Europe, on genetic testing and screening for health care purposes, https://wcd.coe.int/com.instranet.InstraServlet?Command=com.instranet.CmdBl obGet&DocId=601490&SecMode=1&Admin=0&Usage=4&InstranetImage=43355.

This position has been developed in the Recommendation R (97)5 of the Council of Europe on Protection of Medical data (Principle 8.4).[12] According to this Principle, the person subjected to genetic analysis must be informed of unexpected findings if the domestic law does not prohibit the giving of such information; or the person himself has asked for this information; or the information is not likely to cause serious harm to his/her health; or though his/her consanguine or uterine kin, to a member of his/her social family, or to a person who has a direct link with his/her genetic line, unless domestic law provides appropriate safeguards. The person should also be informed if this information is of direct importance to him/her for treatment or prevention.

The recommendation restricts the circumstances in which unexpected findings should not be communicated. In conclusion, the doubtful cases that remain at the moment of deciding on whether to report or not of an unexpected finding are very limited. In cases in which the information does not have a repercussion in the patient's health because the mutation found does not have great significance or there is no therapy or prevention known, or it is not going to be transmitted to the offspring, according to the Recommendation (97)5 of the Council of Europe on the Protection of Medical Data, it is not necessary to inform the patient.

Right of Access and Rectification

Since at this moment there are no better-suited instruments to protect these rights over the sample, it could be appropriate to project the rights that are exercisable in relation to the medical record to apply them to the sample. Although the medical record and the sample are very different items, nonetheless, they share the following common points: (a) both are a medium of data that are health related and which are stored within a hospital center, (b) the property of such doesn't belong to the person, but to the center, (c) specific works are performed by a professional in order to elaborate the medium, which creates an added value to the data, which in turn provides a useful utility for the assistance of the patient.

Due to the aforementioned, we shall say that the Spanish Act on Protection of Data (1999)[13] establishes the affected person's right to access his or her stored data (Article 13). Furthermore, the Patient's Rights Law (Article 18) specifically regulates access to the patient's medical record. If the person has the right to access his or her data in the medical record, then he or she also has the right to access the data of the sample, which in turn needs certain clarification in relation to the scope of the latter. It is necessary to clarify whether the right to access in turn enables the

---

12   Recommendation of the Council of Europe on Protection of Medical Data https://wcd.coe.int/com.instranet.InstraServlet?Command=com.instranet.CmdBlobGet&DocId=560580&SecMode=1&Admin=0&Usage=4&InstranetImage=43009.

13   Spain. (Protection Data Act, 1999). LEY ORGÁNICA 15/1999, de 13 de diciembre, de Protección de Datos de Carácter Personal.

right to know the results of the analysis. Bearing in mind that the right to access is exercisable in relation to the data obtained and through a document that offers an objective reflection of the reality, though not necessarily by the handing over of the medium, then the answer is that the patient doesn't have the right to have handed over the preparation that has been obtained in relation to his or her sample, based on the right to access the data of a personal nature that has been stored.

In fact, when patients have claimed to exercise certain rights within this scope and have not been satisfied, lawsuits have been resolved by applying non-specific criteria whose interpretation has derived in different arguments that are reflected in several Spanish rulings. These rulings show many argumentative differences, but nonetheless we have observed that they also have a point in common. This is that the rights of the patient in relation to his or her sample is framed within the scope of the right to health information and not within a possible right to property, which would easily justify the mandatory nature of the handing over. However, this statement must be made more precise by taking into account the rest of the regulation that is in relation to the protection of data of a personal nature, which would be applicable to the sample of the person affected.

Storage Period

In reference to the storage period, Spanish Law (Patient's Right Law, Article 17) establishes that the health data contained in the medical record shall be kept during the adequate time as established on a case-by-case basis. As a minimum, the medical record shall be kept for five years from the date of medical discharge from each medical assistance. Additionally,

> the clinical documentation shall also be kept for judicial reasons in accordance with the legislation in force. Likewise, this information shall be kept when there is an epidemiological, research, organizational or for the operation of the National Health System reasons. Its processing shall be done in such a manner as to avoid whenever possible the identification of the affected persons.

According to these criteria, the samples shall be stored in case they might be necessary for the assistance of the patient, but if done with other finalities, then an operation must be undertaken to disassociate the identifiable subject. In sum, the routine storage of samples of identifiable persons after surgical extractions will not be possible unless there is a concrete end purpose.

The Right to Be Informed Previously to Obtain and Use the Sample

When the biological sample that is going to be used for biomedical research purposes is not going to be rendered anonymous, then the person concerned, prior to consent, should receive information as to the final purpose of the research, the benefits expected from such research, the identity of the person responsible for the research, that he or she has the right to revoke the consent and its effects, the procedures to render the sample anonymous and the disposition of the sample after the end of the research.[14]

Relating to this topic, Recommendation R(2006) on research on biological material of human origin[15] stipulates that 'information and consent or authorization to obtain such materials should be as specific as possible with regard to any foreseen research uses and the choices available in that respect' (Article 10.2).

The Recommendation R(2006)4 also stipulates in Article 20 that if the proposed use of identifiable biological materials in a research project is not within the scope of prior consent, if any, given by the person concerned, reasonable efforts should be made to contact the person in order to obtain consent to the proposed use.

If contacting the person concerned is not possible with reasonable efforts, these biological materials should only be used in the research project subject to independent evaluation of the fulfillment of the following conditions:

1. the research addresses an important scientific interest;
2. the aims of the research could not reasonably be achieved using biological materials for which consent can be obtained; and
3. there is no evidence that the person concerned has expressly opposed such research use.

The person concerned may freely refuse consent for the use in a research project of his/her identifiable biological materials or may withdraw consent at any time. Refusal to give consent or the withdrawal of consent should not lead to any form of discrimination against the person concerned, in particular regarding the right to medical care.

Finally, when the person has died, biological materials should not be removed from the body of a deceased person for research activities without appropriate consent or authorization and also should not be removed or supplied for research activities if the deceased person is known to have objected to it (Article 13).

Use of Samples for a Purpose Different from the Original

Along the same lines as the comparison between samples and medical records, summing up a rather complicated topic that does not pertain to the matter at hand leads to the conclusion that the use of samples for research and education

---

14   According to the Spanish ruling from the National Audiency of 8 March 2002 (juridical principle, number 6).

15   Recommendation R (2006) 4 of the Committee of Ministers to Member States on research on biological materials of human origin (Adopted by the Commiittee of Ministers on 15 March 2006 at the 958th meeting of the Ministers' Diputies).

would be possible without the consent of the subject only if such sample were anonymous.[16]

On the contrary, if such sample would be linked to an identified or identifiable individual, then the use with 'different purposes' from those that justified its collection would only be possible with the consent of the person affected or without it in the cases that were mentioned before.

On the other hand, the Spanish Act on Protection of Data (1999) stipulates that data compiled with a specific purpose cannot be used for another that is incompatible to it, which must be interpreted as a different purpose.

The Normative Sources

We must make clear that regulations that could be related to the use of biological samples are practically non-existent except for some isolated cases. This contrasts with the need for such.

A. Contributions of International Law (European Commission)

- Recommendation (92) 3 on genetic testing and screening for health care purposes.
- Recommendation (97) 5 on the protection of medical data.
- Recommendation (2006) 4 on research on biological materials of human origin
- International Declaration on Human Genetic Data that has been promoted by UNESCO, which was approved 16 October 2003. It is the first international legal instrument that establishes a set of rules in relation to both the biological samples as well as the data of a personal nature that can be extracted from the samples.

---

16   Spain. Patient's Rights Law 41/2002 in which Article 16.3 stipulates: 'The access to the clinical record for judicial, epidemiology, public health, research or teaching purposes is regulated by Protection Data Law 15/1999 and by General Health Law 14/1986 and other applicable norms in each case. The access to the clinical record with these purposes obliges to preserve the data of the personal identification of the patient separate from that which is of a clinical and assistance nature in such a manner that as a general rule there is an assurance of anonymity, except when the patient has given his/her consent in order not to separate them. There is an exception for the investigations by the judicial authorities in which the unification of the identification data and the clinical-assistance data are deemed indispensable, in which case there will be an observance of what the judges and tribunals require in the corresponding process. The access to the data and document of a clinical record are strictly limited to the specific ends of each case'.

B. Applicable Regulation that is Foreseeable within the European Framework

In reference to the Law of the European Union, there is a growing interest in biobanks and all aspects related to them. Although for the moment there has not been a specific regulation on this matter, some aspects have already been objects of regulation.

- Directive 2001/20/CE on the conduct of clinical trials
- Directive 95/46/EC of the European Parliament and of the Council, of 24 October 1995, on the protection of individuals with regard to the processing of personal data and on the free movement of such data.
- Directive 2004/23/EC of 13 March on setting standards of quality and safety for the donation, procurement, testing, processing, reservation, storage and distribution of human tissues and cells.

A Few Examples of Biobanks Linked to a Research Project

Population genetic studies are undertaken under the protection of specific legislation that tries to solve the problems related to the rights of the data subject and the sharing of the benefits of the research. These are fundamentally designed with two end purposes, at times converging: either as basic research to identify the mutations and the development of medicines or for the use in the clinical application of an individualized medicine that will directly be of benefit to the data subjects. In the first scenario, the objectives can be met with anonymous data and samples, thereby eliminating many of the objections if the anonymity is guaranteed. However, in the second scenario, this doesn't happen though it is compensated with other measures.

Among studies that are currently being developed, we can find the following:

Iceland was the first state to promote specific legislation on the population data banks for health purposes. (Iceland Act on Biobanks, Act No. 110/2000, passed by the Parliament 13 May 2000, accessible at http://ministryofhealth.is/laws-and-regulations/nr/31).

Estonia A law was passed in 2000 on research on human genetics, which establishes the gathering of data that will be obtained through blood samples of three-quarters of the population in a centralized bank. The data and samples will be unlinked and will be at the disposal of a foundation that is dependent on the Ministry of Health. The researchers shall have free access, and the following have been established as rights of the data subject: the voluntary nature of the obtaining of data and samples, the confidentiality of such, their right to solicit the destruction of the data, the right for a data subject to access his or her stored data in the bank, the right not to know and the right to a specific consent.

Tonga   An Australian biotech company has secured exclusive rights to the entire gene pool of the people of Tonga.[17] Autogen Limited will use the genetically unique DNA of Tongans in its hunt for drugs to treat diabetes, cardiovascular disease, hypertension, cancers and ulcers. The research, based on finding links between diseases and particular genes, could make the company hundreds of millions of dollars if it leads to drugs being commercialized. But it is claimed the Tongans, who number 110,000, have not been told of the deal which was finally signed. The company's director of research and development said the deal would bring jobs and a better-funded health system to Tongans.

A research laboratory on Tonga's main island would be built next to the country's only hospital, which was government-owned. Patients at the hospital would be requested to donate blood to Autogen. The blood would be used to extract DNA from which to form genetic pedigrees of family members in the hunt for disease-causing genes. Personnel in charge denied the company was practicing 'bio-piracy' and said that it had followed ethical guidelines set down by the World Health Organization. In November 2000, through negotiations with the government of Tonga, and in particular, with the Minister of Health, Autogen announced an agreement to conduct genetic research for the purpose of discovering disease-related genes in the relatively isolated and homogeneous Tongan population. (http://www.gfbronline.com/PDFs/Fifth_Casestudy3.pdf). According to the agreement, '[t]he Tongan Government will get royalties if anything comes of it, there will be more jobs and the population will get any drugs that come of the research for free'. Patients would be asked for their full, informed consent before samples were taken. Autogen began collecting DNA samples from Tongans early 2001. The DNA of Tonga is valuable to biotech companies because they are more genetically isolated than other populations, where families are made up of people of different ethnic backgrounds.

Québec   Since its creation in Québec in 2002, the CARTaGENE Project[18] has undergone re-structuring though its goal has remained the same: to create an infrastructure for genomics and public health research. CARTaGENE is a project on population genomics for the study of health and disease in aging.

In the coming years, approximately 1 percent of Québec's citizens between the ages of 25 and 69 will be randomly chosen to form a representative sample of the larger population. Recruitment will be done in two phases: *Phase A, focusing on genomic determinants of chronic diseases in the aging population*, will recruit 20,000 people between 40 and 69 living in four metropolitan regions of the province. *Phase B, focusing on public health*, will recruit 30,000 people in the younger age group.

CARTaGENE is a longitudinal study that will collect and analyze DNA, social, health and environmental information. This collection of information will

---

17   Tonga Autogen: http://www.gfbronline.com/PDFs/Fifth_Casestudy3.pdf.

18   Québec. CARTaGENE Project, http://www.cartagene.qc.ca/index2.cfm?lang=1.

be representative of the genomic diversity of Québec's population 25 to 69 years of age. Knowledge in the fields of genomics and public health made possible by CARTaGENE will help researchers to better understand the health problems that occur within the Québec population. The aim is to provide a tool for the validation and proof of genetic research in a modern and diverse population. CARTaGENE will enable researchers to validate the discovery of new genetic factors in a public health context. Researchers will be able to determine if the isolated genetic factors are common throughout the entire population and whether they play an important causal role in the development of a disease. Thus, the surveillance of certain gene factors in a public health context will be possible. This application of knowledge is termed: 'reverse' genomics and is the method used by CARTaGENE. Furthermore, collecting information and DNA from two generations of the population (25–39; 40–69) will enable researchers to validate and isolate gene-gene and gene-environment interactions. 'Reverse' genomics is the application of genomics knowledge from different genetic research methods to the health problems of a given population.

Since 2003, CARTaGENE has been integrated with the Public Project in Population Genomics (P3G). The aim of this international consortium is to harmonize the research tools used by different population projects like CARTaGENE. The objective of this international project is to improve knowledge sharing and efficiency.

United Kingdom   The UK created a health data bank with a wide sample of the population, which will continue to grow with the passage of time, without having it submit to a specific legal framework. In fact, the UK Biobank[19] is a major UK medical research initiative and a registered charity in its own right, with the aim of improving the prevention, diagnosis and treatment of a wide range of serious and life-threatening illnesses – including cancer, heart diseases, diabetes, arthritis and forms of dementia. Researchers are now recruiting 500,000 people aged 40–69 from across the country to take part in this project. They will ensure that safeguards are in place so that data and samples are used only for scientific and ethically approved research.

Spain   The Fundación Genoma España decided to create the National DNA Bank, in which there is an initial provision to include in the first stage a collection of samples of 1,000 representative individuals of the Spanish population and another 300 from minority groups. The samples will be obtained through voluntary blood donors aged 18–28. The main objective is to ease the analysis of the Spanish DNA to the researchers and to allow the possible association of the mutations with certain diseases. The information obtained will be given to the Genotipe National Center and to other public or private research centers that ask for it.

From a legal point of view in Spain, a specific regulation applicable to the obtaining, access and use of biological samples for research purposes that are

---

19   United Kingdom. Biobank. http://www.ukbiobank.ac.uk/about/what.php.

stored in health centers, universities or industry does not exist. On the contrary, other banks of human tissues are regulated:

1. Royal Decree 411/1996. Such tissue shall be destined to implant in patients whose treatment is medically indicated. The most influential parts are those aspects related to the guarantee of quality of such materials in order to protect the health of the person implanted.
2. Royal Decree 185/1993 and Royal Decree 62/2003, whereby the technical requisites and the minimum conditions for blood donation and blood banks are regulated.
3. Royal Decree 412/1996 on gamete banks for use in human reproduction (research as a residual end purpose).

Likewise, at present, there is in Spain a draft bill, 'Biomedical Research Law', that has several chapters dealing with biological samples, genetic analysis and biobanks. These chapters will establish the guiding principles that must be followed when using samples, such as: the protection of data, cost-free status, consent, quality of data, the manner to obtain samples, the information previous to its use, the consent on the use of the sample, the storage and destruction of such, the procedure to create biobanks as well as some of the rights of the data subject and the requisites of genetic counseling before and after carrying out a genetic analysis.

In view of the aforementioned projects, the appropriate procedure is for a project of this importance to be done within a specific legal coverage and with an appropriate management of the benefits, with management that is not limited to specific private companies as the use of public resources is necessary, for example, in the assignment of the data of the medical record records. To sum up, these initiatives and projects should not be stopped; however, we should establish some guarantees of respect to the rights of the participating persons, especially in relation to the terms of the consent and the guarantee of confidentiality.

Conclusions

1. A generic consent for research is convenient, as it will allow the greatest benefit for the banks for the different projects. However, the information on the use of the samples must be specified as far as possible.
2. The consent must be free.
3. Other guarantees in relation to the right to access the stored personal data

must be included.

4. Each granting of data or of identifiable samples must be consented to.
5. The consent must be revocable and entails the rendering anonymous of the sample or the data.
6. The effectiveness of the guarantee, as well as the supervision of the entire project, should be entrusted to an institution that will act as a mediator between the data subjects and the researchers.
7. In general, the population databases will be subject to the same protection basis as the data of a personal nature.

Bibliography

Berg, K. (1994), 'Le respect de la vie privée par opposition à la communication des informationes', in *Ethique et génétique humaine. Actes du 2ᵉ Syposium du Conseil de L'Europe sur la bioéthique,* Strasbourg.

Council of Europe (1992), Recommendation No. R (92) 3 on Genetic Testing and Screening for Health Care Purposes.

Council of Europe (1997a), Recommendation No. R (97) 5 on the Protection of Medical Data.

—— (1997b), Convention for the Protection of Human Rights and Dignity of the Human Being with Regard to the Application of Biology and Medicine: Convention on Human Rights and Biomedicine (Oviedo).

—— (2006), Recommendation Rec(2006)4 of the Committee of Ministers to member states on research on biological materials of human origin.

Directive 95/46/EC of the European Parliament and of the Council (1995) on the protection of individuals with regard to the processing of personal data and on the free movement of such data.

Directive 2001/20/CE of the European Parliament and of the Council (2001), relating to the approach to the legal and administrative provisions and regulations of the Member States about the application of good clinical practices in the conduct of clinical trials in humans.

European Commission (2004), 25 Recommendations on the Ethical, Legal and Social Implications of Genetic Testing (Brussels).

European Society of Human Genetics (2003), Recommendations on data storage and DNA banking for biomedical research: technical, social and ethical issues.

Furness, F. (2003), 'Consent to using human tissue', *British Medical Journal* 327, 750–59.

Gibbons, S. et al. (2005), 'Lessons from European population genetic databases: Comparing the law in Estonia, Iceland, Sweden and the United Kingdom', *European Journal of Health Law* 12, 102–33.

Green, M. and Botkin, J.R. (2003), 'Genetic exceptionalism in medicine. Clarifying the differences between genetic and nongenetic tests', *Annals of International Medicine* 1/138 (7), 571–5.

Iceland Act on Biobanks (2000), Act No 110/2000, passed by the Parliament 13 May, accessible at http://ministryofhealth.is/laws-and-regulations/nr/31.

International Declaration on Human Genetic Data (2003), http://portal.unesco.org/en/ev.php-URL_ID=17720&URL_DO=DO TOPIC&URL_SECTION=201.html

Kegly, J. (1996), 'Using genetic information: the individual and the Community', *Medicine and Law* 15 (3), 337–8.

Knoppers, B.M. (1998), 'Towards a reconstruction of the genetic family: new principles?', *International Digest of Health Legislation* 49 (1), 250–52.

National Bioethics Advisory Commission (2000), Research involving human biological materials: ethical issues and policy guidance, vol. 1: Report and Recommendations. (Maryland), http://bioethics.georgetown.edu/nbac/hbm.pdf.

Nicolás, P. (2006), *La protección jurídica de los datos genéticos de carácter personal,* (edita Comares- Cátedra interuniveritaria Fundación BBVA– Diputación Foral de Bizkaia de Derecho y Genoma Humano, UD-UPV, Spain).

Romeo-Casabona, C.M. (2004), 'Anonimyzation and Pseudonymization: The legal framework at a European Level', in D. Beyleveld et al. (eds), *The Data Protection Directive and Medical Research Across Europe* (Aldershot: Ashgate).

Rothstein (2005), 'Genetic exceptionalism and legislative pragmatism', *Hasting Centre Report* 35 (4), 27–33.

Royal College of Physicians and the British Society for Human Genetics (2006), *The rule of confidentiality in genetic practice: Guidance on genetic testing and sharing genetic information*. A report of the Joint Committee on Medical Genetics.

Sánchez-Ventura, J. (2003), 'Cribado neonatal de hipotiroidismo congénitas', *Jano* LXV/1488, 35–43.

Spanish Royal Academy Dictionary, http://www.rae.cs/rae.html.

VVAA (1990), 'Automated DNA screening: the problems and the possibilities', in Knoppers B.M. and Laberge, C.M. (eds), *Genetic Screening, From Newborns to DNA Typing* (Amsterdam, New York, Oxford: Excerpta Medica).

Chapter 15

Human Biological Materials among Civil, Trade and Health Law: Ethical, Anthropological and Legal Implications of Conflicts of Law System

Catherine Labrusse-Riou

The development of a law regulating those 'things', which are from now on the different products or elements of the human body, detachable and detached from the body for purposes which should be exclusively related to medicine and scientific research, is a complex undertaking. These things belong to several legal systems whose concepts, underlying logics and even principles of justice, are different. Yet it is nearly impossible, in law, to work out a special legal regime which would be free from any reference to legal traditions at the roots of the different fields of the common law. Defining what we call nowadays the 'law of bioethics' and, more precisely, the development of a legal status applying to the elements of the human body, is rendered difficult by the plurality of models offered by the Western legal tradition. Efforts of harmonization show contradictions and strong tensions which have not been overcome neither at the domestic nor the international level.

Conflicts of Normative Systems

This chapter will mostly focus on conflicts which should be resolved by law. Such conflicts are between civil law, commercial law and health law. Civil law keeps the human body in the area of the law of persons and refuses to consider the existence of any classical property right on it. Commercial law or the law of economic transactions tends to consider the human body as a commodity or resource which can be used for lucrative purposes and governed by the principle of free trade. Finally, health law, which is a specific area of the law, borrows as much from public law as it does from private law and is perpetually swinging between the satisfaction of private interests and public needs. Each field of the law has its own representations and its own purposes, which explains the ambiguity as well as the contradictions of the legal regime governing the removal, the assignment, the industrialization and final uses of these products of the body. This initial complexity is made more complicated by the growing impact of European law on the one hand and domestic regulations providing for different regimes governing different products (blood, organs, cells, tissues, gametes, embryos, etc.) on the other hand, despite the existence of general principles applying to all the products. Such plurality of normative sources is made even more complicated by the confused and often conflicting relationship between law and ethics, such relationship failing to be clearly established by the 'bioethical' framework. Certainly, the legal authority of fundamental, constitutional or European rights provides ordinary law with interpretation and direction guidelines. However, they fail to develop more specific legal regimes involving the use of traditional concepts such as contract, property, goods, tort or the arbitration between conflicting fundamental rights. The law of bioethics challenges the content as well as the function of such concepts in a context of high tensions between the interests and the values at stake. Such normative conflicts are common when new problems arise in a particular society. However, it is important to provide a precise analysis if we want to be able to overcome them and develop a law which should be both coherent and in compliance with values going beyond sanitary or economic benefits.

Problems in French Law

This brief analysis will rely mostly on examples from French law. During the past ten years, French law has developed an impressive statutory and regulatory framework in the field of public health through several laws dealing directly or indirectly with the human body as a resource necessary to medicine and biomedical research. If the so-called laws on bioethics of 29 July 1994 have established principles in the Civil Code itself (Article 16 and following), the most fundamental principles being endowed with constitutional value, most of these very detailed regulations belong to the Public Health code. These laws were revised by the law of 6 August 2004, which is also to be revised after a five-year period. The latter does not modify any of the principles. It reinforces the public health purposes and rationalizes scientific and administrative control over biomedical activities. This control is in the hands of a new institution, called the Agency for Biomedicine. As a consequence, the status of the human body is considered even more public and the expansion of donations to science and medicine is significantly reinforced.

There is a first tension between the individual interest of persons and the public interest which explains – but does not justify – exceptions provided for by the law to the requirement of the consent of individual donors. However, the new law has not dispelled the ambiguities nor resolved the difficulties arising from the gratuitous nature of donations for the donor, while public or private companies reprocessing the products of the human body can make great profits from them in some cases. Thus, the question of the distribution of profits arising from a free commodity remains open and calls for the definition of an intermediary status restraining the operation of the sole market's regulation. Finally, French law has greatly reinforced sanitary security requirements as well as the harshness of criminal law penalties, and courts have followed the same policy in the field of tort and damages. This is the necessary counterpart for the power which can from now on be exercised over human bodies; the question is to whom these responsibilities can and must be imputed. In addition, the law confirms the qualification of the products of the human body as 'things', and even as 'goods', and as 'defective goods', which is especially arguable when we deal with human embryos which can be lawfully given to a couple or be lawfully conceived and genetically processed for the purpose of giving cells or tissues compatible with recipients.

French law is mostly characterized as favoring research and biomedicine, whose current interests and demands are satisfied in breach of a few fundamental aspects of ethics, while trying to reinforce the rights of donors. However, it remains vague on the solution to be given to many problems, such as legal qualifications of human biologic material, the nature of rights (property, right to use, limitations and control over their use according to the purposes) and the nature of contracts dealing with this material (bilateral or unilateral contracts). Furthermore, it is extremely difficult to be aware of the practice in the field of research contracts or contracts of assignment of human products between assignor companies and assignee companies. Yet, when such contracts are entered upon, the donors have the opportunity to negotiate their participation and the control of uses. Furthermore, the content of these agreements gives us an insight into the way prices are established and into the lawful character of the rights and obligations of the parties. Legal thinking is deprived of an important source of knowledge of the legal practices in the marketing of the products of the human body.

Such problems are not peculiar to French law. Even if they are differently put in other European countries, they remain fundamentally the same everywhere. At a superior political level, two questions should be answered:

1. Which dominant logic should prevail? A commercial liberal logic, relying mostly on contracts and private property, or a public health-oriented logic, relying on public interests and undertaken by a strong State's intervention?
2. How much should human dignity weigh in establishing forbidden practices or deciding which conditions should be respected for authorized acts? Such limits to be established by law are restrictions to be imposed on both previous logics in the name of public order, in order to avoid the overwhelming power of the market and State on appropriated bodies, since they can be appropriated by pieces.

The answer to practical questions depends on these choices. French law has not made a clear choice and has tried to conciliate everything, and therefore remains characterized by overambiguity, which affects the legal regime governing donations as well as forms and functions of the law itself.

Legal Regime of Donations

French Law refuses explicitly to decide whether the donor is to be considered the owner of her body. It is true, in theory, that authors (Zénati, Revet) support the idea that ownership as an exclusive right of the individual is an appropriate concept in favor of the protection of the donor. However, the extent of the right to determine what shall be done to one's body is limited by public order for the respect of human dignity. These theories remain a minority, and what prevails is the idea that the body is the representation of the person and cannot be considered as a 'thing' subject to rights of property in civil law. In both cases, the removal of a part of the body requires *the free and enlightened consent* of the person, and the will expressed as to the donation is not binding (which might exclude the recognition of a contract or even of a unilateral binding agreement). Although this principle is established and even strengthened in recent laws, there are also many exemptions. The requirement of consent is strengthened and protected by the strengthening of the duties to inform and by the donor's option to object to any changes in the purpose of the use of the removed organs. This is the counterpart to the legal recognition of the rights of the holders (researchers and doctors) to change the purpose of the use initially planned. Even though many precautions are taken in order to protect the freedom of living organ donors, one may not dispute that traditional protections offered by civil law remain inefficient: the defects of consent, for instance, frequent because of pressures likely to be exerted on donors, are not appropriate. Above all, French law highly values the presumption of consent of the person who has not given an express refusal while alive, at least as far as removals on deceased persons are concerned. Moreover, as a removal is a free decision, it should be prohibited to consent in the name of others. Yet, this is not the position of French law as to removals on persons incapable to express their willingness. These limitations and exemptions are based on the old idea that founded the political organicist theories, according to which the human body is a metaphor or an image of the social body. As such, it belongs somehow to the nation. Thus, the law can use it without the express consent of the person for the benefit of scientific research or medicine, in the name of a State-run solidarity between citizens. Traces of the organicist conception of the State and of a biological solidarity between the living and the dead have not disappeared despite strong criticisms and the opposition of the population. Politically, the question has also an important anthropological aspect that utilitarianism must not set aside. Furthermore, this old ideology explains that products of the human body can only be donated for the benefit of medicine or science to institutions authorized and controlled by the State. Such an assignment can only be made by contracts concluded directly between donors and recipients. Less open to criticism, this ideology nevertheless shows the opposition of the French system to the market. However, is there a contract between the donor and the biomedical institution that proceeds to the removal and one that receives the biological product? There is no legal certainty on this question even though improvements in the recognition of individual rights may lead to a contractual organization of biomedical usages of the human body. There is also no certainty that the practice of private commercial institutions, including medical ones, of keeping products or tissue, such as blood from the umbilical cord, for personal aims is lawful.

Now that donations do not aim only at quick transplantations but represent the first stage of a more or less long process of transformation and exploitation which leads on to derivatives, the greatest contradictions are about economic aspects: how to justify the principle of free donations imposed on donors while companies receive products whose commercialization is a source of profits? Since the famous *Moore* case in California, it does not seem that European laws have made any progress to resolve this conflict of interest. Once again, since proposals made to the lawmaker in the 1980s in order to set up a dual status were not accepted, the State could have levied taxes on part of the commercial profits made by the sale of derivatives obtained from a free raw material. However, we still have to think of this end in Europe if we ever want to reconcile free donations (since the body is not a property on an economic point of view) with the aim of general interest for these donations and the return by the market on the production of derivatives from human biological matter. One may, indeed, imagine that two systems co-exist in Europe: one is commercial and the other one is non-profit making, as this exists elsewhere. One may also think that researchers and associations of patients develop networks and systems of contracts with the purpose that, for the general interest, scientific and medical activity not be governed solely by the rules of property and market. Yet, European law should contribute to build a common system, which reconciles social and economic constraints in this matter. The question is very important and is not limited to human biological material. It requires that the legal profession as a whole, creative and concerned by the ethical and anthropological function of the law, gather their technical skills in the management of parts, natural products or derivatives of the human body.

A proposition was made in France for a special legal statute on human body products, which would oblige the firms to give a part of their profits for humanitarian purposes, so that what is coming from free human body donations return to the benefit of humanity (especially for research on rare genetic disease or for medical treatment in developing countries), but this project was not confirmed by the Parliament in France.

Functions of the Law

If law is a technique that offers tools for various politics or social interests, it cannot cut itself off from the meaning of the notions that it builds to this end. These notions are so many representations or images that structure social life and are used as a normative benchmark in the practice. Law, therefore, cannot be totally confused with an instrument, nor reduced to a technique allegedly purely neutral. Bioethics, with the view to the government of the life sciences and biomedicine, has been for a long time the cause of a deep renewal in the legal and political reasoning as to the function of law, its role and limitations. European States or lawyers do not share the same positions according to the philosophy they defend; such oppositions serve only as an obstacle to the harmonization of legislation. Moreover, we notice today, at least in France, a real confusion between the different normative systems and their functions. Although this question exceeds this chapter's topic, the chapter will deal with it nevertheless and will present some data, which are in the background of the problems concerning the ownership of the human body and the rights attached to its circulation.

On the one hand, the efficiency of some legislations which are more restrictive than others, for ethical reasons is endangered by the free circulation of persons and goods to such an extent that it has almost become impossible to prohibit what other neighboring States allow. The methods of private international law cannot prevent this situation. Thus, the French government believed that it was justified to authorize the importation and exportation of embryonic human cells for the benefit of research, a practice prohibited by French law. The authority of law, whatever the opportunity of such a decision, is denied regardless of the competences of the institutions of the State.

On the other hand, divergences appear within the State between the ethical institutions, the scientific authorities of regulation, the judge-made law and the law. This is the sign of the absence of a real consensus despite of the appearance of common positions. Thus, we can fear oppositions between the Agency for Biomedicine, which has great powers, and the National Committee for Ethics, which could lead to the marginalization of ethics in the regulation of biomedical practices. Ethics, whose formation is encouraged by the intensification of the public debate, may go unheeded for lack of an efficient legal translation.

For lack of strong legal constructions capable to resist the pressure of the situations and to fit to the evolution of the techniques, law, which is so necessary, is nonetheless a weak device. For, as Florence Bellivier says (Bellivier 2004), recent French law

> is the product of compromises of unstable values which seriously put to the test law in its normative function (how is the rule established?), law as a tool of management (isn't there a risk that it be exceeded by technical facts?) and in its political dimension (what is its legitimacy to insist upon such social value and not upon such another?).

One may think that we are witnessing a deep crisis of the constitutional State and at least a transformation of the modes of government. Faced with a more or less fantastical power of sciences and techniques taken over by the uncontrollable influence of the global market, this transformation should not make us forget the virtues of the separation of powers, such as the public order of non-negotiable values that allow us to withstand the quick changes of technologies. That is why an increasing number of lawyers wonder, beyond the ethical sources of our societies that we have wrongfully reduced to a conservative moral order or to a natural law, about the anthropological function of the law, that is to say, about the effects of biological practices on human beings and about the law which legitimates them. Eventually, they are open to post-modernity but reject the fashionable idea of post-humanity.

Some French References on the Theme

For more information in national, European and international law, see:

Florence Bellivier and Christine Noiville (2006), *Contrats et vivant, Le droit de la circulation des ressources biologiques* (introduction by Catherine Labrusse-Riou) (Paris: L.G.D.J. coll. Traité des contrats, Direction Jacques Ghestin), 321 and the bibliography.

Florence Bellivier (2004), 'Revue trimestrielle de droit civil', no 4, 795, *Chroniques de législation* no 29, Bioéthique. loi no 2004-800 du 6 août 2004 relative à la bioéthique.

On the anthropological function of law, especially in societies dominated by market, sciences and technique, see:

Alain Supiot (2005), *Homo juridicus, Essai sur la fonction anthropologique du droit* (Paris: Seuil).

Chapter 16

Indirect Commodification of Ova Donation for Assisted Reproduction and for Human Cloning Research: Proposals for Supranational Regulation

Ingrid Schneider

The demand for women's eggs, whether for assisted reproduction or for embryonic stem cell and cloning research, is increasing at an accelerated pace and is leading to transnational oocyte trafficking. These new, competitive 'needs' for ova call for a fresh look at regulatory challenges and the development of adequate policy responses.

The first part of this chapter provides an overview of the regulatory landscape of oocyte donation in Europe and the range of existing regulations. Then it addresses some types of cross-border trade and reproductive tourism, distinguishing between different recruitment schemes, particularly whether oocytes are provided within or outside of the IVF context and whether anonymity of the donor is legally possible or not. It also highlights the bifurcation between different purposes of egg extraction, particularly the challenges raised by ova demands for cloning research.

The second part suggests ten points for supranational minimum standards that should be considered crucial for protecting both donor and recipients interests, as well as the needs of donor conceived children-to-be and the public good. A particular focus is directed to the question of commodification of oocytes with regard to the European principle of non-commercial, voluntary and altruistic donation, which has an important normative and regulatory function. In practice, however, it allows for indirect commercialization of ova by compensation schemes. After a discussion of arguments and rationales pro and contra payment of egg donation, the case is made for a non-commercial, supranational regulatory framework.

Assisted Reproductive Technologies, Cloning Research and Regulation

Development of IVF and Regulatory Regimes

Following the birth of the first 'test-tube' baby, Louise Brown, in the UK in 1978, In Vitro Fertilization (IVF) techniques spread rapidly throughout the world. The numbers of women being treated has steadily increased, accompanied by an expansion of IVF-clinics. While IVF treatments were first developed in the public sector, private clinics, sometimes part of transnational companies, now carry out the bulk of IVF procedures in many countries.

Part of the increase in IVF is explained by expanding its use beyond women with some organic basis for infertility and by the development towards reprogenetics. ICSI (Intracytoplasmic Sperm Injection) can be applied to fertile women to enable her infertile male partner's genetic parenthood. The introduction of another technique, Preimplantation Genetic Diagnosis (PGD), for genetic testing of embryos before transferral to the woman's uterus also encouraged the use of IVF for women with no problems of (in)fertility. Moreover, PGD itself allows not only for the 'negative' selection of embryos with certain traits (for example, a severe genetic disease) but also, at least technically, for 'positive' selection of embryos, for instance, for reasons of sex selection. The advent of embryonic stem cell technologies couples IVF to the fields of transplantation and regenerative medicine.

The challenges posed by IVF and other Assisted Reproductive Technologies have prompted different types of regulation. Some countries have developed legislative regulation by statutory law, both in the penal code and in the civil law. Additionally, in the UK, a centralized regulatory agency, the HFEA (Human Fertilization and Embryology Authority) was founded. Other countries have left governance mainly to self-regulation by the medical community or the clinics themselves. Further regulation of access to the techniques available is also implicit in whether IVF-treatment is covered by a national health system or private health insurance.

The Regulatory Landscape in Europe

The regulatory landscape in Europe can be mapped along a continuum between prohibitive regulation, as in Austria, Germany, Ireland, Norway, Switzerland and, more recently, in Italy and more permissive regulation, as in the UK, the Netherlands, Belgium and Spain. Countries such as France lie somewhere in-between these poles, while several of the new EU Member States have not yet regulated IVF at all. However, while the UK can be seen as having a very liberal regulatory regime, it actually does provide tight controls of clinics, *inter alia* by regular inspections and by requiring them to be licensed (HFEA 2005). Judging by recent trends in regulatory regimes, neither a 'race to the bottom' nor a 'race to the top' would appear inevitable. On the contrary, there is a range of regulatory options and potentials that are dealt with flexibly by the national states, according to respective legal cultures, social debates and conflicts, cultural traditions and regulatory styles.

Table 16.1   Egg donation – Regulation in Europe and international practice

---

- *Prohibited:*
  - Austria, Germany, Italy, Norway, Switzerland
- *Allowed:*
  - Belgium, Denmark, Estonia, Finland, France, Greece, UK, Latvia, Netherlands, Sweden, Slovenia, Slovakia, Spain, Czech Republic, Hungary
- *Not regulated:*
  - Ireland, Lithuania, Luxemburg, Malta, Poland
- *Practiced in extra-EU countries:*
  - Australia, China, Israel, India, Iran, Singapore, South Korea, USA

Source: European Commission 2006, own research

'Reproductive Tourism'

In the last decade, a new branch of – mainly private – fertility centers has emerged that specialize in providing an infrastructure for patients coming from other countries. Often located at tourist sites or near airports of low-cost carriers, they offer special services for clients from abroad (Schindele and Zimmermann 2006).

This so-called reproductive tourism (Blyth and Farrand 2005) is triggered by several factors. One is differences in regulations (see Table 16.1), for example, the prohibition of egg cell donation and PGD in Germany and other countries but not elsewhere. Moreover, more recent requirements for open – non-anonymous – germ cell donation in the UK promote 'egg-cell tourism' towards countries like Spain, the Czech Republic, Russia, Cyprus and Crete, to name just a few, where these restrictions do not exist (Barnett and Smith 2006, France 2006, Tremlett 2006). Another factor encouraging individuals to go abroad for IVF and germ donation is financial: cost differences in obtaining the procedures may motivate women in the US to travel to Europe, South Africa or elsewhere where prices are lower. Still other factors behind the burgeoning of reproductive tourism are related to the structure of a country's health care system, where long waiting periods or apparent shortages in oocytes lure women abroad for treatment.

Analytically, we can distinguish between different types of reproductive tourism and cross-border-trade of gametes and embryos:

- The first, most common, is when the recipient travels to the donor's country.
- The converse, when the donor travels to the recipient, would be a second type.[1]
- A third type involves the shipment only of gametes and embryos from one state to another.[2]
- A fourth type includes cases where medical doctors and researchers emigrate to countries where there is perceived to be a better supply of oocytes with which to work, more financial grants available for research or more permissive regulatory structures for their scientific activities.[3]

Assessments of these instances of 'reproductive tourism' vary. Some consider this movement merely a normal process of Europeanization and legitimate consumer

---

1   According to investigative journalist research, Cyprus and Belize seem to be hubs for cross-country egg trade. Reportedly, the Petra Health Clinic on Cyprus, an offshoot of the Reproductive Genetics Institute in Chicago, has performed egg transferral on several hundred UK women in 2005 who were referred by fertility doctors in Britain. The oocytes were sourced from women from the Ukraine, Russia and Eastern Europe. The clinic's offices in Kiev reportedly paid Ukrainian young women $500 to fly to the Cypriot clinic and donate ova. The international character of these undertakings is also expressed by its health professionals: the clinic's resident director is Russian, the gynecologist trained in Israel. Additionally, the clinic is recruiting egg donors among immigrants from the former Soviet Union who live in Cyprus (Barnett and Smith 2006).

2   The European Parliament (2005) condemned the practice of the GlobalART Clinic in Romania which specialized in the provision of egg cells to citizens from the UK, the US and Israel. Romanian donors received 100–250 US dollars (USD) as financial compensation. Authorized by the HFEA, sperm was sent from the UK to Romania, to be fertilized with donor eggs retrieved from Romanian women. The resulting embryos were sent back to Britain to be implanted. At least two Romanian women were severely harmed by the egg donation process in suffering from acute ovarian hyperstimulation syndrome and did not receive medical care by the GlobalART Clinic, which forms part of a US-Israeli company. 55 British patients from the Bridge Centre fertility clinic in London underwent IVF with oocytes derived from Romania, in total around 400 embryos were imported to the UK in 2005 (Schindele and Zimmermann 2006).

3   An instructive case is the career of the scientist Miodrag Stojkovic. He studied veterinary medicine in Belgrade and later in Munich, Germany, where he became the head of an animal in vitro fertilization lab and learned cloning techniques. Because he wanted to work on human embryos, which is legally prohibited in Germany, he went to Newcastle upon Tyne in the UK, where he contributed to the derivation of Britain's first human embryonic stem cell line in 2002 and succeeded in 2005 to create a cloned human blastocyst. In the end of 2005, he moved to Valencia, Spain to become deputy director at the prestigious Prince Felipe Research Centre (Gramser 2006). In spring of 2006, the Spanish Parliament legalized research cloning (SCNT) experiments. Stojkovic will be obtaining oocytes for stem cell research from the large IVF infrastructure which was also built up for customers from abroad, particularly a large fertility hospital in Valencia that manages 3,000 cycles of fertility treatment per year. His move to Spain was not only motivated by generous

choice. Others view it as disrespect for national legislation and as private undermining of rules which were democratically passed for the public good. Shall we regard these developments as consumers 'voting with their feet'? Or does the clandestine nature of many of these transactions and the gaps in living standards and conditions between individuals in the respective countries raise concerns regarding inequality and injustice? And what about the potential of cross-border trade leading to the erosion of normative standards and to the exploitation of vulnerable segments of the population?

Egg-Cell Donation

Oocyte donation forms a diverse and complex field of medical, social and legal practices. For analyses and normative judgments, it seems first to be necessary to differentiate between the contexts of ova extraction, particularly whether it is taking place within or outside an IVF treatment. Second, different types of procurement and respective regulations of oocyte donation can be analytically distinguished. All of them have both 'advantages' and 'disadvantages', as well as different consequences in terms of the recruitment of donors. Third, the purposes of use – whether ova are given for the ends of reproduction or for research – make a difference. However, in practical reality, there can be overlaps and interconnections between these analytical categories which may affect both procurement and ethical assessment (compare Daniels 2000).

Ova can be provided *within the IVF context*, as donations of so-called spare or surplus oocytes. This practice does not require additional hormonal stimulation of the provider (Rimington et al. 2003). However, it may deprive a woman of egg cells which could otherwise be used to create an embryo for her own reproductive purposes and thus may reduce the donor's chances of becoming pregnant. As well, 'donation' of 'fresh' 'spare' eggs means that the woman cannot have these ova cryopreserved for possible use in a second cycle should the first IVF-cycle be unsuccessful. Moreover, knowing that another woman has given birth to a child of her own genetic material while the egg donor herself remains childless can have difficult psychological effects (Johnson 1999).

Donations *outside of the IVF-context* are fundamentally problematic in terms of the medical professional ethics, insofar as they imply a serious breach of the

---

grants from the Spanish Government, but also by the liberal egg donation practice: the British HFEA had restricted supply for SCNT research mainly to leftover oocytes from IVF that had failed to fertilize in the lab (Sexton 2005). In Spain, anonymous egg donation has become a burgeoning field, with egg providers receiving 600–1,000 euro (EUR) per successful egg retrieval as 'compensation' (Alkorta 2006, Pérez Ybarra 2006). Stojkovic was cited in *Nature*: 'We need fresh human eggs. What you get left over from the IVF clinic is not viable' (Vogel 2006, 517). This means that for cloning research in Spain, not only donated or 'shared' 'surplus' eggs from IVF treatments will in the future be used but also ova which are extracted from women exclusively for research.

first principle of the Hippocratic Oath '*primum non nocere*' (do no harm!). In any treatment, doctors must assess the risks and benefits for a patient, weighing *intra*personally the risks of the medical treatment against its potential benefit. In the case of egg cell donation, however, there is neither a medical indication for the intervention nor any medical benefit for the donor herself, whereas the treatment may severely harm her health and bodily integrity. Therefore, in this respect, there are some similarities between oocyte extraction for reproductive purposes and living organ donation (kidney, part of the liver). Donation and medical intervention are legitimated by the benefit for another person. However, caution and additional safeguards are required. The fact that the benefits and risks of the medical intervention are accounted for *inter*personally is very critical, because if these were generalized as a social norm, anyone and everyone could be damaged or harmed if it was for the sake of another's good. Whether the ethical justification of these medical interventions can fully rest on the informed consent of the donor thus remains a highly contentious issue (Magnus and Cho 2005, 2006, Schneider 2003a, Schneider and Schumann 2003). Oocyte donation for *research* purposes is different insofar as no clear clinical value or benefit for third persons (the stem cell recipients) has as yet been established. It may more be seen in analogy to research on human subjects.[4] However, in this case, 'the risks of the actual procurement process may not be adequately highlighted' (Magnus and Cho 2005, 1747). Moreover, the risks of the hormonal treatment for egg extraction, and the possible psychological effects of egg donation are not yet sufficiently explored (Beeson and Lippman 2006, Check 2006, 607). All these considerations together have implications for what can count as justifiable, qualified and authentic

Table 16.2   Typology of oocyte donation

Oocyte donation	Unpaid	Paid
Anonymous	'altruistic' donation, rarely occurs outside of IVF context	commercial transaction, organized by intermediary
Non-anonymous	'altruistic' donation, mainly between relatives and in close personal relationships	self-organized transaction, or commercial 'yes'-donor
Within IVF-context	'spare' oocytes	'paid egg-sharing'

---

4   'After all, research often requires individuals to expose themselves to risk for the benefit of others (albeit often with the possibility of direct benefit to themselves). This model may also be inadequate for addressing the status of these women, because the consent process is likely to focus on the post-procurement research risks and benefits ... There is nothing experimental being tested on these women. The only research aspect of their experience is use of their tissues' (Magnus and Cho 2005, 1747).

'informed consent' of a potential donor, both concerning the duties of the doctors and researchers and the autonomy of the women involved.

Other distinctions in gamete donation, both within or outside the IVF context, can be made according to whether or not there is payment, and whether or not the donation is anonymous (see Table 16.2). The classic prototype is the 'altruistic donation', which mostly happens between relatives and in close personal relationships (see Yee et al. 2007).[5] However, altruistic donation can affect intricate social relationships, involving the sense of immense and non-repayable gratitude, but also feelings of guilt.[6] Further, difficulties – centering on questions of responsibility, liability and blame – may arise if the child born suffers from a disability, or if oocyte donation results in ill health of the donor. Whether altruistic donation is always voluntary must be questioned, as subtle psychological pressure is not infrequent (Raymond 1990).

Paid donation, frequently anonymous, usually occurs in commercial settings, mostly enabled by intermediaries.

Donations within the setting of IVF usually involve a woman or couple deciding to provide 'surplus' egg cells to another – for reproduction or for research. So called 'egg-sharing' programs, however, often stand for a payment in kind, either in terms of a substantial discount on the costs of IVF treatment for the 'donor', or in terms of speeding up treatment by moving forward on a waiting list. In these ways, then, egg-sharing programs can be regarded as an indirect commercialization of ova donation.

Cloning for Research Purposes (Somatic Cell Nuclear Transfer)

The advent of embryonic stem cell research, particularly cloning for research purposes, has strongly expanded the demand for female egg cells. In Somatic Cell

---

5   Concerning donation from kin or from strangers, there are two guiding ideas which compete with each other: 'procreation should ideally be kept within the family, which ought to lie outside the market. Alongside such views runs the counterargument that providers ought to remain anonymous, and the thought of substituting the gametes of kin is enough for the conceptual brake of incest to be applied' (Edwards 1998, 168).

6   In the context of organ donation, Renee Fox and Judith Swazey have termed these aspects of the gift-exchange dimensions of the transfer of bodily substances 'the tyranny of the gift', a concept arising from Marcel Mauss's (1990) studies on the social nature of the gift: '[W]hat recipients believe they owe to donors and the sense of obligation they feel about repaying "their" donor for what has been given weigh heavily on them. This psychological and moral burden is especially onerous because the gift the recipient has received from the donor is so extraordinary that it is inherently unreciprocal. It has no physical or symbolic equivalent. As a consequence, the giver, the receiver, and their families may find themselves locked in a creditor-debtor-vise that binds them one to another in a mutually fettering way' (Fox and Swazey 1992, 40). For the 'tyranny of the gift' in the context of donor insemination, see Daniels and Lewis 1996, 1527.

Nuclear Transfer (SCNT), the nucleus of an egg cell is removed and replaced by a somatic cell drawn from an adult person. By fusing the enucleated oocyte with the somatic cell, a cloned human embryo is produced. After development in vitro until the blastocyst stage, cells from the inner cell mass are removed, thereby destroying the embryo. The stem cells obtained have the potential to differentiate into various tissue types. Researchers hope to develop the techniques that will let stem cells develop sufficiently to be used for repair or regeneration of the patient providing the somatic cell. In other words, the guiding idea for this research cloning is to provide replacement tissues genetically identical to the somatic cell donor patient, and thus to prevent immunological rejection. However, while therapeutic potential for human embryonic stem cells is promised, it is so far only speculative and hypothetical. Cloning to produce an embryonic stem cell line has not yet been successfully achieved in humans. Currently, SCNT projects have been undertaken in several countries (see Table 16.3).

In cloning research, oocytes are stripped from their reproductive context. However, this can still have an impact on the future fertility of women donating egg cells. In this respect, it is valid to view research cloning as a form of research on human subjects without benefit for the person herself. Specifically, egg donation for research purposes entails serious risks for women while the potential benefits (that is, future therapeutic options) for third persons are hypothetical and highly uncertain (Beeson and Lippman 2006, Magnus and Cho 2005, 2006).

Additionally, research cloning is extremely inefficient. Deducing from figures from animal research, we can calculate that 280 oocytes would be needed to produce a single cloned embryonic stem cell line (Colman and Kind 2000). This makes it very doubtful that cloning techniques to produce embryonic stem cells for treatment can ever be clinically applied unless other ways are found to provide for egg cell resources (such as in vitro maturation of primary oocytes, derivation from embryonic stem cell lines or animal oocytes; see Denn 2006). Cloned stem cells were unnecessary if immunological rejection of foreign stem cells and tissues were to be circumvented (Brown 2006). The huge numbers of women who would be needed to extract sufficient eggs for clinical purposes will never be available. For example, a conservative estimate (50 eggs per patient) by David Stevens in the USA shows that to obtain enough egg cells to seek clone cures for only four diseases (Parkinson's, Diabetes, Alzheimer's, ALS), every woman in the US aged 18–44 (around 55 million) would have to endure two cycles of ovarian hormone hyperstimulation and then undergo laparoscopic surgery.[7] Therefore, some researchers claim that SCNT can only be useful as an indirect research tool, not as the basis for individualized stem cell-based treatments.

---

7   To treat 22 million affected patients, more than 1 million egg cells would be required.   http://www.cloninginformation.org/info/cloningfact/fact-02-05-13.htm   (last accessed 26.05.2009).

'Hwanggate' in South Korea

South Korea was for some years regarded as heaven for human cloning research, with Korean researchers claiming to be highly efficient in producing cloned stem cell lines. The most prominent among them, Dr Hwang Woo Suk at Seoul National University (SNU), was actually considered a hero in South Korea for bringing the country to the forefront of stem cell and cloning research. However, as we have come to know, Hwang's claims of having successfully created for the first time in the world a cloned stem cell line were based on fraud. His study published in 2004, in which he claimed to have produced one stem cell line from 242 egg cells derived from 16 women, allegedly all unpaid volunteers who had signed informed-consent forms,[8] relied on falsified data (Hwang et al. 2004). Similarly, his report (Hwang et al. 2005) of having successfully created 11 patient-specific embryonic stem cell lines also turned out to be false. This time, he claimed to have needed 'only' 185 ova to generate the 11 cloned embryonic stem cell lines, thus allegedly having substantially improved his efficiency ratio to 1:17.

Official inquiries by the SNU investigation committee revealed that Hwang's team failed to produce even one single cloned embryonic cell line. They also brought to light that many more oocytes were procured and used than disclosed in Hwang's two *Science* papers. In their May 2006 report, public prosecutors concluded that from 2002 until December 2005, a total of 2,236 eggs had been collected from 122 women, of whom 71 had been financially remunerated. Payment even continued after 1 January 2005, when the *Bioethics and Biosafety Act* banning such practices went into effect (Wohn and Normile 2006).

According to official inquiries and reports in South Korean newspapers, 20 percent of the women involved in Hwang's research developed ovarian hyperstimulation syndrome from the hormonal drugs used in the process. More than 12 percent were treated in a hospital, and two were hospitalized for additional care (SNU 2006, Min 2006a, b).

This was not all. It also turned out that several female subordinates in Hwang's laboratory were pressured to donate their own oocytes for research.[9] Such donations from his junior researchers occurred in violation of the international standards of ethical conduct for scientists codified in the World Medical Assembly's (1964) Declaration of Helsinki. Interestingly, at least some of the female lab scientists seem to have donated ova voluntarily as kind of a medical self-experiment to

---

8   'Patients voluntarily donated oocytes … [N]o financial reimbursement in any form was paid' (Hwang et al. 2004).

9   Hwang claimed to have been unaware of egg donation by his laboratory members. In the wake of the scandal, it was revealed that Hwang's research team circulated a form asking consent for voluntary egg donation and collected signatures from female technicians. Hwang himself accompanied at least one female student to the hospital. One PhD student was forced to 'replace' oocytes she accidentally spilled with her own ova (SNU 2006; *Korea Times*, 11.1.2006, http://www.lifenews.com/bio1265.html [last accessed 26.05.2009]).

advance their scientific careers. While 35 South Korean women's organizations have filed suit against the government on behalf of women harmed in Hwang's cloning research (Rahn 2006), Hwang still has fervent supporters. More than 1,000 women pledged to donate their egg cells for his future work, mainly motivated by patriotism and hopes for the advancement of biotechnology.[10] Despite its discredit, the South Korean government announced to fund other researchers to continue human research cloning in order to keep Korea's competitive edge.

Following the revelations about the fraudulent South Korean work, the international cloning race has revived, with a number of researchers indicating that they would redouble their own efforts to be the first to clone a human embryo and derive stem cells from it. By early January 2005, the US firm *Advanced Cell Technologies* (ACT) had begun advertising for women to 'be part of the cure' by providing their eggs. In one of the ads, women were addressed thus:

> Which comes first – the egg or the cure? It could happen to you or your loved one: diabetes, heart disease, spinal cord injuries, Parkinson's disease, blindness, strokes, AIDS, MS, cancer, among others. Thousands of Americans die everyday from diseases that could potentially be treated – or even cured – using stem cells. Women 21-35 years old needed to donate eggs for stem cell research project. (All procedures will be carried out at an accredited clinic by certified medical professionals. Travel, hotel and other expenses are covered.) Let your eggs be part of the cure! Please donate your eggs. Call 202-315-3736.[11]

The language used in this advertisement bears testimony to the 'therapeutic misconception' (Magnus and Cho 2005, 1748) often inherent in appeals for egg cell donation. While risks are down played or not even mentioned, the prospects for therapeutic applications are grossly overstated, thus enticing women into exposing themselves to medical risks.[12]

New research approaches which emphasize that they avoid the ethical dilemma of embryo destruction for the creation of stem cell lines include stem cells from parthenogenetic embryos. First successful results of embryonic stem cells created by activating an unfertilized human oocyte using chemicals instead of sperm were recently presented by a team of US and Russian researchers. However, these new

---

10   http://cafe.daum.net/ilovehws (last accessed 26.05.2009).

11   *Washington Express* (a free weekly published by the *Washington Post*) January 3, 2006, 22 (online: http://www.washingtonpost.com/wp-srv/express/pdfs/EXPRESS_01032006.pdf [last accessed 14/11/2008]).

12   'The less restrictive and intrusive the state's legislation regarding third party assisted conception, the greater is the issue of commercialization of human genetic material … In countries permitting extensive commercialization, the issue arises of the status of women offering themselves on the marketplace of the industry of human reproductive services, and also of the intrinsic value of a person created by such means' (Blyth and Landau 2004, 274–5).

Table 16.3   'The race is on...': research cloning (SCNT) projects in 2006/2007

- 2 UK:
    - Edinburgh (Ian Wilmut and Christopher Shaw, King's College London)
    - Newcastle upon Tyne (Alison Murdoch)
- 1 Spain:
    - Valencia (Miodrag Stojkovic)
- 4 USA:
    - Harvard University, Boston
    - UCSF, San Francisco
    - Sloan Kettering Center, New York City
    - Advanced Cell Technology, Massachusetts
- 1 China:
    - Shanghai Institutes for Medical Sciences
- ? South Korea
- Australia*

Note: *See: 'Australia lifts ban on cloning', in: *Nature* 444, 14 December 2006, 799.

Source: Vogel 2006, own research.

stem cell sources continue to be heavily dependent on access to fresh human ova and thus are creating a demand for this resource. Ova for these experiments were extracted from women undergoing IVF in Russian fertility clinics; the female donors received some cost-coverage for their own IVF procedure (Cyranoski 2007b).

The Need for Supranational – European and International – Regulation

International reproductive tourism (Blyth and Farrand 2005, Blyth and Landau 2004, 273–5) and cross-border egg trade is growing. Infertile women from Germany, the UK and Italy are traveling to Southern and Eastern Europe and to Russia to undergo IVF with donated ova (Brodde 2006, France 2006). Egg donors from the Ukrainian capital, Kiev, are flown to Cyprus to get egg cells extracted, which are then to be implanted in women from the UK (Barnett and Smith 2006). The Romanian clinic GlobalART, which had temporarily shut down its services for clients from abroad after a resolution passed by the European Parliament (2005), has resumed its egg extraction operations (Schindele and Zimmermann 2006). The British clinic Bridge Center seems to have moved its cooperation for oocyte delivery from Bucharest to a clinic in Kiev (Abrams 2006).

The demand for oocytes generated by the cloning research race and ambitious national research programs put some pressure on deregulation. A leading stem cell scientist moved from the UK to Spain, expressly because of the better supply with 'fresh' eggs from young women (Vogel 2006). A new bill on Biomedical Research passed by the Spanish Parliament in June 2007 authorizes the use of fresh egg cells for stem cell (SCNT) research, obtained both within and outside the IVF context, that is, even donated explicitly for research (Ley de investigación biomedica, Article 32).[13] The new Act provides that compensation to donors will be regulated by the provisions of the Act on Reproductive Technologies (14/2006), which permit compensation for expenses as well as 'physical nuisances' (Ley sobre técnicas de reproducción humana asistida 2006, Article 5.3). In practice, this means that donors of oocytes for research purposes get the same compensation of around EUR1,000, which egg donors for reproduction purposes are already receiving. According to internal statistics of some Catalan fertility clinics, most egg donors are immigrant women; it is expected that the new demand may increase this tendency, especially as there is no need anymore to have an 'Anglo-Saxon' karyotype to qualify as a donor.[14]

The British HFEA changed its rules[15] in February 2007 as well to allow the donation of oocytes outside the IVF context for cloning research and to increase the level of reimbursement for oocyte donors.[16] Breaking with its former policy guidelines, the HFEA now has permitted women (called 'non-patients') who are not themselves undergoing fertility treatment to donate their ova. In return, female donors receive a compensation of up to 250 British pounds (GBP) covering loss of earnings, as well as 'reasonable expenses', such as travel costs. The HFEA also allowed ova donation through 'egg-sharing' schemes, in which women receive discounted IVF in return for handing over eggs to stem cell researchers. This 'landmark medical ruling' (Campbell 2007) was taken after a public consultation process (HFEA 2006a, b). However, feminist researchers from the social sciences harshly criticized the form and the content as well as the outcome of this HFEA consultation: they concluded that the 'narrow and specific framing of the consultation questions' prevented considering 'the wider social context within which women will be expected to make decisions and the inequalities these

---

13   Spain is proud of having derived five 'national' human embryonic stem cell lines, three of them created in Valencia, two in Barcelona. The research Center Principe Felipe (http://www.cipf.es/Actualidad/?lang=en) (last accessed 26.05.2009) has been authorized to create and bank these embryonic stem cell lines following some legal changes on the previous ART Law (Ley 7/2003, (http://www.derecho.com/xml/disposiciones/min/disposicion.xml?id_disposicion=67459&desde=min) (last accessed 26.05.2009).

14   Personal communication, Prof. Dr. Itziar Alkorta Idiakez, 21.06.2007.

15   Campbell, Denis 2007: Women will be paid to donate eggs for science, in *Observer*, 18 February 2007; Watchdog gives all clear to charitable egg donors, *Guardian*, 21 February 2007, http://www.guardian.co.uk/medicine/story/0,2018207,00.html#article_continue.

16   Preceding this decision, and before the consultation process was closed, the HFEA had issued new directions concerning the level of reimbursement; see Directions given under the HFE Act: Giving and receiving money or other benefits in respect of any supply of gametes or embryos. Ref. D.2006/1, 1 April 2006, http://www.hfea.gov.uk/docs/D2006_1_Directions_on_giving_and_receiving_money.pdf (last accessed 14.11.2008).

schemes will exacerbate and produce'. They also criticized that women were portrayed as having a strong desire to donate their eggs instead of asking 'whether researchers should be allowed to approach women'.[17] Remarkably, a two-page HFEA 'fact sheet' informing women about 'donating your eggs for research' does not even mention the medical risks implied in the process of donation.[18]

In Israel, a new legislative proposal on ova donation passed its first reading in the Knesset on May 8, 2007. The act aims at allowing ova donation from women who are not undergoing IVF treatment for themselves, but are willing to undergo ova extraction solely for donation, for purposes both of donor-aided IVF conception as well as for stem cell and cloning research. The bill strives for reducing the supposed egg shortage in Israel. *Isha L'Isha*, a feminist women's organization based in Haifa issued a position paper strongly criticizing the bill as proposed. They demand that any donation solely for research purposes shall not be permitted. Furthermore, for altruistic ova donations in the IVF context, they propose several measures for protecting vulnerable women from exploitation and medical risks, as well as for preventing abuse by sanctions in the penal law. In their view, ova donations should be subjected to the same regime as organ donation from living donors (for kidneys). Other proposed measures include extended information for prospective donors on health risks, low hormonal stimulation regimes, a maximum of ten ova extracted from each donor and monitoring and follow-up schemes for adverse consequences.[19]

In a striking and unprecedented coalition, 'pro-life' and 'pro-choice' feminists have come together internationally to call for a moratorium on egg extraction for research purposes ('Hands off our ovaries' manifesto 2006).

To sum up, paradoxically, on the one hand, the national and international effect of the Korean stem cell scandal has been 'a tightening of the ethical-legal rules for egg donation' in countries such as South Korea, Singapore and, to some extent, also in the US, and thus, arguably, 'the level of the international playing field has been heightened' (van den Belt and Keulartz 2007, 68). On the other hand, in countries like the UK, Spain and possibly Israel, protective mechanisms for women were repealed in favor of new, liberalized rules which allow for ova donation exclusively for research purposes outside the IVF context, and with more or less considerable reimbursement fees. This means that neither a 'convergence

---

17   Should scientific researchers be allowed to ask women to provide their eggs for disease research? A statement of concerns in response to the current HFEA public consultation: Donating eggs for research: safeguarding donors. December 2006, http://www.cesagen.lancs.ac.uk/events/eventsdocs/HFEA_sourcing_eggs.pdf (last accessed 27.06.2007).

18   HFEA 2007: Donating your eggs for research, http://www.hfea.gov.uk/docs/Eggs_for_research_factsheet_Feb07.pdf (last accessed 27.06.2007).

19   Proposed Legislation on Ova Donation: Isha L'Isha—Haifa Feminist Center's position, available at: http://isha.org.il/default.php?lng=3&dp=2&fl=7&pg=1 (last accessed 26.05.2009).

to the top' nor a 'race to the bottom' can fully capture diverse developments and contradictory tendencies.

This conclusion points to the decisive role of political regulation in the competitive downgrading or upgrading of ethical standards in egg donation both for IVF purposes and for human embryonic stem cell research.

Nonetheless, some alerting country reports and the occurrence of transnational reproductive trade patterns signal the urgent need for supranational political regulation. At the European level, this could be put forward by a directive of the European Union; such legislation would be legally binding on the 27 EU Member States. Recommendations by the Council of Europe would be less mandatory, but would include 46 nations.

The requirements introduced by the EU cell and tissue directive (2004/23/EG), which still await implementation in several member states, will increase safety standards and oversight and can be seen as an important step forward. However, as the directive deals generically with cells and tissues, it does not sufficiently address specific issues raised by germ cells and fertility treatments or research. Therefore, further regulation and harmonization measures on the EU level are needed.

On the international level, regulation by the United Nations could be most powerful if it were passed as an international convention. But even if there were only a non-binding UN declaration, this 'soft law' could set some ethical standards and provide for guidance. The UN Declaration on Human Cloning (59/280) adopted in 2005 called upon the nations 'to prohibit all forms of human cloning', thus entailing both reproductive cloning and research cloning.[20] It also called 'to take measures to prevent the exploitation of women in the application of life sciences' (UN 2005, clauses b and d). Unfortunately, national legislation to bring these calls into effect so far was hardly adopted and implemented. If a complete ban on cloning research shall not be achieved at the national level, then at least strict regulatory measures should be taken.

Supranational regulation and governance cannot and will not mean uniform standards. It can only provide some minimum standards that must be met by all the states which allow egg cell donations to take place within their respective jurisdictions. This shall not prevent a state from maintaining or introducing in its

---

20 Unfortunately, despite the long gestation process, an international cloning convention which was originally intended, could not be achieved. Resolution 59/280 was passed by the General Assembly on a recorded vote of 84 to 34, with 37 abstentions. The Member States having opted for permitting and funding cloning research within their jurisdictions objected or abstained from vote. A policy change within these countries cannot be expected. Thus, the UN passed a somewhat 'radical' declaration, which in many states will probably not be implemented. The alternative would have been to ban reproductive cloning, as it happened, and to permit cloning (SCNT) research on the condition that strict legislative standards be passed to regulate this research. For many reasons, this route was not taken in the course of development.

territory more stringent protective measures. It would not undermine domestic regulation prohibiting egg donation, if democratic decision-making has come to choose this prohibitive way of regulation but would provide some protection for women living under more permissive regimes.

The following paragraphs will propose some rules for supranational regulation which warrant international deliberation.

1. Abolish Anonymous Donation of Germ Cells

In regard to egg donation for reproductive purposes, the best interests of the *children* should be the primary consideration.[21] Because assisted reproduction is viewed as a medical procedure for adults, the children-to-be are often neglected. Unlike adoptees, who have gained the right to their original birth certificates, most of the donor-conceived offspring still do not know how they came to be.[22] The guiding principle should be that the rights of donor-conceived people 'not to be deceived or deprived of information about [their] personal history'[23] must be protected. The welfare and best interests of the child imply the right to know about his or her genetic origin. This should be in compliance with the UN Convention on the Rights of the Child (Article 3, 7, 8)[24] (compare Blyth and Farrand 2004).

Therefore, mechanisms for donor registration should be set up that will enable offspring who wish to know about – and potentially contact – their genetic parent

---

21   See EU Charter (2000), article 24.2.: 'In all actions relating to children, whether taken by public authorities or private institutions, the child's best interests must be a primary consideration'.

22   Interestingly, in several countries such as the UK and the USA, adults conceived by sperm donation have organized and try to trace their genetic fathers. In the UK, the Donor Conception Network has been very active in promoting openness and telling a child of its donor origins (http://www.donor-conception-network.org/) (last accessed 26.05.2009).

23   David Gollancz in House of Commons (2005, Ev 30).

24   UN (1989): Convention on the Rights of the Child. Article 3:1. In all actions concerning children, whether undertaken by public or private social welfare institutions, courts of law, administrative authorities or legislative bodies, the best interests of the child shall be a primary consideration. Article 7:1. The child shall be registered immediately after birth and shall have the right from birth to a name, the right to acquire a nationality and, as far as possible, the right to know and be cared for by his or her parents. 2. States Parties shall ensure the implementation of these rights in accordance with their national law and their obligations under the relevant international instruments in this field, in particular where the child would otherwise be stateless. Article 8:1. States Parties undertake to respect the right of the child to preserve his or her identity, including nationality, name and family relations as recognized by law without unlawful interference. 2. Where a child is illegally deprived of some or all of the elements of his or her identity, States Parties shall provide appropriate assistance and protection, with a view to re-establishing speedily his or her identity.

to have access to the recorded information from a central database when they reach age 18. As we know from adoption research, family secrets are harmful for children (Sorosky et al. 1984, Hartman 1993, Landau 1999, Whipp 1998, Blyth and Landau 2004, Turner and Coyle 2000). Laws cannot force parents to tell the truth to children created by germ cell donation. But at least they can provide instruments to enable donor-conceived offspring to know from where they came to be, if they so wish. It is to be emphasized that non-anonymity requirements do neither confer custody nor liability rights and obligations.

A ban on anonymous donation of genetic material and mandatory identity disclosure may initially lead to some decline in donor rates. However, as experience in several countries that have open (non-anonymous) sperm donation practices has shown, identity disclosure policies mostly just shifted the recruitment of donors towards men who already had children and whose motivation to donate is more reflective and not primarily triggered by financial reasons (Thorn 2002, Blyth et al. 2004).

A *complementary* requirement – the right of *donors* to get information about the outcome of egg donation and to know whether children were born as a result of germ cell donation – also merits consideration. Not to know whether somewhere in this world there is a child – or even several of them – who are genetically related can be a cause of substantial psychological distress for donors. Even if donors don't seem to care about this at the time of donation, or even favor anonymity and 'not-knowing', experience shows that certain life events later on, such as having one's own children, or experiencing disease, life crises or the death of relatives, may kindle the desire to know about one's own genetic offspring. Moreover, some women feel guilty about not having cared for their genetic child or develop some feelings of responsibility for her or him. Having access to some information about children born from their gametes may have positive effects on them (Daniels and Haimes 1998). Interestingly, there are also potentially positive effects on the social parents – the 'recipients' of germ cells. They may seek to get some information on the donor in the face of some particular biographic events (for example, a health problem in the child).

Another useful suggestion is to permit donor-conceived children to search for siblings once they have attained the age of 18, as was proposed in a draft of the Human Fertilisation and Embryology Bill by the UK Government. As experiences from the US and some European countries show, donor-conceived offspring are looking for half-siblings via the Internet to get in touch with them, as a form to fill the gap felt by them about tracing their origins (Schindele 2007). According to the UK bill, which was passed by the House of Commons on 25 October 2008, egg and sperm donors will also be informed of any children seeking their identity.[25]

---

25   Draft UK Tissue and Embryos bill published 21 May 2007, http://www.bionews. org.uk/new.lasso?storyid=3442.

2. Oversight and Quality Control of Clinics and Research

In many countries, there is no regulation of the number of clinics providing services and no monitoring of their performance. Such oversight and quality control is essential to ensure transparency, accountability and trust. The British model of establishing a specialized regulatory agency, the Human Fertilization and Embryology Agency (HFEA), may be instructive in considering the kind of mechanisms needed.

A major element in oversight and quality control is a mandatory register of procedures and outcomes. With a registry and mandatory reporting by clinics, IVF success rates (liveborn baby-take home rates), problems such as multiple pregnancy rates (twins, triplets, etc.), premature birth after IVF and complications such as hyperstimulation syndrome and other serious adverse effects can be recorded and monitored, thereby increasing transparency.[26] Other useful regulatory instruments include regular inspections and licensing schemes, both for IVF treatment and for research with germ cells and embryos, which introduce accreditation and approval requirements (see HFEA 2005).

3. High Standards for Qualified Informed Consent Procedures

Another necessary regulatory requirement concerns the need for high standards for ethical, accountable informed-consent procedures free of conflicts of interest, both for donors and for recipients of germ cells. For qualified informed consent, there must be full, accurate, unbiased information about short- and long-term risks of hormonal stimulation and of oocyte extraction for a woman's health and fertility (Rimington et al. 1999, Beeson and Lippman 2006). However, comprehensive informed consent must not mean a shift of medical responsibility and liability for any of the consequences of egg cell donation to the donor herself.

Complementary measures to protect ova donors that could be required at the national level, include:

- A precondition of having given birth to one or two children before one can be eligible to be an oocyte donor for IVF or for research cloning. Donating egg cells can have implications for future fertility and affect a donor's chance of having her own children later in life. This requirement would provide some means of safeguard for donors should they become infertile as a consequence of the hormonal treatment or from injuries such as inflammation or scars in the retrieval of egg cells.
- Limits on the number of stimulated cycles in an individual woman and low stimulation regimes. It is alarming that, for example, in Spain oocyte donors are sometimes undergoing three to four stimulation cycles per year

---

26   This reporting requirement is established for tissue procurement in the EU tissue directive (23/2004/EC) in Article 7(6).

(Schindele and Zimmermann 2006, Alkorta 2006), in Cyprus even more.[27] As some studies indicate, repeated and strong stimulation may increase the long-term risks of cancer for a woman (Althuis et al. 2005, Brinton et al. 2005, Ahuja and Simons 1998, Rossing et al. 1994).

- Limits on the number of children born after egg donation from a single donor.
- Donor screening for infectious diseases is important both for donor and for recipients. However, screening for genetic disorders or susceptibilities, as is sometimes required, is not free from eugenic undertones and carries the risk of interfering with the donor's right 'not-to-know'. It may also violate data protection rights and even expose women to genetic discrimination and stigmatization.

4. Donor Advocates

Clinics should provide for an independent donor advocate, particularly in the case of 'altruistic donation', to ensure that information provided is unbiased as well as to enable psycho-social counseling for the donor. Where appropriate, we should also consider procedures that are based on ethics committee models for assessing whether a donation is truly voluntary and not forced by psychological pressure or induced by financial offers.[28]

5. Precluding Conflicts of Interest

Conflicts of interest may arise if the same institution or person who carries out donor recruitment also uses the egg cells obtained. Most obvious would be the temptation to push stimulation in order to gain more oocytes, clearly something detrimental to a woman's health and well-being. Therefore, particularly in the case of cloning research, there should be a clear separation of institutions and of personnel in the informed consent process, the procurement of eggs and the use of oocytes obtained.

---

27   According to reports on the situation at the Petra Health Clinic on Cyprus, egg donors are not given any psychological or medical counseling and do receive more money the more eggs they produce. According to local sources, one young woman donated nearly 20 times. At another fertility clinic in Nicosia, some women viewed egg donation as their main source of income, going through the process of being injected with hormones at least five times a year. The payment rate was 350 Cyprus pounds (EUR600) for a cycle in which a woman produced 12 eggs; 500 Cyprus pounds if she produced more (Barnett and Smith 2006).

28   Such a model was introduced as statutory requirement in the German Organ Transplantation Act (1997, §8 [3]) and has been implemented in Germany for assessing organ-donation from living donors.

6. Follow-up and Health Coverage for Adverse Consequences

Follow-up monitoring und ongoing protection for donors must be secured; the specific mechanisms or model implemented will depend on the features of a country's national healthcare system. In general, clinics must give healthcare services at no costs to the woman should there be complications related to the egg extraction. Clinics or the state should also provide for insurance for donors in case of occupational disability or death. Another model would be to oblige the health insurance of the egg recipient to cover the costs of treatment for the donor's ill-health if it can be related to the donation.

7. Non-commercial Donation

Emphasis should be placed on non-commercial donation, even making this a mandatory requirement. This position accords with the deontological principle of the non-commodification of the human body. This principle, a universal norm, derives from the particular status of the human body, which is a precondition for the human existence as a person, and its inalienability (see Schneider 2003b, 2007).

7.1. European norms   A commitment to non-commercialization can draw on Article 3 of the Charter of Fundamental Rights of the European Union (2000). It states that 'in the fields of medicine and biology', the 'prohibition on making the human body and its parts as such a source of financial gain' must be respected.[29] This principle has also been codified in Article 21 of the Convention on Human Rights and Biomedicine of the Council of Europe (1997), wherein it is stated: 'The human body and its parts shall not, as such, give rise to financial gain or comparable advantage'.[30]

The commitment to non-commercial donation is also expressed in Article 12 of the EU Directive on human tissues and cells (2004/23/EC): 'Member States

---

29   'Article 3: Right to the integrity of the person: 1. Everyone has the right to respect for his or her physical and mental integrity. 2. In the fields of medicine and biology, the following must be respected in particular:
- the free and informed consent of the person concerned, according to the procedures laid down by law,
- the prohibition of eugenic practices, in particular those aiming at the selection of persons,
- the prohibition on making the human body and its parts as such a source of financial gain' (EU 2000/C 364/01).

30   This principle was further concretized in Articles 21 and 22 of the Additional Protocol to the Convention on Human Rights and Biomedicine, on Transplantation of Organs and Tissues of Human Origin: 'Article 21: Prohibition of financial gain: 1. The human body and its parts shall not, as such, give rise to financial gain or comparable advantage. The aforementioned provision shall not prevent payments which do not constitute a financial

shall endeavour to ensure voluntary and unpaid donations of tissues and cells'. Unfortunately, non-payment is not laid down as a strictly binding requirement but is only codified as a guiding principle. These standards should also be further specified for germ cell donation.

Article 12 further stipulates: 'Donors may receive compensation, which is strictly limited to making good the expenses and inconveniences related to the donation. In that case, Member States define the conditions under which compensation may be granted'. Thus the exact terms are left to the subsidiarity principle.

Unfortunately, the term 'compensation' establishes a grey zone which allows for commercialization to enter through the back door: exactly what would constitute 'justifiable expenses?' Should compensation only cover reimbursement of out-of-pocket expenses, such as travel costs, or also include lost wages, child care, the time for hormonal 'preparation', etc.? Furthermore, 'compensation' could also be expanded to indemnify for 'inconveniencies', such as pain and suffering or even for other immaterial damages.

Obviously, whether and to what extent to compensate women for providing oocytes are controversial matters. What is clear, however, is that the more 'compensation' is considered as fair, the more it legitimates the sale and purchase of ova. The more broadly expenses and inconveniences are interpreted, the more there is space for indirect commercialization.

It is doubtful whether there can ever be a 'just price' for egg cells. The dilemma for donors thus reduces to how paying 'too much' becomes an undue inducement, while paying 'too little' will always come close to exploitation. For oocyte 'consumers' – the recipients and/or researchers – prices that are 'too high' may work as a disincentive and encourage, among other things, the reproductive tourism outlined earlier. In any case, leaving governance and steering to price bidding on unrestrained and unregulated markets seems to be inadequate.

Some, including this contributor, are very skeptical concerning proposals to dry up transnational egg trafficking by demanding 'higher wages' for the women involved. Of course, brokers or other intermediaries often take the lion's share of profits (Heng 2006, 2007). But it is most uncertain that state-organized procurement would be an adequate alternative. There will never – and cannot ever – be a 'just price' for eggs. In market economies, prices are a result of demand and supply. If

---

gain or a comparable advantage, in particular: – compensation of living donors for loss of earnings and any other justifiable expenses caused by the removal or by the related medical examinations; – payment of a justifiable fee for legitimate medical or related technical services rendered in connection with transplantation; – compensation in case of undue damage resulting from the removal of organs or tissues from living persons. 2. Advertising the need for, or availability of, organs or tissues, with a view to offering or seeking financial gain or comparable advantage, shall be prohibited. Article 22 – Prohibition of organ and tissue trafficking: Organ and tissue trafficking shall be prohibited' (Council of Europe 2002).

prices are too high, the industry will move to another country. In a world where more than a billion people have to live on less than one US dollar per day, it seems to be an illusion to allow paid sale of egg cells and to keep prices up.

7.2. The pros and cons of payment   Of course there is no definite answer to these contentious questions. In the following, I will briefly summarize the pros and cons.

The most common arguments brought forward *in favour of payment* are:

*   Women's work should be remunerated.
*   Her suffering should be compensated.
*   Payment for sperm is already occurring.
*   Egg donation should be seen like the sale of one's labor or as a service for providing a product.
*   If intermediaries (brokers) and doctors are paid anyway, it would be unfair to exclude the donor.
*   And finally, autonomy is invoked, claiming that a woman should be allowed to control her body and to 'own' it as 'property', thus giving her full rights of disposition (see Wilkinson 2003, Andrews 1986, Dickenson 1997).

Counterarguments against payment include:

*   Gametes are unlike work or services; they are about kinship and genealogy.
*   The body can never be completely dissociated from the person. My body is not my property but part of myself as a person.
*   Resulting children are not 'products' and should not be regarded as a commodity (this applies if gametes are used for reproductive purposes).[31]
*   As complications and risks show, there can never be a complete 'control' over one's own body (see Ruhl 2002).
*   Organizing the transfer and exchange of bodily substances in gift relationships (Titmuss 1971) affirms important social values.
*   It is more advisable to restrict 'downstream' commercialization than to commodify the act of donation itself (see Radin 1996, Schneider 2003b).

---

31   The psychological harm possibly caused by paid donation has been expressed in a testimony by Suzanne Rubin: 'How do I reconcile my sense of integrity with knowing that my father sold what was the essence of my life for $25 to a total stranger, and then walked away without a second look back? … How do I learn to live without profound pain and disappointment knowing that this man, who is my father and who is my flesh and blood, "Did it for the bucks?"' (Rubin 1983, 214; for the psycho-social dimensions, see Daniels and Lewis 1996, Daniels 2000, Blyth and Farrand 2005).

This contributor's preference, assuming a country actually allows for any oocyte 'donation', is that this should be restricted to so-called altruistic donation with at most only some minimal compensation provided as reimbursement for necessary expenses. If compensation is too high, this would indirectly amount to commodification and thus undermine the ban on payment.

To illustrate the perils of payment, another advertisement from the US-based IVF and Genetics Institute is instructive: Women are lured into 'donation' by dangling multi-thousand dollar sums. An ad, showing a smiling, cheerful young woman says: 'Help infertile couples experience the joys of parenthood and earn up to $50,000. Become an egg donor. We need healthy women up to age 32. Compensation begins at $5,000! ... To apply online, visit www.gametedonors. com. Confidentiality assured'.[32]

However, in reality, most women are never paid amounts of this magnitude, but much less (around 3,000–5,000 US dollars [USD], Steinbrook 2006). The fertility clinics placing these ads apparently have no intention of paying up to USD 50,000 but rather are trying to attract women for egg extraction recruitment.

7.3 Consequentialist arguments contra payment   Non-payment for human bodily substances, particularly germ cells, is not only a basic ethical principle which reflects cultural and moral norms about the status of the human body and about children. It can also be justified based on consequentialist considerations:

- Paying women to donate egg cells may undermine a proper informed consent. The financial incentive may rule out the adequate consideration of medical and psycho-social risks. It may induce women to take on serious risks without proper understanding or without taking into consideration the potential acute and long-term adverse effects of the medical intervention for egg harvesting.
- Payment can also tempt concealment of important information by the donor, for example, about infections and diseases, in order not to be rejected as a donor. This can have negative effects on the donor herself, as well as on the recipient and the resulting child. (These risks can only partly be countervailed by medical tests and tissue screening procedures).
- The most important reason against payment, in this contributor's opinion, is the fact that any payment may cause a social bias in the recruitment of donors: less well-off women, particularly those in poorer countries, are already more vulnerable to exploitation because of their economic situation. The potential for disproportionate recruitment of low-income women, migrants and young students for their egg cells is high. If women are paid to donate ova, those in financial need may neglect health risks. Payment creates a particular inducement to put themselves at risk to economically

---

32   Advertisement from *The Daily Bruin*, the campus newspaper at the University of California, Los Angeles, January 2005.

disadvantaged women who do not have other ways to earn their living. This contravenes principles of equality and reciprocity. The transfer of ova from 'poor to rich' also touches on hot issues of power differentials, gender inequality and exploitation.

Given the disagreements on the ethics of egg cell donation and the long-lasting controversies on payment, it is likely that consensus may never be reached. In this situation, however, prudence and diligence call for applying the 'precautionary principle'. This means that in cases of doubt, we should opt 'to err on the side of caution' ('*in dubio pro protectione*').

8. National Self-Sufficiency as Guiding Principle

National self-sufficiency through voluntary, unpaid donations should be achieved and be the guiding principle for supranational regulation.[33]

There are several reasons for this provision. Most obviously, because of the existing gaps in living standards and wages between countries, this self-sufficiency would mean that women in poorer countries could not be used to provide ova as resources for those in wealthier conditions. Countries should not be allowed to 'export' problems emerging within their own territory but must look for adequate solutions within their own jurisdictions.

9. Regulatory Framework as Gender-Sensitive, Human Rights-Based Approach

Any regulatory framework that is politically endorsed and implemented must take a human rights-based approach and, thereby, necessarily be gender sensitive. The commitment to a human rights framework can be underlined in a respective preamble to the regulatory text.

---

33 At a first glance, national autarky seems to contravene the EU single market and international free trade. However, this commitment to self-reliance has already been established in the case of blood donations in the wake of the HIV contamination scandals in the early 1990s. The German Blood Transfusion Act (Transfusionsgesetz, 1.7.1998), for instance, in its Article 1 sets as its purpose the safe provision of blood which shall be fostered by the self-supply with blood and plasma. The EU 'Blood' Directive as well affirms the EU's commitment to attain Community's self-sufficiency through voluntarily, unpaid donation (2002/98/EC, Recitals 7, 8, 9, 23, 32). However, several Member States significantly depend on the importation of commercially sourced blood products (see Farrell 2005), and self-sufficiency through voluntary, unpaid donation was not made a mandatory requirement.

10. The State of California Bill 1260 – a Model Legislation for SCNT Research?

The Reproductive Health and Research Bill (Senate Bill 1260), which was passed by the State of California legislature in September 2006, may be seen as an important step into the right direction for those US states and other nations who decided to allow for SCNT research. Bill 1260 regulates the procurement of oocytes for research.[34] It defines women who provide oocytes for research as 'research subjects', triggering federal and state regulatory protections. It ensures that women should be better informed of the risks of egg retrieval and mandates that access and costs for women suffering from adverse reactions are covered. The bill also prohibits employees working in stem cell units using their own human oocytes and their family members to donate ova for the research project. To prevent conflicts of interest, the physicians performing the egg cell retrieval shall not have a financial interest in the outcome of the research and must disclose other relationships. The aspect of the law that has drawn most attention is the limit it places on payment for oocyte donors to reimbursement for direct expenses and for lost wages.[35]

Senate Bill 1260 draws on recommendations for Human Embryonic Stem Cell Research issued in 2005 by a special committee of the US National Academies for Sciences (see Steinbrook 2006) and on policies adopted by the California Institute for Regenerative Medicine and by the state of Massachusetts (Darnovsky 2006). Another important requirement of SB 1260 is that oocytes procured outside of California to be used for cloning and stem cell research taking place within this state shall meet these same standards. Thus, the California bill may have some radiation effect on other US states and may prevent the import of oocytes derived under lower safeguards.

What is missing, though, is a rule impeding researchers in nations that prohibit payment for egg cells to work on stem cells derived from eggs procured by collaborators elsewhere from paid donors (compare Safeguards for Donors

---

34 Oocyte donation for reproductive purposes is not regulated in the Bill on so-called 'assisted oocyte production'.

The law applies only to research conducted in California which is not funded by the California Institute for Regenerative Medicine (CIRM). It does not cover CIRM-funded research because Proposition 71, which led to the foundation of CIRM, prohibited any legislative amendments until January 1, 2008. However, it does close a loophole in CIRM's own regulations that could have encouraged researchers to use non-CIRM money to get oocytes obtained without safeguards (Marcy Darnovsky, personal communication, 05.12.2006).

35 Contrary to the draft proposal for the bill, lost wages are no longer excluded from reimbursable expenses in the Senate Bill 1260 passed. Nonetheless, beyond direct expenses and lost wages, compensation is still prohibited. This makes SB1260 consistent with the rules for the CIRM (California Institute for Regenerative Medicine) and with the US National Academies' guidelines.

2006). Regulatory measures like California's bill will be needed to set enforceable standards and safeguard women's health, should SCNT research be permitted.

Outlook: Shortages as Incentive?

Revelations about reproductive tourism and cross-border trade in oocytes, and about ova acquisition in the wake of the South Korean cloning scandal have created more public sensitivity concerning ethical, legal and social issues. The growing awareness of the manifold problems and risks associated both with egg donation and with cloning research must be translated into comprehensive regulatory models. These should be based on non-anonymity of germ cell donation and provide for registers and quality control of clinics as well as of research to enhance transparency. High standards for qualified informed consent procedures must be combined with other safeguards, such as donor advocates and the preclusion of conflicts of interest. Donors must be followed up for adverse consequences on their mental and physical well-being, and treatment costs be covered. Non-commercial donation of ova should be mandatory, and women who provide egg cells should be reimbursed for their expenses but not paid beyond that. To preclude cross-border trade and exploitation of women, national self-sufficiency through voluntary, unpaid donations should be achieved. Thus, oocyte donation must not follow the market model but must be based on a gender sensitive, human rights approach.

Despite the need for and attraction of both national and supranational regulations on egg extraction, such a regime could lead to an exacerbation of what is said to be an egg cell 'shortage'. This is the risk we are taking. The political goal must not and should not be the 'maximum supply' with ova, but respect for and commitment to humanitarian social values and protection of the health and well-being of the women donors, the resulting children and the (possible future) recipient-patients.

There is not a fixed demand for egg cells. Demand can be increased by medical and social factors, such as postponement of the wish for a child even until after menopause or failure to deal with environmental exposures that harm fertility. This calls for proper consideration of the social conditions of procreation and childrearing. There are no positive rights which would force us to strive for maximalist procurement strategies. Neither is there a 'right to have a child'; there is only a negative right not to be hindered by the state to procreate.

Nor does freedom of research encompass a 'right' to get the respective 'material' delivered. Freedom of research means intellectual freedom, but in their actions, researchers must as a matter of course respect human rights. There also is not – and can never be – a positive duty to participate in biomedical research if we do not want to run into a forced socialization and social obligation of our bodies.

Societies must live and deal with the fact that certain bodily substances are rare, precious and, by many people, regarded as inalienable (Schneider 2008).

However, shortages must not always be seen as negative. They can also provide opportunities to widen the horizon and to engage in creative solutions for the underlying problems, such as involuntary childlessness or severe diseases. In the search for cures, there are many possible strategies and solutions which do not necessarily rely on sensitive bodily substances of others. Shortages in 'material' can encourage approaches to invent other social and technical solutions and even encourage other ways of dealing with the challenges involved.

It may well be that breakthroughs in experimental biology may radically alter the landscape of stem cell research. Research in mice reported by three different research groups[36] in June 2007 (Cyranoski 2007a) suggested that fibroblast cells harvested from skin of adult persons could be turned into 'induced' pluripotent stem cells (so-called iPS cells) by adding a mixture of different proteins. This 'proof of principle' achieved in mice was soon applied to human cells as well. However, the transcription factors which are transferred to the cells using retroviruses must yet turn out to be a safe and efficient procedure. These and other important preconditions still require substantial experimental work (Nishikawa et al. 2008). If safe, specific and efficient reprogramming of human somatic cells towards pluripotency could be induced, then a radical shift in embryonic stem cell and cloning research could be accomplished.

It remains to be seen whether these iPS-achievements can work as valuable research tools and could in the future be applied for patient-specific cell therapies. If so, then the need for female ova and embryos for obtaining pluripotent stem cells would arguably be rendered obsolete. Thus, the procurement of egg cells and embryos, which still constitute the 'ethical heel of Achilles' (van den Belt and Keulartz 2007, 68) for human embryonic stem cell research, could possibly be overcome by new technical means for obtaining pluripotent stem cells for research and potentially for future therapeutic purposes. These research results may radically call into question current research projects in which women are subject to the manifold risks of egg extraction.

However, these interesting experimental achievements should not induce policy-makers to twiddle their thumbs, hoping that technical progress may dissolve complex ethical questions. Funding decisions and regulations for biomedical research and Assisted Reproductive Technologies can strongly impact on technological trajectories and social practices. The implementation of the UN Convention on the Rights of the Child, particularly mechanisms such as donor registries for safeguarding the children's right to know about his or her genetic origin, are crucial as well for enabling donor-conceived offspring to trace their genetic parents. Therefore, it is of utmost importance to continue political deliberations on these issues. The task ahead is to strive for regulations which neither sacrifice women's health today for the sake of highly uncertain medical therapies tomorrow, nor to subject children-to-be to the psychological harms of darkness about their genetic-social origins.

---

36   See Takahashi and Yamanaka 2006, Maherali et al. 2007, Okita et al. 2007.

Acknowledgments

The propositions and recommendations presented in this chapter were discussed with experts, politicians and women's organizations from Western, Southern and Eastern Europe, Russia, Israel, the USA and Canada on several occasions. First at the conference 'European Biopolitics: Connecting Civil Society – Implementing Basic Values', in Berlin, March 17–19, 2006, which was organized by the Heinrich Böll Foundation and the 'Institut Mensch, Ethik und Wissenschaft' (Institute Humans, Ethics, and Science). Second with social scientists, biomedical researchers and lawyers at the workshop 'Commodification and Trust' from the EU-FP6 project 'Property Regulation in European Science, Ethics and Law (PropEur)' in Bratislava, Slovakia, June 23–24, 2006 and finally with members of the European Parliament at the Parliamentary 'Intergroup Bioethics' session on June 21, 2007 in Strasbourg. An earlier version of this chapter was published in *Law and the Human Genome Review*, July-December 2006 (25), 205–41; the present version was substantially revised and updated for publication in this volume. Special thanks go to Marcy Darnovsky and Abby Lippman for important information and support. The views expressed in this article only reflect those of the author. The responsibility for any remaining errors is solely mine.

Bibliography

Abrams, F. (2006), 'The misery behind the baby trade', *Daily Mail*, 17 July.

Ahuja, K.K. and Simons, E.G. (1998), 'Cancer of the colon in an egg donor: policy repercussions for donor recruitment', *Human Reproduction* 13 (1), 227–31.

Alkorta I. (2006), 'Donación de óvulos', *El País*, 28.03.2006. http://www.elpais.com/articulo/salud/Donacion/ovulos/elpsalpor/20060328elpepisal_4/Tes/ (last accessed 26.05.2009).

Althuis, M.D. et al. (2005), 'Uterine cancer after use of clomiphene citrate to induce ovulation', *American Journal of Epidemiology* 161, 607–15.

Andrews, L.B. (1986), 'My Body, My Property', Hastings Center Report, October, 28–38.

Barnett, A. and Smith, H. (2006), 'Cruel cost of the human egg trade', *The Observer*, April 30.

Beeson, D. and Lippman, A. (2006), 'Egg harvesting for stem cell research: medical risks and ethical problems', *RBM online* 13, No. 4.

Blyth, E. and Farrand, A. (2004), 'Anonymity in donor-assisted conception and the UN Convention on the Rights of the Child', *International Journal of Children's Rights* 12, 89–104.

—— (2005), 'Reproductive tourism – a price worth paying for reproductive autonomy?', *Critical Social Policy* 25 (1), 91–114.

Blyth, E. and Landau, R. (2004), *Third Party Assisted Conception Across Cultures* (London, New York: Jessica Kingsley).

Blyth, E., Crawshaw, M. and Daniels, K. (2004), 'Policy formation in gamete donation and egg sharing in the UK – a critical appraisal', *Social Science and Medicine* 59 (12), 2617–26.

Brinton L.A. et al. (2005), 'Ovulation induction and cancer risk', *Fertility and Sterility* 83, 261–74.

Brodde, K. (2006), 'Die Jagd nach den Eizellen', *Greenpeace Magazin,* 3/2006, 72–5, http://www.reprokult.de/EizellenKirstenBroddeGreenpeaceMag_3_06.pdf.

Brown, P. (2006), 'Cloning: Do we even need eggs?', *Nature* 439, 655–7.

California (2006), *Senate Bill (SB) 1260*, introduced by Senators Ortiz and Runner, signed into law by Governor Arnold Schwarzenegger on September 26.

Campbell, D. (2007), 'Women will be paid to donate eggs for science', *The Observer*, 18 February. Check, E. (2006), 'Ethicists and biologists ponder the price of eggs', *Nature* 442 (10), 606–7.

Cobbe, N. (2006), 'Why the apparent haste to clone humans?', *Journal of Medical Ethics* 32, 298–302.

Colman, A. and Kind, A. (2000), 'Therapeutic Cloning. Concepts and Practicalities', *Tibtech* 18, 192–6.

Council of Europe (1997), Convention for the Protection of Human Rights and Dignity of the Human Being with regard to the Application of Biology and Medicine: Convention on Human Rights and Biomedicine. Oviedo, 4.4.1997, http://conventions.coe.int/Treaty/EN/Treaties/Html/164.htm.

—— (2002), Additional Protocol to the Convention on Human Rights and Biomedicine, on Transplantation of Organs and Tissues of Human Origin. Strasbourg, 24.1.2002, http://conventions.coe.int/Treaty/EN/Treaties/Html/186. htm (last accessed 26.05.2009).

Cyranoski, D. (2007a), 'Simple switch turns cells embryonic', *Nature* 447 (7), 618–19.

—— (2007b), 'Activated eggs offer route to stem cells', *Nature* 448, 116.

Daniels, K.R. (2000), 'To give and sell human gametes – the interplay between pragmatics, policy and ethics', *Journal of Medical Ethics* 26, 206–11.

Daniels, K.R. and Lewis, G.M. (1996), 'Donor Insemination: The gifting and selling of semen', *Social Science and Medicine* 42 (11), 1521–36.

Daniels, K. and Haimes, E. (1998), *Donor Insemination. International Social Science Perspectives* (Cambridge: Cambridge University Press).

Darnovsky, M. (2006), 'A Pro-Woman Stem-Cell Policy', *Tom Paine*, October 26, http://www.tompaine.com/articles/2006/10/26/a_prowoman_stemcell_policy. php (last accessed 26.05.2009).

Denn, C. (2006), 'Mining the secrets of the egg', *Nature* 439, 652–55.

Dickenson, D. (1997), *Property, Women and Politics. Subjects or Objects?* (Cambridge: Cambridge University Press).

Edwards, J. (1998), 'Donor insemination and "public opinion" in Daniel and Haimes 1998, 151–72.

EU (2000), *Charter of Fundamental Rights of the European Union* (2000/C 364/01), http://www.europarl.eu.int/charter/pdf/text_en.pdf (last accessed 26.05.2009).

—— (2004), Directive 2004/23/EC of the European Parliament and of the Council of 31 March 2004 on setting standards of quality and safety for the donation, procurement, testing, processing, preservation, storage and distribution of human tissues and cells, http://eur-lex.europa.eu/smartapi/cgi/sga_doc?smart api!celexapi!prod!CELEXnumdoc&lg=en&numdoc=32004L0023&model=g uichett (last accessed 26.05.2009).

European Commission (2006), Report on the Regulation of Reproductive Cell Donation in the European Union. Results of Survey, February.

European Parliament (2005), *Planned egg cell trade. Resolution on the trade in human egg cells.* P6_TA(2005)0074. http://europa.eu.int/eur-lex/lex/ LexUriserv/site/en/oj/2005/ce320/ce32020051215en02510253.pdf (last accessed 26.05.2009).

Farrell, A.M. (2005), 'The emergence of EU governance in public health: the case of EU blood policy and regulation', in Steffen, M. (ed.), *Health Governance in Europe* (London, New York: Routledge), 134–51.

Fox, R. and Swazey, J. (1992), *Spare Parts: Organ Replacement in American Society* (New York: Oxford University Press).

France, L. (2006), 'Passport, tickets, sun cream, sperm. Faced with long waiting lists at home, infertile British women are booking IVF holidays in the sun', *The Observer*, 15 January.

German Transfusion Law (1998), *TFG – Transfusionsgesetz.* 1.7. 1998, BGbl. I 1998, 1752.

Gramser, S. (2006), 'Leading stem-cell biologist heads across Europe', *Nature* 439, 240.

Hands off manifesto (2006*), Keep your hands off our ovaries!* Campaign launched 8 March 2006. http://www.handsoffourovaries.com/manifesto.htm (last accessed 26.05.2009).

Hartman, A. (1993), 'Secrecy in Adoption', in Imber-Black, E. (ed.), *Secrets in Families and Family Therapy* (New York: W.W. Norton).

Heng, B.C. (2006), 'The advent of international "mail-order" egg donation', *British Journal of Obstetrics and Gynaecology* 113, 1225–7.

—— (2007), 'Should fertility specialists refer local patients abroad for shared or commercialized oocyte donation? ', *Fertility and Sterility* 87 (1), 6–7.

HFEA (Human Fertilisation and Embryology Authority) (2005), *Facing the Future.* Annual Report 2004/2005 (London).

—— (2006a), Donating eggs for research: safeguarding donors – consultation document. September 2006.

—— (2006b), SEED Report. A report on the Human Fertilisation & Embryology Authority's review of sperm, egg and embryo donation in the United Kingdom. http://www.hfea.gov.uk/docs/SEEDReport05.pdf (last accessed 26.05.2009).

House of Commons (2005), *Human Reproductive Technologies and the Law.* Fifth Report of Session 2004–05, vol. II.

Hwang, W.S. et al. (2004), 'Evidence of a pluripotent human embryonic stem cell line derived from a cloned blastocyst', *Science* 303, 1669–74.

—— (2005), 'Patient-specific embryonic stem cells derived from human SCNT blastocysts', *Science* 308, 1777–83.

Johnson, M.H. (1999), 'The medical ethics of paid egg sharing in the UK', *Human Reproduction* 14 (7), 1912–18.

Ley de investigación biomedica (Biomedical Research Act) (2007), passed by the Parliament in Spain on 20 June 2007.

Ley sobre técnicas de reproducción humana asistida (Act on Assisted Human Reproduction) (2006), Ley 14/2006, Spain, in force 26 May 2006, *Boletín Oficial del Estado*, núm. 126, 27 mayo 2006, 19947–19954.

Landau, R. (1999), 'Planned orphanhood', *Social Science and Medicine* 49 (2), 185–96.

Magnus, D. and Cho, M.K. (2005), 'Issues in Oocyte Donation for Stem Cell Research', *Science* 308, 1747–8.

—— (2006), 'A Commentary on Oocyte Donation for Stem Cell Research in South Korea', *The American Journal of Bioethics* 6 (1), W23.

Maherali, N. et al. (2007), 'Directly Reprogrammed Fibroblasts Show Global Epigenetic Remodeling and Widespread Tissue Contribution', *Cell Stem Cell* 1, 55–70, http://www.cellstemcell.com/content/article/fulltext?uid=PIIS1934590907000203 (last accessed 26.05.2009).

Mauss, M. (1990), *The Gift. The Form and Reason of Exchange in Archaic Societies* [1923] (London: Routledge).

Min, J.K. (2006a), 'Stem Cell Researcher Used More Eggs Than Reported', 13.1.2006, http://english.ohmynews.com/articleview/article_view.asp?menu=&no=266656&rel_no=1&back_url= (last accessed 26.05.2009).

—— (2006b), 'Hwang Guilty of Fraud: SNU Investigation finds the Korean stem cell scientist fabricated claims', 13.1.2006, http://english.ohmynews.com/articleview/article_view.asp?no=268365&rel_no=1 (last accessed 25.05.2009).

Nishikawa, S., Goldstein, R., and Nierras, C. (2008), 'The promise of human induced pluripotent stem cells for research and therapy', *Nature Reviews Molecular Cell Biology*, 13 August 2008.

Okita, K., Ichisaka, T. and Yamanaka, S. (2007), 'Generation of germline-competent induced pluripotent stem cells', *Nature advance online publication*, 6 June 2007, http://www.nature.com/nature/journal/vaop/ncurrent/full/nature05934.html (last accessed 26.05.2009)

Pérez Ybarra, R. (2006), 'Donar óvulos, altruismo con recompense', *El País*, 11.07.06.

Radin, M. (1996), *Contested Commodities* (Cambridge: Harvard University Press).

Rahn, K. (2006), 'Ova donors to file compensation suit', *The Korea Times*, 6 February.

Raymond, J. (1990), 'Reproductive gifts and gift giving: the altruistic woman', *Hastings Center Report*, December, 7–11.

Rimington, M.R., Simons E.G. and Ahuja K.K. (1999), 'Counselling patients undergoing controlled ovarian stimulation about the risks of ovarian hyperstimulation syndrome', *Human Reproduction* 14 (11), 2921–2.

—— (2003), 'Should non-patient volunteers donate eggs?', *Reprod Biomed Online* 6 (3), 277–80.

Rossing, M.A. et al. (1994), 'Ovarian tumors in a cohort of infertile women', *New England Journal of Medicine* 331, 771–6.

Rubin, S. (1983), 'Reproductive Options I. A Spermdonor baby grows up', in Zimmerman, J. (ed.), *The Technological Woman: Interfacing with Tomorrow* (New York: Praeger), 211-15.

Ruhl, L. (2002), 'Dilemma of the Will: Uncertainty, reproduction, and the rhetoric of Control', *Signs* 27 (3), 641–63.

'Safeguards for donors' (2006), *Nature* 442 (7103), 601.

Schindele, E. (2007), 'Spenderkinder. Auf der Suche nach den genetischen Wurzeln', *SWR-Wissen*, Radiosendung vom 30, April 2007, http://www.swr. de/swr2/programm/sendungen/wissen/-/id=2058430/property=download/ nid=660374/1thl8cy/swr2-wissen-20070430.rtf (last accessed 26.05.2009).

Schindele, E. and Zimmermann, I. (2006), 'Rohstoff für das Mutterglück. Der globale Handel mit Eizellen', *WDR 3 Diskurs*, Radiosendung vom 04.07.2006, http://www.wdr.de/radio/wdr3/bilder/sendung/wdr_3_diskurs/20060704_ schindele_eizellenhandel.pdf (last accessed 26.05.2009).

Schneider, I. (2003a), '"Reproduktives" und "therapeutisches" Klonen', in Düwell, M. and Steigleder, K. (eds), *Bioethik. Eine Einführung* (Frankfurt am Main: Suhrkamp), 267–75.

—— (2003b), 'Gesellschaftliche Umgangsweisen mit Keimzellen: Regulation zwischen Gabe, Verkauf und Unveräußerlichkeit', in Graumann, S. and Schneider, I. (eds), *Verkörperte Technik – Entkörperte Frau. Biopolitik und Geschlecht* (Frankfurt am Main/New York: Campus), 41–65.

—— (2003c), '"Pro-life" and "Pro-choice": Overcoming the misleading controversy', *International Conference 'Within and Beyond the Limits of Human Nature'*, Center for Genetics and Society & Heinrich Böll-Foundation, 12–15 October 2003, Berlin. http://www.glow-boell.de/media/de/txt_rubrik_2/Schneider_Pro_Life.pdf (last accessed 26.05.2009).

—— (2007), 'Die Nicht-Kommerzialisierung des Organtransfers als Gebot einer Global Public Policy', in Taupitz, J. (ed.), *Die Kommerzialisierung des menschlichen Körpers* (Berlin: Springer), 109–26.

—— (2008), 'Die soziale und rechtliche Regulation des Transfers von Körpersubstanzen: Kategorien, Klassifikationen und Normbildungsprozesse', in Steineck, C. and Döring, O. (eds), *Kultur und Bioethik: Eigentum am eigenen Körper* (Baden-Baden: Nomos), 26-50.

Schneider, I. and Schumann, C. (2003), 'Stem cells, therapeutic cloning, embryo research – women as raw material suppliers for science and industry', in ReproKult (ed.), *Reproductive Medicine and Genetic Engineering. Women between Self-Determination and Societal Standardisation* (Cologne: Federal Centre for Health Education), 70–79, http://www.reprokult.de/e_forum_3.pdf (last accessed 26.05.2009).

Sexton, S. (2005), 'Transforming "waste" into "resource": From women's eggs to economics for women', *Reprokult workshop at Femme Globale Conference, hosted by Heinrich Böll Foundation, Berlin, Germany*, http://www.thecornerhouse.org.uk/pdf/document/eggs.pdf (last accessed 26.05.2009).

'Should scientific researchers be allowed to ask women to provide their eggs for disease research?' A statement of concerns in response to the current HFEA public consultation: Donating eggs for research: safeguarding donors. Cesagen statement. December 2006, http://www.cesagen.lancs.ac.uk/events/eventsdocs/HFEA_sourcing_eggs.pdf (last accessed 27.06.2007, no longer available).

SNU (2006), 'Summary of the Final Report on Professor Woo Suk Hwang's Research Allegations by Seoul National University Investigation Committee', *International Herald Tribune*, 10.1.2006. http://www.iht.com/articles/2006/01/10/asia/web.0110clone.text.php?rss (last accessed 26.05.2009).

Sorosky, A.D., Baran, A. and Pannor, R. (1984), *The Adoption Triangle: Sealed or Opened Records: How They Affect Adoptees, Birth Parents, and Adoptive Parents* (New York: Anchor Press/Doubleday).

Steinbrook, R. (2006), 'Egg donation and human embryonic stem-cell research', *New England Journal of Medicine* 354 (4), 324–6.

Takahashi, K. and Yamanaka, S. (2006), 'Induction of pluripotent stem cells from mouse embryonic and adult fibroblast cultures by defined factors', *Cell* 126, 663–76.

Thorn, P. (2002), 'Die Gesetzgebung im Bereich der Reproduktionsmedizin – internationale Entwicklungen und Diskussionen', *Ethik in der Medizin* 14, H.2, 103–9.

Titmuss, R. (1971), *The Gift Relationship: From Human Blood to Social Policy* (New York: Pantheon).

Tremlett, G. (2006), 'Spain becomes the destination of choice for fertility tourists from Britain', *The Guardian*, 12 May.

Turner, A.J. and Coyle A. (2000), 'What does it mean to be a donor offspring? The identity experiences of adults conceived by donor insemination and the implications for counselling and therapy', *Human Reproduction* 15 (9), 2041–51.

United Nations (1989), *Convention on the Rights of the Child*. Adopted and opened for signature, ratification and accession by General Assembly resolution 44/25 of 20 November 1989.

—— (2005), *United Nations Declaration on Human Cloning* (59/280). Resolution adopted by the General Assembly at its 82nd meeting, 8 March 2005. http://www.un.org/law/cloning/ (last accessed 26.05.2009).

van den Belt, H. and Keulartz, J. (2007), *Worldwide cultural differences in socio-ethical views in relation to biotechnology*. A report commissioned by the COGEM (Netherlands Commission on Genetic Modification).

Vogel, G. (2006), 'Picking up the pieces after Hwang', *Science* 312, 516–17.

'Watchdog gives all clear to charitable egg donors', *Guardian*, 21 February 2007, http://www.guardian.co.uk/medicine/story/0,2018207,00.html#article_continue (last accessed 26.05.2009).

Whipp, C. (1998), 'The legacy of deceit: A donor offspring's perspective on secrecy in assisted conception', in Blyth E., Crawshaw, M. and Speirs J. (eds), *Truth and the Child 10 Years on: Information Exchange in Donor Assisted Conception* (Birmingham: British Association of Social Workers).

Wilkinson, S. (2003), *Bodies for Sale: Ethics and Exploitation in the Human Body Trade* (London: Routledge).

Wohn, Y. and Normile, D. (2006), 'Prosecutors allege elaborate deception and missing funds', *Science* 312, 980.

World Medical Assembly (1964), *Declaration of Helsinki. Recommendations guiding physicians in biomedical research involving human subjects*. http://www.cirp.org/library/ethics/helsinki/ (last accessed 26.05.2009).

Yee, S., Hitkari, J.A. and Greenblatt, E.M. (2007), 'A follow-up study of women who donated oocytes to known recipient couples for altruistic reasons', *Human Reproduction* 22 (7), 2040–50.

Chapter 17

Accessing Genetic Information: Anomalies Arising from the Regulation of Genetic Material and Genetic Information in the UK

Alison Hall[1]

Over the last decade, a consequence of our ever-increasing knowledge about the human genome is that regulators and legislators have been forced to address the challenge of providing robust and proportionate frameworks by which to control access to human genetic material and to the information it contains. As advancing technologies provide the capability to glean ever-increasing knowledge from minute amounts of material, this seems to demand increasingly rigorous controls to be placed upon such material and information. This chapter examines the recent regulatory changes to the governance of human cellular material (through the Human Tissue Act) and information (through the prospective introduction of personalized electronic medical records) in the United Kingdom. It focuses in particular upon how effectively these frameworks can be applied to cases in which the interests of family members collide and conflict.

The Governance of Human Cellular Material

An Introduction to the Human Tissue Act 2004

Despite a growing acknowledgment that the existing law regulating the access to and use of human tissue was out of date (*Human Tissue Act* 1961), arguably it was media attention that ultimately provided the leverage for legislative change. Successive reports revealed the widespread practice of retaining organs and tissues without the knowledge and consent of families (Department of Health et al. 2001a, Department of Health et al. 2001b), but it was the personal stories and widely reported events at Bristol (Learning from Bristol 2001) and Alder Hey (Report of

1   I am grateful for the feedback provided by participants at the PropEur conference organized by the Centre for Global Ethics, University of Birmingham (21–22 September 2006), to Dr Kathleen Liddell for her helpful insights and suggestions and to my colleagues Dr Ron Zimmern and Dr Hilary Burton at the PHG Foundation for reading and commenting upon earlier drafts of this paper.

the Inquiry into the Royal Liverpool Children's Hospital 2001) that elevated these events to a status of a scandal and fueled pressure for reform.

Historical analysis of the genesis and evolution of the resulting Human Tissue Bill is illuminating. As scandal after scandal hit the headlines, the Government's intention changed from trimming and refining existing legislation to wholesale replacement by new reforming legislation, prompted by Alan Milburn's statement in 2001 that 'the law will be changed to enshrine the concept of informed consent' (Hansard 2001). The Bill that was introduced into Parliament in 2003 went beyond righting the wrongs suffered by families deprived of the chance to influence the fate of the bodies of their dead relatives. As well as rectifying the deficiencies of existing legislation, the Bill challenged the traditional paternalistic relationship between doctor/researcher and patient and represented a diversification in regulatory scope. The resulting Act is both prescriptive and restrictive: prescribing future practice and imposing sanctions for breaches. By seeking to entrench tissue use that is contingent upon the prior consent, it demands a shift in culture and practice. Moreover, since the scope of the Act extends to areas not contemplated in pre-legislative debate, such as the regulation of material from the living as well as the dead,[2] and builds on recommendations from the Human Genetics Commission providing for an offense of non-consensual analysis of DNA,[3] the enforced culture shift is comprehensive (Human Genetics Commission [HGC] 2002, para. 360, Human Tissue Act 2004, s. 45). The Human Tissue Authority is also established as the competent authority pursuant to the EU Directive on Tissues and Cells, and the Act sets up systems of licensing and inspection for certain prescribed activities, including the storage and use of material for human application (Directive 2004/23/EC, Human Tissue Act 2004, s. 16).[4]

Regulating the Retention, Storage and Use of Human Cellular Material

The starting point for the principal part of the Act is the stipulation that activities including the removal, storage and use of human material are lawful[5] if done

---

2   The Act (which received Royal Assent on 15 November 2004 and was implemented on 1 September 2006) also regulates such diverse areas as transplantation, public display and anatomical examination.

3   That of holding cellular material with the intention of analyzing the DNA within it without consent otherwise than for an excepted purpose.

4   These activities include the carrying out of post mortem examinations; the removal, storage and use of bodies of and relevant material from deceased persons (excluding transplantation); the storage of a dead body or relevant material from a human body (living or dead) for use for a scheduled purpose or using any of the above for the purpose of public display.

5   If normal rules of statutory interpretation apply, this might suggest that an activity identified in s.1 HTA performed for a purpose outside Schedule 1 might be unlawful. There is no evidence that this was the legislative intention: the Act is silent as to whether consent is needed for nefarious acts such as eating human tissue or making leather from an

with 'appropriate' consent for specified purposes. These purposes, identified as *'scheduled purposes'* include research, transplantation, obtaining scientific or medical information from one person for the benefit of another and public display. They do not include the medical treatment or diagnosis of the person from whom the material was derived. Exemptions apply where material from the living and the dead is used for purposes sanctioned by the state, such as criminal justice or pursuant to the authority of the coroner or procurator fiscal. Other provisions exempt material from the living from the requirement for consent, where it is used for service related purposes, including clinical audit, education or training relating to human health, performance assessment, public health monitoring and quality assurance (Human Tissue Act 2004, s. 1(10), Schedule 1, part 2).

Thus, where material is to be removed, stored or used for a scheduled purpose, appropriate consent[6] is required to legitimize action. In the absence of consent, an offense is committed (Human Tissue Act 2004, 5). The Act prioritizes the donor's wishes over those of family members: where the donor has failed or chooses not to consent, consent is required from a ranked hierarchical list of 'qualifying relatives', who by virtue of their social and genetic relatedness to the individual establish a claim to make decisions about how the material should be treated.[7]

By establishing a regulatory framework for using human material which promotes the interests of the tissue donor, the Act arguably promotes the donor's autonomy interests. Where, however, these are unclear or waived, generally those with the greatest consanguinity rank above those who are more distantly related.[8] If disagreements occur between those of equal consanguinity, the Act provides no mechanism for resolution. In such circumstances, the consent of any one person claiming the highest ranking suffices: consents trump refusals.[9]

---

amputated leg. Contributor, Human Tissue Workshop (Bioethics Research Project, King's College Cambridge Research Centre and CGKP, 20–21 January 2004) (Chatham House Rules) cited in Liddell and Hall 2005, 183.

6   Although the Act uses the term 'consent', in many ways the term is synonymous with 'authorization' used in equivalent Scottish legislation, the Human Tissue (Scotland) Act 2006.

7   The list includes (in order of rank), spouse or partner, parent or child, brother or sister, grandparent or grandchild, niece or nephew, stepfather or stepmother, half-brother or half-sister and friend of long-standing (Human Tissue Act 2004, s. 27(4)).

8   The exception is the spouse or partner whose claim depends upon establishing a social relationship with the deceased rather than a genetic one.

9   However, the Codes of Practice offer some guidance on resolving the conflicting claims of relatives of equal consanguinity. For example the Post Mortem code suggests that, 'Careful consideration should be given before proceeding on the basis of one person's consent if there are overwhelmingly strong objections' and where there are differences of opinion, decisions will need to be made on a case by case basis (Human Tissue Authority 2006, paras 53–4).

The Governance of Cellular Material Held for DNA Analysis

The Human Tissue Act imposes a different regulatory regime upon *cellular* material held for DNA analysis. Sub-cellular material including DNA is excluded from the Act's scope. Here, the driver for legislative change lay not in the organ retention scandals which hit the headlines in the late 1990s but rather in the concerns of the Human Genetics Commission, that there should be 'a new offence to cover particular cases where the wrongful obtaining or disclosure of genetic information for non-medical purposes amounts to a gross intrusion on the privacy of another' (Human Genetics Commission 2002, para. 3.59).

This formulation by the HGC of a criminal offense built upon the House of Commons Science and Technology Select Committee's earlier recommendation that 'misuse of genetic information should be both a criminal and civil offence' (House of Commons Science and Technology Select Committee 1995, para. 225). In the event, the HTA only establishes a criminal offense rather than a spectrum of criminal and civil remedies,[10] providing no basis for the claim of civil damages by those distressed by the non-consensual use of tissue. Given the provenance of these sections, it is significant that the Act expressly excludes sub-cellular material including extracted DNA from its scope.

In contrast to the formulation in the rest of the Act, these sections state that DNA analysis of cellular material regulated by the Act is unlawful except where exemptions apply. The criminal offense created by the Act consists of three elements:

- The *holding* of bodily material[11] (effectively any cellular material but not sub–cellular material such as extracted DNA)[12]
- With the intention of *analyzing the DNA within it without qualifying consent*
- For a *non–excepted purpose* (Human Tissue Act 2004, s. 45).

By criminalizing the holding of cellular material for DNA analysis, the effect of the Act is to curtail the generation of identifiable genetic information rather than to regulate genetic information itself.

---

10   For a more comprehensive discussion, see Liddell and Hall 2005.

11   Bodily material 'means material which – (a) has come from a human body, and (b) consists of or includes human cells' (Human Tissue Act 2004, s. 45(5)).

12   Guidance from the Human Tissue Authority clarifies that extracted DNA and plasma extracted DNA should not be regarded as 'relevant material', but the extent to which this guidance is also applicable to the definition of bodily material in the Act is not made explicit. A purposive interpretation would suggest that these distinctions also apply to bodily material by virtue of Schedule 4, para. 11, which includes authorizations given pursuant to s. 1(1) and s. 1(10)(c) as excepted purposes (Human Tissue Authority 2007a).

Unlike the rest of the Act, the DNA analysis provisions are not limited in territorial scope to England, Wales and Northern Ireland; they apply to Scotland as well. This creates some difficulties with terminology, as the Scottish equivalent of the Human Tissue Act (Human Tissue [Scotland] Act 2006) establishes a different regime for the use and storage of tissue than its English counterpart;[13] hence the requirement for 'qualifying consent' rather than 'appropriate consent' and reference to 'bodily' rather than 'relevant' material.

As with the principal part of the Act, some types of DNA analysis are excepted altogether,[14] and stricter controls are imposed upon material from the deceased than material from the living for certain service-related health uses. This allows the latter to be analyzed for clinical audit, education and training and public health monitoring without consent.

Because of the provenance of the DNA analysis offense, it is not entirely surprising that initial media attention focused on 'DNA theft' as exemplified by the offense of non-consensual paternity testing. Thus the Act prescribes that paternity testing of a minor child requires the consent of a person with parental responsibility;[15] in the absence of the requisite consents, non-consensual paternity testing is unlawful. Although these provisions may prevent the children of celebrities being targeted by unscrupulous journalists, entrenching parental choice in such circumstances is not without difficulty. The Act fails to resolve situations where those sharing parental responsibility, such as two parents (or a parent and a local authority) fail to agree about whether testing should proceed.[16] The Codes of Practice stress that while on the face of the Act, a single consent may sanction testing, account may legitimately be taken of vehemently held objections. Although this contextualized approach has its merits, it undermines one central objective of the HTA, namely to provide clarity about who should give consent. The ambiguity applies wherever opinions are potentially opposed, such as where genetic testing is carried out for the benefit of family members.

---

13 For example, as previously noted, it provides for 'authorisations' rather than 'consents' and establishes a statutory right for tissue blocks and slides from the deceased to be retained as part of the deceased person's medical record rather than being returned to relatives. Significantly it excludes material derived from the living (Human Tissue [Scotland] Act 2006, ss. 38–9).

14 Such as the state sanctioned analyses already noted and analysis for the medical diagnosis and treatment of the person from whom the sample was taken.

15 Defined by the *Children Act* (1989) to include the mother (regardless of marital status) and the father, if married, or if not married at the date of the child's birth, acquired by court order or parental responsibility agreement or other authorized authority.

16 A putative father may have a vested interest in a child's paternity remaining ambiguous if clarification of paternity carries financial liability. However, for the purpose of child support, a refusal to take a DNA paternity test may allow a presumption of parentage to be made (Child Support Agency 2008).

Obtaining Scientific or Medical Information for the Benefit of Another

One consequence of criminalizing the deceitful or non-consensual analysis of cellular material is that material held in the context of clinical genetics may be caught by the Act where material from one family member is analyzed for the benefit of another. Hence, qualifying consent is now required for the purpose of 'obtaining scientific or medical information about a living or deceased person which may be relevant to any other person (including a future person)' (Human Tissue Act 2004, Schedule 1, part 1, para. 4),[17] such as where DNA is needed from one family member as a positive control to clarify another's susceptibility to a genetically inherited disease.[18]

Where the material held for DNA analysis is from a *deceased* person, lawful testing is contingent upon consent being obtained from *any* person holding any of the specified degrees of social or genetic relatedness within the list of qualifying relatives: the list is unranked.

In contrast to the rest of the Act (in which there is a linear relationship between degree of relatedness and power to influence decision-making), this lack of hierarchy seems to evidence a determination not to give primacy to either social or genetic relationships. Thus the views of those with a social relationship, such as a spouse or partner, are accorded equal weight with those who are genetically related. However, the failure to prioritize relationships by degree of consanguinity makes it more difficult to resolve conflicting autonomy interests, particularly if the autonomy interest of one person can only be respected at the expense of another. Even if such a model authorizing DNA analysis on the basis of consanguinity were adopted, as previously noted, this would fail to resolve conflicts within a nuclear family if there are disagreements between those with claims of equal strength (Ngwena and Chadwick 1993).

The consent requirements which apply to bodily material from the *living* are quite different. They provide that a competent person (whether an adult or child) may *veto* the use of their material irrespective of the reasons and timing of their refusal. However, the rights conferred over this material are not transferable; so an adult may not appoint a nominee to give qualifying consent (although authorization by a nominated representative may be sufficient for certain types of DNA analysis involving existing holdings).[19]

Thus, in the main, the Act seems to exemplify an individualistic and autonomous model of decision-making in which the role of consent is to provide procedural justification for future action.[20] There are some concessions in the Act towards

---

17   The scope of this purpose includes analysis for reproductive choice.

18   This comparison is necessary because polymorphisms at primer binding sites (unique to a particular family) might result in a false negative test.

19   Compare *Human Tissue Act* 2004, s. 4 and Schedule 4, paras 7 and 11.

20   Beyleveld and Brownsword (2007) are critical of such simplistic accounts. Instead they favor locating consent within a Gerwithian inspired community of rights.

a more proportionate model which balances comparative risks and benefits, but these seem to be prompted by expediency rather than any ethical imperative. For example, as the Bill proceeded through Parliament during 2004, it became apparent that there was no mechanism for using cellular material from those lacking capacity to consent for scheduled purposes pending the implementation of the Mental Capacity Act in 2007.[21] This omission potentially could have terminated essential research using tissue from those lacking capacity to consent. Recognizing that it is in the public interest to continue with such research and that problems arose because of a lack of synchronicity between the Human Tissue Act and the Mental Capacity Act, the gap was plugged by regulations which came into force in September 2006.[22]

Upholding the right of an individual to make autonomous decisions regardless of proximate risk may well be contrary to the public interest and disproportionate in certain circumstances.[23] The genetics community unsuccessfully lobbied for a judicial mechanism in the Act that could overturn the autonomous refusal of an individual who knowingly inflicted harm on a relative by refusing to allow his or her own material to be tested for that other's benefit.[24] This proposal was rejected on the basis that this would 'drive a stake thought the heart of the Bill because it goes against its basic principle; namely that people should be able to decide what happens to their bodily material' (Hansard 2004).[25]

Instead, provisions allow deemed consent to be given by the Human Tissue Authority or Court of Sessions in prescribed circumstances provided that there is no evidence that the donor has died or lacks capacity (Human Tissue Act 2004, s. 7 and Schedule 4, para. 9). Additionally, applicants must prove either that it is not reasonably possible to trace the potential donor or that the potential donor has refused to respond to requests for consent. Testing must be justified in terms that it 'is desirable in the interests of another person (including a future person)' (Human Tissue Act 2004, Schedule 4, para. 9(2)(c)). An additional qualifier that '[t]here is

---

21   The *Mental Capacity Act* 2005 was implemented progressively from 1 April 2007, with the majority of the Act being implemented on 1 October 2007.

22   The Human Tissue Act 2004 (Persons Who Lack Capacity to Consent and Transplants) Regulations (2006) provided for deemed consent to the use of material from an adult lacking capacity to consent for the purposes of transplantation and obtaining information relevant to another person, provided that the proposed use was in the best interests of the person lacking consent. The regulations also provided a mechanism for material to be used in clinical trials and intrusive research as defined by the *Mental Capacity Act* 2005 pending that Act's implementation.

23   See Manson and O'Neill (2007) who demonstrate the shortcomings of a conception of informed consent based upon a narrow view of individual autonomy.

24   Such as where a relative is unable to determine her risk of inheriting a familial cancer syndrome (such as BRCA1), because she is denied access to a relative's bodily material for mutation analysis and opts instead to have a bilateral mastectomy.

25   Baroness Andrews in response to a draft amendment allowing the High Court to overturn a refusal from a competent adult to a proposed use of tissue.

no reason to believe that the donor has refused consent' adds weight to the view that the ethical determinant of making such an order is to maximize autonomous choice.

The Human Tissue Authority has published guidance setting out the extent of these exemptions (Human Tissue Authority 2007b).[26] This guidance requires certain information to be made available to the prospective donor, including the detail of the analysis to be performed, whether the DNA analysis is to be used to determine paternity and a requirement that should the donor intend to refuse consent to the proposed testing he or she should immediately inform the Authority. There is no additional requirement placed upon the applicant to include a justification for the proposed DNA analysis or any obligation to set out the advantages and disadvantages of proceeding. It is assumed that such information is implicit from the nature of the DNA analysis to be carried out.[27] If the information to be gained from the proposed analysis concerned the imminent onset of a severe genetically inherited condition for which a cure or therapy was available, then a utilitarian analysis might suggest strong indications for allowing the testing to proceed without consent.

Where a prospective donor can be traced but has failed to communicate a consent decision, the requirement that 'reasonable efforts have been made to get the donor to decide whether to consent to the use of material for that purpose' imposes practical constraints upon geneticists and counselors. Some argue that a provision of this sort is unethical because it could be used to impose information upon a donor who does not wish to know a diagnosis. In such a situation, even though the prospective donor's autonomous rights of refusal have been respected, the geneticist may have made the essence of the information known by trying to contact him. Another prerequisite for granting such an order is that the tissue donor has notice of the application which again precludes the prospective donor from exercising the ethical right not to know a diagnosis.[28] Laurie cogently argues that concepts such as autonomy or confidentiality are not rich enough to provide the ethical justifications for such a claim, partly because of limitations in scope or because they may be susceptible to preconceived value preferences. Instead he argues that an interest or right 'not to know' lies in spatial privacy so that those contemplating disclosure undertake a comprehensive and reflective assessment of the potential benefits and harms of proceeding with the disclosure (Laurie 2002, 257). Moreover, the donor

---

26   This guidance sets out the evidence required to establish that it is not reasonably possible to trace the donor, (Human Tissue Act 2004, Schedule 4, para. 9(2)) and that reasonable efforts have been made to get the donor to decide [whether or not to give consent] (Human Tissue Act 2004, Schedule 4, para. 9(3)).

27   This assumption is misguided. For example, the justification for genetic testing for inherited breast cancer genes such as BRCA1 or BRCA2 is strengthened if many first degree relatives are affected at an early age.

28   By implication, this right is denied to the applicant who must supply details of the proposed analysis as part of the application to the Human Tissue Authority.

cannot be said to be exerting an autonomy right in any real sense because full information and knowledge of the consequences of a choice are required to be a 'moral chooser' (Benn 1988). If we acknowledge a right 'not to know a diagnosis' in the context of genetic testing, then it would seem that an individualistic approach derived from the ethical principle of autonomy as exemplified by the Human Tissue Act fails to ground this right.

The fact that the applicant for 'deemed consent' is not required to justify the merits of his or her application, also suggests a minimal contribution from other types of ethical theory, such as utilitarianism or a 'four principles' approach (Beauchamp and Childress 2001).[29] Neither have confidentiality nor informational privacy been appealed to in this context. Arguably these latter concepts have more resonance when applied to the regulation of genetic information and particularly in the context of governmental plans to implement electronic patient records.

The Governance of Genetic Information

Implementing an Electronic Patient Record System: an Introduction

National Health Service Connecting for Health[30] is an ambitious program of information technology reform, set to modernize data storage and use within the NHS which, it is claimed, will improve patient care and services and enhance patient autonomy. Within ten years, the program aims to provide a matrix of secure electronic links between 30,000 general practitioners and 300 hospitals, enabling identifiable patient information to be transferred between them and giving patients access to their personal health and care information.[31] The thrust of the original reforms was to locate two distinct types of records (described as Summary and Detailed Care Records respectively) on a central electronic spine, so to afford universal access (contingent upon password and access status)[32] to patient records in England (excluding Wales, Scotland and Northern Ireland) with phased implementation to 2010.[33] Originally, the Summary Care Record was to contain

---

29   Namely, beneficence, non-maleficence, autonomy and justice (Beauchamp and Childress 2001).

30   The origins of the program to introduce on-line access to electronic patient records in England and Wales lie in the 1998 Information for Health strategy. This was replaced by the National Programme for IT in October 2002 (after numerous iterations) and in April 2005, NHS Connecting for Health was established as a single national provider for the NHS with responsibility for delivering the National Programme with the aim of full implementation by 2010 (under the rubric 'Connecting for Health').

31   For a historical account of the project, see National Audit Office (2006).

32   Access will be afforded via a smart card to those who are able to demonstrate both that they occupy an appropriate role and have a legitimate relationship with the patient.

33   Electronic prescription services connecting prescribers and dispensers together with the provision of private and secure access to HealthSpace were partially operational

all vital elements for an emergency admission, including details of prescriptions, allergies and summary medical history, and the Detailed Care Record an integrated record of primary and secondary care. Both elements were to be held within a centralized system. However, the system has evolved so that the Detailed Care Record is likely to be held at local rather than national level (House of Commons Health Committee 2007).[34] These proposals impact upon the existing legal and ethical governance of genetic information.

Legal Analysis: UK Common Law

In contrast to human material, where there have been tentative attempts to formulate rights of property over tissue, in common law it is well established that personal information is not capable of being owned. While case law has established that '[T]here can be no proprietorship in information as information because once imparted by one person to another, it belongs equally to them both', the records in which that personal medical data are recorded are not the patient's property (*Breen v. Williams* 1996, Pattenden 2003, para. 19.04).[35] Within the NHS these records are owned by the relevant NHS institution and ultimately the Secretary of State: in a private health care setting, they are the property of the doctor or the clinic where the patient was seen (McHale 1999). The law does however recognize various intellectual property rights in certain types of information subject to specified conditions and imposes statutory restrictions on data processing and sharing (UK Intellectual Property Office 2007, *R. v. Department of Health* 2001).[36]

UK Statutory Law: the Data Protection Act (DPA) 1998

The legal basis for the regulation of genetic information from the living in England and Wales is the Data Protection Act 1998.[37] This Act influences the exchange of information in a variety of ways:

---

by late 2008 and links between systems operational by 2010.

34   The scope of this enquiry (commenced February 2007) was to determine the extent to which personal health information will be stored on electronic systems and rights of opt out, who will have access to this information, whether confidentiality can be adequately protected and how such information is to be used for purposes other than delivery of care. Current progress on the development of the infrastructure needed to deliver the systems also fell under the remit of the enquiry.

35   While the law recognizes intellectual property rights in information, such as copyrights, designs, patents and trademarks, a comprehensive analysis of these rights falls outside the scope of this paper.

36   Case law has also established that a proprietary interest in abstract information cannot be vested in an individual.

37   The Data Protection Act (1998) implements the European Data Protection Directive 95/46 (1995). The Article 29 Data Protection Working Party (2007) has published guidance

- It sets out the parameters for consent required to process genetic information
- It identifies a number of principles of data processing

It also confers

- Subject access rights to data subjects; and
- A right to request cessation of processing should data subjects have experienced (or might in the future experience) substantial damage or distress.

These rights may conflict with the professional obligations of health care professionals to record their actions, and patients have historically had no legal right to dictate the form or content of records made by clinicians or stipulate where they will be held provided that they comply with data processing principles. Such rights over records are distinct from rights to process or access the personal information itself.

On its face, the scope of the DPA is limited to the processing of *identifiable* data from the *living*, providing that the processing of data requires consent unless alternative justifications apply (Information Commissioner's Office 2007). One such exception, set out in Schedule 3 of the DPA allows for the processing of personal data without explicit consent provided that it is:

necessary for medical purposes and is undertaken by -

a. a health professional

b. a person who in the circumstances owes a duty of confidentiality which is equivalent to that which would arise if that person were a health professional (Data Protection Act 1998, Schedule 3, para. 8(1)).

Thus the processing of data within clinical genetics will generally fall under this exception since it involves the processing of sensitive personal data within a confidential relationship for *medical purposes*, (defined in this context as preventative medicine, medical diagnosis, medical research, the provision of care and treatment and the management of healthcare services).[38]

Data protection legislation imposes a raft of generalizable principles of data processing, which are sometimes difficult to interpret in the context of genetic information. For example, the DPA establishes the right of access for data subjects to make requests of health professionals or data controllers as to whether 'personal

---

on the concept of personal data, which suggests how interpretative differences between the Act and the Directive are liable to be treated in future.

38   Or as Article 29 Data Protection Working Party (2004) expresses it – 'an obligation of medical secrecy'.

data' relating to them is being or has been processed (Data Protection Act 1998, s. 7(1)(a)). This implies a correlative duty to disclose the records in which that data is recorded. The extent of this duty may be difficult to gauge in clinical genetics since the legislation reserves the right but not an obligation for a professional to withhold information relating to a third party.[39] In assessing the reasonableness of disclosure concern must be had for any duty of confidentiality owed to a third party, the steps taken to secure consent, the capacity of the third party to consent and any express refusal (Pattenden 2003, para. 19.33). The law is less clear where that third party is also a family member,[40] particularly if he or she is a child. Where that disclosure concerns a child, health professionals may have difficulty distinguishing between respective rights of access of parents and children, particularly where information has been disclosed by a child to the health professional on the basis that it will not be disclosed to a parent or where the child expressly refuses parental access.[41]

The fact that some genetic information cannot readily be de-identified, particularly in the context of rare disorders, strains the regulatory scope of the DPA, which is limited to identifiable data relating only to the living. Critics argue that the process of de-identification also strips the data of its richness and context and that individuation could achieve the same ethical imperative of safeguarding privacy but without imposing equivalent burdens on secondary use (Manson and O'Neill 2007).

This debate informs divergent views as to whether or not the Data Protection Act derogates too far from the Data Protection Directive from which it originates and whether it should apply to pseudonymized data[42] and data relating to the dead (Gertz 2004). A more recent opinion from the Article 29 Data Protection

---

39   However, the information must be disclosed if the third party consents (Data Protection Act 1998, s. 7(4)(a), or if it is reasonable in all the circumstances to comply with the request without the consent of the third party (Data Protection Act 1998, s. 7(4)(b)). Where the third party is employed in the public sector, for example as a social worker, disclosure may occur unless it is likely to cause serious harm to that person's physical or mental health or condition or the third party is a health professional who compiled or contributed to the record or was involved in the care of the data subject.

40   The Article 29 Data Protection Working Party (2004) acknowledged that sharing information granted family members a distinctive legal status. They suggested that other family members could be regarded as data subjects in their own right or that they could be granted a distinctive right of information 'of a different character, based on the fact that their personal interests may be directly affected'.

41   This is because the DPA seems to afford a universal right of access which is not limited to those with mental capacity to consent. Pattenden argues that the best reading of this provision affords access to 'an individual or the person with parental responsibility for that individual' (Pattenden 2003, para 19.75).

42   For example, see the recommendations of the Privireal project, a European Commission Framework 5 funded project examining the implications of the Data Protection Directive 95/46/EC in relation to medical research and the role of research ethics committees (Beyleveld et al. 2004, Privireal 2005, Article 29 Data Protection Working Party 2007b).

Working Party (2007b) has clarified the interpretative guidance applied at the European level. For example, the opinion cautions against a mechanistic approach but promotes a flexible approach that prioritizes the protection of data subjects' rights and interests. In the context of key-coded or pseudonymized data, emphasis is placed upon a contextual assessment as to whether the individual is 'likely reasonably' to be identified (Article 29 Data Protection Working Party 2007b, 20).[43] By applying this contextual approach, the opinion acknowledges that data relating to one person (B) held in the file of another (A) may still be B's personal data, and that information about family history held in the medical records of a number of family members constitutes personal data relating to *each* of those members and as such is subject to certain protections.[44]

Access to Health Records Act 1990

Where data are processed from the health records of a person who has died, rights to access that information for the benefit of family members is dependent upon circumstances. There are no subject access rights to deceased people's information pursuant to the Data Protection Act, but legislation provides explicitly for health information to be accessed by personal representatives or pursuant to a claim arising out of the patient's death subject to the rights of the record holder to deny access if it would cause serious harm to the physical or mental health of any other person or identify a third person who has not consented to being identified (Access to Health Records Act 1990, s. 5(1)). The extent to which health care professionals are lawfully able to share information about a deceased person is subject to a continuing duty of confidentiality, which is itself open to interpretation. Professional guidance recognizes a limited duty of confidentiality after a patient's death dependent upon circumstances (General Medical Council 2004). The practical question for geneticists is how these conflicting rights and duties should be mediated.[45]

---

43   To this extent, it is argued that since the coded links to research subjects are retained by pharmaceutical companies to enable treatment under certain circumstances: 'such key-coded data constitutes information relating to identifiable natural persons for parties that might be involved in the possible identification and should be subject to the rules of data protection legislation'.

44   The Opinion also offers another clarification, confirming that although DNA samples are sources out of which biometric data are extracted, they are not themselves biometric data. Nevertheless, as technological advances have made DNA scans a reality, the arguments for applying specific protections to biometric data have become more insistent. For national regulatory guidance see Information Commissioner's Office 2007. The extent to which these arguments can be applied to the processing of records from deceased persons is contingent upon the legitimacy of derogation of UK data protection law from the Directive.

45   Contrast the argument that it is appropriate for the living to access medical information from the records of deceased family members if that information could have implications for their health (Australian Law Reform Commission 2007).

Ethics and Genetic Information

The common law and DPA entrench obligations to keep health information confidential, and this requirement remains a cornerstone of medical practice. The central role of genetic counseling within genetic medicine has arguably encouraged a client-centered approach which is often supportive of autonomy-based ethical theory. However, an increasing number of clinical genetics professionals have sought to challenge the role of individual autonomy in genetic medicine, claiming instead that genetic information should be regarded as jointly owned by family members. This model would allow more freedom to share genetic data among family members, allowing predictive test information to be used more effectively within families and promote evidence based care (Lucassen 2007, Clarke 2007).

Governance: the Care Record Guarantee

In addition to legal controls placed upon data processing, in order to promote public trust and confidence in electronic patient records it was recognized that additional reassurance was needed to dispel fears about the lack of confidentiality and security of personal information held within the system. Initially this took the form of an NHS Care Record Guarantee designed to establish 'the rules that will govern information held in the NHS Care Records Service when it goes live'. The Guarantee covers all aspects of access to NHS records, including controls, monitoring and emergency access.

The first version of the Guarantee published in May 2005 advocated 12 core principles, adopting an NHS centered approach that did not seem to acknowledge the legitimacy of sharing information for health or research purposes outside the NHS without consent. A revised version, published in July 2006, moderated these 12 core principles, and a subsequent revision published in August 2007 incorporated further changes to take account of the Mental Capacity Act 2005 and the changes to the specification of the electronic patient record systems since the inception of the project (NHS Care Record Development Board 2005, 2006 and 2007). The way that the Guarantee is now framed has interesting philosophical and clinical consequences. Although the revisions reflect the recognition that there may be important health service uses outside the NHS for which it may be impracticable to obtain consent for data subjects (for example, large scale epidemiological research projects involving public health monitoring), in other ways they seem to restrict information sharing inappropriately. For example, commitment 3 includes the statement:

> We will not share health information that identifies you (particularly with other government agencies) for any reason other than providing your care, unless: you ask us to do so; we ask and you give us specific permission; we have to do this by law; we have special permission for health or research purposes; or

we have special permission because the public good is thought to be of greater importance than your confidentiality (NHS Care Record Development Board 2007).

This much is uncontroversial. However, the examples of permissible data sharing given by way of illustration explain that information that *names* an individual[46] might be used or shared without consent where permission has been given by the Patient Information Advisory Group (PIAG).[47] Examples relate to medical research or to maintaining cancer registers or where a breach of confidentiality is justified to prevent serious crime, serious risks to public or NHS staff or to protect children (NHS Care Record Development Board 2006, 2007).

These examples seem more circumscribed than the earliest draft which framed legitimate sharing in terms of avoiding putting *somebody else* at risk and would include a family member in the context of mutation analysis (NHS Care Record Development Board 2005). This omission in the latest versions of the Guarantee is problematic in that it could be seen to place limits upon the legitimate sharing of genetic information among health professionals for the benefit of family members.

The Guarantee also provides for patients (or data subjects) to impose limits upon how a provider may share certain types of information by placing that information in a virtual sealed envelope. This mechanism is relevant because as plans for an electronic health record are implemented, there remains a lack of consensus as to the extent to which patients can and should be able to prescribe to their health providers the extent and nature of the electronic records made about them and the rights that such sealing would confer (House of Commons Health Committee 2007, paras 75, 76).[48]

Although not yet implemented, the concept of a 'sealed envelope' facility is likely to apply to both the Summary Care Record and the Detailed Care Record. Since sealing is a mechanism by which the confidentiality of patient information within the NHS Care Records Service can be protected (NHS Connecting for Health 2006a), genetic information was identified as a candidate for this approach in early policy statements because of its perceived sensitivity. However, the policy rhetoric seems to have shifted from restricting access to certain types of information to imposing limits on sharing of certain clinical encounters or even single entries in a medical record. The restrictions to be placed upon sensitive information by data subjects reflect the patient's preferences for access. At the outset, before systems

---

46   This wording is curious and does not mirror data protection legislation since an individual may be identifiable without being named.

47   The Ethics and Confidentiality Committee of the National Information Governance Board replaced PIAG with effect from 1 January 2009, but the remit of the committee and personnel remain essentially unchanged.

48   Patients also do not have a legal right to prevent their demographic data being held centrally (which is deemed necessary for the proper administration of the NHS).

are fully operational, patients may only exert blunt control over their records (National Audit Office 2006, 31, House of Commons Health Committee 2007).[49] There are two elements of choice in this process: first, individuals have a degree of choice as to whether paper records may be *uploaded* to create an electronic care record (limited in the first instance to the summary care record). Individuals choosing to exercise this right either prevent a summary care record form being uploaded onto the spine or prevent the downloaded material from being visible by creating a blank record (British Medical Association 2007a and 2007b).[50] Alternatively, patients may opt to prevent *sharing* in all circumstances including direct patient care, or only allow sharing within the DCR system within which the original record was created.[51]

Even once systems are fully operational, questions remain about the range of options that will be offered to data subjects and the functionality of the systems to exert that control (for example, to limit sharing by the type of information or by the source or potential recipient).[52] It seems likely that they will not permit the data subject to deny access to the author of the entry or to their workgroup.[53] However, once a set of sensitive information has been identified, the data subject has the choice of sealing the envelope or sealing and locking it. Both options are only available following discussion with a clinician: a data subject may not unilaterally restrict access without involving a clinician or another 'trained individual' who has a responsibility to advise the consequences of the patient's choice (NHS Connecting for Health 2006b, 9).[54]

Where data is sealed, the patient retains control over access to that information, since access is contingent upon users outside the author's workgroup seeking permission from the patient. A potential user operating outside the author's workgroup will be advised of the existence of sealed information by a flag. Breaking the seal on the basis of the best interests of the patient (for example where they are unconscious or lack capacity) is only justifiable where a clinician working outside the author's workgroup can demonstrate that the public good

---

49   Estimates suggesting that the sealed envelope function would become operative in respect of Summary Care Records in 2008 (House of Commons Health Committee 2007, para. 91) have been overly optimistic.

50   The original download will still be traceable within the audit trail.

51   In certain circumstances this limitation could prevent data sharing between primary, secondary and tertiary providers at local level.

52   Indeed, these questions formed the basis for a public consultation in 2008 by NHS Connecting for Health on additional uses of patient data.

53   The lack of clarity surrounding the configuration of the detailed care record system, the definition of a workgroup and who may be accorded access has been described as an 'explanatory vacuum'. The effect of limiting data sharing to within workgroups is likely to be very variable and dependent upon the size of the DCR system and the extent to which detailed care records are pooled (House of Commons Health Committee 2007, para. 229).

54   Guidance provides additionally for 'someone else trained to explain the implications for [the patient's] health' to advise on opting out.

advanced by breaking the seal will reduce the harm to specific individuals or the public in general, and that this outweighs the harm done by breaching patient confidentiality. There is no justification for breaching a seal solely on the basis that it is in the patient's best interests, even if the patient is unconscious (NHS Connecting for Health 2006a, Appendix A, 14). This places the clinician who wishes to breach a patient-imposed seal in an impossible situation. By denying access to the sealed information, the clinician is also denied the means of justifying a claim on the basis of public interest, suggesting that the rights given to clinicians in these circumstances are largely rhetorical and are likely to be extremely circumscribed in practice.

In contrast, where information is sealed and locked, this means that it is only accessible to the author and his or her workgroup. No alert will be generated to other potential users unless they are servicing a subject access request from the patient. Given that under current plans, the only mechanism for patients to access their detailed care records is by making a formal data subject access request (NHS Connecting for Health 2006b, 11), it seems likely that the number of subject access requests will increase once electronic patient records are fully implemented, with contingent implications for Caldecott guardians.

Moderation in the Light of Experience

Clinical Engagement

Although there is support for the broad objectives of the program, there are fears about the way in which it is likely to be implemented and widespread cynicism about the efficacy of previous large scale information technology projects (fueled by the perception that historically policy makers have appeared to ride roughshod over patient rights). Given that the program has encountered significant challenges as financial targets are exceeded and key players have dropped out of the project, it is not surprising that professional and public confidence in the project has been eroded. This is exemplified by evidence from general practitioners (Carvel 2006) and senior academics in computing which revealed widespread dissatisfaction with the proposed reforms and unwillingness amongst GPs to cooperate with initial plans to upload patient records without explicit consent (British Medical Association 2006 and 2007b, House of Commons Health Committee 2007, para. 194, Ev 164).[55] Recognizing this lack of clinical engagement, a ministerial task force was established in July 2006 with the purpose of reconciling the ethical differences between Connecting for Health and the professional groups regarding

---

55 Concerns voiced by professional organizations, including the British Medical Association, claimed that 'uploading clinical data without explicitly asking the patient could jeopardise the trust and relationship between doctors and patients, as well as violating a patient's right to confidentiality'.

implied or explicit consent. Facing imminent collapse, the emergent compromise solution signaled three significant concessions. The first is the acknowledgment that the initial upload of a patient's summary care record onto the central spine is dependent upon a hybrid opt in/opt out system (rather than solely to opt out as originally envisaged). Following a mass mailing, patients are asked to consent to the creation of a summary care record and are informed that if they do not respond within an initial period (by alerting their general practitioner) non-responders will be deemed to have given implied consent to sharing. This approach relies upon the cooperation of GPs to alert patients to the fact that the notice period has begun and if necessary provide patients with a printout of their summary record (British Medical Association 2007a). These plans will give scope for patients to 'ask for their summary care record not to be shared or uploaded at all' (Ministerial Taskforce on the Summary Care Record 2006, para. 4.13). The second concession concerns the structure of the summary care record. In its original format, the record was to be information rich, containing free text medical history and diagnostic data. Current plans for a pared down version contain only details of current medical status, relevant drug prescriptions and historical information about severe adverse reactions. Perhaps the most significant concession is for the detailed care record (comprising more sensitive information, such as detailed medical history, discharge letters, etc.) to remain locally held. Centralized record keeping will, initially at least, only apply to the limited summary care records.[56] This distinction between centralized and localized record keeping is significant from a legal perspective because of developments in European law (Article 29 Data Protection Working Party 2007a). Following a critical report,[57] the hybrid consent model has been modified even further to allow for an additional explicit consent to be sought at the point at which the data was to be accessed and used 'consent to view'. Functional details of this change remain unclear, including the extent to which it might be exercised where patients suffer a loss of capacity to consent during the process.

Evidence from the Pilot Schemes

This debate continues to receive substantial adverse media attention, and perhaps because of this, any empirical analysis of rights and responsibilities is problematic. Preliminary evidence from the pilot schemes commenced in March 2007 yielded opt out rates (that is, patients who request no summary care record upload) of

---

56   The extent of these concessions has become apparent in oral evidence given to the Parliamentary Health Committee enquiry on the electronic patient record (House of Commons Health Committee 2007).

57   University College London (2008) Summary Care Record Early Adopter programme: an independent evaluation by University College London.

around 0.34 percent[58] while pooled rates from a wider geographical spread were around 0.81 percent with an additional 0.03 percent imposing restrictions upon data sharing (University College London 2008). However, concerns remain about those whose interests may not have been adequately reflected in pilot schemes (University College London 2008, 91).[59]

Reflections and Implications

These legislative and regulatory changes seem to demonstrate a lack of coherence in policy development in respect to human tissue held for DNA analysis and genetic information, and point to the development of two distinctive models of governance. One approach, exemplified by the provisions of the HTA that relate to the DNA analysis of material from the living, is grounded in individual autonomy: the other approach, exemplified by access to genetic information in the context of electronic patient records, whilst seeming to take account of a range of public and private interests, appears to be failing to balance those interests effectively by using mechanisms that are not demonstrably reliable or efficacious.

Clinical Genetics

The sealed envelope facility seems to create an interest or right that is more akin to what Graeme Laurie has identified as a right of 'informational privacy' (Laurie 2002). This can be distinguished from a right grounded in confidentiality because a confidential relationship is not a necessary prerequisite. Once this commitment is fully operational, it could have significant implications for clinical genetics. The traditional approach of clinical geneticists is to collate genetic information from a variety of family members and record it in the form of family pedigrees. Since the Connecting for Health initiative also confers a right for data subjects to view their Summary Care Record on a dedicated webspace called HealthSpace, geneticists will have to be much more systematic in identifying the parts of patient records which use information from other family members and in reviewing those entries by seeking consent to disclosure from third parties or sealing. This suggests a departure from the ways in which geneticists have traditionally recorded

---

58   Initial pilots represented only 11 G.P. practices within a single geographical location and excluded a small minority of practices that chose not to participate in the pilot.

59   It is not clear the extent to which different systems of consent will impact upon vulnerable groups such as the elderly or those who are not registered with a general practitioner. Pilot projects began in April 2007, and continuing empirical research is urgently needed.

information (Parker and Lucassen 2004),[60] and a move towards individualized patient records or standardizing a duplicate set of notes.[61] Both systems seem likely, at least in the short term, to lead to less effective patient care (Academy of Medical Sciences 2006, Chapter 3), and a generalized proscription on sharing genetic information is likely to be unworkable across the NHS given that routine encounters with patients in the primary health care sector already yield highly predictive genetic information for family members (such as cholesterol or blood pressure readings).

If one family member were to opt for a sealed envelope approach, it would make it difficult to validate clinically important information for other family members and use family history to assess risk calculations for complex multi-factorial genetic disease, such as some inherited forms of breast and colorectal cancer.

Data Sharing within the NHS

Health professionals are used to mediating their actions according to the sensitivity of information disclosed to them. A deficiency of these proposals is that they promote an 'all or nothing' approach to data processing. The adoption of systems which *label* certain types of information as inherently more sensitive than others regardless of content[62] is likely to fuel differences between specialties or workgroups in the amount of information that is routinely sealed and/or sealed and locked and arguably seems likely to encourage a multi-tiered system of data sharing within the NHS. Legal standards for clinical specialties are likely to diverge depending upon whether information is regarded as sensitive or not. In the short term, it seems likely that the records made by clinical geneticists may have more stringent access controls placed upon them than other types of encounter. In the longer term, this analysis may be too simplistic, for as complex genetic testing and evaluation become rolled out into mainstream medicine, the primary healthcare team may play an increasingly important role in evaluating genetic risk factors and managing the sharing of information between family members.

---

60   Parker and Lucassen examine the ethical basis for regarding genetic information as jointly owned by the family rather than an individual.

61   The process of integrating electronic and paper records is likely to generate 'significant challenges' to ensure that pre-existing duplicate registrations are eliminated, and none created (Department of Health 2006, part 1, para. 25).

62   Evidence points to sensitive information being characterized in different ways depending upon context: thus concerns in relation to sexual health and inherited genetic disease were around the release of potentially discriminatory information *outside* the NHS, rather than within it, but other types of information such as termination of pregnancy and mental health were perceived as being potentially discriminatory if disclosed *within* the NHS (NHS Information Authority et al. 2002, NHS National Programme for Information Technology and *Health Which?* 2003).

Domestic law does not provide clear direction to health professionals who grapple with decisions about disclosing health information within families. The failure of the common law concept of confidentiality to accord a right to relatives of a proband to control the flow of familial genetic information towards themselves is identified as problematic (Laurie 2002, 243). Increasingly, lawyers and ethicists have looked to ethical frameworks for interpretative guidance. For example, in his analysis of privacy and genetic information, Laurie concludes that while a statutory duty to respect a right not to know genetic information may be imposed upon employers, insurers or the state: '[t]o exclude family members from this duty is simply an admission that the law does not always have a role to play in determining what should be done with genetic information' (Laurie 2002, 265).

If Laurie's analysis is correct, seemingly the law has little to contribute where a relative who is potentially at risk refuses to engage with the healthcare system at all, either to acknowledge genetic risk or to seek diagnosis or treatment (Care Records Development Board, Ethical Advisory Group 2004). Laurie argues that in these circumstances the regulatory limbo could be filled by the concept of 'spatial privacy' (Laurie 2002). There seems to be room for a more pragmatic approach which recognizes a limited role for the judicial system to arbitrate between two conflicting sets of private and public interests in certain exceptional circumstances.[63] The importance of context is also a theme of Manson and O'Neill's critique of informed consent in bioethics. They argue that the data protection legislation fails to offer a satisfactory approach to informational privacy on the grounds that 'it invests some types of information with intrinsic ethical significance, at the expense of analyzing the epistemic and ethical norms that specify informational and communicative obligations, and on the second–order informational obligations that secure their performance' (Manson and O'Neill 2007).

These comments seem particularly relevant to the development of electronic sealed envelopes within an electronic health records system.

Data Sharing between Parents and Their Incompetent/Minor Children

Context also becomes paramount and the respective claims difficult to judge where there are disagreements between parents and their children as to what constitutes the best interests of the child. In the context of clinical genetics these judgments may be finely balanced. There is continuing debate as to whether non-paternity should be disclosed (Lucassen and Parker 2001, Lucast 2007) or whether it can be in a child's best interests to carry out a test which may reveal a late onset genetic

---

63   Indeed, there may be a case for reforming the Human Tissue Act to allow judicial intervention in the form of an order by the court allowing DNA analysis to proceed in the absence of consent from a living donor where the interests of family members are opposed. This would allow any potential interference with privacy interests to be judged on the basis of whether they are necessary and proportionate.

condition.[64] Debates around non-paternity are particularly problematic since respecting one partner's autonomy rights may only be possible at the expense of denying those of the other.[65] Legal analysis suggests that although disclosure of non-paternity may interfere with the right to respect for a private and family life, this interference could be justified under article 8(2) of the Human Rights Act as being necessary for 'the protection of health and morals' and 'the protection of the rights and freedoms of others' (Human Rights Act 1998, Art. 8).[66] In the absence of relevant legal precedent, clinical practice has been to seek both partners' consent to disclosure as part of the informed consent procedure prior to testing, but as Lucast points out, seeking consent to disclose non-paternity does not mitigate the ethical problems involved. Indeed Lucast argues that the best strategy is not to seek consent to disclosure of non-paternity as part of the informed consent procedure but to disclose it if necessary to keep 'the child in question central' by warning the woman ahead of time and disclosing the information in a sensitive and supportive fashion.

The determination of what constitutes best practice in information disclosure continues to be determined by professional groups themselves (*Bolam* 1957, *Pearce* 1998) since clinical negligence is framed by professional opinion. Increasingly however, good practice is dictated by accessing 'expert' information, and high powered search engines enable patients to access the same information as their health professionals. Crolla (2003) thus argues: 'The doctor-patient relationship has accordingly shifted from the linear model with the physician as the controller to a matrix model with the patient or patients at the centre' with the result that patients could be found contributarily negligent for failures in their own care.[67] The lack of relevant case law in the sharing of genetic information is problematic, and changing practices regarding the sharing of information between parents and children are also relevant. Legal precedent provides that a competent child can veto the disclosure of medical information to his or her parent if the doctor agrees that it is in the best interests of the child to do so (*Gillick* 1985, *Axon*

---

64   See the Human Fertilisation and Embryology Authority (2006) consultation on pre-implantation genetic testing for cancer susceptibility.

65   Such as when the woman wants non-disclosure of non-paternity. The alternative strategy for the counselor of blaming a child's condition on a rare spontaneous mutation in the context of a recessive disease such as cystic fibrosis 'constitutes a deception on the counsellor's part, however – one which contradicts her principal function as information provider. That is, it undermines the entire point of counselling' (Lucast 2007, 47).

66   The disclosure of non-paternity engages the right to respect for a private and family life.

67   Once the obligation to use the Internet as a resource becomes a standard part of clinical practice healthcare (because it satisfies a competent body of professional opinion), the failure to access knowledge on the Internet could become grounds for a claim in negligence. In her analysis of patient held records, Gertz (2007) suggests that the logical endpoint of a mistake in patient held records is 'the rather astonishing conclusion that the patient herself must be held liable for the harm she suffered'.

2006; McHale and Fox 2006, 576–621).[68] At stake is the fact that the confidence in the healthcare system might be compromised if healthcare professionals are not regarded as keeping disclosures confidential. In contrast, competent children have no veto over disclosure to parents unless that non-disclosure is in the child's best interests (*Gillick* 1985, NHS Care Record Development Board 2007, General Medical Council 2007).[69]

Implications for Research

The focus of the planned reforms has been improvements to patient care in the short term, by sharing information among providers. In the longer term, the fact that research is needed to generate evidence-based improvements in care has not received enough recognition, and the fundamental role that research plays in promoting evidence-based healthcare is not given a high profile within current versions of the Care Record Guarantee. The rationale for preventing the sharing of identifiable data outside the NHS has been to bolster public trust in medical services by emphasizing the confidential nature of this relationship. Building on the importance of medical confidentiality, honorary contracts have traditionally been the mechanism for researchers to gain access to patient-identifiable information in the course of carrying out research which is clearly in the public interest. However, the primacy of consent-driven electronic systems suggests another model for patient participation in research, which enables a proactive patient to record a generic willingness to be invited to participate in research (Care Record Development Board 2007, recommendation 6).

Rationalizing Information Governance: the Creation of a National Information Governance Board

The situation has been compounded by fragmented data governance within the Department of Health and the NHS[70] and the lack of a consistent judicial remedy for breaches of privacy arising from misuse of patient electronic data. Cayton (2006) identified nine separate bodies or groups with responsibility for information governance within the NHS. Of those, none was identified as being authoritative,

---

68   Note, however, that parental consent may overrule a competent minor's refusal in the context of an abortion.

69   Although the most recent version of the Care Record Guarantee does go some way to acknowledge that both parents and their competent and non-competent children may have conflicting claims over personal health data (NHS Care Record Guarantee 2007), contrast the approach of the HTA, which in the context of holding cellular material for DNA analysis, favors consents (from parents) over refusals (from competent children), presumably on the assumption that consents are more likely to be in the best interests of the donor of the tissue and the least restrictive outcome.

70   See also general guidance, such as NHS Information Authority (2003).

lines of accountability were lacking and implementation was disjointed and patchy.

> The coherence, clarity and consistency in the way information is governed within and between the various bodies involved in the development, delivery and monitoring of NHS care and services will need to be improved to support an electronic NHS ... [But] in order to meet the necessary standards of confidentiality, security, safety and consistency we will need national standards locally implemented and monitored and nationally enforced.

The same report (Cayton 2006, recommendation 3) called for a National Information Governance Board to be established to oversee this process. The concept of independent oversight is not new: regulators and policy-makers have already grappled with the constraints placed upon the sharing of information. In the wake of professional advice from the General Medical Council published in 2000, many GPs stopped sending confidential patient information to cancer registries. A law was passed to clarify the lawfulness of such data sharing in 2001, which provided that identifiable patient information could be shared without consent for certain medical purposes in the public interest (Health and Social Care Act 2001, Academy of Medical Sciences 2006, Chapter 2).[71] The Patient Information Advisory Group (PIAG) was set up to manage the statutory exemptions, but evidence submitted to the Academy of Medical Sciences suggested that researchers found the PIAG process to be 'overly bureaucratic and lengthy' (Academy of Medical Sciences 2006, para. 2.3.3.(4)) and that it has had the effect of ratcheting up existing legal standards. Undoubtedly, some of PIAG's past difficulties were caused by interpretative problems caused by overlapping exemptions provided by the common law and the DPA, but if PIAG's replacement (the Ethics and Confidentiality Committee of the National Information Governance Board) is to be more effective than its predecessor, it must be equipped to deal with the breadth of data sharing which already exists within the NHS (NHS Connecting for Health 2006b, NHS Care Records Service 2006).[72] Also at stake is the absence of consistent judicial remedies for breaches of privacy arising from misuse of the patient electronic care record and the heterogeneity of sanctions arising from similar disclosures (Care Record Development Board 2007, para. 5.3.5).

---

71   Such as cancer registries, communicable disease surveillance, medical research requiring geographical location and for the purpose of anonymization.

72   See, for example, the use of pseudonymized data mediated by the secondary uses service (SUS) for secondary purposes, such as healthcare planning, commissioning, public health, clinical audit, benchmarking, performance improvement, clinical governance and research.

Policy Developments: More Systematic and Comprehensive Data Sharing

While refinements to the framework for sharing summary care records have tended toward seeking a more explicit consent for each episode of data sharing, in other policy contexts, particularly in relation to data sharing between public authorities, there is an opposing trend of more systematic sharing of data without consent. If implemented, such data sharing will have to be compliant with a voluntary code of practice and will be subject to increased sanctions for deliberate or reckless breaches of data protection principles.[73] These reforms follow recommendations made by the Data Sharing Review (Thomas and Walport 2008): provisions in the Coroners and Justice Bill (2009) to allow information sharing orders to be made through secondary legislation mandating data sharing among government departments on the basis that they can be justified on the grounds of necessity and proportionality, and that they reflect a fair balance between the public interest and the interests of any person affected by it were subsequently withdrawn. This withdrawal followed criticisms that their effect might be to allow primary legislation (even the Human Rights Act and Data Protection Act) to be undermined, without sufficient Parliamentary scrutiny.

However other policy initiatives in the Health Bill (2009) provide for an NHS Constitution, supported by a handbook which contains explicit rights for patients to 'be notified of opportunities to join in relevant ethically approved research'. These policy developments may well have an impact upon research practices, by modifying the extent and nature of direct contact between patients and researchers and may signify other developments in policy.[74] As well as changes to the legislative environment, there have been developments in the way that privacy and confidentiality interests have been enforced through the courts.

Refining the Legal Framework

(a) The nature of the confidential relationship: the effect of European and International case law Recent developments in European and international case law have raised the possibility of the development of a privacy tort outside a confidential relationship. This might have relevance where genetic information is used outside a medical setting, for example, in paternity testing or is shared among relatives. The traditional relationship between a healthcare professional and the patient has historically been viewed as the archetype of a confidential relationship

---

73   Criminal Justice and Immigration Act (2008) amends the Data Protection Act 1998 to add an additional section 55(A).

74   The Government response to the Data Sharing Review mandates the National Information Governance Board to amend the NHS Care Record Guarantee to highlight the use of personal information for research (Ministry of Justice [2008]).

since it usually comprises all the elements identified in case law:

> First, the information itself ... must have the necessary quality of confidence
> about it. Secondly, that information must have been imparted in circumstances
> importing an obligation of confidence. Thirdly, there must be an unauthorised
> use of that information to the detriment of the party communicating it (Coco
> 1969 in Mulheron 2006).

This traditional model, in which the doctor-patient relationship is protected by the equitable remedy of breach of confidence has been challenged both in case law in the UK, the European Court, Australia and New Zealand and in professional guidance (British Medical Association 2005). A privacy tort could be invoked where there is a failure to satisfy all the elements of the confidential relationship, but the case for an equitable remedy for breach of privacy can still be made out. The significance of privacy has been down-played in the context of healthcare because until recently, privacy was regarded as but one strand of a confidential relationship. Recent legal precedent from the European Court and judicial comment in *Douglas v. Hello! Ltd* 2006 has added judicial weight to the view that English law must be brought into compliance with the European Court of Human Rights (ECHR) by developing jurisprudence to protect and respect privacy (Mulheron 2006, 696). This suggests that an independent tort of privacy would be viable outside a confidential relationship even if it might be difficult to implement in practice. However, the development of such a tort would be subject to certain provisos, namely that the extent of privacy owed by the professional depends upon the nature of the sensitivity of the disclosure and must be proportionate (*Australian Broadcasting Corp v. Lenah Game Meats Pty Ltd* 2001, *Campbell v. Mirror Group Newspapers Ltd* 2004, Australian Law Reform Commission 2007).

(b) The evolving influence of human rights legislation   Two cases lend weight to the prospect of an independent tort of privacy being justiciable in the UK. The first case concerned the interpretation of different rights under the Human Rights Act, namely conflicting claims to privacy and freedom of expression (*Max Mosley v. News Group Newspapers Limited* [2008]) and is significant to the extent that it clarified the role of the court in arbitrating such claims. The Honorable Mr Justice Eady noted the paradigm shift from 'old-fashioned breach of confidence' to the courts' protection of 'information in respect of which there is a reasonable expectation of privacy'. The motivation for this shift, he argued, was the Human Rights Act 1998, which, through incorporating provisions of the European Convention on Human Rights and Fundamental Freedoms, provided the

necessity for greater congruence between domestic and international law. Rather than providing a forum for weighing up conflicting interests, the court's role was to provide for an 'intense focus' upon the individual facts of the case, which is likely to involve a determination of the relative worth of one person's rights against those of another.[75]

The second case, heard in the European Court of Human Rights, concerned the extent to which democratic societies may seek to justify their interference with individual rights to a private and family life[76] on the grounds that such interference is 'necessary and proportionate' (*S and Marper v. The United Kingdom* [2008]). Both applicants claimed that the ongoing retention of their fingerprints, cellular samples and DNA profiles on the UK national forensic database after criminal proceedings against them had been respectively acquitted or discontinued was contrary to Articles 8 and 14 of the Human Rights Act.[77] The court noted that such retention and storage of data should be regarded as 'having direct impact on the private-life interest of an individual concerned, irrespective of whether subsequent use is made of the data'.[78] In its judgment it found that the blanket and indiscriminate retention 'fails to strike a fair balance between competing public and private interests' and 'constitutes a disproportionate interference with the applicants' right to respect for private life and cannot be regarded as necessary in a democratic society'.[79]

Taken together, these cases suggest a greater willingness on the part of the judiciary to recognize a general tort of privacy and to question the extent of the margin of appreciation that can be claimed by Member States.

(c) Identifying the sensitivity of the information   While the justification for a separate privacy tort may be most pressing in the absence of a confidential relationship, problems remain in identifying the boundaries of the tort and in determining its applicability to the sharing of information among family members by healthcare professionals. Rachael Mulheron has postulated a framework for privacy which builds upon a three-fold categorization of privacy rights proffered by a Privacy Taskforce from the Canadian Departments of Communication and Justice. One of

---

75   The presiding judge found in favor of the claimant and concluded that he had 'a reasonable expectation of privacy in relation to sexual activities' and that there was no justification for intrusion on the personal privacy of the claimant (by clandestine recording, publication and posting video extracts on the web).

76   Pursuant to Article 8 of the Human Rights Act (1998).

77   Namely, the rights to respect for private and family life (Article 8) and the right to enjoy Convention rights and freedoms without discrimination (Article 14). Unlike other member states, the UK alone permitted the systematic and indefinite retention of DNA profiles and cellular samples of those from whom criminal proceedings have been discontinued or who are subsequently acquitted.

78   Paragraph 121, *S. and Marper v. The United Kingdom* [2008] ECHR 1581.

79   Ibid., paragraph 125.

these categories is defined as privacy in the information context which

> is based essentially on the notion of dignity and the integrity of the individual, and on their relationship to information about him. This notion of privacy derives from the assumption that all information about a person is in a fundamental way his own, for him to communicate or retain for himself as he sees fit ... Nevertheless he has a basic and continuing interest in what happens to this information, and in controlling access to it (Mulheron 2006, 698).

Although genetic information, in a most profound way, satisfies the criterion of being *in a fundamental way his own*, by its very nature, these rights over genetic information are not exclusive. Thus in the context of genetic information, it is both disproportionate and misguided to seek to protect sensitive information by creating rights of exclusion: at stake are the inferences that can be made from that information (Manson and O'Neill 2007, 136).[80]

The judgment in the case of *S. and Marper v. The United Kingdom* lends support to the view that the sensitivity around the continued retention and storage of DNA profiles and cellular material derives from the nature and amount of personal information that can be extracted from those samples. However, the judgment goes on to note that such sensitivities are not affected by strategies to reduce the identifiability of samples (by coding), by the fact that information can only be extracted using technological aids or that its dissemination will be limited to a discrete and identifiable number of persons.[81] This seems to indicate that privacy rights under the Human Rights Act may still be engaged even if the data is no longer identifiable or even if it is not ever extracted or processed. This part of the judgment would tend to support a genetic exceptionalist view[82] that the distinctive nature of DNA implies that it should be afforded special protection. This suggests that all users of cellular samples and DNA profiles should be mindful of the potential sensitivities that arise.

(d) Redefining the scope of the duty owed to relatives in the context of electronic health records Instead of questioning the nature of the rights over genetic information (and the correlative responsibilities arising from them) an alternative approach adopted in some jurisdictions is to modify the tort of negligence to delineate the scope of the duty of care owed by health professionals to at-risk relatives. Unfortunately, this demonstrates a striking lack of consensus. Precedent from the Florida Supreme Court establishes that it is possible for a physician to owe a duty of care to someone other than his or her patient,

---

80 As Manson and O'Neill point out, the class of genetic information is both inferentially fertile and heterogeneous.

81 *S. and Marper v. The United Kingdom* [2008] ECHR 1581, paragraphs 72-75.

82 As discussed in Human Genetics Commission (2002) Inside Information: balancing interests in the use of personal genetic data.

although the extent of that duty is only to 'known' and 'identifiable' individuals who are at risk. Thus a physician owes a duty of care 'to the children of a patient to warn the patient of the genetically transferable nature of the condition for which the physician is treating the patient', a duty discharged by warning the patient (*Pate v. Threlkel* 1995, Laurie 2002, 267). Expert evidence in this case that it was a doctor's professional obligation to warn of these dangers was also persuasive.

In another US case, a New Jersey Appellate Court went further, confirming not only that a physician owes a duty of care to all 'members of the immediate family of the patient who may be adversely affected', but that in certain cases this duty trumps the patient's right to confidentiality (*Safer v. Estate of Pack* 1996, 1192-3). The court found that in the case of a physician treating a patient diagnosed with familial adenomatous polyposis,[83] the extent of this duty extended to warning those at risk, in this case the patient's 10-year-old daughter, of the heritable nature of the condition so that preventative measures might be taken. The significance of this case is that the judge refused to rule out warning the relative directly, concluding in this case that 'the duty to warn of avertable risk from genetic causes, by definition a matter of familial concern, is sufficiently narrow to service the interests of justice'.[84]

No directly referable case has been brought to court in the United Kingdom. However these US precedents might have limited applicability to an English setting since the formulation of negligence in English law is more complex than in US systems (which rely upon foreseeability of risk): English precedent relies upon three elements – duty, breach and damage. If such a case were to come to court, in order to prove a claim, an at-risk relative would have to prove that a duty of care was owed to him or her, that the physician was in breach of this duty and that proximate damage was caused by the clinician's non-disclosure. Grubb (2004) argues that English courts might have no choice in recognizing liability where the risks of harm are real and substantial and if a third party's life is at risk.[85] However, it is likely that the threshold for disclosure will be higher where the proband has explicitly requested that information remain confidential, particularly if the genetic information has been placed within a virtual sealed envelope and has been sealed or sealed and locked. In such a situation it may be difficult for a third party relative to claim that a health professional is in breach of his duty of care by failing to disclose relevant information. If such a case came to court and a duty of care to disclose genetic information were to be recognized within the English

---

83   Familial adenomatous polyposis is a hereditary disease which without treatment invariably leads to metastatic colorectal cancer.

84   Per Kestin, JAD.

85   The ECHR held that Article 2 of the ECHR required state authorities to take positive action to avert a real and immediate risk to life of an identified individual(s) from the criminal acts of a third party (*Osman v. UK* 1998, Grubb 2004, para. 5.73).

legal system, this would conflict directly with the right of veto accorded to tissue donors in the HTA.

(e) Specific legislation to outlaw genetic discrimination   Although the main focus of this chapter has been an examination of the rationale for sharing genetic material and information within the clinical setting and the concerns about the confidentiality and privacy aspects which arise when the concerns of family members are opposed, it is worth noting that the sharing of genetic information among data subjects and third parties in the context of insurance or employment may have significant implications for the data subject.[86] In the UK, there are plans to introduce consolidating legislation which brings together anti-discrimination legislation, and a consultation has addressed the possibility of introducing specific legislative controls against genetic discrimination (although in the absence of evidence of widespread genetic discrimination, it is likely that the *status quo* will be maintained [Department of Education and Skills et al. 2007]).

A case for a consistent approach to the regulation of DNA and genetic information   The preceding analysis has suggested that the regulation of genetic material and genetic information within the UK is not consistent. This is problematic because experience has shown that legal complexity, combined with criminal sanctions has fostered a 'hands off' approach. This disjunction between sample and information regulation is especially problematic for researchers. Thus as Hervey and McHale argue:

> The absence of a single regulatory regime governing research use of information and of samples may lead to considerable practical difficulties for researchers. So for example, at Member State level, this may mean that one legal regime governs the retention and use of samples, and a totally separate regime applies to the use of information (Hervey and McHale 2004, 188).

As increasingly complex disease-mutation associations are identified, an exceptionalist approach which awards genetic material or genetic information special status will become increasingly unsustainable. This is because the determination of genetic risk and susceptibility to common complex disease will inevitably become part of healthcare delivery. The legal and ethical challenge is to modify the systems of regulation within the UK to reflect that there is a spectrum of sensitivity attached to differing types of material and/or information

---

86   The moratorium limiting the use of genetic tests by insurers subject to certain financial limits (due to expire in 2014) is noteworthy because as the expiry date for the moratorium becomes closer, it is predictable that fear of discrimination may deter patients from seeking tests that have clinical validity and utility (Department of Health and Association of British Insurers 2005).

and a proportionate need for protection. Such an approach has been adopted in the recent European Protocol on Genetic Testing for Health Purposes, the scope of which is the analysis of chromosomes, DNA and RNA and 'any other element enabling [equivalent] information to be obtained'.[87] In this legislation, the defining factor is the nature of the information which can be obtained from the material rather than the characteristics of the material itself. In the context of genetics, factors such as disease penetrance, prevalence, severity of the condition and the availability of treatment may all be important, but so will family history and perhaps routine biochemical tests. As science progresses, the justification for other determinants (such as biomarkers or epigenetics) to be used as a proxy for ill health or disease susceptibility will become ever more pressing. There is a need for a proportionate regulatory regime that accommodates these medical and scientific advances.

Conclusions

The Human Tissue Act purports to grant autonomy rights to living competent adults and children which allow them to veto the use of their material even if it is for the benefit of others. However, the Act simultaneously provides for deemed consent if tissue donors cannot be traced or fail to respond to requests for consent.[88] A lack of response may mask a wish not to know a genetic diagnosis, a right which is difficult to accommodate within a regulatory framework crudely based on autonomy interests. To insist that patients are informed of a genetic diagnosis against their will in the name of promoting patient autonomy is also misguided. As Pellegrino has pointed out: 'To thrust the truth or the decision on a patient who expects to be buffered against news of impending death is a gratuitous and harmful misinterpretation of the moral foundations for respect for autonomy' (Pellegrino 1992).

The model also seems to break down where the autonomy interests of relatives collide, with consents being prioritized over refusals. In one sense this is a pragmatic solution which facilitates the continued use of cellular material despite paying lip service to the importance of consent.[89] In other respects, policy

---

87   The Additional Protocol to the Convention on Human Rights and Biomedicine, concerning Genetic Testing for Health Purposes, was made on 28 November 2008. Only those countries which have already signed or ratified the Convention on Human Rights and Biomedicine may join as signatories to this Protocol and neither the United Kingdom nor Germany have signed or ratified the Convention.

88   These rights are exercisable by the Human Tissue Authority and/or the Scottish Court of Sessions.

89   As we have seen, there is acknowledgment of public interests in tissue in the context of research using material from those lacking capacity to consent and for the purposes of criminal justice or pursuant to the coroner's authority.

makers have failed to follow their own dicta that the Human Tissue Act should not interfere with medical treatment and diagnosis or with research. As we have seen, the Act could have a significant impact on the practice of medical genetics, particularly where family members disagree.

Similarly, the proposed controls on electronic patient information seem to confer some rights upon data subjects to limit data sharing. However, the exceptions to these rights are not clearly articulated, creating 'public' interests in the genetic information of individuals which are undermined by practical difficulties in exerting those interests. These difficulties are compounded by the blurred epistemic boundary between genetic information and tissue and a lack of understanding that autonomy-based models are inappropriate to describe some types of genetic information. Together, these recent policy developments suggest that the regulation of genetic information is not systematic or grounded in common ethical or legal theory. This makes these policy developments difficult to interpret and recent legislation problematic to implement.

In the absence of a clear ethical framework, the structure put in place for a determination of conflicting interests within the Human Tissue Act would benefit from additional robustness[90] and transparency.[91] The lack of determinative judicial precedent in this complex and difficult area (*Safer v. Estate of Pack* 1995, *Pate v. Threlkel* 1996) exposes clinicians and researchers to criticism and possible liability: a minority of clinicians may seek to manage the conflicting interests of family members by not recording potentially sensitive information electronically to avoid causing distress (which could inadvertently lead to substandard patient care and exposure to claims of negligence). The lack of a coherent and transparent system also threatens to erode public trust in the confidentiality of the patient-clinician relationship and to undermine the basis upon which health care is delivered. It is ironic that these pressures towards duplication and fragmentation of record keeping within the NHS arise just at the time when the impact of human rights legislation is likely to require the justification of any interference in these rights in terms of necessity and proportionality.[92] Until the rights over genetic information and tissue are refined and liability issues resolved, the clinicians and researchers on whom the burden of recording, processing and sharing genetic information falls are placed in a difficult position, which may only be resolved by judicial intervention.

---

90   The Human Tissue Act requires review by a committee of members of the Human Tissue Authority who may have no collective experience of clinical genetics.

91   Regulations in respect of these powers are yet to be made.

92   The correct approach is to recognize that neither right has precedence over the other. There has to be an intense focus on the comparative importance of the specific rights being claimed; the justifications for interfering or restricting each right have to be taken into account, and the proportionality test has to be applied to each (Mersey Care NHS Trust v. Ackroyd 2006).

Bibliography

Academy of Medical Sciences (2006), Personal data for public good: using health information in medical research.

Access to Health Records Act 1990 (c. 23), London, HMSO.

Article 29 Data Protection Working Party (2004), *Working Document on Genetic Data* 12178/03/EN WP91, http://ec.europa.eu/justice_home/fsj/privacy/docs/wpdocs/2004/wp91_en.pdf (accessed 2 June 2009).

Article 29 Data Protection Working Party (2007a), *Working Document on the processing of personal data relating to health in electronic health records (HER)* 00323/07/EN WP 131 [adopted 15 February 2007], http://ec.europa.eu/justice_home/fsj/privacy/docs/wpdocs/2007/wp131_en.pdf (accessed 2 June 2009).

Article 29 Data Protection Working Party (2007b), *Opinion 4/2007 on the concept of personal data* 01248/07/EN WP 136, http://ec.europa.eu/justice_home/fsj/privacy/docs/wpdocs/2007/wp136_en.pdf (accessed 2 June 2009).

Australian Broadcasting Corp v. Lenah Game Meats Pty Ltd [2001] 208 CLR.

Australian Law Reform Commission (2007), *Review of Australian Privacy Law: Health Services and Research*, 1559–1712, http://www.austlii.edu.au/au/other/alrc/publications/dp/72/Part%20H.pdf (accessed 2 June 2009).

Benn, S. (1988), *A Theory of Freedom* (Cambridge: Cambridge University Press).

Beauchamp, T. and Childress, J. (2001), *Principles of Biomedical Ethics*, 5th Edition (Oxford: Oxford University Press).

Beyleveld, D. et al. (2004), *Implementation of the Data Protection Directive in Relation to Medical Research in Europe* (Aldershot: Ashgate).

Beyleveld, D. and Brownsword, R. (2007), *Consent in the Law* (Oxford: Hart Publishing).

Bolam v. Friern Hospital Management Committee [1957] 2 All ER 118, 1 WLR 582, 1 BMLR 1.

Breen v. Williams [1996] 138 DLR 259, 271, 264, 288, 301–02.

British Medical Association (2005), *Confidentiality as part of a bigger picture – a discussion paper from the BMA*. http://www.bma.org.uk/ethics/confidentiality/ConfidentialityBiggerPicture.jsp (accessed 2 June 2009).

British Medical Association (2006), *BMA Statement on Connecting for Health* (updated November 2006) (no longer available online).

British Medical Association (2007a), *Connecting for Health – The NHS Care Records Service –England*. http://www.bma.org.uk/Archive/taskforcereport.jsp (accessed 2 June 2009).

British Medical Association (2007b), *Guidance on the NHS Care Records Service*. http://www.bma.org.uk/Archive/ncrs2.jsp (accessed 2 June 2009).

Campbell v. Mirror Group Newspapers Ltd [2004] UKHL 22 [2004] 2 AC 457.

Canadian Departments of Communications and Justice (1972), Privacy and Computers (Ottawa: Information Canada), 13 cited in Mulheron (2006), n. 149.

Care Record Development Board, Ethics Advisory Group (2004), Ethical issues of consent to recording and disclosure of health records.

Care Record Development Board (2007), Report of the Care Record Development Board Working Group on the Secondary Uses of Patient Information.

Carvel, J. (2006), 'Patients win right to keep records off NHS computer', *Guardian Unlimited* (updated 16 December 2006), http://society.guardian.co.uk/health/story/0,1973337,00.html (accessed 2 June 2009).

Cayton, H. (2006), *Information Governance in the Department of Health and the NHS.* http://www.connectingforhealth.nhs.uk/crdb (accessed 2 June 2009).

Child Support Agency (2008), *Child Support Agency: What happens if someone denies they are the parent of a child?* http://www.csa.gov.uk/en/PDF/leaflets/new/CSL304.pdf (accessed 2 June 2009).

Children Act 1989. (c.41), London; HMSO, http://www.opsi.gov.uk/ACTS/acts1989/Ukpga_19890041_en_2.htm (accessed 2 June 2009).

Clarke, A. (2007), 'Should families own genetic information? No,' *BMJ* 335, 23.

Cayton, H. (2006), *Information Governance in the Department of Health and the NHS*, http://www.connectingforhealth.nhs.uk/crdb (accessed 2 June 2009).

Coco v. A.N. Clark (Engineers) Ltd [1969] RPC 41, 47 (Megarry J.) cited in Mulheron, R. (2006), 'A potential framework for privacy? A reply to *Hello!'* *Medical Law Review* 69 (5), 679–713.

Coroners and Justice Bill 2009 (c. 29), accessed 29 January 2009.

Council of Europe (2008), *Additional Protocol to the Convention on Human Rights and Biomedicine, concerning Genetic Testing for Health Purposes.*

Crolla, D. (2003), 'Cyberlaw: A Potent New Medicine for Health Law on the Internet', in Callens, S. (ed.) (2003), *E-Health and the Law* (London: Kluwer Law International).

Data Protection Act 1998, (c. 29) London: HMSO.

Department of Education and Skills et al. (2007), 'A Framework for Fairness: Proposals for a Single Equality Bill for Great Britain'.

Department of Health and the Association of British Insurers (2005), *Concordat and Moratorium on Genetics and Insurance.*

Department of Health (2006), *Records Management: NHS Code of Practice,* http://www.dh.gov.uk/en/Publicationsandstatistics/Publications/PublicationsPolicyAndGuidance/DH_4131747 (accessed 2 June 2009).

Department of Health (2007a), Information Security Management: NHS Code of Practice.

Department of Health (2007b), *NHS Information Governance – Guidance on Legal and Professional Obligations,* http://www.connectingforhealth.nhs.uk/systemsandservices/infogov/policy/legal/lglobligat.pdf (accessed 2 June 2009).

Department of Health, Department for Education and Employment and the Home Office (2001a), *Report of a Census of Organs and Tissues Retained by Pathology Services in England* (London: The Stationery Office).

Department of Health, Department for Education and Employment and the Home Office (2001b), *The Removal, Retention and use of Human Organs and Tissue from Post-Mortem Examinations: Advice from the Chief Medical Officer* (London: The Stationery Office).

Directive 95/46/EC of the European Parliament and of the Council of the 24th October 1995 on the protection of individuals with regard to the processing of personal data and on the free movement of such data. *Official Journal of the European Communities* (23.11.95) No. L281/31.

Directive 2004/23/EC of the European Parliament and of the Council on setting standards of quality and safety for the donation, procurement, testing, processing, preservation, storage and distribution of human tissues and cells. *Official Journal of the European Communities* (07.04.04) No. L102,http://eur-lex.europa.eu/LexUriserv/LexUriserv.do?uri=CELEX:32004L0023:EN: HTML(accessed 2 June 2009).

Douglas v. Hello! Ltd [2006] QB 125.

General Medical Council (2004), *Confidentiality: Protecting and Providing Information* http://www.gmc-uk.org/guidance/current/library/confidentiality. asp (accessed 2 June 2009).

General Medical Council (2007), 0-18 years: guidance for all doctors.

Gertz, R. (2004), An analysis of the Icelandic Supreme Court judgement on the Health Sector Database Act 1:2 SCRIPT–ed 241@: http://www.law.ed.ac.uk/ahrc/script-ed/issue2/iceland.asp (accessed 2 June 2009).

Gertz, R. (2007), An Electronic Health Record for Scotland: Legal Problems Regarding Access and Maintenance 4:1 SCRIPT–ed 152@: http://www.law. ed.ac.uk/ahrc/script-ed/vol4-1/gertz.asp (accessed 2 June 2009).

Gillick v. West Norfolk and Wisbech Area Health Authority [1986] AC 112, [1985] 3 All ER 402, [1985] 2 BMLR 11 (HL).

Grubb, A. (ed.) (2004), *The Principles of Medical Law*, 2nd Edition (Oxford: Oxford University Press).

Hansard (2001), [Alan Milburn, House of Commons Committee] 31 January 2001, at col. 178.

Hansard (2004), [Baroness Andrews, House of Lords Grand Committee] 16 September 2004, at col. GC 480.

Health Bill 2009 (c.18).

Health and Social Care Act 2001 (c. 15) (London: HMSO)

Hervey, T. and McHale, J. (2004), *Health Law and the European Union* (Cambridge: Cambridge University Press). http://www.opsi.gov.uk/ACTS/acts2001/10015--g.htm#60 (accessed 2 June 2009).

House of Commons Health Committee (2007) HC422-1 *Electronic Patient Record*. The Stationery Office, http://www.publications.parliament.uk/pa/cm200607/cmselect/cmhealth/422/422.pdf (accessed 2 June 2009).

House of Commons Science and Technology Select Committee Third Report (1995), Vol. 1: 41-1 *Human Genetics: the science and its consequences* (London: HMSO).

Human Genetics Commission (2002), Inside Information: Balancing Interests in the use of personal genetic data.

Human Fertilisation and Embryology Authority (2006), *Choices and Boundaries.*

Human Rights Act 1998 (c. 42) (London: HMSO).

Human Tissue Act (1961), (c.54) (London: HMSO).

Human Tissue Act (2004), (c.30) (London: HMSO), http://www.opsi.gov.uk/acts/acts2004/20040030.htm (accessed 2 June 2009).

Human Tissue Act 2004 (Persons Who Lack Capacity to Consent and Transplants) Regulations (2006), SI 2006/1659 (London: HMSO), http://www.opsi.gov.uk/SI/si2006/20061659.htm (accessed 10 October 2007).

Human Tissue Authority (2006), *Code of Practice – Post Mortem Examination.* http://www.hta.gov.uk/_db/_documents/2006-07-04_Approved_by_Parliament_-_Code_of_Practice_3_-_Post_Mortem.pdf (accessed 2 June 2009).

Human Tissue Authority (2007a), *Relevant Material* (updated 22 February 2007 and 24 November 2008). Available at: http://www.hta.gov.uk/guidance/licensing_guidance/definition_of_relevant_material.cfm (updated November 2008) (accessed 2 June 2009).

Human Tissue Authority (2007b), *Non consensual DNA testing (revised guidance).* http://www.hta.gov.uk/guidance/non-consensual_dna_analysis.cfm (accessed 2 June 2009).

Human Tissue (Scotland) Act (2006), (asp. 4), http://www.opsi.gov.uk/legislation/scotland/acts2006/20060004.htm (accessed 2 June 2009).

Information Commissioner's Office (2007), Data Protection Technical Guidance: Determining what is personal data.

Laurie, G. (2002), *Genetic Privacy: A Challenge to Medico-Legal Norms* (Cambridge: Cambridge University Press).

Learning from Bristol: The Report of the Public Inquiry into Children's Heart Surgery at the Bristol Royal Infirmary 1984–1995 Cm 5207 (2001), http://www.bristol-inquiry.org.uk/final_report/report/index.htm (accessed 2 June 2009).

Liddell, K. and Hall, A. (2005), 'Beyond Bristol and Alder Hey: the future regulation of human tissue', *Medical Law Review* 13, 170–223.

Lucassen, A. (2007), 'Should families own genetic information? Yes', *BMJ* 335, 22.

Lucassen, A. and Parker, M. (2001), 'Revealing false paternity: some ethical considerations', *The Lancet* 357 (9261), 1033–5.

Lucast, E.K. (2007), 'Informed consent and the misattributed paternity problem in genetic counselling', *Bioethics* 21 (1), 41–50.

Manson, N. and O'Neill, O. (2007), *Rethinking Informed Consent in Bioethics* (Cambridge: Cambridge University Press).

Max Mosely v. News Group Newspapers Limited [2008] EWHC 1777 (QB).

McHale, J. (1999), 'The general practitioner and confidentiality' in Dowick, C. and Frith, L. (eds), *General Practice and Ethics: Uncertainty and Responsibility* (London: Routledge), 73, cited in Pattenden (2003).

McHale, J. and Fox, M. (2006), *Health Care Law: Text and Materials, 2nd Edition* (London: Sweet and Maxwell)

Mental Capacity Act 2005 (c.9), http://www.opsi.gov.uk/acts/acts2005/20050009.htm (accessed 2 June 2009).

Mersey Care NHS Trust v. Ackroyd [2006] EWHC 107 (QB).

Ministerial Taskforce on the Summary Care Record (2006), *Report of the Ministerial Taskforce on the NHS Summary Care Record*.www.connectingforhealth.nhs.uk/publications/care_record_taskforce_doc.pdf (accessed 2 June 2009).

Ministry of Justice (2008), Response to the Data Sharing Review Report.

Mulheron, R. (2006), 'A potential framework for privacy? A reply to *Hello!*', *Medical Law Review* 69 (5), 679–713.

National Audit Office (2006), *Department of Health: The National Programme of IT in the NHS*. http://www.nao.org.uk/publications/nao_reports/05-06/05061173.pdf (accessed 2 June 2009).

National Health Service Act 2006. (c. 41) (London: HMSO).

Ngwena, C. and Chadwick, R. (1993), 'Genetic diagnostic information and the duty of confidentiality: ethics and the law', *Medical Law International* 1, 73–95.

NHS Care Record Development Board (2005), Care Record Guarantee, Version 1.

NHS Care Record Development Board (2006), Care Record Guarantee, Version 2.

NHS Care Record Development Board (2007), Care Record Guarantee, Version 3. http://www.nigb.nhs.uk/guarantee/crs_guarantee.pdf (accessed 2 June 2009).

NHS Care Records Service (2006), *Your health information, confidentiality and the NHS Care Records Service*. http://www.connectingforhealth.nhs.uk/systemsandservices/scr/documents/confidentiality.pdf (accessed 2 June 2009).

NHS Care Records Service (2007), Guidance on Managing Requests for No Summary Care Record during the period of the Early Adopter Programme.

NHS Connecting for Health (2006a), *Sealed Envelopes Briefing Paper: Selective Alerting Approach*. http://www.connectingforhealth.nhs.uk/crdb/sealed_envelopes_briefing_paper.pdf (accessed 2 June 2009).

NHS Connecting for Health (2006b), Guidance for the NHS about accessing patient information in new and different ways and what this means for patient confidentiality (no longer accessible online).

NHS Connecting for Health (2007), Care Record Development Board. http://www.connectingforhealth.nhs.uk/crdb (accessed 2 June 2009).

NHS Connecting for Health (2008), Consultation on Public, Patients, and Other Interested Parties' Views on Additional Uses of Patient Data.

NHS Constitution for England (2009).

NHS: Handbook to the NHS Constitution for England (2009).

NHS Information Authority, The Consumer's Association and Health Which? (2002), Share with Care! People's Views on Consent and Confidentiality of Patient Information.

NHS Information Authority (2003), *What You Should Know about Information Governance*.https://www.igt.connectingforhealth.nhs.uk/KnowledgeBase/KB%5CIG%5CIG_Leaflet_FV.pdf (accessed 2 June 2009).

NHS National Programme for Information Technology and *Health Which?* (2003), *The Public View on Electronic Health Records*.

Osman v. UK [1998] 5BHRC 293.

Parker, M. and Lucassen, A. (2004), 'Genetic Information: a joint account?', *British Medical Journal* 329, 165–7.

Pate v. Threlkel 661 So. 2d 278 (Fla Dist Ct App1995).

Pattenden, R. (2003), *The Law of Professional–Client Confidentiality: Regulating the Disclosure of Confidential Personal Information* (Oxford: Oxford University Press).

Pearce v. United Bristol Healthcare NHS Trust [1998] 48 BMLR 118 (CA).

Pellegrino, E.D. (1992), 'Is Truth Telling to the Patient a Cultural Artefact?', *Journal of the American Medical Association* 268, 1734–5, cited in Laurie, G. (2002).

Privireal Project (Privacy in Research Ethics and Law) (2005), *Recommendations Made to the European Commission*. http://www.privireal.org/content/recommendations/#Recc (accessed 2 June 2009).

R (on the application of Axon) v. Secretary of State [2006] EWCA 37 (Admin), [2006] All E.R. (D) 148

R v. Department of Health ex. parte Source Informatics Ltd [2001] Q.B. 424 (CA).

Report of the Inquiry into the Royal Liverpool Children's Hospital (Alder Hey) (2001) (Redfern Report), HC 12–11 (London: HMSO), http://www.rlcinquiry.org.uk/download/index.htm (accessed 2 June 2009).

S. and Marper v. The United Kingdom [2008] ECHR 1581.

Safer v. Estate of Pack [1996] 677 A. 2d 1188 (N.J. Sup Ct App Div).

Thomas, R. and Walport, M. (2008), *Data Sharing Review Report*, http://www.justice.gov.uk/docs/data-sharing-review-report.pdf (accessed 2 June 2009).

UK Intellectual Property Office (2007), *Patents: Basic Facts*. http://www.patent.gov.uk/p-basicfacts.pdf (accessed 2 June 2009).

University College London (2008), Summary Care Record Early Adopter Programme: an independent evaluation by University College London, http://www.ucl.ac.uk/openlearning/documents/scrie2008.pdf (accessed 2 June 2009).

Wellcome Trust (2007), Public Attitudes to Research Governance: A qualitative study in a deliberative context.

Chapter 18

Biobanks for Research: The German National Ethics Council's Opinion

Jochen Taupitz

Collections of Human Bodily Substances as a Promising Instrument of Medical and Pharmaceutical Research

Human bodily substances are an important resource for establishing the causes and mechanisms of a large number of disorders, in particular those widely disseminated among the population.[1] The more thoroughly the human genome is understood, the more it is becoming possible to identify the role not only of external factors such as environmental agencies or lifestyle but also of hereditary predispositions (genes) in their causation. Scientific interest here as a rule centers not on individuals but primarily on very large population groups. For this reason, collections of human bodily substances and the associated medical data have taken on enormous significance in modern medicine.[2] Lately these collections have even acquired a specific name: 'biobanks'.

The majority of current biobanks are relatively small collections devoted to particular diseases, established, for example, in university departments and comprising a few hundred to a few thousand donor samples.[3] These biobanks will remain significant in the future. In addition, some countries are in the process of setting up large-scale population-wide biobanks that will permit not only research on individual disorders but also the investigation of a broad range of health-related issues.[4] Biobanks are increasingly also being established in the pharmaceutical sector.

---

1 See Nationaler Ethikrat 2004, 9 et seq., 23 et seq.

2 Recently Mand 2005, 565.

3 Cf. Zentrale Ethikkommission 2003, 2; in-depth to the different types: Nationaler Ethikrat 2004, 28 et seq.

4 For population-related biobanks in-depth and with examples, see Nationaler Ethikrat 2004, 35 et seq.

Donor Protection

Fundamental Considerations

While biobanks hold out the prospect of significant breakthroughs in medical and pharmaceutical research, they also arouse anxiety and distrust. The main concern is protection of donors – that is, of the individuals whose bodily substances and medical data are used for research.[5] Specific statutory provisions on the permissible use of human bodily substances do not as yet exist in Germany.[6] Jurisprudence and judicial practice must therefore apply the existing general legislation in such a way as to establish a specific doctrine whereby donors are appropriately protected. It is quite clear that this leads to some uncertainty – and to disputes about the right level and means of protection.

Three aspects of protection must be distinguished. The first is protection of living human beings and their bodies – that is to say, the conditions that should govern the extraction or separation of bodily substances from a donor's body. The second has to do with the conditions that should apply to the use of bodily substances lawfully obtained from a donor's body for research purposes. The main issue here concerns donors' rights in respect of bodily substances once severed from their bodies. The third and last aspect involves the conditions applicable to use of donors' medical data – that is, specific information.

Extraction of Bodily Material from a Person's Body

The principal consideration here is the donor's right of self-determination. This right is protected not only by the German Constitution but also by the criminal and civil law through the right to physical inviolability.[7] It is a fundamental precept that an action on a person's body may be carried out only with that person's informed consent.[8] This applies equally to medical actions: a doctor has no right to treat a patient capable of exercising self-determination without that patient's consent, let alone against his[9] will. The right of self-determination comes even more fully into play where an action on a person's body is performed for the purposes of

---

5   For the rights of donors of biological material, see Bellivier/Noiville 2004, 89.

6   Halàsz 2004, 1 et seq; Mand 2005, 565 et seq.; Nationaler Ethikrat 2004, 24; Zentrale Ethikkommission 2003, 4; in general, for the permissible use of human blood, Schröder and Taupitz 1991, 1 et seq.

7   Spranger 2005, 1084 et seq.; Tag 2000, 1 et seq.

8   For example, see German Federal Constitutional Court: BVerfGE 52, 131, 168 et seq.; German Federal Court of Justice: BGHZ 29, 46, 49 et seq.; BGHZ 106, 391, 397 et seq.; Deutsch and Spickhoff 2008, 163; Halàsz 2004, 207 et seq.; Laufs 2002, §61 No. 14; Schröder and Taupitz 1991, 23 et seq.; Wagner 2004, §823 No. 665.

9   The masculine form is used throughout for convenience, and it should be understood as including the feminine.

research.[10] For this reason, the extraction of bodily substances from a person's body and the collection of personal information, in both cases for subsequent use in biobanks for medical research, must be subject to the consent of the individual concerned.[11] The consent is effective if the donor has the capacity to give consent, the consent is given voluntarily and the donor has been appropriately informed of the purposes, nature, significance and implications of the collection and use.[12]

Reuse of Lawfully Extracted Bodily Substances

However, it is legitimate to enquire whether the requirement of consent still applies where bodily substances lawfully extracted from a person's body are to be reused for research. This question arises in particular with samples which were originally taken for medical reasons in the interests of a patient, for example, for diagnosis or therapy, and which may then be used for research rather than being disposed of. This kind of multiple sample use is extremely valuable for medical research, but in the past it usually took place without explicit patient consent.[13]

To determine whether such reuse of bodily substances is lawful only if the person from whom they were taken has expressly consented to such use, it is necessary to establish what right that person has to 'his' bodily substances once separated from the body.

Rights to Substances Separated from the Body: Property and Personal Rights

According to current prevailing opinion,[14] two rights to bodily substances separated from the body of a living subject exist side by side (cumulatively).

First, on separation from the body, the bodily substance becomes an 'ordinary' chattel. Upon the separation, the person from whom the substance was taken becomes its owner. That person may subsequently transfer his property in the chattel to someone else (that is, he may assign the chattel), or he may relinquish the property right, thus allowing anyone else to take possession of the chattel.

Second, the right of self-determination of the person from whom the sample was taken persists in respect to his entire body even after the separation of a part of the body or of a bodily substance. The main reason why this right of self-determination, which is called the 'general personal right' or 'general right of personality', continues to attach to the chattel is that the bodily substance contains

---

10   Deutsch and Spickhoff 2008, 917 et seq.
11   Nationaler Ethikrat 2004, 48 et seq.
12   Mand 2005, 572 et seq.; Nationaler Ethikrat 2004, 56 et seq.
13   Nationaler Ethikrat 2004, 25.
14   Schröder and Taupitz 1991, 42 et seq. with numerous references; Taupitz 1991, 209; Deutsch and Spickhoff 2008, 547; Halàsz 2004, 35 et seq.; Freund and Weiss 2004, 316; Freund 2005, 453; Müller 1997, 49 et seq.; Nationaler Ethikrat 2004, 45; Zentrale Ethikkommission 2003, 5.

the genes of the person from whom the sample was taken – that is, the building blocks of that person's genetic identity and individuality.

Differences between Property Right and 'General Right Of Personality'

Different persons may be entitled to each of these two rights – the property right and the 'general right of personality'. For instance, as a rule, a patient who leaves his bodily material with a doctor without comment may be presumed thereby to assign it to the doctor.[15] The doctor thus becomes the owner of the bodily material. However, this does not mean that the doctor can do what he likes with it. Instead, he must respect the patient's continuing 'general right of personality'. The situation is rather like that of a love letter: although the recipient becomes the owner of the letter, he must not, for example, publish it without the sender's consent.[16]

Therefore, if the 'general right of personality' of the person from whom the bodily substance was taken to the substance persists, the question arises whether the assigning of the bodily substance to the doctor has any significance at all, or whether the doctor must nevertheless, owing to the 'general right of personality', obtain the patient's individual consent for any kind of use.

The first point to be made is that violations of property rights incur sanctions under both civil and criminal law, whereas the 'general right to personality' is protected by civil law only. Hence, a doctor who violates the patient's property right faces criminal-law sanctions (prison or a fine). In addition, the doctor may in certain circumstances have to pay damages to the patient under civil law. The doctor will face neither of these sanctions if, as stated, he has become the owner of the bodily substance. Conversely, if he violates the 'general right of personality', he will not be liable to a penalty. At most, the patient can demand damages and, in extremely unusual circumstances,[17] also compensation for intangible harm – that is, for non-economic damage (*pretio doloris*). In other words, a doctor will face severe sanctions if he violates a property right, whereas infringement of the 'general right of personality' has virtually no adverse consequences.

Another important consideration is that any action affecting property rights carried out without the owner's consent is unlawful. This is not so in the case of the 'general right of personality'. This right is deemed to have been violated only if the outcome of a 'comprehensive balancing of interests' is that the interests

---

15   Halàsz 2004, 60 et seq.; Nitz and Dierks 2002, 401; Schröder and Taupitz 1991, 94; Zentrale Ethikkommission 2003, 5; for a different opinion, Freund and Weiss 2004, 316; Freund 2005, 455.

16   Cf. Schack 2005, No. 52 et seq. with numerous references.

17   According to the decisions of the courts, there must have been a 'severe' violation of the personal right that cannot be compensated for in any other way than by a pecuniary settlement (rather than, say, by retraction of a defamatory statement).

of the holder of the relevant right have indeed been substantially affected.[18] For instance, an attempt to produce a second, genetically identical person by cloning a cell taken from his body would surely constitute a violation of his personal rights.[19] Conversely, the interests of the person concerned can scarcely be said to have been substantially affected if cells from the body are used for scientific instruction or research in anonymized form and in a situation to which the genetic individuality of the person concerned is irrelevant. Balancing the interests involved, the high weight of freedom of research also has to be taken into account.[20]

Therefore, a given use of body cells must be examined in terms of whether it really does affect the personal interests of the person from whom they were taken. If this is found to be so in a specific case, the use is unlawful and can be rendered lawful only if the consent of the holder of the right is obtained. If, on the other hand, these interests are deemed to be unaffected, the researcher does not require the consent of the holder of the right, as his action is lawful even without such consent. Nor, in these cases, need he inform the donor of the projected use, as information would be necessary only as a condition and basis for consent. In other words, if property in the bodily substance has been assigned to him, the researcher may use the substance secretly for his own purposes if and to the extent that he does not unlawfully violate the 'general right of personality' in so doing.

Another important criterion for determining whether interests of the donor are affected by the projected use of 'his' bodily substances is whether they are to be used together with personal data or in anonymized form.[21] After all, the use of substances already separated from a donor's body cannot present a *physical risk* to him; any risk arises mainly from the use of the *information* accruing from the analysis of his bodily substances. For instance, he may himself be given information that he did not wish to receive, in which case his right not to know will have been violated.[22] Alternatively, other people (for example, employers, insurance companies or family members) might obtain information about him that gives rise to the danger of discrimination and stigmatization.[23] For this reason, since the use of bodily substances already separated from the body of a person carries mainly *informational risks,* and since the regulation of such risks falls within the purview of the data protection laws, the values inherent in that legislation can also

---

18   Cf. German Federal Court of Justice: BGHZ 13, 334, 338; BGHZ 31, 308, 312 et seq.; BGHZ 36, 77, 82 et seq.; BGHZ 50, 133, 143; Deutsch 1992, 163; Müller 1997, 51; Taupitz 1991, 210 et seq.; Taupitz 1992, 1092; Nationaler Ethikrat 2004, 45 et seq.; Zentrale Ethikkommission 2003, 6.

19   Cf. Schröder and Taupitz 1991, 65.

20   Spranger 2005, 1085 et seq.

21   Fundamental to the relevant right of self-determination on personal data, see German Federal Constitutional Court: BVerfGE 65, 1 et seqq. – *census of population*; see for the judgments before: BVerfGE 27, 1 et seq.; BVerfGE 27, 344 et seq.; BVerfGE 32, 373 et seq.; cf. Jarass 2004, Art. 2 No. 44.

22   Cf. to the right not to know: Taupitz 1998, 583 et seq. with numerous references.

23   Nationaler Ethikrat 2004, 68 et seq.

be adduced for specifying the conditions under which human bodily substances may be used in biobanks.

Implications for the Storage and Use of Human Bodily Substances In Biobanks: Uncertainty and Disagreement

Although the basic legal position described above is essentially undisputed, considerable disagreement exists on the specific conclusions. The uncertainty arises mainly from the extremely ill-defined requirement of a 'comprehensive balancing of interests' stipulated for determining whether the 'general right of personality' has been violated. The disagreement centers on the following questions:

- When human bodily substances are used, in what cases is the individual consent of the relevant donor required, and in what cases can it be dispensed with?
- In cases where individual consent is required, is there a need for specific consent in which, for example, a precise research project is mentioned, or can blanket consent suffice?
- Can consent be granted for use for a specified time only, or is consent without a time limit sufficient?
- Should donors be given a choice of declarations of consent providing for different degrees of permission?
- What information must donors be given in order for their consent (where required) to be valid?
- Should donors be eligible to share in any eventual benefits?
- Should biobanks be subject to state licensing and supervision?
- In what cases should an interdisciplinary ethics commission be involved, as required by the laws governing certain fields of research on human subjects (for example, research on pharmaceuticals or medical devices and research using X-rays)?

The German National Ethics Council's 2004 Opinion

In view of the legal situation outlined above and, in particular, of the resulting uncertainties, in 2004 the German National Ethics Council issued recommendations on the use of human bodily substances in biobanks:[24]

1. The central element of all regulatory proposals must be the donor's right of self-determination. This means that the collection of bodily substances from his body and the gathering of personal data, in both cases for subsequent use in biobanks for the purposes of medical research, must be

---

24   Nationaler Ethikrat 2004, 1 et seq. (The English version of this document can be found at http://www.ethikrat.org/_english/publications/opinions.html).

subject to the donor's consent. The consent is effective if the donor has the capacity to give consent, the consent is given voluntarily and the donor has been appropriately informed of the purposes, nature, significance and implications of the collection and use.

2. The requirement of consent must also apply whenever samples and data obtained for other reasons – for example diagnosis or therapy are subsequently to be used for research. This kind of multiple sample use is extremely valuable for medical research, but in the past it usually took place without explicit consent. To ensure that these samples remain available for research in the future, the process of obtaining consent must not be unnecessarily complicated. A form-based declaration that the samples may also be used for medical research subject to appropriate donor protection conditions ought to suffice.

3. If samples and data lawfully obtained for diagnostic or therapeutic reasons are subsequently used for medical research, the requirement of consent may be waived if the samples and data are completely anonymized. Since no relation to the person then exists, donor interests calling for protection are not at issue. However, if the donor has expressed a contrary wish at the time of collection of the samples, it must always be respected. The same applies if the samples and data have been pseudonymized and the research worker has no access to the code, so that he cannot by himself relate them to the person concerned. In this case, as in that of anonymization, the researchers lack the possibility of relating samples and data to their donors. Ensuring the observance of data protection requirements is a matter for the data protection officer.

4. Under Germany's current data protection legislation, the requirement of consent may also be waived in the case of samples and data lawfully obtained for diagnostic or therapeutic purposes if, although the samples and data are to be used in personalized form, the scientific interest in the conduct of the research project substantially outweighs any interest of the donor in exclusion from use and if the purpose of the research cannot be achieved in any other way, or can be achieved only with disproportionate effort and expense. Even so, donor consent to the research should be obtained if reasonably possible. This exceptional situation ceases to be of practical relevance if, when bodily substances are collected for diagnostic or therapeutic purposes, precautionary consent is obtained for their use for medical research purposes. 'Exceptional situations' also includes cases where personalized samples and data obtained with donor consent for a specific research project, such as research on particular diseases, are to be used for research on further diseases. This exception need not be invoked where wide-ranging consent was granted at the time of collection of the

samples. If an exceptional situation is to be invoked, an ethics committee must first be involved and have issued a favorable opinion (see Regulatory Proposal 17).

5. The scientific potential of biobank samples and data can often be fully exploited only if their use is not confined to individual research projects specifiable in advance. Donors should be able to give generalized consent to the use of their samples and data for the purposes of medical – including genetic – research.

6. The same applies to consent relating to the duration of storage and utilization of samples and data. Donors should be able to consent to the use of their samples and data for an indefinite period. Moreover, compulsory time limits on the storage of samples and data appreciably limit the scientific value of biobanks. Epidemiological studies may extend over several decades. It must also be possible at any time to withdraw consent given to the use of samples and data for an unlimited period (see Regulatory Proposal 10 below).

7. Modern research is dependent on national and international cooperation and networks. For this reason, donors should also be able to consent to the transfer of samples and data from biobanks to third parties for the purposes of medical research. However, except in circumstances prescribed by law, the transfer must take place only in anonymized or coded form, with the recipient in the latter case having no access to the code. Should the recipients' research require an association with personalized data, this may be provided only by an officer of the biobank to which the donors originally entrusted their samples and data. All transfers of samples and data to third parties must be fully documented for future reference.

8. Subject to donors' consent, transfer of an entire biobank should be permissible, provided that the recipient is subject to standards of donor protection and quality assurance equivalent to those applicable to the original institution in charge of the biobank. Transfer of a biobank without donor consent is acceptable only if the samples and data have first been anonymized. Transfers of existing biobanks to third parties with the inclusion of personalized donor data ought to be possible only with the approval of an ethics committee.

9. Whether donors should be able to choose between declarations of consent providing for different levels of authorization ultimately depends on the purpose of the research. The absence of options does not constitute a violation of the right of self-determination, for it is up to the donor to decide whether or not to participate in the research under the specified conditions.

10. Donors must have the right to withdraw their consent to the use of their samples and data at any time. It should not be possible to waive this right. However, there should be provision for donors to allow samples and data to continue to be used, in the case of withdrawal, if they are anonymized – that is, if their personalization has been eliminated.

11. Consent must always be subject to the furnishing of appropriate information on all circumstances recognizably relevant to the donor's decision. These as a rule include:

   - the voluntary nature of participation;
   - the purposes, nature, extent and duration of the proposed use, including the possibility of genetic analyses;
   - the extent of, and conditions for, the possible transfer of samples and data;
   - the possibility or otherwise of communication of research results to the donor;
   - information on the possible consequences of the communication of results of genetic analyses for the donor and his relatives, including possible obligations to divulge (for example to insurance institutions);
   - the form of data storage and combination;
   - anonymization or pseudonymization of samples and data;
   - other ancillary donor protection measures;
   - any provision for State access to samples and data;
   - the right to withdraw consent;
   - the fate of samples and data if consent is withdrawn and if the biobank closes down;
   - any commercial prospects of the proposed research (including the possibility of filing patent applications on the results);
   - issues of payment of expenses, remuneration or benefit-sharing.

   It should not under any circumstances be possible to dispense with the provision of this information.

12. The information need only cover personal risks to the donor arising directly in connection with the use of samples and data in biobanks. The general risk that existing safeguards might not be observed, or the possibility that research results obtained by means of the biobank might lead to undesirable societal trends, cannot form part of the information provided by the research worker.

13. If individual communication of research results to the donor is agreed, he must also be told, as a part of the information to be given, that he must divulge these details in certain circumstances – for instance, when

concluding new employment or insurance contracts in the future. In addition, where such individual communication to the donor has been agreed, the findings must be imparted by a person with the appropriate counselling skills. This applies in particular to the communication of results of genetic diagnosis.

14. To protect donor privacy, when biobank samples and data are stored and used, personal information allowing inferences as to donor identity shall as far as possible be concealed by coding. Organizational measures shall be adopted to ensure that the code and the encrypted data are stored and administered separately from each other.

15. There is no need for a general approval requirement for biobanks. The collection and use of human bodily substances and personal data are part of the normal course of medical research. They do not as a rule carry any particular risks to donors and are covered by the established standards governing medical research. For this reason, blanket prior oversight by an authority is not necessary. However, it might be appropriate to require the licensing of large-scale biobanks – along the lines of the national biobank planned in the United Kingdom – that are relatively permanent organizations combining a number of different major resources under a single umbrella. In this case, a crucial regulatory consideration, in addition to donor protection, would be a guarantee of appropriate access to an infrastructure important for research.

16. Under the current data protection legislation, biobanks are in all cases subject to the supervision of a data protection officer, who must, where appropriate, be appointed specifically by the institution and who is responsible for ensuring compliance with the legal requirements applicable to the handling of personal data. As a rule, no other internal or external supervisory body will be necessary. Different arrangements may be indicated for large-scale biobanks with divided organizational responsibilities, which might need higher level coordination and oversight.

17. Prior to the conduct of a research project involving the use of biobank samples and data, it should be necessary for the consent of an ethics committee to be obtained where

   • bodily substances are to be collected from a donor's body for research purposes;
   • the project calls for the linking of samples to personalized data;
   • bodily substances in personalized or pseudonymized form are to be transferred to external researchers;

- existing biobanks are to be transferred *in toto* to third parties with the inclusion of personalized donor data;
- exceptional situations are to be invoked (see Regulatory Proposal 4).

The involvement of an ethics committee and the need for its favorable opinion are intended to ensure that a narrowly worded consent is not exceeded, that a consent in broad terms is not inappropriately given an even wider interpretation and that exceptional situations in which consent may be waived are not illegitimately invoked.

18. On the other hand, there should be no requirement for an ethics committee to be involved if samples and data are anonymized. In this case there is no particular need for donor protection.

19. Donors must be protected by an obligation of confidentiality on the part of all concerned with the establishment and use of biobanks. Where not provided for by law, the obligation of confidentiality must be imposed by the institution itself, for instance, in its statutes or by contract.

20. Donors will often grant biobanks the right to use their samples and data for medical research with hardly any limitation of content and time. This seems reasonable only if this application (that is research) is strictly adhered to. For this reason, confidentiality of research must be enshrined in law, to preclude any access to samples and data other than in the context of research. This protection should also, in all cases, extend to access by the State.

21. The risk of results of genetic diagnosis being used in society to discriminate against people on the grounds of their genetic characteristics must be precluded by statutory regulation of fields in which the relevant information can be used in discriminatory ways, for instance, by stipulating restrictions on the use of genetic findings in the sphere of employment and insurance. Specific provisions for biobanks are not necessary.

22. Owing to the sometimes excessive importance hitherto assigned to the genetic element of physical and, in particular, mental characteristics in both the general and the scientific debate, the possibility cannot be ruled out that research results associating diseases with genetic endowment may be perceived as stigmatizing by those concerned and in their social environment. This perception reflects an overvaluation of genetic factors that fails to do justice to the significance of other conditions of human life (such as education, experience or environment). It must be corrected by

information, not by regulation of research.

23. Genetic analyses of samples may also generate information applicable to a donor's relatives. Donors should nevertheless be able to consent to the analysis of their own samples without the need for the relatives' consent. However, information on their genetic status must not be forced on relatives.

24. Genetic analyses of donor samples may result in findings concerning the genetic particularities and risks of patients suffering from a specific disease or of ethnic groups in which such diseases are particularly prevalent. The relevance of the results to these groups cannot constitute grounds for a requirement of group consent in addition to the consent of individual donors. The particular problems presented by research on indigenous populations do not arise in Germany.

25. People incapable of giving their consent are just as entitled as those possessing that capacity to information on the use of their samples and data and the results of the relevant research. The collection and use of such subjects' samples and data should be conditional on their having as far as possible given their consent, or at least not having shown any sign of refusal. In the case of someone who lacks the capacity to give consent, the decision must always be made, after the required information has been imparted, by the legal or duly authorized representative. Medical research involving people who lack the capacity for consent is, however, currently a matter of intense debate in a number of fields (for example, pharmaceutical research). A detailed resolution of these issues is beyond the scope of an opinion on biobanks. Instead, it is necessary to develop universally applicable principles combining proper protection of those incapable of giving their consent with – as far as possible – a recognition of the need for research for the benefit of others.

26. Deceased persons' samples and data can be obtained and used by biobanks on the same conditions as those applicable in the case of living individuals. If the deceased has not given the necessary consent during his lifetime, his next of kin can supply it, provided that this does not conflict with the deceased's wishes, expressed or presumed, during his lifetime.

27. For thorough utilization of the scientific potential of biobanks, access should be granted to as many research workers as possible. This requirement should be allowed for in the determination of the form of donor consent and when public funds are allocated for the establishment of biobanks. However, research workers who have contributed preliminary work of their own to the establishment of a biobank should be accorded

priority of use for a certain period.

28. To a greater extent than was usually the case in the past, biobanks should be structured and maintained in accordance with uniform scientific standards. Adequate quality assurance measures are the only way to guarantee that biobanks will remain usable for a variety of research projects for an extended period.

29. The establishment of biobanks should be subject to the principle of unpaid donation. The tendency to pay expenses at a level approaching that of actual remuneration should be counteracted. This would not only address any ethical reservations about commercialization of the human body, but also prevent any undermining of solidarity.

30. In consideration of the possibility of economic gain accruing from the subsequent exploitation of research results, forms of benefit-sharing for the individual donors or donor groups concerned or for society are being debated. However, as a rule, individual donors will not be able to benefit, if only because the contribution of an individual donor to the result of the research and the return on it is almost impossible to determine. Benefit-sharing at a level higher than that of the individual, in the form of voluntary contributions to welfare funds, is conceivable and desirable. Compulsory funds, however, would compete with State corporate taxation and with the balancing of private gain and public benefit which it is intended to bring about. The regulatory issues of principle associated with the establishment of such funds extend far beyond the matter of biobanks.

Concluding Remarks

The recommendations of the German National Ethics Council have met with a predominantly positive response in the debate among representatives of the relevant disciplines. It remains to be seen how far they will influence the current discussions on the drafting of a law on genetic diagnosis.

Bibliography

Bellivier, F. and Noiville, C. (2004), 'The commercialisation of human biomaterials: what are the rights of donors of biological materials', *Journal of International Biotechnology Law* 1, 89–97.

Deutsch, E. (1992), 'Das Persönlichkeitsrecht des Patienten', *Archiv für die civilistische Praxis* 192 (1), 161–80.

Deutsch, E. and Spickhoff, A. (2008), *Medizinrecht*, 6th Edition (Berlin: Springer).

Freund, G. (2005), 'Nabelschnurblut und das Zustimmungserfordernis bei der Gewinnung und Verwendung menschlicher Körperstoffe', *Medizinrecht* 23 (8), 453–58.

Freund, G. and Weiss, N. (2004), 'Zur Zulässigkeit der Verwendung menschlichen Körpermaterials für Forschungs- und andere Zwecke', *Medizinrecht* 22 (6), 315–19.

German Federal Constitutional Court:

(a) Mitglieder des Bundesverfassungsgerichts(eds) (1970), Entscheidungen des Bundesverfassungsgerichts, Volume 27.

(b) Mitglieder des Bundesverfassungsgerichts (eds) (1972), Entscheidungen des Bundesverfassungsgerichts , Volume 32.

(c) Mitglieder des Bundesverfassungsgerichts (eds) (1980), Entscheidungen des Bundesverfassungsgerichts, Volume 52.

German Federal Court of Justice:

(a) Mitglieder des Bundesgerichtshofes und die Bundesanwaltschaft (eds) (1954), Entscheidungen des Bundesgerichtshofes in Zivilsachen, Volume 13.

(b) Mitglieder des Bundesgerichtshofes und die Bundesanwaltschaft (eds) (1962), Entscheidungen des Bundesgerichtshofes in Zivilsachen, Volume 36.

(c) Mitglieder des Bundesgerichtshofes und die Bundesanwaltschaft (eds) (1967), Entscheidungen des Bundesgerichtshofes in Zivilsachen, Volume 46.

(d) Mitglieder des Bundesgerichtshofes und die Bundesanwaltschaft (eds) (1969), Entscheidungen des Bundesgerichtshofes in Zivilsachen, Volume 50.

(e) Mitglieder des Bundesgerichtshofes und die Bundesanwaltschaft (eds) (1989), Entscheidungen des Bundesgerichtshofes in Zivilsachen, Volume 106.

Halàsz, C. (2004), *Das Recht auf bio-materielle Selbstbestimmung* (Berlin: Springer).

Hanau, P., Lorenz, E. and Matthes, H.-C. (eds) (1998), *Festschrift für Günther Wiese zum 70. Geburtstag* (Neuwied und Kriftel: Luchterhand).

Jarass, H.D. (2004), 'Art. 2 [Allg. Handlungsfreiheit, Allg. Persönlichkeitsrecht, Leben und körperliche Unversehrtheit, Freiheit der Person]', in H.D. Jarass and B. Pieroth (eds) (2006), *Kommentar zum Grundgesetz*, 8th Edition (München: C.H. Beck).

Jarass, H.D. and Pieroth, B. (2006), *Kommentar zum Grundgesetz*, 8th Edition (München: C.H. Beck).

Laufs, A. and Uhlenbruck, W. (eds) (2002), *Handbuch des Arztrechts*, 3rd Edition (München: C.H. Beck).

Laufs, A. (2002), 'Die ärztliche Aufklärungspflicht', in Laufs, A. and Uhlenbruck, W. (eds), §§61–8.

Mand, E. (2005), 'Biobanken für die Forschung und informationelle Selbstbestimmung', *Medizinrecht* 23 (10), 565–75.

Müller, R. (1997), *Die kommerzielle Nutzung menschlicher Körpersubstanzen* (Berlin: Duncker und Humblot).

Nitz, G. and Dierks, C. (2002), 'Nochmals: Forschung an und mit Körpersubstanzen – wann ist die Einwilligung des ehemaligen Trägers erforderlich?', *Medizinrecht* 20 (8), 400–403.

Rebmann, K., Säcker, F.J. and Rixecker, R. (eds) (2004), *Münchener Kommentar zum Bürgerlichen Gesetzbuch*, vol. 5, 4th Edition (§§ 705–853) (München: C. H. Beck).

Schack, H. (2005), *Urheber- und Urhebervertragsrecht*, 3rd Edition (Tübingen: Mohr Siebeck).

Schröder, M. and Taupitz, J. (1991), *Menschliches Blut: verwendbar nach Belieben des Arztes?* (Stuttgart: Enke).

Spranger, T.M. (2005), 'Die Rechte des Patienten bei der Entnahme und Nutzung von Körpersubstanzen', *Neue Juristische Wochenschrift* 58 (16), 1084–90.

Tag, B. (2000), *Der Körperverletzungstatbestand im Spannungsfeld zwischen Patientenautonomie und Lex artis* (Berlin: Springer).

Taupitz, J. (1991), 'Wem gebührt der Schatz im menschlichen Körper?', *Archiv für die civilistische Praxis* 191 (1), 201–46.

Taupitz, J. (1992), 'Privatrechtliche Rechtspositionen um die Genomanalyse – Eigentum, Persönlichkeit, Leistung', *Juristenzeitung* 47 (22), 1089–99.

Taupitz, J. (1998), 'Das Recht auf Nichtwissen', in P. Hanau, E. Lorenz and H.-C. Matthes (eds), 583–602.

Wagner, G. (2004), '§823 [Schadensersatzpflicht]', in K. Rebmann, F.J. Säcker and R. Rixecker (eds) (2004), *Münchener Kommentar zum Bürgerlichen Gesetzbuch*, vol. 5, 4th Edition (§§ 705–853) (München: C.H. Beck).

Internet-based References

'Biobanks for research', *Nationaler Ethikrat*, Opinions page (published online 17 March 2004), http://www.ethikrat.org/_english/publications/opinions.html (home page) (accessed 28.05.2009).

'(Weiter-)Verwendung von menschlichen Körperteilen für Zwecke medizinischer Forschung', Zentrale Ethikkommission, Statements page (published online 20 February 2003), http://www.zentrale-ethikkommission.de/10/index.htm (home page) (accessed 28.05.2009).

Chapter 19

European Regulations on Human Tissue and Cells Transplantation

Ján Koller

Introduction

Tissue banking in Europe started during World War II in the UK with the banking of skin for severely burned pilots. The first tissue bank on the European Continent was established in 1952 by Dr Rudolf Klen in Hradec Kralove, former Czechoslovakia,

The first attempt to harmonize legislation of the European states on transplantation issues was done by the Council of Europe (CoE) as early as 1978. The document called 'Recommendation (78)29 on harmonization of legislation of member states relating to removal, grafting and transplantation of human substances' (Council of Europe 1978) was published and distributed to all the Member States of the CoE. The first official global set of recommendations for transplantation of both organs and tissues was outlined by the World Health Organization (WHO, WHA Resolution No 40.13, 1987). They presented a proposal for setting up Guiding Principles for organ transplantation which outlined the basic ethical principles used up to the present time. These principles pertained not only to organs, but also to tissues and cells as well. The core of these principles lay in voluntary and unpaid donations. They also required that the human body and its parts could not be the subject of commercial transactions. In the light of the principles of distributive justice and equity, donated organs should be made available to patients on the basis of medical need and not on the basis of financial or other considerations. Following extensive discussions four years later, the WHO Guiding Principles were approved by the World Health Assembly (WHA) in 1991 as WHA Resolution No 44.25 (World Health Organization 1991). The pioneering effort of WHO in the field of organ and tissue transplantations was later followed by the Council of Europe and by the European Parliament and continues up to the present time (World Health Organization 2006).

WHO Guiding Principles (GP)

Because of their importance, the original text is included here of all nine WHO Guiding Principles of human organ transplantation, as appeared in the WHA Resolution 44.25/1991.

- *Guiding Principle 1:* Tissues can be removed from the bodies of deceased persons for the purpose of transplantation, if any consents required by law are obtained, and there is no reason to believe that the deceased person objected to such removal.
- *Guiding Principle 2:* Physicians determining that the death of a potential donor has occured should not be directly involved in organ (tissue) removal from donor and subsequent transplantation procedures or be responsible for the care of potential recipient.
- *Guiding Principle 3:* Organs (tissues) for transplantation should be removed preferably from the bodies of deceased persons. Adult living persons may donate organs, but in general they should be genetically related to the recipients. An organ can be removed only after the donor gives free consent.
- *Guiding Principle 4:* No organ should be removed from the body of a living minor for the purpose of transplantation. Exceptions may be made under national law in the case of regenerative tissues.
- *Guiding Principle 5:* The human body and its parts cannot be the subject of commercial transactions. Accordingly, giving or receiving payment for organs (tissues) should be prohibited.
- *Guiding Principle 6:* Advertising the need for or availability of organs with a view to offering or seeking payment should be prohibited.
- *Guiding Principle 7:* It should be prohibited for physicians and other health professionals to engage in organ transplantation procedures if they have reason to believe that the organs concerned have been the subject of commercial transactions.
- *Guiding Principle 8:* It should be prohibited for any person or facility involved in organ transplantation procedures to receive any payment that exceeds the justifiable fee for services rendered.
- *Guiding Principle 9:* In the light of the principles of distributive justice and equity, donated organs should be made available to patients on the basis of medical need and not on the basis of financial or other considerations.

The Essence of GP 1991 included:

- preference for deceased over living donors.
- preference for genetically related over unrelated living donors.

As preconditions of all cases there was required:

- Obtaining informed consent by competent person.
- Consent granted free of undue influence or pressure.
- Non-commercialization of organs, tissues and cells for transplantation.
- Fair distribution of organs, tissues and cells to recipients.

In addition to these basic principles there were also challenges that needed to be confronted. In countries with relatively few healthcare institutions, there were problems with detection and identification of potential donors. This resulted in insufficient supply of suitable donors. On the other side it was proved that progress in science enabling usage of live donors more extensively showed at least equal, or better, results than with deceased donors. Other mostly ethical problems arose with unrelated live donors. Since physicians usually do not like to challenge claims of 'relationship', using unrelated donors claiming to be volunteers seemed to be quite acceptable.

Another group of problems was pertaining to the requirement of non-commercialization. Some leaders in transplantation believe that 'incentives' will increase the rate of organ or tissue donations. There are ethicists who see prohibitions on payments as paternalistic interference with personal autonomy. In some countries organ donation programs are linked to commercialized tissue operations, where human material is a commodity. One of the major problems that some countries either do not have or do not enforce is *prohibitions of organ trafficking* and may allow, or even support '*transplant tourism*'.

European Regulations and Standards

WHO Guiding Principles have been implemented into all relevant subsequent documents (regulations, rules, guides, ethical codes, etc.) pertaining to organ, tissue and cell transplantation. The implementation included not just official bodies, but professional associations as well.

The European Association of Tissue Banks (EATB) was founded in 1991 to promote science, research and teaching in the field of tissue banking and related sciences, in Europe and more widely, and to publish safety and quality standards for Tissue Banking. EATB is a non-commercial, non-profit professional organization which is seated and registered in Berlin, Germany. The founder and first president of EATB was Dr Rudiger von Versen. The first comprehensive international set of General Standards for Tissue Banking was prepared and issued by the EATB in 1994 (European Association of Tissue Banks 1994a). The separate EATB Ethical Code (European Association of Tissue Banks 1994b) was attached as an Annex to the Standards. Neither the General Standards nor the Ethical Code deal with the issue of the property of organs/tissues/cells for transplantation purposes.

In 1999, the Council of Europe with 46 Member States set up a working group of experts for safety and quality assurance for organs, tissues and cells for transplantation. As an output of this effort, in 2002 the first edition of the CoE Guide to Safety and Quality Assurance for Organs, Tissues and Cells was published. The second, updated, edition of the Guide was published in 2004, and the third, revised, edition in 2007 (Council of Europe 2007). This Guide was designed to serve as a recommendation for the CoE Member States for regulation of organs, tissues and cells transplantation. This Guide is so far the only document which includes issues of organs, tissues and cells for transplantation. With regard to transplantation ethics, the CoE produced an important document, 'Additional protocol to the convention on human rights and biomedicine, on transplantation of organs and tissues of human origin', which was adopted by the Committee of Ministers in Strasbourg on 24 January 2002 (Council of Europe 2002). This document aims at setting ethical requirements on key aspects of transplantation practices.

Since 1 January 2007, the European Union (or European Communities) includes 27 Member States. On 31 March 2004, the European Parliament and the Council issued Directive 2004/23/EC, on setting standards for the quality and safety for donation, procurement, testing, processing, preservation, storage and distribution of human tissues and cells (European Communities 2004), which was implemented into national legislation of all 27 Member States. In addition to this 'Mother Directive', two more Directives containing technical requirements have been issued (European Communities 2006a and 2006b).

CoE Guide to Safety and Quality Assurance for Organs, Tissues and Cells

Safety and quality assurance in organ and tissue transplantation is an essential element of the right of the patient to safe healthcare of good quality (Council of Europe 2004). Safety includes provision of organs, tissues and cells for transplantation, where the risk of transmission of diseases can be minimized. It includes also traceability of the products from the donor to the recipient and vice versa. In addition, other risks, such as from operative interventions and other procedures, shall be kept at a minimal possible level. The Guide provides guidance for all those involved in the transplantation of organs, tissues and cells to minimize the risks to donors, recipients and healthcare personnel and to maximize their quality and thereby the rate of transplant success.

The document is composed of seven chapters.

Chapter 1 deals with general considerations, benefits and risks of transplantation and ethical and legal issues. The role of the state is in creating a legal framework within which transplant services can operate. There is also a need to set up and control a body responsible for the allocation and distribution of organs, tissues and cells. Organizational issues are relevant, particularly for maintaining traceability, to guarantee anonymity and to assure a transparent and fair allocation system.

Chapter 2 is on quality management. It is important to operate an effective quality assurance program including risk assessment and management. The basic elements of the quality management system should include clear organizational structure and accountability, clear and effective documentation, control of processes, requirements for personnel, facilities and equipment, detection, investigation and corrective actions for non-conformance.

Chapter 3 addresses the selection of donors. The main principle of donor selection should be to maximize the benefit and minimize the risk of transplantation for the recipients. It is very important to have an active donor detection system for cadaveric donors, which can increase the donation rate significantly. With respect to living donation, the Guide reinforces the importance of voluntary and unpaid donations, stressing the importance of appropriate relationship between donor and recipient as defined by law. If there is no family relationship, the donation should be approved by an independent body. In any case, the living donor should receive appropriate information about the risks of donation and should give a free consent, which he can withdraw any time without any reason preceding donation. Written informed consent is required for donors of surgical residues as well.

Chapter 4 deals with organ retrieval and preservation, describing technical aspects related to both cadaveric and living donations.

Chapter 5 covers tissue and cell procurement. Techniques of procurement, processing, preservation, packing, labeling and distribution of tissues and cells are described in detail. Specific issues pertaining to hematopoietic progenitor cells banking were also included in this part of the Guide.

Chapter 6 deals with tissues and cell establishments. It is of utmost importance to follow the quality and safety requirements in establishments where tissues and cells are processed. Requirements for the design of the facilities, functioning of the equipment, validation of processes, etc. are described. Distributed tissue and cell products should be appropriately packed, labeled, stored and transported to the end-users in order to retain their biological properties and to preserve their pre-defined quality. The importance of accurate documentation and record keeping is stressed as well. Records relevant to safety and quality of tissue and cells products should be stored for a minimum of 30 years.

Chapter 7, the last chapter, is devoted to transplantation practices. This includes the description of activities related to pre- peri- and post-transplant periods. Special attention is addressed to donor-recipient match, management of waiting lists and the importance of both donors (live donors) and recipients follow-up following donation/transplantation.

Appendices of the Guide contain list of participants, list of references to standards, definitions and the Steering Committee of Bioethics (CDBI) Additional Protocol 2002 to the Convention of Human Rights and Biomedicine.

The CoE Guide proved to become a very useful reference manual for all kinds of transplantation, and the only one where issues on transplantation practices were also included. It is important that the different European bodies agree on the main principles of transplantation safety, quality and practices. Stressing the non-profit principle of donations contributes to the protection of the donor against any abuse, which could be detrimental to his/her health. It also contributes to protection of health of the recipients as concerns can arise about safety requirements when trade is involved.

European Directives on Setting Standards of Quality and Safety on Donation, Procurement, Testing, Processing, Preservation, Storage and Distribution of Human Tissues and Cells (HTCs)

In order to guarantee the safety and quality of human tissues and cells for human applications in the EC Member States, the European Commission started to develop new regulations under Article 152 of the Treaty of Amsterdam. Their principal aims are to protect the recipients of human tissues and cells from transmitted diseases and other risks arising from poor quality material and, by protecting recipients, to safeguard the wider public health. Following several years of preparations and discussions, finally on 31 March 2004, Directive 2004/23/EC of the European Parliament and the Council on setting standards of quality and safety for the donation, procurement, testing, processing, preservation, storage and distribution of human tissues and cells was adopted by the European Parliament. It was published on 7 April 2004.

Directive 2004/23/EC

The main aim of the Directive is to set up a unified framework in order to ensure high standards of quality and safety with respect to the procurement, testing, processing, storage and distribution of tissues and cells across the Community and to facilitate exchanges of HTCs and products derived from HTCs for patients receiving this type of therapy. The Community provisions ensure that human tissues and cells, whatever their intended use or source, are of comparable quality and safety. The establishment of such standards, therefore, will help to reassure the public that human tissues and cells that are procured in another Member State, will carry the same guarantees as those in their own country.

The Directive should apply to *all HTCs for human applications* including:

- Hematopoietic peripheral blood, umbilical-cord (blood) and bone-marrow stem cells.
- Reproductive cells (eggs, sperm).
- Fetal tissues and cells.
- Adult and embryonic stem cells.

The Directive *excludes*:

- Blood and blood products (covered by other Directives – 2002/98/EC).
- Human organs.

- Organs, tissues, or cells of animal origin.
- Tissues and cells used as an autologous graft, within the same surgical procedure and without being subjected to any banking process.
- Human tissues and cells for research purposes, such as when used for purposes other than application to the human body, e.g., *in vitro* research or in animal models.

The Directive covers tissues and cells intended to be used for industrially manufactured products, including medical devices, only as far as donation, procurement and testing are concerned. This Directive should not interfere with decisions made by Member States concerning the use or non-use of any specific type of human cells, including germ cells and embryonic stem cells and should establish high standards for safety and quality for each one of the steps in the human tissues and cells procurement, processing preservation and application.

Each Member State shall designate the competent authority, or authorities, responsible for implementing the requirements of this Directive. As in all the transplantation issues, ethical principles should be followed as well. Tissue and cell donation and application programs should be founded on the philosophy of voluntary and unpaid donation, anonymity of both donor and recipient, altruism of the donor and solidarity between donor and recipient. Member States are urged to take steps to encourage a strong public and nonprofit sector involvement in the provision of tissue and cell application services and the related research and development. In the case of living donors, the Directive requires that the health status of the donor shall not be altered by the donation. The dignity of the deceased donor should be respected, notably through the reconstruction of the donor's body. The identity of the recipient(s) should not be disclosed to the donor or his/her family and vice versa.

The Directive respects the fundamental rights and observes the principles reflected in the Charter of Fundamental Rights of the European Union and takes into account as appropriate the Convention for the Protection of Human Rights and Dignity of the Human Being with regard to the application of biology and medicine.

Confidentiality and personal data protection measures should be in place An accreditation system for tissue establishments and a system for notification of adverse events and reactions linked to tissue and cell activities should be established.

Inspections and control measures should be organized, and they should be carried out by officials representing the competent authority to ensure that tissue establishments comply with the provisions of this Directive.

Requirement for qualification, education and training of personnel participating in both tissue banking and inspection activities should be in place.

The best possible scientific advice available in relation to the safety of tissues and cells in the light of the rapid advance in biotechnology knowledge and practice in the field of human tissues and cells should be provided.

An adequate system to ensure the traceability of human tissues and cells should be established. 'Traceability' means the ability to locate and identify the tissue/cell during any step from procurement through processing, testing and storage to distribution to the recipient or disposal. This also implies the ability to identify the donor and the tissue establishment or the manufacturing facility receiving, processing or storing the tissue/cells and the ability to identify the recipient(s) at the medical facility/facilities applying the tissue/cells to the recipient(s). Traceability also covers the ability to locate and identify all relevant data relating to products and materials coming into contact with those tissues/cells. It should be enforced through accurate substance, donor, recipient, tissue establishment and laboratory identification procedures as well as record maintenance and an appropriate labeling system.

Importation/exportation of HTCs, delivery and/or receipt of HTCs and/or their products to/from EU Member States are considered as distribution. Regulations for importation/exportation pertain to delivery/receipt of HTCs and/or their products to or from the third countries. The competent authority shall take all the necessary measures to ensure that imports/exports of HTCs meet the quality and safety standards equivalent to those contained in this Directive.

Appropriate penalties should be applied by member states The Directive uses the term 'tissue establishment' and defines it as a tissue bank or a unit of a hospital or another body where activities of processing, preservation, storage or distribution of human tissues and cells are undertaken. It may also be responsible for procurement or testing of tissues and cells.

The text of the Directive is divided into seven chapters including 32 articles.. One Annex containing information to be provided on the donation of tissues/cells is attached.

Chapter I includes objectives, definitions, as well as the scope and implementation of the Directive.

In Chapter II obligations on the Member States' authorities are described. These were listed in the previous paragraphs and include also an obligation for reporting and establishing a publicly accessible register of tissue establishments.

Chapter III concerns donor selection and evaluation and includes also the issues of consent, selection evaluation and procurement.

Chapter IV contains the issues of quality management, responsible person, personnel, tissue and cell reception, processing, packing and labeling, storage, distribution and the relationship between the tissue establishment and third parties.

Chapter V sets up requirements for exchange of information, coding and penalties.

Chapter VI deals with the list of technical requirements which will specify in details the particular activities.

Chapter VII specifies the issues of transposition into Member States' national regulations and entry into force, which took place following publication of the Directive in the Official Journal of the European Union on 7 April 2004.

This Directive was adopted by the European Parliament and the Council and included a list of so- called 'technical requirements', which were subsequently elaborated by comitology procedure by the European Commission. The two sets of technical requirements were approved by the Commission and published as European Commission Directives 2006/17/EC and 2006/86/EC.

The deadline for implementation of Directive 2004/23/EC to Member States' regulations was 7 April 2006. Report on the state of implementation in the Member States shall be sent to the Commission.

Directive 2006/17/EC

This European Commission Directive of 8 February 2006 implements the requirements of Directive 2004/23/EC (so-called 'Mother Directive') regarding certain technical requirements for the donation, procurement and testing of human tissue and cells. The Directive contains nine Articles and four Annexes. The Directive and its Annexes describe in more detail than the 'Mother Directive' the following issues:

- Requirements for the procurement of human tissues and cells.
- Selection criteria for donors of tissues and/or cells (excluding reproductive cells donors).
- Laboratory tests required for donors.
- Selection criteria and laboratory tests required for donors of reproductive cells.
- Cell and/or tissue donation and procurement procedures and reception at the tissue establishment.
- Requirements for direct distribution to the recipient for specific tissues and cells.

The deadline for implementation of Directive 2006/17/EC to Member States' regulations was 1 November 2006.

Directive 2006/86/EC

The second European Commission Directive of 24 October 2006 implements the requirements of the 'Mother Directive' regarding traceability requirements, notification of serious adverse reactions and events and certain technical requirements for the coding, processing, preservation, storage and distribution of human tissues and cells. This Directive contains 13 Articles and seven Annexes.

The Directive describes in great details the following important technical requirements:

- Requirements for the accreditation, designation, authorization or licensing of tissue establishments.
- Requirements for the accreditation, designation, authorization, licensing of tissue and cell preparation processes at the tissue establishments.
- Requirement for notification of serious adverse reactions and serious adverse events including communication of information between competent authorities and the Commission and reporting.
- Information on the minimum donor/recipient data set.
- Information contained in the European Coding System.
- Examples of reporting forms are attached.

The deadline for implementation of Directive 2006/86/EC to Member States regulations was 1 September 2007.

Impact of the Directives on Tissue Establishments

The adopted Directives will have a major impact on all the tissue establishments in the Member States, including procurement organizations, processing centers, laboratories providing biological testing of the donors and, of course, the tissue establishments themselves. All the above mentioned institutions will need to implement the requirements of the Directives into their everyday practices. This will include, particularly, the necessity of new accreditation, designation, authorization or licensing (further referred to as 'accreditation') of tissue establishments from the competent authorities. The basic condition for 'accreditation' will be that the tissue establishment will follow the whole range of rules, conditions and requirements which have been set up by the new Directives. Not only the tissue establishments but also all the tissue preparation processes will need to be 'accredited'. Stricter requirements for donor selection, facilities, preparation processes, personnel, equipment qualification, maintenance and repair, education and training of personnel, validation of processes, quality management, etc. have been established. The adoption of the new requirements will require, especially at the start of the Directives implementation, a major workload on the tissue establishments' personnel and a major increase of their expenditures. Possibly some smaller tissue establishments or hospital tissue banks will not be able to follow the new regulations and will be closed. A new system for reporting adverse events and reactions as well as for inspections of tissue establishments needs also to be established. The new European coding system is still in the phase of development and does not exist yet. The Directives were aimed and adopted as technical documents. They say nothing specific about the property of organs/ tissues/cells for transplantation purposes

Bibliography

Council of Europe (1978), Recommendation (78)29 on harmonization of legislation of member states relating to removal, grafting and transplantation of human substances, www.coe.int.

—— (2002), Additional protocol to the convention on human rights and biomedicine, on transplantation of organs and tissues of human origin (Strasbourg: Council of Europe Publishing).

—— (2004), *Health, Ethics and Human Rights. The Council of Europe Meeting the Challenge* (Strasbourg: Council of Europe Publishing).

—— (2007), *Guide to Safety and Quality Assurance for Organs, Tissues and Cells* 3rd Edition (Strasbourg: Council of Europe Publishing).

European Association of Tissue Banks (1994a), General Standards for Tissue Banking, www.eatb.de.

—— (1994b), Ethical Code for Tissue Banking, www.eatb.de.

European Communities (2004), Directive 2004/23/EC of the European Parliament and the Council on setting standards of quality and safety for the donation, procurement, testing, processing, preservation, storage and distribution of human tissues and cells (Official Journal of the European Union, 7 April). .

—— (2006a), Directive 2006/17/EC of the European Commission as regards certain technical requirements for the donation, procurement and testing of human tissue and cells (Official Journal of the European Union, 2 February).

—— (2006b), Directive 2006/86/EC of the European Commission Directive as regards traceability requirements, notification of serious adverse reactions and events and certain technical requirements for the coding, processing, preservation, storage and distribution of human tissues and cells, 25 October *Official Journal of the European Union,*.

World Health Assembly (WHA) (1987), Resolution No. 40.13 (World Health Organization).

World Health Organization (1991), Guiding principles of human organ transplantation. WHA resolution 44,25/1991 (Geneva: WHO publishing), www.who.int.

—— (2006), Aide-Mémoire on Key Safety Requirements for Essential Minimally Processed Human Cells and Tissues for Transplantation (Geneva: World Health Organization).

Index